Corruption, Class, and Politics in Ghana

Ohio University Research in International Studies

This series of publications on Africa, Latin America, Southeast Asia, and Global and Comparative Studies is designed to present significant research, translation, and opinion to area specialists and to a wide community of persons interested in world affairs. The series is distributed worldwide. For more information, consult the Ohio University Press website, ohioswallow.com.

Books in the Ohio University Research in International Studies series are published by Ohio University Press in association with the Center for International Studies. The views expressed in individual volumes are those of the authors and should not be considered to represent the policies or beliefs of the Center for International Studies, Ohio University Press, or Ohio University.

Corruption, Class, and Politics in Ghana

Ernest Harsch

Ohio University Research in International Studies
Africa Series No. 100

Ohio University Press
Athens

Ohio University Press, Athens, Ohio 45701
ohioswallow.com
© 2024 by Ohio University Press
All rights reserved

To obtain permission to quote, reprint, or otherwise reproduce or distribute material from Ohio University Press publications, please contact our rights and permissions department at (740) 593-1154 or (740) 593-4536 (fax).

Printed in the United States of America
Ohio University Press books are printed on acid-free paper ∞ ™

Library of Congress Cataloging-in-Publication Data

Names: Harsch, Ernest, author.
Title: Corruption, class, and politics in Ghana / Ernest Harsch.
Other titles: Research in international studies. Africa series ; 100.
Description: Athens : Ohio University Press, 2024. | Series: Ohio university research in international studies. Africa series ; 100 | Includes bibliographical references and index.
Identifiers: LCCN 2024017319 | ISBN 9780896803435 (paperback) | ISBN 9780896803428 (hardcover) | ISBN 9780896803442 (pdf)
Subjects: LCSH: Political corruption—Ghana. | Political corruption—Ghana—Public opinion. | Public opinion—Ghana. | Ghana—Politics and government.
Classification: LCC JQ3029.5.C6 H35 2024 | DDC 364.132309667—dc23/eng/20240415
LC record available at https://lccn.loc.gov/2024017319

For Eloise and Nabeel

Contents

List of Illustrations
ix

Acknowledgments
xi

Abbreviations
xiii

1
Local Realities, Global Narratives
1

2
Chiefs and Colonial Bureaucrats
15

3
Nationalism and Patronage
43

4
Path to Plunder
69

5
From Mutiny to Revolution
88

6
"We No Go Sit Down"
108

7
Justice Fast and Rough
145

8
Shifting State Agendas
167

9
Elections and Money
195

10
Corruption the Democratic Way
224

11
Vigilance from Above and Below
248

12
For a Society Just and Fair
281

Notes
291
Bibliography
335
Index
359

Illustrations

Table

7.1. Occupations of defendants before Ghana's public tribunals   157

Figures

10.1. Corruption Perceptions Index for Ghana   227
10.2. Ghana government performance in fighting corruption   229

Acknowledgments

This book had a long gestation, beginning with research during visits to Ghana as a journalist in the 1980s and later in pursuit of graduate and postgraduate studies, some of which overlapped with work as managing editor of the United Nations quarterly magazine *Africa Renewal*. Over the years, more than two dozen individuals in government, academia, civil society, and other spheres graciously agreed to be interviewed on record, and their views are cited here. Many others also helped in various ways. At the recommendation of Dr. Kwame Ninsin, I approached Professor Joseph Ayee at the University of Ghana, Legon, who kindly hosted me for several months as a research affiliate in the Department of Political Science. In turn, his colleagues at the university's Institute of African Studies helped me locate documentation and allowed me to work from their center. Professor Emmanuel Gyimah-Boadi, founder of the Ghana Center for Democratic Development, generously shared his insights on various occasions, as did his associate Dr. Baffour Agyeman-Duah. Ken Attafuah passed me a copy of his unpublished manuscript on the public tribunals and provided details of the workings of the Commission on Human Rights and Administrative Justice, of which he was a director. The late Valerie Sackey and her able colleague at the Castle Information Bureau, Opoku Acheampong, helped open doors to high government officials in the 1980s. Yao Graham of the Third World Network–Africa, former University of Ghana vice-chancellor Akilagpa Sawyerr, Yaw Akrasi-Sarpong, Kwame Karikari, Nii K Bentsi-Enchill, and numerous other Ghanaians assisted me in crucial ways during my sojourns to Ghana. Nicholas Goudé of the UN Development Program enabled me to join a journalist tour that took me for the first time to Ashanti and the north. A variety of international experts working on corruption issues put up with my sometimes-impertinent questions, among them Transparency International Chairman Peter Eigen, Michel van Hulten of the World Bank, and Georg Kell of the UN Global Compact. Numerous editors permitted me to share my preliminary findings and thinking about Ghana through their publications, most notably Margaret Novicki at *Africa Report*. And when she later worked for the United Nations in Accra, she provided a congenial base of operations and helped connect me with some of her many contacts. This book also benefited from feedback to early research presentations at the University of Ghana, Columbia University, and University of KwaZulu/Natal (South Africa), as well as to an annual meeting of the US African Studies Association. I would additionally like to thank the New School for Social Research in New York for its Chiune Sugihara Dissertation Fellowship, which helped defray some early research costs. I am especially grateful to the late Charles Tilly, who mentored my work at the New School and pushed me to ask difficult questions, maintain a comparative perspective, and better highlight the wider significance of the processes of political and social change under way in Ghana and neighboring Burkina Faso, with material from the latter country yielding two earlier books. Finally, I would like to express my gratitude to the two anonymous reviewers who read the manuscript for Ohio University Press, especially for their suggestions about how to better underscore the book's central arguments and contributions.

Abbreviations

AFDCs	Armed Forces Defence Committees
AFRC	Armed Forces Revolutionary Council
ALU	Association of Local Unions
ARPB	Association of Recognized Professional Bodies
CDD	Center for Democratic Development
CDRs	Committees for the Defence of the Revolution
CHRAJ	Commission on Human Rights and Administrative Justice
CMB	Cocoa Marketing Board
CPC	Cocoa Purchasing Company
CPI	Corruption Perceptions Index
CPP	Convention People's Party
CVC	Citizens' Vetting Committee
ECOWAS	Economic Community of West African States
EOCO	Economic and Organized Crime Office
ERP	Economic Recovery Programme
GACC	Ghana Anti-Corruption Coalition
GBA	Ghana Bar Association
GBC	Ghana Broadcasting Corporation
GIHOC	Ghana Industrial Holding Corporation
GII	Ghana Integrity Initiative
GNFC	Ghana National Farmers Council
GNPC	Ghana National Petroleum Corporation
GTP	Ghana Textile Printing
IMF	International Monetary Fund
INCC	Interim National Coordinating Committee
JFM	June Fourth Movement
KNRG	Kwame Nkrumah Revolutionary Guards
MFJ	Movement for Freedom and Justice

Nadeco	National Development Company
NAL	National Alliance of Liberals
NCD	National Commission for Democracy
NDC	National Democratic Congress
NIC	National Investigations Committee
NLC	National Liberation Council
NLM	National Liberation Movement
NMC	National Media Commission
NMP	National Mobilization Programme
NPP	New Patriotic Party
NRC	National Redemption Council
ORC	Office of Revenue Commissioners
PBD	Produce Buying Division
PDCs	People's Defence Committees
PIAC	Public Interest and Accountability Committee
PNDC	Provisional National Defence Council
PNP	People's National Party
PPP	People's Progressive Party
PRLG	People's Revolutionary League of Ghana
SFO	Serious Fraud Office
SMC	Supreme Military Council
TUC	Trades Union Congress
UAC	United Africa Company
UGCC	United Gold Coast Convention
UGFCC	United Ghana Farmers Cooperative Council
UP	United Party
WDCs	Workers Defence Committees

1

Local Realities, Global Narratives

In Ghana, as elsewhere in the world, exposing high-level corruption can be risky. Close to midnight on January 16, 2019, journalist Ahmed Hussein-Suale left his home in the Madina neighborhood of Accra, the capital, to check on an ill nephew. As his car slowed at a crossroads a hundred meters away, two men on a motorbike pulled alongside. They fired into the car, the first bullet hitting Hussein-Suale in the neck. According to eyewitnesses, one of the gunmen then walked up to the shattered window and fired twice more into his chest. By the time emergency responders got Hussein-Suale to the nearby Pentecost Hospital, he was dead. Just thirty-one years old, he left behind a wife and three children.[1]

Noting the absence of any evidence of a robbery attempt, police investigators said the crime bore the hallmarks of a targeted assassination. The killing of journalists has been rare in Ghana: the year before, the Paris-based Reporters without Borders ranked the country first in Africa on its press freedom index. Yet Hussein-Suale was no ordinary journalist. He was a key member of the Tiger Eye team of investigative reporters led by Anas Aremeyaw Anas, renowned for exposing corrupt judges, government officials, football administrators, and other authoritative figures. Usually operating undercover with hidden cameras, they shot graphic video evidence of bribe taking and malfeasance of all sorts. Their methods—and their success in prompting Ghanaian authorities to dismiss or prosecute some of the errant individuals—not only turned Anas and his colleagues into folk heroes. They also made them powerful enemies.

If Hussein-Suale's killers intended to dissuade journalists, they failed. In the immediate wake of the murder, numerous aspiring reporters applied to join Tiger Eye. Two months later, Anas and his team released another video, capturing on film officials of an interministerial committee on small-scale gold mining taking bribes to evade regulations.[2]

The Tiger Eye documentaries often drew audiences in the thousands. Yet Ghanaians also had many concerns other than corruption. Would the country's economic performance hold—and provide more benefits for not only the wealthy but also the poor? How could Ghana's schools improve? Would affordable medical care be available? Could women enhance their prospects in a male-dominated society? How could farmers be more productive, amid climate change and threats to farmland from mining and logging? When would party leaders, whether in government or opposition, place the national well-being above their own partisan interests? Could the notoriously slow, inefficient, and venal bureaucracy be sufficiently reformed to provide better services to ordinary citizens? In 2019, a public opinion poll conducted by the Ghana Center for Democratic Development (CDD-Ghana), an independent think tank and research center, found that corruption ranked as only the eighth most worrisome problem in the country, after economic and social difficulties such as high unemployment and poor roads, education, and health care.[3]

Yet corruption clearly was a common concern. Ghanaians were often very passionate about the issue. For officials worried about the impact of corruption on the government's effectiveness and image, it was a dire threat. As a commission of inquiry put it in 1975, "Mounting corruption leads to cumulative incompetence of the governmental machinery. Faith in government is a very important ingredient in a government's ability to mobilise public support for its policies, programmes and projects. Corruption is a deadly virus that is eating its way into the body politic. If it is not checked and brought under control it will seriously undermine the effectiveness of the present or any future government of Ghana."[4]

Corruption was also a preoccupation at the lower rungs of society. Many ordinary Ghanaians found dishonesty and cheating, especially by those in authority, to be morally reprehensible. They rued its impact on their lives, whether through shakedowns of motorists at police checkpoints or school administrators seeking "gifts" from parents to admit their children. As occurred elsewhere in Africa,[5] some of the most irritating instances seemed to be the small ways in which people encountered petty corruption in their routine, day-to-day dealings with civil servants and other lower-level state personnel. But they also resented "grand" corruption at the summits of power, including as a symptom of wider political and social injustices. Repeatedly, from British colonial times through the establishment of a stable electoral system at the end of the twentieth century, Ghanaians voiced anger at the corruption and high living of those at the top.

Consider just two of many instances: In August 1982, at a time when the radical regime of Flight Lieutenant Jerry Rawlings was encouraging public action against corruption, employees of the Ghana National Farmers Council ousted their former secretary-general for "embezzlement of huge sums of our money." That official, they explained, had "exploited and cheated us illiterate farmers for long. We shall not allow it any more."[6] A decade and a half later, many thousands of opposition party supporters poured into central Accra to protest the economic and political policies of Rawlings's then-ruling party, the National Democratic Congress. They marched, danced, sang, and carried banners proclaiming "Stop the corruption!"[7]

From time to time, people talked to pollsters. In a June 2008 survey of 1,200 Ghanaians by the CDD-Ghana, respondents most often perceived the police, tax authorities, courts, government agencies, parliament, presidency, and local government councils as corrupt. A clear majority felt that corruption was increasing.[8] A decade later, in 2017, the CDD surveyed a wider sample of 2,400 Ghanaians, finding strong perceptions of corruption surrounding most of the same occupations. On the overall trends, views were mixed: a third thought corruption had increased; slightly over a third, that it had decreased; and a fifth, that there was no change. By a wide margin, most believed that a person's social position was an important factor: while ordinary Ghanaians were seen as having little chance of using bribery to avoid paying taxes, going to court, or registering land that did not belong to them, between two-thirds and three-fourths of respondents believed that a rich person could do so.[9]

As this book demonstrates, class matters. I employ the concept here loosely, given the prevalence of ambiguous, fluid, and overlapping forms of class distinctions in Ghana and elsewhere in Africa, among both those who toil for a living and those at the upper reaches of society.[10] Just as class position can influence one's overall opportunities and outlooks, it may intersect with corruption in particular ways. Whether in terms of economic activity, property, or some other marker of social differentiation, a person's place in society can determine how corruption affects them and color how he or she views corruption, its links to the broader social and political system, and what remedies appear most appropriate. Put starkly, corruption favors the rich. Those who are already wealthy have the resources and connections (including access to foreign partners, markets, and financial networks) to illegally evade or distort state laws and regulations and bribe officials to look the other way. Corruption also favors the politically powerful, who are much better placed than lower officials—let alone ordinary citizens—to embezzle public funds or appoint friends and family members to advantageous positions. By combating such expressions of graft and malfeasance, opponents may fight not only for cleaner government but also against underlying social inequities and class inequalities.

Often, Ghanaians' perceptions of corruption also differed considerably from those of foreign observers. From external perspectives, Ghana had long been doing relatively well. The Berlin-based Transparency International's annual corruption rating, known as the Corruption Perceptions Index, was the best-known international measure. The index was compiled by combining the results of more than a dozen international surveys and then assigning a composite score for each country. Ranking those scores, in 2018 Transparency International placed Ghana at 78 out of 180 countries in the world, from least to most corrupt, thus somewhat below the global midpoint. But within sub-Saharan Africa, Ghana's ranking fared notably better, at 11 out of 49; that is, only 10 other African countries were considered less corrupt and 38, more corrupt. Nor was the country's performance static: Over time, Ghana's absolute score—scaled from 0, most corrupt, to 100, least corrupt—generally improved. In 1998, the first year Ghana was included in the Transparency International index, it was 33; two decades later, in 2018, it was 41.[11]

The discrepancies between external and domestic views of corruption in Ghana in part reflected differences in what was measured. Transparency International's index relied on surveys from international financial rating agencies and thus gave considerable weight to aspects of corruption related to external financial flows, investment conditions, and so on. Yet many Ghanaians felt the pinch differently. They saw it up close. In Ghana, as in Kenya, Nigeria, Sierra Leone, and other African countries,[12] ordinary people often had notions about corruption that were at odds with the standard conceptions of international donors, investors, and trade partners. And their definitions of corruption drew less from the law books than from their experiences with corruption's real social and political contexts.

Dominant Discourse

Although local debates and discussions about corruption have been rich, only some voices from Ghana and other African countries reached the international conference halls that mapped out the most common anticorruption remedies. The standardized agenda favored and promoted by the international financial institutions and major donor agencies—and oversimplified by the international media—privileged mainly the concerns of Africa's elites and of multinational corporations.[13]

There was some perversity in the anticorruption posture of many in the industrialized North. While bemoaning corruption in Africa and other poor regions, they minimized graft in their own countries as incidental aberrations and largely ignored their historical—and ongoing—role in fostering corruption elsewhere. Some states had abetted the slave trade, colonized much of Africa, and openly pillaged its natural resources. Subsequently, many continued to aid a succession of kleptocratic regimes, as their corporations extracted super profits and handed out bribes to secure access to Africa's minerals, oil, timber, and other wealth. Their banks and offshore tax havens enabled corrupt African presidents and ministers to launder and hide their ill-gotten riches. It was thus with some indignation that South Africa's parliamentary speaker, Frene Ginwala, addressing a European business ethics conference in 1996, highlighted the fact that many industrialized countries still considered foreign bribes to be legitimate tax-deductible "business expenses."[14]

In the late 1980s, some Northern governments and corporations began to edge away from the most egregious types of business practices and seek to tamp down on overt foreign bribery, in part to save costs. Their overall remedies bore a strong probusiness imprint that reflected underlying assumptions about the proper roles of state and market, in which the state was often regarded as an obstacle to market development.[15] While the specific measures recommended to fight graft varied, they generally revolved around a core model of liberal democracy, with formal political pluralism, drastically reduced state economic involvement, and unfettered markets and entrepreneurship. Most Africans welcomed greater democracy and political liberty, but many also contested some of the other assumptions.

One of the first formulations of the anticorruption agenda of the Northern "development community" came in a major 1989 World Bank report on Africa. Although it dealt primarily with economic policies, it also addressed state institutions. "Africa requires not just less government but better government," the World Bank affirmed, with corruption curbed and state activities oriented toward supporting productive activities rather than rent seeking.[16] In an era of constrained financing, World Bank officials also worried that "widespread corruption is siphoning away both domestic and foreign aid resources."[17]

Soon, Transparency International was founded in 1993, under the chairmanship of Peter Eigen, who told me that he had resigned from the World Bank two years earlier because raising corruption issues was then still "out of bounds" within that institution. Initial funding came from multinational corporations (including General Electric, Boeing, Merck, Rio Tinto Zinc, and Tate & Lyle). With that constituency in mind, the organization placed a particular accent on the need "to build bridges" for firms that might have engaged in extensive bribery but wanted to move away from corrupt practices.[18] Transparency International lobbied on corruption issues internationally, promoted national chapters in dozens of countries—including Ghana—organized conferences, and published reports. In 1995 it began issuing its annual Corruption Perceptions Index. Despite the promarket assumptions underlying some of its work, Transparency International and its chapters also involved academics, political figures, and representatives of nongovernmental organizations, giving depth to its local analyses.

By the late 1990s, the World Bank recognized some of the shortcomings of its earlier approach, admitting that its "overzealous rejection of government" had "tended to overshoot the mark" to the extent that "the good was as often cut as the bad." Instead, it argued, the emphasis should shift to strengthening state effectiveness: "Development without an effective state is impossible."[19] While that modified view of the state permitted limited social welfare functions—at least in providing certain public goods "undersupplied" by the market—there nevertheless remained a tendency by some officials to equate state welfarism with corruption and patronage.

To combat corruption specifically, the World Bank often proposed a checklist of typical remedies, many of them formulated in technical terms and supposedly nonpolitical: eliminating policy "distortions" that provided opportunities for corruption, raising civil service salaries to private sector levels, hiring and promoting civil servants on the basis of merit not patronage, enhancing the monitoring of officials, establishing clear rules and an independent judiciary, naming ombudsmen to hear citizens' complaints, and creating anticorruption commissions to investigate serious allegations. Beyond institutional reform, the World Bank did stray onto political terrain by also suggesting major changes in governing systems, arguing that democracy provided a better framework for combating corruption, through the scrutiny of opposition parties, civil associations, and an independent press.[20]

Who would enact such reforms? For the World Bank, successful transformation would be "crafted by dynamic leaders,"[21] that is, from above, by members of the political elites or at least those willing to embrace the international financial institutions' prescriptions. And in the face of inevitable skepticism about the feasibility of relying on administrators and politicians who were part of the prevailing networks of corruption, World Bank and International Monetary Fund (IMF) officials went a step further: They simply tagged explicit governance and anticorruption conditions onto their lending criteria, in hopes of strengthening local authorities' "political will" and avoiding backsliding.[22] Whether African leaders genuinely believed in that agenda or simply feigned acceptance to obtain the offered loans and aid grants, the Northern powers' ideas and prescriptions for "good governance" soon shaped the dominant anticorruption discourse.

African Critics

The World Bank/IMF vision of a noncorrupt state kept honest by competitive market forces and external pressure appeared to be shared by some of Africa's elites, including in Ghana. For many African critics of the earlier and very austere structural adjustment programs—often implemented by authoritarian regimes—the shift toward some acknowledgment of citizens' aspirations for transparency and democracy was welcome. Yet analysts across the continent raised many concerns. Skeptics worried about the practical problems of waiting on genuine reform from above. They questioned the extent to which Africa's former colonial powers were committed to a new democratic era. And they objected to the persistence of the economic liberalism and promarket policies underlying the Northern institutions' conception of the proper role of African government, which generally excluded notions of an active developmental state that could effectively deliver health, education, and other essential public services, favor greater social equity, and promote broad-based development.[23]

Among international scholars of corruption, some leaned toward the advocates of liberalism. But some were as skeptical as the African critics. Michael Johnston argued that either economic or political liberalization without a strong state or political and social institutions held little prospect for improved citizen participation or cleaner government. Liberalization in such a context would instead yield "choices for a powerful few, insecurity and deprivation for the many, and illicit connections between wealth and power."[24]

By exploring in detail the experiences of Ghana, this book highlights the main shortcomings and fallacies underlying the anticorruption perspectives of the Northern financial institutions, governments, and donor agencies. It does so in two main ways. First, contrary to standard approaches that see corruption as a malady in its own right, I demonstrate that in many essential respects it is more a symptom of deeper social and political problems. And second, as a result, combating corruption cannot be effective by implementing narrowly focused technocratic reforms, as prescribed by the main international and elite anticorruption organizations. Rather, combating corruption requires major societal mobilization and political change. Ordinary citizens, who often feel the impacts of corruption most acutely, have much to contribute to the struggle against it and may see its wider connections to unjust power relations more clearly than do reformers who come from the elites.

As the evidence and analysis in this book emphasize, corruption is a profoundly political phenomenon. The nature of the regime in power influences the avenues and opportunities for corruption. Authoritarian governments—whether characterized by patronage or predation, and with little open scrutiny—permit the politically connected to take advantage of weaknesses in the management of state resources. Electoral regimes usually have formal mechanisms for accountability yet paradoxically tend to have looser systems of control. Contrary to the view that equates democracy with good governance, electoral systems do not eliminate corruption; they may open new avenues for opposing it but sometimes do little more than change its forms and framework.

In several other respects as well, this book challenges, or at least questions, several recurrent features of the standard approaches to corruption:

- *History.* Corruption—and the importance of opposing it—was not first identified in the 1980s and 1990s by foreign financiers, aid officials, and governance experts. Reactions to corruption have had a long history in Ghana. From the checks on abusive chiefly authority in the indigenous societies of earlier centuries to the popular movements that resisted British exactions and the venality of colonial-supported "traditional authorities," and from the people's anticorruption committees of the 1980s to more contemporary citizens' movements, Ghanaians did not have to take cues from outside to demand accountability from their leaders.

- *Disaggregation.* The multiple manifestations of graft in Ghana and the varied ways in which Ghanaians reacted to them show that corruption must be disaggregated into its component parts. Corruption is not a single, uniform phenomenon. Attempts to define it in clear and comprehensive legal terms have been notoriously complicated, bedeviling academics and policymakers alike.[25] The 2003 United Nations Convention against Corruption avoided any definition, instead citing a range of specific acts that could be considered corrupt.[26] Commonly, analysts have identified an array of activities, including outright theft; embezzlement; misuse of state property; nepotism; abuse of public authority to exact payments, privileges, and favors; and collusive, crony-like relations between public officials and private businessmen. Ghana's national anticorruption plan for the decade 2015–24 contented itself with the vaguest of definitions: "the misuse of entrusted power for private gain."[27]

- *Context.* Given the absence of a universal definition, corruption also must be examined in context. It cannot be understood in isolation from the specific social and political meanings that individuals and institutions attach to it. As some scholars have noted, corruption can be adequately identified and analyzed only within its concrete circumstances, and each form may have a different consequence.[28] Depending on what other social or political problems prevail, corruption may pale by comparison. As the editors of a collection on corruption around the world noted, "There are worse evils and injustices in human society than corrupt practices."[29] And where corruption is deemed a major malady, its social meanings and implications may be as varied as the divisions and stratifications of society itself. Those at the top who benefit may be disproportionately male or from certain ethnic groups and thus seen by others as unfairly profiting from their position. Often, corruption reflects social and economic inequalities, favoring the rich to the disadvantage of the poor. As a workers' committee at the Bank of Ghana viewed it, "The exploitation of man by man and the possession by some individuals of more of the general wealth than they need is a manifest departure from natural law and the beginning of distortions and corruption in the life of the human community."[30] Meanwhile, ostentatious displays of wealth by those in public office could be interpreted in quite divergent ways: to political supporters as a demonstration of the patron's ability to hand out favors, but to his opponents as a sign of likely illicit acquisition and disdain for the disadvantaged. The differing social meanings people attach to the misuses of power and resources also account, in turn, for the often messy, contradictory, and limited outcomes of official anticorruption campaigns—not everyone pulls in the same direction.

- *Private actors.* Contrary to most official anticorruption programs and media portrayals, which focus overwhelming on graft by state officials and employees, unscrupulous private businessmen are also often involved. Many ordinary Ghanaians, in fact, see little reason to distinguish fraudulent conduct by market actors from corrupt dealings by public officials; both are considered exploitative. Frequently individuals from both the public and private worlds may be implicated. Such instances dated back to the colonial and immediate postcolonial eras. The 1975 commission of inquiry on corruption (quoted above) found "no intrinsic difference between corruption committed by or in respect of a public officer and corruption by or in respect of an officer of a private organisation."[31] Following the reintroduction of multiparty electoral politics in the early 1990s, there were numerous scandals involving businessmen and officials of both major political parties. Besides highlighting the roles of local merchants and business operators in abetting official corruption, some scandals also exposed the involvement of foreign businessmen and companies.

- *Politics.* Just as corruption itself is deeply political, so is opposition to it. Denunciations of corruption are often useful in waging political contests. As Steven Pierce observed in his study of corruption in Nigeria, "People talk about corruption in order to achieve specific political ends."[32] For leaders who just come into office, trying predecessors on corruption charges can help win credibility for the new regime while simultaneously weakening opposition. However partisan such efforts, they nevertheless can disrupt old systems of elite impunity and bring at least a partial measure of justice. For antigovernment opponents, denouncing corruption is a powerful tool for delegitimizing incumbent officeholders and mobilizing followers. In Ghana and elsewhere in Africa, noted Jean-François

Médard, "the theme of corruption is becoming more and more a political resource.... It is the battle horse of populist opposition."[33] Indeed, added Sidney Tarrow, from the scandals of prerevolutionary France to the downfall of the regimes in Eastern Europe and the former Soviet Union, "the importance of corruption, and especially of popular belief in corruption, may turn out to be a constant in the overthrow of authoritarian regimes."[34]

- *Institutions.* In the long run, new institutions for accountability and the ongoing monitoring of public resources, as many official governance programs suggest, have been more important than episodic prosecutions of corrupt leaders or bureaucrats. But institutions are far from enough. Elites, especially those in political power, are highly adept at weakening, delaying, sidestepping, or simply ignoring the anticorruption codes and bodies they agree to establish. As Ghanaian political scientist Kwame Ninsin observed, although the 1992 constitution provided for a significant body of laws and institutions for the effective management of public finances and minimization of corruption, elite domination ensured that "they are unable to function effectively and when they act, they are unable to act impartially."[35]

- *Popular vigilance.* Finally, as Ghana's experience has amply shown, reducing corruption requires more than small circles of elite reformers. It also requires popular vigilance by wider sectors of society. It needs grassroots activists and other citizens alert to instances of malfeasance, able to publicly expose them, and organized enough to apply pressure on the authorities to act. As a workers' committee at the Tarkwa gold mine affirmed in 1982, employees "must be vigilant at their various work places" to "check abuses and corrupt practices."[36] Decades later, in the wake of revelations that numerous politically connected businessmen had obtained irregular state funding, those businessmen were able to avoid repaying the funds until a civil society group, OccupyGhana, won a Supreme Court suit in 2017 compelling repayment.[37] Based on their experience, many Ghanaians have limited expectations of initiatives from above. They have come to believe that popular scrutiny and mobilization are necessary to ensure that officials and institutions take stronger action against corruption—and the political and social injustices that feed it.

While Ghana's case is in certain respects unique, citizens in other African countries—indeed, around the world—will recognize some of its features. Beyond the widespread experience of colonial domination and its legacies, independent Ghana has been governed, at different points, by a full spectrum of regime types: single-party, military, revolutionary, multiparty. And while its systems of corruption may not have been the most debilitating, the forms and dynamics they took will have some familiarity across much of Africa, whether characterized as instances of "the politics of the belly" or "state capture."[38] The modest successes of Ghanaians in exposing and combating the phenomenon may also stir some inspiration beyond the country's borders.

2

Chiefs and Colonial Bureaucrats

Before British colonial authorities drew the boundaries of the state today known as Ghana, the territories that eventually constituted the area were inhabited by various indigenous societies. Some of their symbols and social values continue to resonate in Ghanaian political life. And their mechanisms for enforcing accountability of chiefs and other persons of authority prefigured contemporary strategies for ensuring government transparency and constraining abuses of office. Those controls were in place long before colonial administrators sought to impose their own notions of "good governance."

Ghana's precolonial entities spanned a wide spectrum, from decentralized societies governed by lineage elders to local chiefdoms covering modest populations and expanses of territory, to more centralized and hierarchical kingdoms—most notably Asante, which ruled over major populations, engaged in conquest, and extracted tribute from subjugated peoples. These societies' degrees of "stateness" roughly correlated with two elements: the local economy's ability to produce surpluses beyond the bare necessities of familial or clan survival, and the exigencies of warfare and military defense, factors that have been identified in state-making processes elsewhere.[1] The former permitted the accumulation of wealth by some and the emergence of more specialized and nonproductive occupations, such as warriors, priests, and chiefs. Prior to colonial conquest, the possibility of social surpluses often depended on population density and the availability of labor, rainfall and the fertility of soils, the forms of organization of agricultural production, and linkages to external trade routes and markets (initially, local produce exchanged for fabrics and other manufactured goods brought by trans-Saharan caravans, and later, under the influence of European outposts along the coast, accelerated trade in gold and slaves). Prior forms of social organization also mattered, as traditional mechanisms of wealth redistribution and communal solidarity constrained the extent of stratification and individual accumulation. However, war, conquest, migration, and the gradual spread of market relations tended over time to erode such traditional controls.

While they lasted, customary constraints and checks on the authority of elders and chiefs, combined with limited opportunities for enrichment, made it difficult and sometimes risky for those in positions of power to step beyond their socially defined duties and obligations. That did not make precolonial African societies either democratic or socially just. Women, social juniors, commoners, immigrants, war captives, and slaves—the majority in many such societies—had little or no voice in the management of affairs. Popular interpretations of "tradition," as far as they left behind any historical evidence, sometimes diverged quite dramatically from the dominant versions handed down by the chiefs' oral historians and praise-singers. Nevertheless, the constraints and checks on those in authority were real, if limited.

Among the peoples at the more decentralized end of the spectrum were several similar groups straddling the border between present-day Ghana and Burkina Faso, known variously as Lobi and Dagari, among others. They had no chiefs and therefore no defined territorial organization. Their main social units were small farming groups of related families led by a patrilineal elder. Within them, surpluses of millet, the main staple, were redistributed by depositing the harvests of all fields, both familial and collective, into common granaries, to which everyone had access, especially in times of shortage.[2]

The Ewe of southeastern Ghana similarly had no tradition of strong indigenous chiefship, although certain groups occupied slightly different portions of the spectrum of stateness. Those of Abutia, in the northern part of the Ewe territories, have a founding myth of flight from an oppressive chief in what is today Togo.[3] Until 1870, the highest authorities were lineage elders, but around that time there emerged the *fia* (a term that German and British colonial administrators later translated as "chief"), which appears to have been modeled on nearby Akan chieftaincies. According to Michel Verdon, they were in fact more like "ritual custodians." Their authority did not extend beyond the village and was limited to presiding over judicial cases and summoning a council of elders, which governed by consensus. The fia himself traditionally had to be young, humble, and respectful of the population; was subject to prosecution like any other villager; and could be "destooled" (removed from the stool, the traditional symbol of office). The fia received no tribute of any kind; as a result, "none of them could accumulate wealth by virtue of their position."[4]

The Anlo Ewe of the coastal region moved further in the direction of chieftaincy. Through the seventeenth century, they had only local military leaders and lineage elders. But following a series of wars with neighboring societies between 1730 and 1742, Anlo society became more militarized, and some commanders were able to transform themselves into chiefs, borrowing the title *awafia* from the Akwamu chiefdom (which governed Anlo for a time). Meanwhile, new sources of wealth developed from technological innovations in Anlo salt production and the involvement of Anlo traders in the burgeoning river-borne trade in slaves, ivory, and manufactured goods between interior societies and European ships along the coast. Rich traders gained broader authority by helping to finance Anlo military campaigns, enabling some to create their own stools, known as *hozikpui* (wealth stools). None of these chiefs, however, had any rights to collect taxes or tolls, while effective authority over land and people remained with the lineage and clan elders.[5]

Among the Krobo, an Adangme group directly west of Anlo, a similar process developed, spurred on the one hand by an increase in wealth from Krobo preeminence in the nineteenth-century palm oil trade and on the other by the proximity of Akan warfare and the raids that accompanied the growth of slave trading. By the end of the 1830s, political authority had shifted from priests to war leaders and paramount chiefs, known as *konors*, to some extent modeled on Akan political structures and under the influence of Akan refugees assimilated into Krobo society.[6]

Apart from Asante itself, one of the larger precolonial polities within Ghana's current borders was the Gonja kingdom, originally established in the sixteenth or seventeenth century by mounted warriors moving southward from the upper Niger River. They subdued several small local groups and by the nineteenth century had established an extensive polyglot empire north of the Akan chiefdoms. Power in Gonja remained diffuse, despite the kingdom's military tradition, ongoing wars with neighboring societies, and own slave-raiding expeditions. The ruling dynasty was divided into several segments residing in different territorial divisions of the kingdom, while the chieftaincy rotated among the major divisions. The rotational system, combined with chiefs' obligations to share revenue with the rest of the community, inhibited long-term concentration of property in one segment of the ruling estate. Moreover, for any chief to be installed, the cooperation of both the Muslim and commoner estates was required. And while the central political authorities posted administrative chiefs to most villages, the latter were always assisted by local shrine priests and "masters of the earth" who represented the original peoples of the area. Finally, there was a strong tradition in some of the divisional capitals of providing sanctuary to people fleeing the punishment or exactions of a paramount or other chiefs.[7]

The history of the Akan peoples, who today make up about half the population of Ghana, moved across the entire spectrum, from small, localized societies to various contending chiefdoms to a relatively powerful, centralized state, Asante. Blessed with deposits of gold, the Akan were drawn into the world economy as early as the fifteenth and sixteenth centuries by way of European mercantile outposts along the "Gold Coast," as those foreigners called it. Akan merchants not only traded locally mined gold but also served as middlemen for gold, slaves, and other goods from elsewhere in West Africa. That trade, combined with the impressive output of the region's forests and agriculture, stimulated social differentiation. Achievement through the accumulation of wealth came to be codified positively in the dominant value system, with richer entrepreneurs known most simply as *obirempon* ("big men," a term that has persisted in contemporary Ghanaian political discourse). In part, however, their wealth was still viewed in collective terms, as a symbol of community prosperity more generally. Numerous social prohibitions continued to discourage lavish spending, the squandering of accumulated wealth, or the wholesale transmission of property to one's descendants. But eventually the most successful obirempon institutionalized their wealth in chiefship, converting economic clients into political retainers and adopting various regalia to symbolize their new political authority.[8]

Still, Akan chiefs were subject to checks on their power and authority. Upon taking office, many had to swear formal oaths stipulating their responsibilities to the community and the conduct expected of them while they occupied the royal stool. By the early seventeenth century, there also began to emerge structured *asafo* companies among most of the Akan peoples, especially the coastal Fante. Originating as warrior organizations, the asafo soon extended their activities to include collecting taxes and tolls, maintaining law and order, clearing roads, building marketplaces, and providing communal labor. All able adult males were eligible and expected to participate in the companies, which "connoted the third estate or common people." Their members were referred to politically as *mbrantsie* (youngmen), as distinguished from the *mpanyinfu* (chiefs and elders).[9] The most important political function of the asafo companies was to serve as a popular voice in the selection or removal of chiefs. According to Maxwell Owusu, "The members of the Asafo had a sacred duty to safeguard the interests of the wider local community against rulers or leaders who misused or abused their power."[10]

By the end of the seventeenth century, the nascent Asante state, centered in Kumasi, had achieved supremacy over other Akan chiefdoms. The following century it became an expansionist power, subjugating neighboring Akan and non-Akan peoples through conquest and the imposition of taxes and tribute, with the empire at its height covering a large portion of present-day Ghana. More than other, localized chiefdoms, the Asante state, headed at the pinnacle by an *Asantehene* sitting on a throne (the Golden Stool), displayed a considerable gulf between the ruling aristocracy, the *asikafo* ("men of gold," associated with the state and long-distance trade), and the village communities over which the state governed.[11] In the characterization of Catherine Coquery-Vidrovitch, Asante was a "clearly differentiated *class* society," in contrast to neighboring societies in which the basic social unit remained the extended family.[12]

Perhaps more important than the emergence of clearer distinctions in social position, as McCaskie noted, was that state office came to be separated to a greater degree from the subsistence, matrilineal bases of the social order as the "older, historic ties of organic continuity between state and society" were progressively weakened.[13] Beyond its considerable implications for all those on the lower rungs of Asante society (not to mention the slaves, war captives, and subject peoples who had no jural claim on the state), this dissolution meant two things for the accumulation process: the amassing of wealth was channeled increasingly through state channels, while simultaneously the avenues for accumulation outside the state were narrowed considerably. Although the amassing of wealth in gold, people, land, and food stocks had begun much earlier, as McCaskie observed, "in the eighteenth and nineteenth centuries, participation in the office-holding structures of the state became the key to accumulation of these resources; membership in the state became the only certain avenue to the possibility of acquiring great wealth. The state sought ways in which to monopolize the (re)sources of enrichment, and means by which to determine access to them."[14]

That shift made it much more difficult for individuals to become obirempon simply through trade or control over productive resources outside the office-holding echelons of state service. According to McCaskie, "All the successive levels of upward mobility, from insertion through aggrandizement, advancement and reward, depended on having access to opportunities sanctioned by the state." In turn, heavy death duties, inheritance taxes, fines for infractions of Asante law, and other controls prevented the dynastic transmission and consolidation of wealth. Thus "the emergence of a class of hereditary property owners was blocked, and the state effectively retained a monopoly over access to wealth and its redistribution."[15]

Meanwhile, as the nineteenth century progressed, the central Asante state became increasingly bureaucratized, with a proliferation of state offices. Ivor Wilks's massive study of Asante in that period described the development of a complex and differentiated administration, with numerous departments to oversee trade, military recruitment, and financial matters—including separate offices of the treasury, mint (which managed the common currency, gold dust), and revenue assessment and collection.

In principle, the power of the Asantehene was not absolute, and he usually acted upon the advice of a council representing the various Asante provinces and chiefdoms.[16] Yet in practice, political and administrative power often continued to be exercised in a highly personalized manner, symbolized by the very wide prerogatives of the Asantehene and his appointees to levy taxes, impose fines, and utilize stool (state) funds. Under the circumstances, it might be somewhat misleading to describe departures from established norms governing the utilization of Asante state resources with references to contemporary notions of state corruption, originally derived from European contexts marked by more delineated public and private realms.[17] Nevertheless, the concept of a public treasury had at least begun to emerge—as distinct from the Asantehene's household treasury—and specified norms governed the uses of such funds. Careful records were kept and audits were conducted regularly. If funds fell short through mismanagement or apparent theft, those deemed responsible were executed. Punishment was not systematic, however, and politically powerful or favored individuals could get off lightly. In 1817, for example, an influential royal counselor was discovered to have accepted a bribe to misrepresent a case brought before the Asantehene; though bribery was a capital offense, he was only fined twenty ounces of gold.[18]

In periods of broader political and social tensions, perceived violations of customary standards of taxation or the use of stool funds contributed to conflict. By the last half of the nineteenth century, heavy taxation, nepotism, and the arbitrary imposition of fines and seizures of property were deemed to have become excessive, especially under the Asantehenes Kofi Kakari (1867–74) and Mensa Bonsu (1874–83). In Asante historical memory, Kakari was judged to have squandered state property, including on numerous concubines, and to have violated historic norms in promotions, taxation, and judicial fines. He eventually was "destooled"—ousted from office—for removing gold ornaments from a sacred mausoleum and giving royal jewels to his wives for their personal adornment. Mensa Bonsu, his successor, was considered as—if not more—avaricious and extortionate; in addition, he executed many noblemen simply to seize their wives and properties.[19] That spurred disgruntlement among the Asante provincial aristocracy. More immediately, such practices provoked the emergence in 1879–80 of a movement, called *odomankama*, which used interpretations of Asante religious beliefs to directly challenge the legitimacy of the Asantehene. The participants in the movement "located the source of all of the ills of contemporary Asante in what they saw as the state's deviant and corrupt subversion of and turning away from fundamental prescriptions."[20] After a failed assassination attempt against Mensa Bonsu, the Asantehene suppressed the movement by exterminating much of its membership.

In both cases, however, irregular or extortionate financial conduct was but one factor in the opposition to the monarchs. Kakari also was blamed for military losses by the Asante army, while Mensa Bonsu's increasing reliance on widespread executions and other forms of repression pushed a section of the junior aristocracy to ally with lower social strata in a popular movement that finally overthrew him in 1883 and briefly took power in Kumasi.[21] Not only were two Asantehenes ousted one after the other, but the rate of destoolments of other chiefs also increased notably, from an average of one every 5–6 years during the previous 120 years to nearly two dozen during the decade and a half of the two Asantehenes' successive reigns.[22] Whether those lower chiefs were destooled for incurring the displeasure of their superiors, through factional infighting, or because of popular opposition, the phenomenon reflected heightened political instability in Asante overall. The mid to late 1880s were troubled years, marked by growing demands by provincial officeholders for the return of seized properties and the outbreak of open civil war among rival factions in Kumasi—all in a context of mounting pressure from British forces securely implanted in the coastal regions.

European Conquest

Well before the first glimmers of colonial ambition, European maritime powers established commercial outposts along much of the coastline of the Gulf of Guinea. The opportunity to trade for gold, ivory, kola nuts, and slaves attracted to the Gold Coast merchants and chartered companies from Portugal, Holland, Denmark, England, and even the German principality of Brandenburg. Between the mid-fifteenth and late sixteenth centuries, they built a score of forts and castles at harbors and river mouths along the 170 miles of shore between Winneba and the Assini

River, now Ghana's westernmost border. For a long time, those early European interlopers demonstrated little interest in the societies that lay inland, as long as the trade routes stayed open and the Fante and Ga, who lived along much of the coast, did not cause them undue trouble.

Most European competitors had pulled out by the late eighteenth century; the British remained the dominant power, managing affairs through a council of merchants based in the harbor town of Cape Coast. By then, Asante had emerged as the paramount Akan state, exercising a strong hold over the interior trade routes and posing a serious military threat to neighboring societies, such as the Fante, an Akan people whose chiefs had renounced their loyalty to the Asantehene in Kumasi. Briefly, at the start of the nineteenth century, the merchants' council supported Asante's ambition to resubjugate the Fante but then reversed itself, realizing that the British bargaining position would be weakened if Asante succeeded in extending its rule down to the coast. That decision soon led to the creation of an informal British "protectorate" over the territory. In 1821 London took direct responsibility for the coastal forts, placing them under the authority of the governor of Sierra Leone, Sir Charles MacCarthy. Tensions between Britain and Asante immediately escalated. On the pretext of defending the Fante chiefdoms against Asante, Sir Charles launched a military drive on Kumasi in 1824 but was killed at Nsamankow. Two years later, the Asante army, during a renewed march seaward, was defeated by an alliance of coastal forces backed by the British. Overall, however, Britain's position remained weak, and in face of continued Asante power, it prudently bided its time.

For the next half century, Britain gradually consolidated its position in the Gold Coast, though not without difficulty. Progressively greater British incursions into various facets of Fante life incurred widespread anger. London's fiscal conservatism dictated that the colony's administration raise much of its own revenue, leading to an attempt in 1852 to impose an annual poll tax of one shilling per person. Stiff opposition erupted. Ordinary

Fante resented the fact that the bulk of the taxes were used for civil servants and administrative functioning, with only 8 percent earmarked for schools and roads, while chiefs objected to tax collectors' efforts to supplant them. Collecting the tax proved next to impossible, and in 1864 the authorities abandoned it.[23]

Many Fante chiefs also chafed at the gradual whittling away of their power and authority. They believed the nature of their subordination to the Cape Coast authorities should have been similar to the relations that prevailed within traditional Akan society, in which a lower chief's allegiance to a superior meant only a commitment to render military service, not abandonment of sovereignty over local laws and customs. Against those traditional conventions, the British authorities sought to impose their own laws and courts and in various other ways circumscribed the power of chiefs. That push provoked a major reaction. In 1865 many of the chiefs in the Gold Coast, with prevalent popular support, came together to form the Fante Confederacy. The confederacy explicitly sought internal self-government and adopted a constitution providing for a king-president, supported by councillors and a national assembly of local dignitaries. Over the next few years, it began establishing its own state apparatus and instituted a tax in the Fante districts to raise revenue for officials' salaries and other expenses. Many Fante, who a few years earlier had resisted the British authorities' poll tax, were quite willing to financially support the confederacy. (With the appearance of distinct state revenues and state officials, the Fante Confederacy experienced at least a few cases of corruption, including an instance in which a Fante official traveling on confederacy business submitted a false expense claim.)[24]

The confederacy also formed a military force, initially with volunteers but later through organized recruitment and training. By early 1869, it had raised an army of 15,000. While not directly challenging the British presence, the Fante Confederacy did try to expand its control by eliminating the Dutch and Asante influences in the western parts of Fante territory. The Fante army defeated the

Dutch at Komenda but failed to take Elmina, the most formidable of the Dutch forts. Meanwhile, the British authorities in Cape Coast grew alarmed at the confederacy's influence, which not only posed a potential threat to British dominance in the Fante areas but also had inspired the formation of a Ga Confederation in the Accra region. Rather than attacking the Fante Confederacy militarily, the British administrators played on local rivalries to turn Fante chiefs against each other, including by paying "subsidies" to some. Those divide-and-rule tactics compounded other difficulties facing the confederacy, among them the military setback at Elmina and the fact that the wartime disruptions in Fante trade made it difficult for many districts to pay the taxes levied on them. As a consequence, the confederacy collapsed in 1873.[25]

Almost immediately the British launched another war with Asante. It culminated in the sacking of Kumasi in 1874 and a treaty obliging the Asantehene to formally renounce any claims to territories within the Gold Coast. But that outcome still left Asante a strong, independent power. The insecurity of the British position prompted London to tighten and expand its control over the coastal region, "in the interest of civilization and of commerce," as one British MP put it.[26] The British bought out the remaining Dutch forts, including Elmina, proclaimed a formal protectorate over the Gold Coast, and within a few years had seized new territories to the east, inhabited mainly by Ewe. A governor was appointed, and the capital was shifted from Cape Coast to Accra, considered healthier for Europeans.

The rest of the century saw further indigenous resistance. People in the inland and maritime states of the protectorate repeatedly protested renewed efforts to impose taxes, British interference in chieftaincy disputes, regulations for compulsory labor, the formation of municipal councils that excluded African representation, and attempts to undermine traditional land tenure arrangements. Opposition to British land policy was so great that the colonial authorities had to abandon some of their plans to control land allocations and introduce freehold tenure.[27]

Above all, British officials in Accra worried about the continued survival of an independent and militarily formidable Asante. Despite the 1874 treaty renouncing further territorial claims, the Asante leaders in Kumasi still aspired to bring all Akan areas within their empire. Beyond the constant military tensions this generated, the example of Asante's power—combined with the direct agitation of pro-Asante political factions within the protectorate—complicated Britain's efforts to consolidate power over the region. Asante's strength also blocked any prospect of British expansion farther into the interior. Those worries turned to dismay when, in the wake of the Asante civil war of 1884–88, the victorious alliance installed Prempeh as the new Asantehene (Britain had covertly supported the losing faction). Within a few years, Prempeh succeeded in reuniting all six of the core Asante states and restoring Kumasi's authority over most of the outer ones, unleashing a wave of renewed Asante nationalism. Prempeh also made major progress toward regaining Salaga, which would have enabled Asante's external trade to bypass British control through Lomé, then under German occupation. At a time of growing competition among European colonial powers to stake their effective claims in Africa, another worry for London was Prempeh's success in opening new arms supply routes through French-controlled Côte d'Ivoire. Especially alarming were Prempeh's efforts to forge an alliance with Samori Touré, who in the 1880s had forged a powerful Dyula state in defiance of French military forces; Samori has been considered "the greatest military organizer and empire-builder in the history of West Africa."[28]

Before such an alliance could be consolidated, British forces moved quickly and massively into Kumasi in January 1896. They captured Prempeh and exiled him first to Sierra Leone and later to the Seychelles Islands off the east coast of Africa. When in March 1900 the Gold Coast governor traveled to Kumasi to announce that Prempeh was not returning and to demand that the Asante turn over to Britain the Golden Stool, the symbol of their nationhood, a vast rebellion erupted across Asante to drive the

British out. Well organized and operating under the authority of Yaa Asantewaa, Asante's "queen mother," the rebel forces inflicted heavy losses on the British. But by the end of the year the British had received reinforcements from Nigeria, Sierra Leone, and elsewhere, the rebels' stocks of ammunition were running out, and some important Asante chiefdoms had defected to the British. The rebellion was put down. More than a dozen of its central leaders were captured and exiled to the Seychelles. In 1891, Asante was officially annexed to the Gold Coast, as the crown colony called "Ashanti."[29] The same year, a British protectorate was proclaimed over the kingdoms of the Northern Territories, and during World War I Britain occupied a portion of Togoland, formerly ruled by Germany, thereby fixing the Gold Coast's easternmost boundaries.

Colonial State Making

Imposed through conquest, the new colonial state continued to rest on force and the threat of force, regardless of home office self-justifications about bringing "civilization," economic development, and social progress to Africa. Military garrisons and local constabularies remained vigilant and ready to act and sometimes did so with great brutality. Colonial taxation and especially the imposition of various forms of compulsory labor required considerable coercion, almost on a routine basis. In parts of the Gold Coast with a history of resistance, the British imported Hausa troops from Nigeria and gave them wide latitude to brutalize and extort the local population.

Yet force alone could not suffice. This was not a colony of large-scale European settlement, as in eastern or southern Africa. Given the inhospitable climate and prevalence of debilitating diseases, few British personnel were willing to live in the colony. Nor was the Colonial Office keen to shoulder the cost of large military garrisons. So once the initial resistance to conquest had been suppressed, the authorities shifted toward greater civil administration.

Numerous state institutions were introduced at both central and local levels. Senior positions were filled by British nationals and junior posts by Africans who had learned to speak, and perhaps read and write, English. Those institutions—to collect taxes, count and categorize residents, build and maintain roads, recruit labor, draft laws and regulations, police, provide sanitation and basic health services, and conduct numerous other routine tasks—were often modeled on those of the metropole. But since they were externally imposed, not built up through a protracted process of social interaction as they had been in Europe, they enjoyed very little legitimacy. The colonial administrators sometimes accommodated local concerns but ultimately were accountable to their ministries in London, not to the African peoples they governed. So however much the governors in Accra desired local support and cooperation, the nature of the colonial state severely limited the possibilities. Even the tiny strata of African merchants, chiefs, and "scholars" (literate youngmen) who actively engaged with the colonial authorities often did so with underlying resentment and tension. This was true even in the Fante areas, where prolonged exposure to market relations and the spread of English literacy had conditioned a greater number of Africans to bureaucratic, nontribal forms of administration.

Very early, realizing the difficulties of trying to extend their administration's direct presence much beyond the main towns, Gold Coast authorities opted for a patronage relationship with chiefs and other local dignitaries, paying them stipends to ensure order among their subjects and followers. Although many British officials spoke in terms of preserving the traditional status of the chiefs, some, such as a certain Captain Lees, explicitly viewed the chiefs as simple agents of colonial administration, stating that their power "should rest rather upon English authority, than upon their innate right."[30] Despite the serious limits of their traditional authority, chiefs served as key linchpins between the overall colonial state and the subject population.

Whatever chiefs' continued weight and influence, ultimate power remained with the central colonial administrations, represented at the local level by the district commissioner. In contrast to the administrative checks and separations of authority that prevailed in London and among many precolonial polities in Africa, those local officials exercised varying degrees of "fused power," to borrow Mahmood Mamdani's apt term.[31] They not only wielded executive authority but also legislated. Although responsible for implementing general colonial policy, poor communications between the capital and the districts left the commissioners considerable leeway in drafting local rules and regulations, occasionally in ways not anticipated or desired by their superiors. They likewise carried out judicial functions, both directing the new British law courts and supervising or acting as judges of appeal over the traditional courts that continued to operate, with limited jurisdictions, under chiefs and elders.

As elsewhere in Africa, those colonial officers "used their prerogatives to cultivate patronistic relationships with those under their command, accommodating social forces that they feared they could not control." In the process, they "created new privileged groups within African societies or allowed established powerholders to sustain their status and wealth."[32] Whatever local patronage arrangements the functionaries fashioned, ultimately those were backstopped by the colonial state's coercive power.

To staff central and provincial administrative offices, African civil servants were required, including clerks, messengers, drivers, guards, and record keepers of various kinds. Others were needed to communicate directives to indigenous populations and provide information about local political and social structures to European administrators. In the coastal regions, with their long exposure to European traders and the presence of some missionary-run schools, Africans literate in English were generally not hard to recruit. But in the more recently conquered Ashanti and the Northern Territories, it often was necessary to staff offices with Fante and other coastal civil servants.

In training such administrative staff, indeed in the very act of establishing new bureaucratic institutions, British authorities sought to introduce concepts of public accountability and organizational behavior similar to those that were supposed to prevail back home. But such standards were not adhered to scrupulously. The reports and correspondence of officials are full of complaints about the conduct of African civil servants, with some regarding Africans as inherently corrupt. One Gold Coast administrator claimed that he had met only two or three honest "native government servants" during his tenure, although others disputed such a sweeping characterization.[33]

While the colonial administration may have suffered some losses due to financial diversion by its civil servants, ordinary people were the main victims. It was not uncommon for an African state employee to use his position to extort money, goods, or services from local villagers or poor urban residents. Such conduct does not appear to have overly bothered the colonial authorities if it was not so excessive that it provoked active resistance. Indeed, despite the occasional verbal or written complaints about corruption, the general stance of senior officials was quite tolerant. Permitting African staff to misuse their positions for personal or familial interests was one way to help them supplement their meager salaries at little direct cost to the colonial treasury, while simultaneously cementing their loyalty to the colonial service. In that respect, the colonial administration functioned as much along patronage lines as according to bureaucratic norms, setting patterns of conduct that were to last long after its departure.

The authorities had other reasons to distrust their African staff. The involvement of so many literate Africans in the insurgency of the Fante Confederacy and in subsequent protest movements in the coastal regions left many colonial officials highly suspicious of the political sympathies of educated Africans in general. By the turn of the century, there thus developed a marked reluctance to recruit many more skilled Africans into the administration, for fear that they might ultimately use their organizational abilities and positions against the colonial order itself.

That was despite the scarcity of British personnel. As of 1922, there were only 89 British political administrators in the Gold Coast, one for every 27,253 people in the south, for every 17,425 in Ashanti, and for every 34,204 in the Northern Territories.[34] Clearly, the capacities of the colonial administration to directly govern were extremely limited. The authorities needed other means of anchoring their rule. So they leaned more heavily on the chiefs.

Indirect Rule

In their relations with chiefs, British colonial administrators often justified their practice in the language of "indirect rule," that is, a broad policy of leaving much local authority in traditional hands. Lord Lugard, who first formalized indirect rule in northern Nigeria, characterized it as a policy of cooperation, not subordination, with British resident administrators acting in advisory capacities and chiefs in local executive roles, albeit with some modifications in their traditional responsibilities in matters such as justice and taxation. The chiefs, Lugard argued, should have "well-defined duties and an acknowledged status equally with the British officials."[35] This, he hoped, would preserve their legitimacy in the eyes of local populations and thereby facilitate political stability.

In reality, British professions of cooperation and respect for tradition were often little more than rhetoric designed to justify coercive domination. They made it clear to chiefs who the real rulers were, often interfered in chieftaincy succession disputes to ensure the selection of favored candidates, and came down heavily if local circumstances threatened to escape control.

A few early British governors of the Gold Coast proposed appointing more district commissioners to live in rural areas and work directly with chiefs. But the Colonial Office in London agreed only to appoint some traveling officers to periodically tour rural areas to hear complaints, receive taxes, and make reports. It disclaimed any intention of curtailing the powers of chiefs simply because they did not always administer justice in accordance with British legal notions. In some respects, the Colonial Office proclaimed in 1880, the powers of chiefs should be strengthened, since the administration in Accra was not able to substitute its own authority in "the inaccessible wilds and impenetrable forests of the interior."[36]

The precise tenor of the relationship varied by region. In the south, the emphasis of various initiatives and laws to define the role of chiefs was colored by memories of the chiefs' defiance, especially their support for the Fante Confederacy. Accordingly, the Native Jurisdiction Ordinance of 1878 explicitly reduced chiefs' powers by giving the administration authority to subdivide chiefdoms, set aside particular bylaws, dismiss chiefs, and permit defendants tried before traditional courts to appeal the judgments to English colonial courts.[37] After affirming the administration's supremacy over chiefs, the ordinances then sought to protect chiefs from challenges from below. They removed most popular checks on chiefly authority, stipulating that no chief could be removed (destooled) without government confirmation. The Native Administration Ordinance of 1927 then expanded the chiefs' authority in judicial matters. To further ensure their cooperation, it also widened the range of revenues available to chiefs, including fees and fines from court cases and payments for travel and attendance at provincial council meetings.[38]

The administration's attitude toward chiefs in Ashanti followed a trajectory similar to that in the south. Although some British officials expressed open admiration for the way the old Asante empire had indirectly governed its non-Akan vassal states in the north,[39] they were not yet ready to apply similar indirect-rule methods in Ashanti. The first three decades of British rule instead emphasized bringing the once-powerful kingdom under firm control. Not only was the top of the chiefly hierarchy removed with the deposition and exile of Prempeh in 1896, but many other chiefs were also deported. They were replaced by appointees deemed loyal to the British, some from disgruntled factions of royal lineages. Some were not even natives of the local communities over which they were enstooled. Ashanti chiefs subsequently posed no major challenges to overall British domination, and as the authorities in Accra grew more confident, they gradually shifted toward again strengthening chiefs' administrative and judicial powers. A 1924 ordinance established separate chiefly treasuries. That same year the government allowed Prempeh to return from exile; although he was not permitted to resume his traditional post as Asantehene, he was installed two years later as *Kumasihene*, chief of the Kumasi division, a position he held until his death in 1932. In 1935 the authorities went a step further by allowing Osei Agyeman Prempeh II to be enstooled as Asantehene, thus formally reconstituting the old chiefly elite as a key regional component of the colonial state.

The Northern Territories presented quite different scenarios. The British authorities regarded some districts as too socially decentralized to govern effectively, so they unilaterally created hierarchical chieftaincies. Among the Tallensi, ritual *nam* chiefs, who previously had limited authority, were elevated to executive status, with the power to govern much wider areas. Elsewhere, lineage elders with some claim to being representative were promoted to chieftaincies. In Bolgatanga and Sekoti, some local "big men," who had wealth but no recognized traditional authority, were simply proclaimed chiefs. Where chieftaincy systems existed prior to British rule and the chiefs had signed treaties of "protection" with the new colonial authorities, the latter usually tried to work with them from the outset, sometimes giving them responsibilities that went far beyond those sanctioned by custom.

Dagomba, one of the more hierarchical states in the northeast, followed a trajectory like that of Ashanti. At first, the British authorities forbade recognition of the paramount chief, the *Ya Na*, whose capital, Yendi, was then under German rule in neighboring Togo. The tenure of the lower-level Dagomba chiefs was made conditional on continued British approval, and a few were deposed. After Germany's defeat in World War I and the incorporation of Yendi into the Northern Territories, the Ya Na's paramountcy was again recognized, but British officials routinely intervened in Dagomba disputes over succession to the throne.

More generally, Dagomba chiefs saw their coercive and judicial powers curtailed, and they were obliged to forcibly recruit local labor for British construction projects. As one British administrator commented in 1928, "In reality the chiefs are practically powerless; they have neither revenue nor authority; they have tended to become mere sergeant-majors through whom the Administration can address the rank and file."[40] By the 1930s, however, under the combined influences of a European economic slump (which brought retrenchments in the colonial administration) and the growing power of officials in Accra who were more ideologically committed to indirect rule, policy in the Northern Territories shifted toward strengthening the chiefs as more autonomous agents of colonial administration. An acting chief commissioner explained that the goal was to give "a more particular acknowledgement than . . . heretofore, to the standing and authority of Chiefs over their people, and to clothe them with powers, enforceable by law, which they had not previously exercised."[41] Those included powers to arrest, fine, and collect "tribute taxes." Henceforth, all chiefly appointments were made directly by the Ya Na, and for life. There were no longer any opportunities for ordinary subjects or lineage elders to remove unpopular, incompetent, or even incapacitated chiefs.

In all regions, the enhanced powers accorded to chiefs, combined with the removal of traditional checks on their conduct, facilitated abuses. Although chieftaincy treasuries were formally established to support official activities and local development projects, there were no effective mechanisms of accountability. Chiefs and other members of their immediate entourages frequently dipped into the treasuries for personal use. Some collected tribute payments that were never deposited into the treasuries, using the revenue for local patronage purposes. Acting as judges, chiefs sometimes imposed heavy fines for even minor breaches of local customs and administrative regulations. Acting as labor recruiters for the government, some conscripted more than the required number, diverting the extra laborers to work on their own farms. As the *Gold Coast Independent*, a weekly newspaper reflecting the views of African intellectuals in the south, commented on the British policy of indirect rule in 1919: "Is it any wonder that selfish and avaricious Chiefs who have greedily drunk of this new wine, have become intoxicated?"[42]

The many references to chiefly misconduct in official reports and correspondence suggest that the British authorities were aware of the phenomenon. Only rarely, however, did they discipline any chief. As Lord Hailey later commented in 1938, the stool treasuries in the coastal colony and Ashanti were not supplemented by any government contribution, and therefore "they are not unnaturally regarded as available mainly for expenditure on stool purposes, including the personal needs of the chief and his councilors; their expenditure is not controlled by administration, and large sums are wasted on litigation regarding stool lands."[43] In the Northern Territories, some local administrators opposed the Accra government's plans to increase the powers of the Dagomba chiefs, arguing that since some of the highest-ranking chiefs "are the worst grafters," further enhancing their authority would only "cause a system of graft to be born like unto which Tammany Hall is an infant."[44] In 1934, the "Mbadugu affair," involving a court elder of Dagomba's Ya Na, exposed an extensive system of chiefly corruption that included cattle rustling, skimming profits from a mess contract for the Yendi prison, and the outright buying of chiefships.[45]

Elsewhere in the north, in the Zuarungu and Bawku districts, the exactions of chiefs became so resented that much of the popular violence expressed during the anticolonial "Bongo riots" of April–June 1916 was aimed directly against them. Those chiefs had been installed over formerly chiefless peoples, enabling the chiefs to use their authority to conscript labor and mandate payments from local communities and divert some of those resources to their own use. According to Roger Thomas, they were able to exploit British backing "to aggrandize themselves materially at the expense of their subjects."[46]

In Ashanti, there were 166 recorded destoolments of chiefs during the forty-three years after Prempeh's formal inauguration as Asantehene in 1888, a rate of 3.9 annually. Some were removed by Prempeh or other superior chiefs or by British authorities after Prempeh's deportation in 1896. But many who were judged too corrupt or accommodating to the British also were ousted through popular protest movements. As a chief commissioner of Ashanti complained in 1905 about efforts to depose the chief of Jasua, "if petty extortion were accepted as sufficient grounds to depose a Chief, nearly all the Chiefs of Ashanti would have to be removed from their stools." He felt that the movement by the people of Jasua, specifically, "was premeditated in order to rid themselves of a 'Government man.'"[47]

The most widespread and sustained popular protests against corrupt and abusive chiefs developed in the coastal provinces during the 1910s and 1920s. In several Akan communities, the asafo companies of precolonial days were revived, often led by literate or prosperous commoners. They spearheaded the destoolment of many unpopular chiefs. In the district of Akim Abuakwa, the asafo companies, which previously had been considered subordinate to the chiefs, exhibited greater political independence from about 1913 onwards, successfully removing many chiefs and even challenging the position of the area's Omanhene. In Ashanti, a British official reported, "a chief had only to make himself in the mildest degree unpopular and the *asafo* would promptly destool him by the simple ceremony of seizing and bumping his buttocks three times on the ground."[48] Although the British had circumscribed the authority of the chiefs, who now answered to the central government and not their subjects, colonial policies had left more popular institutions such as the asafo relatively unaffected. The companies "continued to enjoy their traditional freedom of expression, which thus constituted a relatively greater threat to the authority of the Chief."[49]

The asafo of Kwahu was the best-documented case of this phenomenon. In 1915 the youngmen of Kwahu decided to revive the old asafo companies as an outlet for economic and political grievances. Two years later they adopted a veritable "Magna Carta" that included calls for an end to extortion by the chiefs' and elders' tribunals and a prohibition on the use of bribes by candidates in elections to the provincial council. While opposition to chiefly corruption was a central concern, it was expressed within a wider spectrum of grievances over colonial policy that also encompassed demands for centralizing trade in foodstuffs and controlling market prices. By the end of the decade, the Kwahu chiefs were complaining to British officials that the asafo were undermining all established authority in the area.[50]

Throughout the coastal colony, Governor Gordon Guggisberg reported in 1925, there had been 109 destoolments of head chiefs over the previous two decades.[51] Alarmed by the trend, British authorities moved to curtail the independent power of the asafo companies by severely punishing some of their leaders, co-opting others as representatives on the chiefs' advisory councils, strengthening the authority of chiefs to dismiss troublesome asafo leaders or disband entire companies, and most important, amending legislation to make the removal of any chief contingent upon government approval. According to Governor Guggisberg, such measures brought down the number of destoolments of head chiefs to just one in 1925 and two in 1926.[52] Opposition to corrupt and abusive chiefs continued in other forms, however, through the press, public meetings, and campaigns to pressure chiefs to boycott the administration's advisory provincial councils. Denunciation of chiefs and their subordination to British authority would repeatedly resurface in the later nationalist agitation for independence.

Custom's Contradictory Legacies

Beyond the direct interactions between chiefs, their subjects, and the colonial state, custom had a wider, lasting impact by continuing to influence the social norms and standards of both elites and non-elites. While each community had its own mix of customs, "tradition" in its most general form shaped attitudes toward graft and corruption in two contradictory ways. One justified or at least glossed over questionable self-enrichment practices. The other regarded such conduct as antisocial and abhorrent, a violation of the communitarian ties of solidarity and reciprocity that historically marked many of Ghana's local societies.

The educated children of the better-off indigenous elites were often the first to secure jobs within the colonial administration. For them, social solidarity was primarily expressed through continuing ties of allegiance to members of their own social and kinship networks. As elsewhere in Africa, some saw little reason to remain loyal to the colonial authorities' imposed institutions and little or nothing wrong with diverting state resources toward their own enrichment or that of their families and acquaintances.[53] A later official commission of inquiry into corruption in Ghana highlighted some problems with kinship solidarity: "Although the principle of being your brother's keeper is a good one, the corollary that your brother must keep you can be a major source of corruption. It breeds parasitism within the extended family and encourages indolence and abject dependence on others."[54]

At the same time, while some readily accepted the acquisition and accumulation of wealth through irregular means, others regarded such conduct as a violation of still prevalent notions of community welfare and equity. Across the Akan societies of Ghana, for instance, there were innumerable sayings, maxims, proverbs, and tales that derided selfishness and greed or extolled the virtues of generosity, truthfulness, sharing, and communitarianism. Among many other expressions, C. A. Ackah cited the proverb "It takes one man to kill an elephant, but it is a whole town that consumes it," which not only portrayed "the importance of beneficence" but also suggested that "a good act should produce the greatest happiness of the greatest number."[55]

By protecting chiefs against sanctions motivated by such popular social norms, the colonial authorities reduced accountability and provided greater scope to abuses and violations. So too did the broader social and economic changes that accompanied British rule. Greater market activity—especially the massive expansion of cocoa farming—the growth of cities and towns, and the steady increase in the size and reach of the state apparatus all presented new openings for accumulation by some Ghanaians. As early as the nineteenth century, some indigenous traders along the coast or in major river towns became wealthy, initially during the slave trade and later as exporters of palm oil, rubber, and other commercial crops.[56] Some operated independently, others as commission agents for European trading companies. As British colonial rule was imposed over the Asante empire, local African entrepreneurs secured "new opportunities for the pursuit of wealth."[57] The process was contradictory and uneven, however. As the big European commercial houses consolidated their domination and in 1929 amalgamated to form the giant United Africa Company, many African traders found themselves squeezed out by the UAC's price fixing and monopolies.[58] Chiefs also went into business. Some engaged in large-scale cocoa farming. Others became building contractors, transport owners, timber exporters, and commission agents for British commercial houses.

Increases in wealth accumulation in turn influenced prevalent social attitudes. Among the LoDagaba in the north, the greater differentiation of wealth, boosted in part by the exaction of tribute by British-appointed chiefs over a people that previously had no or only weak chieftaincies, tended to undermine traditional egalitarian inheritance practices in favor of concentrating inherited property within the more immediate family group.[59]

Among many at the lower rungs of society, however, displays of wealth and avaricious behavior continued to stir popular resentment and disgust. Traders and other profiteers were a common target of such antipathy. Some saw African merchants as being no less ruthless than Europeans, prompting frequent complaints of unfair trading practices. Intellectuals called on African businessmen to exhibit "greater business integrity and high moral purpose," that is, to act not only in their own interests but also that of the wider community.⁶⁰ Among the Frafra of northeastern Ghana, wrote one researcher, "the abiding impression ... was that the most common sources of surplus income were manipulation of markets, theft, usury, speculative deals and a host of more or less dishonest operations, which enabled the sharp manipulator to acquire capital without contributing directly to the production of social welfare."⁶¹

While such customary suspicions of individualistic wealth acquisition were common, other social changes fostered new attitudes driven more by class than tradition. In the countryside, the growth of cocoa and other commercial agriculture saw not only the emergence of better-off farmers but also many landless (or land poor) farm laborers. Many others flocked to Ghana's expanding cities and towns in search of wage work or opportunities to make a living from petty trading or crafts, but often the migrants simply swelled the ranks of the urban poor. The growth of industry and mining created a working class that was numerically quite significant. By 1960, the first year in which a relatively reliable census was conducted, there were 250,000 employed in manufacturing, 48,000 in mining, and another 171,000 in construction, utilities, and transport, out of a total nonagricultural labor force of 992,000.⁶²

For the most part, the concerns expressed by African workers in petitions, strikes, and union rallies revolved around standard labor issues such as wages and working conditions—and as the nationalist struggle for independence began to heat up in the late 1940s, extended to explicitly political demands as well. Occasionally, workers' grievances were also directed against cheating and corruption by superiors in the workplace and local administration. In Obuasi, the main town in the gold mining region of Ashanti, residents expressed much bitterness over the "rake-off" system, in which African labor recruiters extorted payoffs from anyone wanting to work in the mines. Out of a dozen strikes recorded in the gold mines between 1930 and 1937, strikers raised demands in two of them either against the rake-off system or against timekeepers soliciting bribes. As labor militancy mounted in the late 1940s and 1950s, rank-and-file union members increasingly accused their leaders of taking payoffs from employers or the government.[63]

More widely, greater social differentiation and stratification also stimulated an increase in contemporary civil organization. That had already begun in the coastal areas during the early years of colonial rule, but it flourished in the years before and during World War II, with a proliferation of trade unions, professional bodies, business associations, farmers' unions and cooperatives, groups of literate "school leavers," hometown associations, and many others. Eventually such groups lent greater popular vitality not only to the growth of the anticolonial movement but also to struggles against graft, fraud, profiteering, and other expressions of antisocial conduct.

3

Nationalism and Patronage

For the British colonial administration, the peoples of the Gold Coast did not constitute a nation. They were disparate tribes too primitive to govern themselves in the foreseeable future and more likely to compete than to cooperate toward a common purpose. The structures of the colonial state seemed designed to keep it that way. Except for the tiny strata of urbanized workers, artisans, professionals, merchants, and public employees, most Africans had only a tenuous and indirect link to the state in Accra, through the intermediaries of their traditional chiefs. Moreover, although the Gold Coast was under a single governor, its constituent parts—the coastal colony, Ashanti, Northern Territories, and the Togoland trust territory in the east—had different administrative systems, regulations, and patterns of governance.

Yet that broad framework established a new configuration for imagining what the Gold Coast might one day become. Despite the immediate intentions of the Colonial Office in London or its administrators in Accra, more and more Africans under their rule began to search for at least a limited voice in shaping their circumstances. Advisory councils of chiefs and other selected African dignitaries established in the interwar years marked a small step in that direction but soon demonstrated their limits. Increasingly,

African intellectuals and other thinkers turned toward the most readily available model, that of the European nation-state. They started to dream of an "imagined community" of their own.[1] Those nationalist pioneers initially used the English colonial name for their territory, the Gold Coast. But by the 1950s leaders such as Kwame Nkrumah had fixed on an alternative—and explicitly African—name: Ghana. It had no direct antecedents among any of the peoples of the Gold Coast, referring back instead to the storied Ghana Empire that ruled a large area farther north, covering today's southeastern Mauritania and western Mali, for half a millennium from about 700 to 1240.[2] However borrowed in its origins, "Ghana" nevertheless soon became the preferred name, signifying its people's desire for an independent state.

Their imaginings acquired increased power as other parts of the British Empire (above all India) and the wider colonial world mobilized to assert national independence. As those anticolonial revolutions gained momentum, the identification of nationalism with freedom became irresistible. Thus the territorial boundaries originally imposed by foreign conquerors over the Gold Coast's different peoples were transformed into a framework that would draw them together and foster a mass movement to throw off the bonds of empire.

That transformation did not only mark a shift in territorial perspective; it also had a social component. The old African elites, especially the chiefs most closely allied with the colonial authorities, saw their authority weaken as individuals from more plebeian social strata built up followings and assumed leadership roles. As elsewhere in colonial Africa in the wake of World War II, agitation by workers, ex-servicemen, export-crop producers, associations of urbanized "youngmen" (commoners), and others proliferated.[3] Some of their demands and activities were spurred by economic and social grievances, and many emerged as sharp critics of the traditional chiefs they largely viewed as agents of the colonial order. A 1951 commission of inquiry into the chiefs' customary tribunals found a widespread view that many such courts were tainted by "the vice of corruption, and ... other defects [such as] dilatoriness, somnolent inattention, illiterate incomprehension, using the court as a political weapon."[4]

As other parts of the British Empire gained independence, the notion of "self-government" soon caught on. One of the first groups in British-ruled West Africa to raise the idea was the United Gold Coast Convention (UGCC), formed in 1947. It was led by lawyers, merchants, and professionals, including some belonging to the official semi-elected legislative and local government councils. As part of its general call for moves toward self-government, the UGCC favored replacing the chiefly representatives on those councils with fully elected members, that is, educated commoners. Overall, however, its criticisms were tame, perhaps because many of the group's leaders came from chiefly families. Its main leaders were also socially elitist, with one of its original mission statements calling for establishment of a "property owning democracy."[5]

Soon a more militant current developed within the UGCC. It was led by Kwame Nkrumah, who returned home in December 1947, first from a sojourn in the United States and then nearly a dozen years in London working with a variety of nationalists and Marxists from across Africa and the Caribbean. His wing of the UGCC crystallized at a time when polite petitions drafted by skilled lawyers seemed increasingly inadequate. The leaders of Nkrumah's current were of humbler social background: primary school teachers, clerks, storekeepers, petty traders, and small-scale businessmen. Their followers were humbler still: ordinary laborers, irregularly employed migrants recently arrived from the villages, elementary and junior secondary-school leavers, and sundry youngmen and "verandah boys" of no fixed occupation or residence. As Nkrumah succeeded in pushing the UGCC to link up with the colony's militant youth associations, many more people flocked to the convention's rallies, which became increasingly large and rowdy.[6]

Early 1948 was a time of widespread social unrest, fueled in part by rising prices and other economic grievances. The first initiatives for action came from outside the UGCC. In January, a month-long boycott was launched by small-scale traders and consumers against European goods imported by big colonial trading houses, to press them to reduce prices. Several chiefs sided with the popular movement and backed the boycott. No sooner did the trading houses agree to cut their profit margins, ending the boycott, than a new constituency moved into the streets—ex-soldiers recently returned from serving in Britain's war efforts. At the call of an Ex-Servicemen's Union, thousands embarked on a march in late February to the governor's castle. When a police detachment tried to block the marchers and some stones were hurled, police shot to death several demonstrators. That set off angry uprisings across Accra and eventually in Kumasi and other towns, leading to another dozen deaths over the next two days. The government halted the unrest only by declaring a state of emergency.[7]

While the main UGCC leadership sought to distance itself from this popular anger, Nkrumah saw the protests as a rebuke "of the UGCC leaders' caution and a simultaneous yearning for his vision of mass mobilization."[8] The unrest also provided an opportunity to press the British authorities much more forcefully. Local organizations of literate young men, farmers, and others began demanding self-government not in the distant future but "as early as possible" or "in the shortest time possible."[9] In June 1949, at a rally of 60,000 people in Accra, Nkrumah formally broke from the UGCC to establish the Convention People's Party (CPP). The new organization's constitution called explicitly for political independence, "for removing all forms of oppression and for the establishment of a democratic government," and for "complete unity of the people" through maintenance within a newly independent state of all the territory's constituent parts—the Colony, Ashanti, Northern Territories, and Trans-Volta/Togoland regions.[10] Toward those goals, the CPP launched a campaign of "positive action," with many rallies, street protests, and other mobilizations. In January 1950, the Trades Union Congress (TUC), many leaders of which also belonged to the CPP, called a national general strike supported by the CPP. The successful work stoppage, combined with large street gatherings, prompted the authorities to again declare a state of emergency. They arrested and jailed TUC and CPP leaders, including Nkrumah. That only increased those leaders' popularity.[11]

Faced with the prospect of further unrest if it failed to make any concessions, the British Colonial Office that same year opted for a course of gradual "self-government" for the Gold Coast. The first step was establishment of a new Legislative Assembly but with less than half its seats directly elected, the remainder chosen indirectly through territorial electoral colleges, some selected by the European Chambers of Commerce and Mines, and a few appointed by the governor. Setting aside misgivings about the assembly's limitations and the British authorities' evident favoritism toward the UGCC and other more conservative groups, the CPP put up candidates in the February 1951 elections. That poll—the first unrestricted adult franchise election in sub-Saharan Africa—brought the CPP a stunning victory, carrying all five municipal seats and twenty-nine of the thirty-three rural electoral colleges. Additional support from indirectly elected non-CPP representatives from the Northern Territories gave the party a strong working majority in the new assembly. The colonial authorities, while deeply distrustful of the CPP's radical nationalism, freed Nkrumah from prison, and he became the "leader of government business." Because of the CPP's dominance in the assembly, he was named prime minister the following year.

Building a Party Machine

From that point on—with the CPP having at least one foot inside the state—two different strategies of political mobilization unfolded in parallel. For Nkrumah and his closest party allies, the dominant approach remained one of organizing and motivating their followers around issues, chiefly building a common national identity beyond the ethnic particularisms pursued by the CPP's conservative rivals, pressing for social reform, working toward full political independence for Ghana, and, in a spirit of pan-Africanism, supporting freedom struggles across Africa. Much of the CPP's popular following came from its image as a champion of common folk and the most steadfast opponent of colonialism, as well as from Nkrumah's personal stature on the African stage, at a time of widespread hopes and agitation across the continent. But another mobilizational strategy, largely domestic, also began to develop: the use of financial and political resources now available to CPP officeholders to lay the foundations of a patronage machine, to reward clienteles, win over new allies, and undercut competitors.

The use of patronage by those in authority was of course not unique to Ghana. It was evident in numerous ex-colonies in Latin America and Asia and would soon become prevalent throughout the rest of Africa as well—not to mention in Europe and other more developed societies where it had been common for some time. The erection of patron-client networks, however, appears especially pervasive where states are weak and legal institutions not well established. When laws, courts, police systems, and other official mechanisms for protecting citizens are absent or ineffective or lack legitimacy, patrons can provide their followers with useful benefits: extending some measure of protection and supplying scarce jobs, educational opportunities, health care, business licenses, and other services, if not to everyone, then at least to those within the network.[12] From that perspective, patronage fills an institutional void. Its networks might be small and local, or they may be linked together in pyramid-type structures that encompass large sectors of the population and reach the summit of social and political power.[13] For those holding central state office, relations with local patrons serve to extend their authority, at least indirectly, into areas they cannot otherwise reach on their own.[14] The colonial authorities understood as much, which is why they not only tolerated existing forms of clientelism but also encouraged the creation of new ones.[15] The CPP soon learned that where its efforts to mobilize around national issues fell short, patronage resources could provide an extra draw to help integrate the poor and disadvantaged into its broad nation-building project.

From the bottom to the top of any patronage network, there usually are a variety of middlemen and brokers, who, in the words of René Lemarchand, "help bridge the proverbial gap between the elites and the masses."[16] A village-level patron, for example, may be a client of a district patron, who in turn may work with a regional or national figure. Such go-betweens are key figures deciding how to allocate jobs, resources, or other favors. Because of their critical positions, they not only keep the overall network functioning but also have considerable leeway to act in their individual interests. That may entail diverting money or goods for their personal use or on behalf of their families or friends, or to finance autonomous power bases not fully under the control of those higher up the chain.

Patronage and corruption are thus closely related, although their dynamics are not the same—and their consequences are sometimes quite contradictory. Those tensions became evident in the different attitudes of Ghanaians toward various patronage practices or exposures of graft among state or party officials. Supporters of opposition parties were more likely to see all such behavior by CPP figures as corrupt and reprehensible. Yet party followers were generally more tolerant if its leaders were seen to be acting for the common good, and critical only of particularly blatant displays of individual greed.

Self-Government and the "Hungry Man"

Throughout the six years in which Nkrumah and his CPP participated in government under the waning shadow of the British crown, they maintained an emphasis on popular mobilization toward the achievement of national goals, such as greatly expanded education and health care, and above all, independence. But with at least some provisional control over parts of the state, they could also begin utilizing other methods of rule, including coercion and the selective allocation of public resources. According to Maxwell Owusu, a seasoned Ghanaian analyst, the CPP started to direct police against its political rivals at the local level. More significantly, the party "demonstrated its ability to incorporate traditional leaders and other local influentials through a combination of cooptation, persuasion, bribery, coercion, and selective appeals to traditional symbols, rituals and values."[17]

The power of financial inducement was most evident during elections. While the CPP had few resources other than membership dues and many small contributions to wage the 1951 campaign, by 1954 it was able to attract more sizable sums from business circles eager to curry favor with those most likely to win the leadership of an independent Ghana. Expectations of future material benefits also carried some weight in the candidate-selection process. In the 1954 elections, for example, "to have one's own village candidate elected could affect the siting of a local court, a district council headquarters, a new school, a borehole, a power station. In short, a candidate was an investment, and the dividends could be high."[18]

Given the potential rewards of office, the competition to be nominated on the CPP ticket was fierce. "Election contractors" emerged to canvass local constituency executives and facilitate the nomination of particular candidates. In voting as well, the CPP had a clear advantage over its competitors, since it was already able to influence how state resources were allocated. In the Northern Territories, a common allegorical fable about Nkrumah had him consorting with "mummy water," a mythical figure, half-fish, half-woman, who supplied him with unlimited quantities of money as needed.[19] The CPP's financial power was indeed very real. Some party officials sought to display that muscle by explicitly threatening to block funds to constituencies that elected opposition candidates.

Despite temptations to rely on patronage, some in the CPP refrained from such methods. One contemporary researcher found "little graft or corruption among the militant left wing, whose members, emulating Nkrumah, live in comparative simplicity, some of them in the slum areas in Usshertown in Accra."[20]

Others in the party leadership were more susceptible, seizing financial opportunities not only to build up the party machine but also to line their own pockets. Their actions elicited denunciations from the CPP's left wing, which accused them of abandoning their revolutionary ideals in exchange for dipping their hands into the "honeypot."[21] Several CPP ministerial secretaries were found guilty of corruption in the issuance of government contracts and sentenced to prison. In November 1953, Minister of Communications and Works Joseph Adam Braimah, the only minister from the Northern Territories and not himself a member of the CPP, resigned amid rumors of corruption. He admitted accepting a "gift" from an Armenian construction contractor and in turn charged that several fellow ministers had taken bribes in other deals. A subsequent commission of inquiry could not substantiate Braimah's allegations but did find that a venture involving a Greek contractor and Krobo Edusei, one of the most prominent CPP leaders, "was such as inevitably to lead to suspicion."[22] British personnel were not above questionable dealings themselves. Another commission of inquiry into a dispute over a 1954 land compensation claim found collusion between a private British-owned cocoa company and "almost all of the senior expatriate officers of the Lands Department."[23]

One of the CPP's most important patronage vehicles was the Cocoa Purchasing Company (CPC). Although created in 1952 as a subsidiary of the Cocoa Marketing Board, a colonial entity, the company was CPP-run from the outset. All but one of its directors were party members. With substantial assets, a regular staff of 700, and some 1,800 "receivers" who bought up farmers' cocoa on commission, the CPC in practice often exerted greater day-to-day influence than its parent enterprise. The company's loans were overwhelmingly partisan in orientation, going entirely to members of the CPP-affiliated United Ghana Farmers Council. That set the company at loggerheads with cocoa farmers in Ashanti who supported a regional opposition party. In 1956 yet another commission of inquiry concluded that the company was essentially "a political weapon" of the party. It also found that a few CPC officials benefited personally. According to the commission, the company's managing director, A. Y. K. Djin, "did connive at irregularities committed by certain employees" and "defrauded the company" by using its employees and vehicles to sell or transport goods from his private construction firm. Although many of Djin's malpractices had been known, the commission observed that Nkrumah failed to punish him. Djin nevertheless was eventually forced to resign."[24]

In looking the other way, Nkrumah was not alone. Most of the CPP's rank and file and supporters were similarly forgiving. Railway and harbor workers in the strongly unionized town of Sekondi-Takoradi reportedly responded to accusations of CPP corruption: "We know the CPP has squandered money; we will vote for them to squander even more," and "It is the hungry man who eats. The present Assembly members are now satisfied. So we will vote them again."[25] Joe Appiah, a CPP leader who had gone over to the opposition, later recalled Takoradi workers telling him that the opposition "is full of lawyers, doctors, professors and too many wise men who may indulge in corruption too cleverly, to defy detection. So in the end it might be better to vote in the not-too-clever Nkrumah and his CPP; at least we can always catch them out when they indulge in further corruption and bribery."[26]

Opposition parties and independent candidates nevertheless tried to gain political mileage out of the scandals surrounding the CPP by lacing anticorruption themes into their campaign rhetoric. In the 1954 and 1956 elections, they decried CPP corruption and campaigned for "good government." In a typical speech, K. A. Busia (who years later became prime minister) claimed, "During the last five years of CPP rule, we have had an increase in bribery and corruption on an unprecedented scale." Local opposition activists in Keta issued an Ewe-language election leaflet accusing CPP members of being "thieves, rogues, traitors, double-tongued receivers of bribes, givers of bribes and gangsters."[27]

Some of those labels could have applied as easily to key figures in the opposition. The National Liberation Movement (NLM), a disparate ethnic and political coalition centered around top Asante chiefs, raised funds in dubious ways and engaged in strong-arm tactics against CPP supporters in areas where the opposition dominated. Shortly after the NLM's formation, in the wake of the 1954 elections, the chiefs' Kumasi State Council openly voted funds for the party coffers, in violation of customary regulations governing the use of royal revenues. The Asanteman Council, headed by the Asantehene, was an elaborate system of economic patronage, and during the 1956 elections it used its authority to arrange favors for leading NLM figures. Those included allocating land plots for petrol stations to individual NLM supporters, with the understanding that a portion of the revenue earned from the Shell or Mobil concessions would be channeled to the party.[28]

The CPP, in its own campaign rhetoric, was quick to point out such practices and derided opposition leaders for their wealth, elitism, and conservative social views, themes that played well with most ordinary voters. The party also acknowledged instances of bribery and corruption within the administration but tended to minimize them as transitional growing pains that ultimately would be overcome with independence. The CPP's 1954 election manifesto, for example, pledged that the party "will continue to do everything it can to purge the body politic of all malpractices of this kind, which are part of the legacy of over a hundred years of the imperialist colonial system, from which our country is just emerging."[29] Whatever the weight of corruption issues on actual voting patterns—and by most indications it appears to have been minimal—the CPP was able to secure comfortable majorities in both polls, taking 72 out of 104 assembly seats in the 1954 election and 71 in 1956.

Though yielding a legislative majority, those outcomes nevertheless revealed that the CPP's support was not as sweeping as its leaders claimed, both in the north, where it came in second, and in Ashanti, where the NLM and an allied party took 13 of the 21 constituencies.[30] Beyond its regional bases, however, the opposition had failed to defeat the CPP at the polls nationally and opted instead for extraparliamentary action, including threats of armed revolt and secession.[31] Nkrumah and the CPP, which long favored establishing a strong central state (against the opposition's proposals for a loose federation), responded by going after the powers of local chiefs, many of whom supported the opposition. Various changes in local government and laws gradually reduced chiefs' ability to utilize royal treasuries or draw revenue from sitting in judgment over traditional courts. As a result, in the six years of CPP administration before independence, "chiefs had lost most of their local government and local judicial functions. Their command of patronage had been profoundly undermined by their loss of control of stool [royal] revenues."[32]

Although Nkrumah enjoyed formally cordial relations with the British governor-general, many of the expatriates in the colonial administration were quite hostile to the CPP. The authorities in London were also uneasy and during the final steps in the transition to independence constrained Nkrumah's ability to modify the constitution. The British also imposed regional assemblies intended to weaken the CPP's goal of building a strong centralized state in Accra.

Nevertheless, with the CPP in a dominant political position and Nkrumah enjoying high political stature at home and abroad, the Gold Coast finally acceded to independence on March 6, 1957, as Ghana. It thus became only the second sub-Saharan colony (after Sudan) to break free of direct European rule, sending a strong signal of encouragement to African nationalists and revolutionaries throughout the region.

Limits of a Nationalist Revolution

The strong popular base and radical nationalist outlook of the CPP leadership gave the new government a revolutionary allure. Benefiting from Ghana's pioneering role, Nkrumah was able to assume the status of nation-builder not only within Ghana but also on a continental stage. At the United Nations and in other international arenas, the Ghanaian leader championed the cause of anticolonial movements in the British, French, Belgian, and Portuguese empires, as well as the struggles against white minority rule in southern Africa. As the continent's league of independent states expanded in the early 1960s, his was a prominent voice in the pan-African debates that ultimately established the Organization of African Unity, winning Nkrumah further prestige as one of the "fathers" of African nationalism.[33]

Domestically, the most immediate challenge was building the Ghanaian state. The country's new leaders set to the task with considerable vigor. Nkrumah and his colleagues envisaged a "modern" state, capable of imposing its will throughout the territory, able to secure sufficient resources through taxation and foreign trade to help finance the country's economic and social development, and with enough power to overcome any domestic or external threats. In their eyes, that required a strong central state. Despite the limits on state sovereignty that the departing British authorities had sought to impose, the CPP succeeded in gaining control of the regional assemblies. Then in 1960 a massive 90 percent "yes" vote in a referendum approved a new constitution making Ghana a "sovereign unitary republic." In the process, Nkrumah became president, with extensive executive powers.[34] Over time many more Ghanaian civil servants were recruited and trained, and the military and police forces were expanded significantly. By the early 1960s, most British expatriates in the officer corps and senior civil service ranks had been replaced by Ghanaians.

Once formal independence was achieved and the remaining ties to Britain loosened, Nkrumah was able to translate his movement's earlier popular support into an initial stock of political capital for the new government. Much was expected of it, but much also seemed possible.

With reform squarely on the agenda, the first decade of independence brought some notable achievements in the social and economic spheres. In line with the CPP's profession of a broadly socialist outlook, the government took an increasingly interventionist approach to economic development, codified with the launching in 1961 of a seven-year development plan that assigned a preponderant role to the public sector. Nkrumah spurred a major industrialization drive to lessen Ghana's dependence on cocoa, its main export crop. Railways were improved, and a modern road network and artificial deepwater port at Tema were built. A national shipping line and airline were established. Scores of state enterprises arose, employing more than a third of the workforce. On the social front, school attendance was greatly expanded. A campaign to teach illiterate adults how to read and write brought Ghana one of the highest literacy rates on the continent at the time. Access to health care expanded considerably.

With the CPP's emphasis on the leading role of the state, Ghanaian timber merchants, big cocoa farmers, and other businessmen found themselves squeezed by new regulations and taxes. Meanwhile, the government sought to attract foreign capital to help finance its ambitious industrialization plans. The most dramatic example was a giant hydroelectric dam and aluminum smelter complex on the Volta River, built with financing from the World Bank and US Kaiser company.[35]

The CPP leadership's conception of a stronger, more centralized state also had repercussions in the political realm, including resulting in further hardening relations with the fractious, ethnically organized opposition. Claiming a need to preserve national unity, the authorities harassed and detained prominent figures of the Ashanti-led National Liberation Movement. Many leaders and members of the Muslim Action Party, a key NLM ally, were deported, even though some had lived most of their lives in Ghana. A minor revolt in the Trans-Volta region, led by supporters of the Togoland Congress, was crushed militarily. In Accra, a popular movement among the indigenous Ga had developed against both Fante "outsiders" and corrupt local CPP officials, leading to a series of strikes and rallies. The dissidents formed a political ethnic association, the Ga Adangme Shifimo Kpee (Ga Standfast

Nationalism and Patronage

Association), to which the CPP responded with arrests and attacks by armed gangs.[36] A new law prohibiting any political party based on ethnic, racial, or religious criteria forced the dissolution of most such groups and impelled the leaders of the former NLM to combine with other currents to launch the United Party. But further police crackdowns on the opposition virtually eliminated its presence in the legislature, so that Ghana effectively became a one-party state even before a 1964 referendum made it official.

The fact that the conservative opposition drew significant support from traditional chiefs provided additional impetus to the CPP's reform of local government.[37] While some party circles were virulently antichief, the authorities stopped short of eliminating chieftaincy entirely, which would likely have provoked popular outrage, especially in Ashanti. Although many Ghanaians viewed especially venal or decrepit individual chiefs with great distaste, they did not necessarily reject the institution as such. The government's legislation and decrees on the chiefs thus had two main goals: first, to clearly subordinate chiefs to the state machinery; and second, to purge them of publicly scorned or politically unacceptable figures.

Chiefs progressively lost direct access to much of their royal treasuries, and taxation was taken over by local government councils. Cabinet decrees replaced chiefs sitting on local courts with other individuals. A new act on recognizing chiefs placed them under the minister of local government, who could withdraw recognition if he considered it "expedient in the public interest."[38] Commented one scholar, "The CPP government, unlike its more nervous and much less powerful colonial predecessors, could now override customary law and insist upon the primacy of the national government's view of the propriety of individual enstoolments and destoolments."[39]

The authorities withdrew official recognition from hundreds of chiefs, including some high-ranking paramount chiefs, singling out those who had sided in any way with the opposition, and replaced them with figures favorable to the CPP. They even created new chieftaincies or upgraded minor ones to paramount status as a way of rewarding chiefly supporters. Many Brong paramount chiefs were won over in 1959 with the creation of a new region, Brong Ahafo, carved out of the old Ashanti Region.

In essence, the CPP government ended up replicating portions of the colonial administration's system of chiefly indirect rule, albeit with reduced powers and a more codified link to both the central government and strengthened local direct-rule institutions. But in one significant respect the new policy was more retrogressive than the old. By placing the sole power of destoolment in government hands and criminalizing unsanctioned local destoolment proceedings, it trampled on the robust tradition by which commoners previously could remove unpopular chiefs. With an end to popular sanction from below, the new system made it more tempting for chiefs to abuse their authority. Their tenure was secure as long as they displayed continued loyalty to the CPP and their conduct was not so egregious that it caused serious unrest.

With the role of chiefs diminished, the main local agents of the central state were henceforth individuals in the bureaucratic and political apparatus, represented in the villages by the CPP branch leaders and at the district and regional levels by appointed commissioners. Although the CPP continued to profess ideals of democracy and popular inclusion, there were few avenues in the new system of local government for genuine public debate. Loyal CPP members might sometimes transmit grievances upwards through party channels, but otherwise local state administrators and party commissars wielded considerable power. In Swedru, for example, the local district commissioner functioned as a policeman, set up a vigilante unit to control crime, and settled cases that should have gone to the courts.[40]

"Self-Seekers and Careerists"

Much of the significance—and drama—of Ghana's first decade of independence lay in the Nkrumah government's efforts to transform the state, economy, and society it inherited from its colonial predecessor. Few Ghanaians remained indifferent to those changes. Some energetically supported the CPP leaders' policies and initiatives. Others thought they did not go far enough. Yet others, especially among the old elites and supporters of the political opposition, virulently decried Nkrumah and his comrades as reckless "communists" who were ruining the country and trampling citizens' individual freedoms. In the broad sweep of what was happening in Ghana at the time, corruption was but one issue among many. And overall, it was not a particularly important one, except in the eyes of opposition politicians or others who failed to benefit from the CPP's extensive patronage.

Corruption nevertheless did increase perceptibly. Some analysts, especially those influenced by neoliberal thinking, maintained that the government's active and extensive intervention in economic affairs inevitably brought waste, inefficiency, corruption, and economic decline.[41] While such a direct cause and effect may be debatable, the specific circumstances at the time—rapidly changing economic and social structures, weak state regulatory capacities, and a multiplication of state agencies and enterprises—did bring many new opportunities for public personnel to engage in corrupt practices. And as the political leadership moved increasingly toward authoritarian methods and one-party rule, the possibilities for either judicial or public scrutiny of officials' conduct diminished. Moreover, as the social scientist James Scott pointed out, the context was strongly marked by the CPP's move away from popular mobilization and toward the practices of a typical patronage machine, in which the support of various clienteles was secured through partisan distribution of state resources, jobs, business licenses, and other favors.[42] That helped foster a general climate in which informal dealings and personalistic conduct by state and party officials did not seem out of place. Insofar as patronage practices helped the CPP outmaneuver its political rivals or strengthen its hold over the machinery of the independent state, they even appeared to some of those involved, patrons and clients alike, as arguably patriotic.

However, distinguishing between "ordinary" political patronage and self-serving enrichment was often difficult. The ministers and party leaders who lined their pockets certainly saw no reason to do so. As they channeled funds into the CPP's coffers or distributed resources to its followers, some took advantage to benefit themselves and those close to them. Nkrumah seemed to overlook such dealings as long as the individuals remained politically loyal. But sometimes the scramble exceeded tolerable limits, prompting sporadic crackdowns. Several government commissions investigating trade-related malpractices uncovered illegal sales of import licenses by both low-level and senior officials in the Ministry of Trade; the commissions also pointed to widespread tax evasion by private sector importers.[43]

Most dramatically, Nkrumah, in an infamous "dawn broadcast" on April 8, 1961, lashed out at CPP leaders and senior government officials known to be accumulating inordinate wealth and property:

> I have stated over and over, that members of the Convention People's Party must not use their party membership or official position for personal gain or for the amassing of wealth.... In spite of my constant clarifications and explanations of our aims and objectives, some party Members in Parliament pursue a course of conduct in direct contradiction with our party aims. They are tending, by virtue of their functions and positions, to become a separate social group aiming to become a new ruling class of self-seekers and careerists. This tendency is working to alienate the support of the masses and to bring the National Assembly into isolation.[44]

Over the following months, the president decreed that party members could not own more than two houses, two cars, or land worth more than £500, although those limits were not consistently enforced. Some of the most visibly corrupt leaders were forced out. Among them were Finance Minister K. A. Gbedemah and the powerful former interior minister Krobo Edusei, whose exploits—including permitting his wife's importation of a solid gold bed—had become legendary and quite embarrassing to Nkrumah.[45]

Despite the purge, the CPP's basic methods of functioning did not change appreciably. Corruption persisted, although its extent was not fully evident at the time. Only after the February 1966 military coup and subsequent establishment of about forty commissions of inquiry into the affairs of the Nkrumah era did many of the particulars eventually emerge. Despite the clear partisan bias of the officers who ousted Nkrumah and sought to smear his image, many officials emerged with relatively unblemished records. But many did not. The wealth of detail in the commission reports demonstrated that corruption had spread among significant portions of the state and party hierarchy. It appeared most prevalent where officials had discretionary powers for major trade or investment decisions, especially in sectors involving foreign companies or local businessmen. Some instances of fraud or embezzlement by public officials were reported. But the most common involved taking bribes—or "commissions"—for awarding construction contracts, selling import licenses, or approving investment projects.

One of the commissions concluded that the system of issuing official import licenses signed by the trade minister "provided the framework within which bribery and corruption reigned supreme, organised on a systematic basis with committees and agents operating in different sectors and at different levels of society." One of the ministers, A. Y. K. Djin, was reported to have had secret interests in a private trading enterprise for which he authorized an exceptionally high level of imports. Another, Kwesi Armah, was found to have regularly charged "commissions" of 10 percent on the import licenses he approved.[46] Another commission looked at the Timber Marketing Board, established in 1960 as the sole buyer and seller of logs, and the Timber Cooperative Union, a business association. With fierce competition for logging concessions, timber cutters frequently used bribery to secure them, paying off both board officials and the ministers responsible for land grants.[47]

Many inquiries showed clear patterns of personal self-aggrandizement. But the dominant dynamic was that of political patronage, as highlighted most clearly by the investigation of the National Development Company (Nadeco), one of several agencies used to raise party finances and bolster its influence. Set up in October 1957, Nadeco was a consulting and insurance firm that brokered deals between the government and foreign and local businessmen. Its board of directors comprised mainly CPP figures. According to a commission of inquiry that later sought to unravel Nadeco's affairs, the enterprise was essentially "a storehouse for all bribes with which the C.P.P. was to be organized and maintained."[48] The commission acknowledged that the funds generally went into CPP coffers, sometimes passing through the individual bank accounts of Nadeco and party officers. Perhaps because the commission was appointed by a regime politically hostile to the CPP, it tended to interpret the sometimes-contradictory evidence in the worst possible light for the individuals involved, minimizing the institutional political motivations behind the rake-off system and playing up appearances of personal enrichment.

Those biases were most evident in the commission's treatment of Nkrumah, presenting him as a "swindler" bilking businessmen of huge sums for his personal use. Yet the commission also heard evidence that in a deal to acquire the old colonial-era Leventis trading house, a £750,000 payment into an account allegedly controlled by Nkrumah was intended to set up a "trust for the people of Ghana," with the specific purpose of "building hospitals, colleges and schools."[49] A later commission of inquiry and government report on Nkrumah's accumulated property holdings followed an approach similar to that of the Nadeco commission. It mixed together state, party, and personal funds in ways that portrayed Nkrumah as personally corrupt, claiming that on the day of the coup he had a net worth of more than £2.3 million. That sum was based, however, upon a notion of "de facto ownership," since almost all the properties and accounts were not in Nkrumah's name but in the names of various associates and institutions, such as Nadeco and several other enterprises. Nkrumah's legal holdings, while not insubstantial, were modest: several houses and other properties in Ghana worth just under £60,000, not counting several bank accounts totaling £340,000.[50] Those accounts could possibly have been intended for a mix of political and personal uses.

What about other government and CPP leaders? Three later inquiries (the Sowah, Jiagge, and Manyo-Plange commissions) investigated the assets of fifty-nine leading party and state officials believed to have engaged in illegal practices. Some held title to substantial assets. A portion of their accounts were probably used in the typical fashion of political patrons to distribute "gifts" and other favors to their clienteles to build support for the CPP. Many clearly also augmented their personal lifestyles, buying flashy cars, building houses for their relatives, or acquiring consumer durables such as freezers, which then were still luxuries in Ghana. The most common acquisition was real estate. A majority of CPP figures named in the commission reports had more than one or two houses to their name; some had five, seven, eleven, or in the exceptional case of Krobo Edusei, twenty-seven houses, along with various farms and plots of land. Those who had at some point been ministers, regional commissioners, or heads of state corporations usually had the most, using their ownership of multiple houses to draw rental incomes. A few had small fleets of trucks, which they rented out.[51] In such ways, and contrary to the CPP's socialist rhetoric, many officials seemingly used at least some of their dubious funds to launch business careers, mainly of a rentier variety.

Similar developments were evident in some CPP affiliates. They too served as vehicles for distributing political patronage to their members. In the process, some leaders were able to dip into those resources for their own ends. For example, the Workers Brigade, a public works agency, saw the theft of funds by senior officials, pilfering of wages and materials, shady contracts, and irregular land grants by CPP-aligned chiefs.[52] The Bureau of African Affairs, a semicovert office that helped arrange financing and training for anticolonial guerrilla movements in Angola and elsewhere, also suffered some diversions of funds by its top officers.[53]

Another entity was the United Ghana Farmers Cooperative Council (UGFCC), as the United Ghana Farmers Council had been renamed. In the early 1960s, the council was given direct responsibility for purchasing farmers' crops on behalf of the cocoa board. A later commission of inquiry revealed that the buying process was rife with fraud and corruption. According to farmers' testimony, the purchasing officers frequently rigged the weighing scales to pocket the difference, sometimes delayed actual weighing until they were paid a "consideration," or delayed payments to farmers so that they could use the funds for short-term loans, upon which they earned interest. Some higher-level UGFCC officials imposed special levies on members and misused the funds or demanded "tributes" from the purchasing clerks, prompting the latter to divert even more from farmers.[54] According to one analyst, the UGFCC became "an instrument for the social advancement of a new class of trader-bureaucrats, concerned with monopolising commercial opportunities and using public office as a platform for private entrepreneurship."[55]

Nor was the Trades Union Congress immune. A later commission detailed "a catalogue of malpractices, irregularities and misuse of funds involving even some of the topmost officials of Congress."[56] In part because of their handsome salaries and perks, the main leaders of the TUC and most of its affiliated national unions tended to defend the policies of the CPP and government, even if those policies contradicted the interests of rank-and-file union members.[57] One researcher noted that the greatest abuses by senior union officials seemed to be committed by those who were most insecure in their tenures. Knowing that the CPP could intervene at any time to remove them, "they needed to act quickly before losing access to sources of wealth."[58]

While many other government supporters tended to suffer such malpractices in silence, workers, with a more extensive history of struggle, did not. Although some explicitly objected to the ostentatious living styles of some government officials, many also felt aggrieved over a range of other issues, including the perceptible decline in real wages in the early 1960s, the authorities' heavy-handed approach to the unions, and the corruption and business dealings of their own union leaders.[59] The most dramatic challenge to the government came in September 1961, when railway and harbor workers in the adjoining industrial towns of Sekondi and Takoradi embarked on an illegal strike that lasted two and a half weeks. Many workers were still broadly pro-CPP, but they bypassed their party-affiliated union structures to protest the imposition of a 5 percent compulsory savings deduction from their wages. Other grievances reflected opposition to the government's authoritarian union policies and to official corruption, especially within the National Housing Corporation. One analyst of the strike detected signs of "strongly anti-elitist and anti-corruption attitudes among Ghanaian workers, and especially skilled manual workers. For they, unlike some clerical and administrative executives, enjoy few opportunities for benefiting from corrupt practices, or gaining promotion through patronage, while suffering directly from managerial and governmental corruption, to which they tend to attribute government's lack of finance for raising wages."[60]

Such concerns echoed the grievances of many other people in Sekondi-Takoradi, and the strikers enjoyed broad public support. Bus drivers and city employees joined the strike, soon paralyzing the towns, while market women helped sustain it by bringing food to the strikers. The strike leaders, some of whom previously had been active in *asafo* companies, the semimilitary commoners' associations, hit a resonant cultural chord by using traditional battle cries, sounding gong-gongs, and wearing red head- and armbands, signifying their readiness for war in the custom of the old Fante armies. If the political challenge of the strike were not already evident to the authorities in Accra, the strike leaders made it absolutely clear when they warned that if the parliament did not accede to the people's demands, they would march on the capital and disband it. Alarmed officials declared a limited state of emergency in Sekondi-Takoradi, and Nkrumah implied that the strikers might face treason charges if they persisted. Such intimidation and the depletion of the strikers' funds ultimately forced them back to work. The government promptly followed up by detaining many strikers and supporters and dismissing union officials who had sided with the rank and file.[61]

The Sekondi-Takoradi strike was a rare instance of public defiance of the central authorities. It was all the more significant because it came from a sector considered to be among the Nkrumah government's staunchest supporters. In that, it also pointed to an erosion of the CPP's popular base. Corruption clearly was a factor, but only one among many. As one analyst of corruption in the Nkrumah era emphasized, corruption remained mainly an elite phenomenon and "was neither as pervasive nor as ultimately destructive to Ghana's politics and economy as the popular image would suggest."[62] For many Ghanaians, economic difficulties, state inefficiency, growing authoritarianism, and other issues also weighed heavily. Corruption, moreover, does not appear to have been as conscious or centrally planned as the later commissions of inquiry tended to portray it. According to Herbert Werlin, in a review of the Ghanaian anticorruption commissions, rather than viewing corruption under the CPP as strictly a result of arbitrary power or excessive state intervention in economic affairs, "what needs to be emphasised is that corruption really emerges from the absence of power. It was the weakness of the Nkrumah régime—its inability to control what went on rather than its totalitarian façade—which facilitated corruption."[63]

That weakness made the February 23, 1966, coup that brought down the Nkrumah government easier. Although the cabal of army and police officers who seized power justified their takeover, in part, by citing the financial misconduct of the CPP old guard, their primary motivations lay in a combination of domestic and foreign policy concerns. Much of the army's officer corps had been trained by

British instructors, within Ghana and in Britain, and had absorbed their ethos of conservatism and institutional professionalism. That, combined with the fact that a majority of the officers were Ewe or Ga, ethnic groups with a history of antipathy to the CPP, meant that the military hierarchy was more politically inclined toward the opposition than to Nkrumah's "scientific socialism." The involvement of some army and police personnel in two assassination attempts against Nkrumah and in several purported coup plots had only heightened Nkrumah's distrust of the regular officer corps. In the early 1960s, the government began devoting an increasing share of military spending toward building up alternative security and intelligence forces politically loyal to the CPP. That stirred not only officers' resentment over an erosion of their own perks and financial benefits but also fears (probably justified) that the government would eventually try to push aside the old army entirely.

On top of such corporate concerns, the officers were alarmed by Nkrumah's foreign policy, especially his efforts to involve Ghana militarily in a quest for pan-African liberation and unity. The several thousand Ghanaian troops Nkrumah dispatched to the Congo in 1960 to aid Patrice Lumumba got bogged down in the confusion of the United Nations intervention, leading to high casualties and a mutiny by one of the Ghanaian battalions. By 1964–65, some of the officers involved in the Congo debacle had joined with others to begin actively plotting the coup, a process that was accelerated by Nkrumah's growing use of Soviet and Cuban military support, the establishment of training bases in Ghana for insurgents from other African countries, and his efforts to push the Organization of African Unity to intervene militarily against the Rhodesian white minority regime. While Ghanaian officers clearly had their own reasons for mounting a coup, there also is evidence that they received prior approval, and possibly some support, from the US Central Intelligence Agency and other Western powers.[64]

When the coup makers finally launched "Operation Cold Chop" while Nkrumah was traveling abroad, they succeeded relatively quickly and easily. Most regular officers appeared to support the coup at least tacitly, while Nkrumah's more loyal security forces were taken by surprise and offered only light resistance. The CPP, with a formal membership of two million, virtually collapsed. Whatever else it signified, the coup demonstrated how dependent the CPP had become on continued access to state patronage resources, as well as how much its initial base of committed popular support had eroded during its years in power.

4

Path to Plunder

When they overthrew Nkrumah, the leading officers of the Ghanaian army and police established a governing junta, the National Liberation Council (NLC). Since the armed forces had only limited prior access to the state's central budgetary and procurement structures, it was able to take over with a relatively clean reputation. The eight-member council declared at the outset that it would not hang onto power but turn the reins over to an elected civilian government. While there were conflicting views among its members about the pace and mechanisms of the transition, the NLC seemed agreed on one thing: fixing the outcome so that the conservative opposition would eventually assume office and Nkrumah's Convention People's Party (CPP) could not come back.

Although the CPP failed to mount any real resistance to the coup and was immediately banned, while Nkrumah took up exile in Guinea, the party nevertheless remained a political force. It had former leaders and activists throughout the country, in the state administration, and in numerous social and professional organizations. So one of the NLC's prime tasks was to undermine the CPP's surviving structures and bases of support. The enormous number of commissions and inquiries into the practices of the Nkrumah government and CPP were designed to discredit them and justify their exclusion. While many of the commissions' findings were based at least partly on real transgressions, their interpretations often leaned toward exaggeration, rationalizing judicial proceedings against some and the political disqualification of many others.

The NLC assault on Nkrumahism also marked a shift in social orientation. Gone were the days of populism and appeals for the mobilization of the poor and downtrodden. The military council looked instead toward Ghana's old social elites.

Many (but not all) of the previous measures to limit the powers of traditional chiefs were reversed. More than two hundred chiefs appointed by the previous government lost their recognition and a comparable number were demoted in chiefly status, while scores of paramount and other chiefs deposed under the CPP were restored to their positions.[1] The NLC's interventions in chieftaincy matters were not always crudely partisan, however, as in Anlo, where it blocked efforts to oust a pro-CPP paramount chief, and in Yendi, where it overruled a local effort to use military and police force in a succession struggle among the Dagomba.[2] A new constitution drafted in 1969 by a constituent assembly appointed by the NLC created, for the first time, a National House of Chiefs, comprising representatives of regional houses of chiefs and serving as an appeals court on matters relating to customary law.[3]

However much the NLC tried to re-enhance the authority of the chiefs, their local power remained contested and sometimes subject to accusations of corruption. In Ejura, in northern Ashanti, the highest-ranking chief and his elders were accused by the Ejura Ratepayers and Farmers Association of illicitly selling community land to a "white American" agricultural company in 1968. The *Ejurahene* (chief) later told a commission of inquiry that he had leased the land in exchange for "drink"—an initial payment of 10,000 cedis (₵, the new currency), with another ₵5,000 due in six years. Not only was the deal made without consulting the farmers (three hundred of whom were subsequently evicted) but also the proceeds, instead of being deposited in the royal treasury, were "used by the said Ejurahene and his Elders for their private purposes," the commission found. In denouncing those customary leaders, a memorandum of the Ejura farmers' association did not question traditional norms and authority as such but rather the "complete abuse of the powers and positions vested" in the chief and elders. In the farmers' eyes, the Ejurahene's conduct was "most unroyal."[4]

In urban areas, the military council concentrated its favors and programs on the middle and upper classes. The numerous commissions and other statutory bodies set up by the NLC provided posts for many lawyers, who had fared poorly under the CPP. Lawyers, chiefs, private businessmen, doctors, and other professionals accounted for the largest blocs in the constituent assembly.[5]

In economic policy, the NLC moved sharply away from the previous government's reliance on the public sector. By mid-1968, 66,000 workers, or 10 percent of the total salaried workforce, had been dismissed. The government ordered the closure of almost all projects begun—or even nearly completed—with funding from the Soviet bloc and sold off numerous state farms and other enterprises. Many of those businesses went to foreign companies, not Ghanaians. The NLC also established close ties with the International Monetary Fund and World Bank, receiving several significant loans in exchange for currency devaluation, privatization, and a general reduction in public investments and state economic activity.[6]

Without party support structures, the NLC relied on two main state pillars: the uniformed services and the state bureaucracy. The army ensured order nationally, while the police, given their detailed knowledge of local conditions, were assigned to suppress any incipient opposition. In the state bureaucracy, after some purges, senior civil servants and administrators were given additional powers—and exempted from accountability. While the NLC's commissions of inquiry investigated the conduct of Nkrumah-era bureaucrats, none targeted those who served the military council. Only after the NLC had left the scene did some malpractices come under scrutiny, as in the case of Justice Annie Jiagge, who headed one of the NLC's most prominent commissions and was found to have been improperly allocated two houses through her husband, the head of the state-run Tema Development Corporation.[7]

The NLC's reliance on civil administrators, combined with the resurgence of chiefly power in the countryside, prompted one scholar to note a striking similarity "between the former colonial and the new military government. Support for policies at the centre in favour of administration and administrators, and rule at local level by a combination of chiefs and centrally appointed advisors, was characteristic of the British, and it re-emerged under the N.L.C."[8]

Another consequence of NLC rule was a further expansion of the armed forces. From 1965 to 1969, the military budget more than doubled, although government spending in general increased by only 10 percent (and spending on agriculture was slashed by 35 percent). Meanwhile, all military officers and ranks were granted full exemption from income taxes and housing, electricity, and water charges. Aside from such institutionalized "plunder of the state treasury,"[9] there were few signs of outright corruption within the top officer corps at the time. As party activities resumed in the lead-up to the 1969 elections, General Joseph Ankrah, chairman of the NLC, was accused of sanctioning the covert allocation of funds for his campaign efforts and as a result was forced by his colleagues to resign from the council. Further down the ranks, however, there were many allegations of corruption of ordinary policemen, while auditors' reports of local government bodies, public boards, and state corporations found widespread embezzlement, misappropriation, and theft. According to the auditors, total estimated losses reached $37.9 million between 1967 and 1969, equivalent to 5 percent of national budget expenditures.[10]

At times, grievances over corruption surfaced during popular agitation. Protesting students at some secondary schools, teacher training colleges, and universities accused administrators of corruption, nepotism, and other malpractices. At the University of Science and Technology in Kumasi, the NLC acquiesced to student demands and ousted the vice-chancellor, but at the

University of Ghana, Legon, student unrest was quelled by police action and threats of expulsion.[11] Workers also became restive, marked by a sharp increase in 1968–69 in the number and size of strikes, with mineworkers playing an especially militant role. Aside from raising economic grievances, many strikers denounced corruption among state enterprise managers and leaders of their own unions.[12] The NLC's response, as in a May 1968 Prestea goldfields strike, was to accuse the workers of "hooliganism" and boost the police presence.[13]

Civilian Interlude

True to its promises, the NLC began preparations for a withdrawal to barracks and a handover to elected civilians. After a resumption of open political life was authorized, more than twenty parties emerged by May 1969. Only five, however, met the council's criteria to take part in parliamentary elections that August. A majority of seats were won by the Progress Party, which represented the old opposition to Nkrumah and was strongly favored by the military council. Its leader, K. A. Busia, became prime minister. With many of Nkrumah's old colleagues still barred from electoral activity, the only party even vaguely aligning itself with the Nkrumahist tradition, the People's Action Party, remained a marginal force. The National Alliance of Liberals (NAL) came in second, with 30 percent of the votes and 29 of the parliament's 140 seats. Although led by a former Nkrumah cabinet minister, K. A. Gbedemah, its platform was little different from that of the Progress Party, nor was it distinguishable in the social composition of its candidates, many of whom were lawyers, businessmen, merchants, and teachers. In fact, none of the election manifestos of the various parties fundamentally challenged the military council's broad vision for Ghana, reflecting the legal and ideological limits the NLC placed on the campaigns.[14] Even after Busia became prime minister, the NLC, then chaired by General A. A. Afrifa, retained a direct hand in governmental affairs through a three-member presidential commission, until Afrifa was replaced in 1970 by a civilian.

The resumption of civilian rule meant that decisions over budgetary and economic affairs and over the national allocation of public goods and services were back in the hands of party notables. The tendency toward patronage politics that was evident under Nkrumah's CPP became even more pronounced. The biggest difference was that the previous pan-Africanist and socialist ideological justifications were replaced by a more laissez-faire outlook that clashed less starkly with the pursuit of individual self-interest. As one political scientist put it, in the election campaign and subsequent proceedings in the parliament, "the parties gradually became elaborate patronage networks serving the interests of a narrow segment of the population, mostly the professional, chiefly, and administrative occupational groups. Therefore, the parties became in a sense more a means for the disbursement of goods and services than a well-formed vehicle for the expression of public opinion."[15] The likelihood that patronage would dominate the electoral process was so evident that even before the campaigns some Ghanaian intellectuals, keen to reduce the politicians' "arrogance, abuse of power, corruption, and vice," had strongly urged mechanisms to publicly vet candidates, monitor party operations, and hold elected officials more accountable.[16] Neither the NLC nor the parties it permitted to run had any interest in such supervision, however.

In the process of distributing resources, Busia's Progress Party held the greatest advantages. Its election manifesto had vowed to "wage war on corruption," and Busia, prior to his election, had overseen the work of the Centre for Civic Education, which sought to educate the public about corruption and democratic values.[17] But the party's cabinet ministers and parliamentary deputies soon developed elaborate and extensive networks of patronage and graft. A series of investigations by a commission of inquiry into bribery and corruption, conducted while the Busia government was in power but not released until shortly after its ouster, uncovered numerous malpractices. Although some began in the NLC era, most took place under the Progress Party. The cases included corruption in the Ports Authority, smuggling by border guards and police, payments by businessmen in exchange for contracts and licenses, kickbacks in the hiring of casual labor for public construction projects, and solicitation of bribes by judges and other court officials.[18] Busia, a former professor of sociology, was well aware of what was going on and once remarked that, aside from himself, "there is not a single honest person in my cabinet."[19]

There was much public doubt over whether the prime minister was actually an exception. The suspicions were confirmed after Busia's ouster when an assets investigation committee determined that some of his houses, businesses, and foreign bank accounts were obtained with illicit funds, both at the time of his political association with the NLC and later as prime minister. Some of the details of the assets of Busia and several of his key associates, including a minister of lands and education, pointed to a new development compared with the Nkrumah era: not only did officials use their illicit funds to acquire fixed properties such as land and houses, but to a greater extent they also set up or bought shares in legally licensed private businesses, from trucking, wood supply, and trading enterprises to pharmacies and nightclubs.[20] In that way, corrupt officials were able to take advantage of the government's probusiness economic policies to profit doubly, first by pilfering the public till and then by using the proceeds to diversify into lucrative private ventures.

Also to an extent greater than before, Busia's style of government, including the allocation of patronage resources, exhibited an unmistakable ethnic bias. The Progress Party drew the bulk of its electoral support from the Akan peoples, including the inland Asante and Brong and the coastal Fante. For the most part, Ewe and Ga, who had tended to vote for Gbedemah's NAL, were excluded from the distribution of jobs and development projects. Not one of Busia's top forty cabinet or subcabinet appointees was an Ewe. When Busia purged the civil service in 1969 of five hundred career bureaucrats, not a single Akan was among them. That same year he pushed through the parliament an Aliens Expulsion Act, which led to the deportation of thousands of non-Ghanaian Africans and angered the local Muslim community, since many of the deportees were Muslims long resident in Ghana. The ethnic favoritism of the Busia government was a sharp departure from the policies of both Nkrumah and the NLC, which had sought to maintain some measure of ethnic balance in their political appointments.[21]

Throughout Busia's time in office, Ghana suffered a serious economic crisis, exacerbated by a sharp fall in the production of cocoa, the principal export. That brought lower rural incomes, cutbacks in government spending, and a further decline in jobs and working conditions. Public discontent increased, especially as poor Ghanaians compared their own circumstances with the ostentation and wealth of senior government officials and private businessmen and merchants. The incidence of strikes mounted and more frequently turned violent. When the Trades Union Congress (TUC) opposed the imposition of a "national development" levy on all workers in mid-1971, the government responded by trying to dissolve the national TUC structures. The unions fought back and reconstituted the TUC under its existing leadership, in the process winning overt support from the student movement as well. The students also had become increasingly militant, with the National Union of Ghana Students staging protests against the government's policy of "dialogue" with apartheid South Africa and the failure of members of the parliament and cabinet to publicly declare their assets, as stipulated by the constitution. The government often tried to quell labor strikes and student protests with police crackdowns, although repression had only limited effect. Then in December 1971, following recommendations from economic advisers from the World Bank, the International Monetary Fund, and Harvard University, Busia declared a massive 44 percent devaluation of the cedi. While the earlier austerity measures and job cuts had hit poorer Ghanaians especially hard, the devaluation tended to hurt middle- and upper-class Ghanaians most, since many depended on imported goods, which had become more expensive with the drop in the cedi's value.[22]

From Redemption to "Kalabule"

Busia succeeded not only in becoming widely unpopular but also in alienating important sectors of his original base of support. Among those who turned against him were segments of the military's middle and junior officer corps, who were aggrieved by cutbacks in their benefits and resentful over the government's ethnic favoritism and propensity to promote politically connected officers over the heads of their peers.

Carrying through on coup plans that apparently were already under consideration a year earlier, a small group of conspirators led by Lieutenant Colonel Ignatius K. Acheampong seized key installations in Accra on January 13, 1972, and proclaimed the ouster of the Busia government (while the prime minister was abroad for medical treatment). The coup makers immediately set up a ruling junta, the National Redemption Council (NRC). As the highest-ranking member, Acheampong became chairman of the thirteen-member council. The NRC was ethnically diverse, although with a numerical overrepresentation of Ewe officers. The reduction in Akan dominance, combined with the fact that most of the officers had seen their career advancement blocked under the NLC and Busia governments, led one analyst to characterize the NRC as a "coalition of the 'outs.'"[23]

Acheampong openly acknowledged that one of the motivations for the coup was the officers' corporate self-interest, that Busia had "started taking from us the few amenities and facilities which we in the armed forces and the police enjoyed even under the Nkrumah regime."[24] But he also sought broader justification by denouncing the Busia government's corruption and malpractices, as well as its "doctrinaire attachment to a free market economy."[25] He promptly appointed a commission to investigate the assets of former government members and reversed Busia's currency devaluation.

At first, Acheampong's NRC took a mildly populist stance and sought some reconnection with Nkrumah's political legacy. A few months after Nkrumah's April 1972 death in exile, Acheampong permitted his body to be reburied in Ghana and presented a eulogy that, while acknowledging Nkrumah's "shortcomings," nevertheless praised him as a "great leader."[26]

In economic policy, the NRC returned to a heavy reliance on public enterprises and state interventionism, including tight controls over currency transactions and imports. Striking a nationalist note, the council repudiated some £66 million in foreign debt to British companies and suspended repayments on other loans. Emphasizing equity, the regime redirected developmental spending toward Ghana's poorer areas, with less for the more advantaged Akan regions. Acheampong appointed the most ethnically balanced cabinet since independence. Extolling the virtues of self-reliance, he also urged Ghanaians to grow more food, in part through the promotion of traditional *nnoboa* self-help work parties. The government tried to foster a sense of national mobilization by the citizenry as a whole, while the established patrons of the previous years experienced a diminution in their direct influence over state affairs.[27]

Many such initiatives were initially popular with Ghanaians, generating hopes that austerity and self-serving politics might give way to a period of national revival. But the moment did not last. By the middle of the decade, a deep crisis had set in, marked by a convergence of severe economic difficulties, a hardening of Acheampong's rule, and a veritable explosion of corruption.

After some years of higher food production, successive droughts during 1974–78 brought decline and scarcity. By 1975 world cocoa prices had started to fall, and the cost of oil imports rose, making it much harder to pay for the inputs needed to keep industry and agriculture productive. The government tried to cover its public spending by printing more money, which stoked inflation and eroded living conditions. Though extensive on paper, the military council's supervision and control over trade and other economic activities deteriorated and the black market thrived.

Meanwhile, Acheampong's authoritarian inclinations became more pronounced as the top decision-making circles narrowed.

Within a few years of taking power, the NRC ceased to operate as a collective body, as Acheampong assumed more powers for himself. In October 1975 he purged the junta and reconstituted it as the Supreme Military Council (SMC). He then promoted himself to the rank of general. While the NRC had always depended on a small circle of patronage brokers, under the SMC it became smaller still. Many of the networks of civilian "big men" who had been influential in the immediate post-Nkrumah years and under the Busia regime were excluded from virtually all access to state resources. And as Michael Johnston has argued in other contexts, a sense of exclusion can heighten people's grievances and provide a powerful impetus for action by opposition groups.[28] In Ghana, only a small group of civilian newcomers were included, and that occurred in an arbitrary and haphazard manner. Acheampong's SMC thus alienated weighty segments of Ghana's established social elites. It also outraged many bureaucrats and professionals by reducing their opportunities and interfering heavily in the bureaucracy and judiciary (for example, the chief justice, Samuel Azu Crabbe, was simply fired by the SMC in 1977). As the council provoked powerful elite antipathy, other signs of instability emerged, including a succession of four alleged coup plots by the end of 1975. A couple may have been real, but at least one appeared concocted by the SMC to cover a purge of Ewe officers (including Captain Kojo Tsikata, a radical pan-Africanist who was to later play a major role in the Rawlings government).[29]

The acquisition of more arbitrary powers by Acheampong's inner circle of senior officers gave them unprecedented opportunities for short-term financial gain, with a strongly predatory hue. Top military figures used their positions to grab a portion of the illicit earnings that previously were largely monopolized by civilian politicians, bureaucrats, and businessmen. Some came through institutional channels: every member of government was allocated special twice-annual subsidies as well as personal import licenses, enabling them to buy goods abroad with scarce foreign exchange and then resell them domestically at steep mark-ups. Most, however, was obtained informally and illegally. The officers running the Cocoa Marketing Board practically depleted the agency's funds.[30] Government members routinely signed contracts or authorized import licenses in return for kickbacks or company shares.

According to later mandatory asset declarations, more than two dozen senior officers—a few from the NLC era but most from Acheampong's regime—managed to amass significant property holdings and business interests.[31] There was an acceleration in the trend, already evident under Busia, by which officials invested their proceeds not only in land and rental housing but also in industrial, commercial, and other enterprises. One of the significant developments under the SMC, noted Eboe Hutchful, "is the extent to which both active and retired military and bureaucratic officials have come into possession of *capital* as such, invested typically in agriculture, bulk-haulage, luxury transport systems, real estate, and the acquisition of company shares."[32] In that respect, noted Kwame Ninsin, elite corruption in Ghana could be viewed as a form of "primitive accumulation," borrowing Karl Marx's concept.[33]

Some officers preferred an old standby, farming. Significant public investments were devoted to transforming the more arid and impoverished northern regions into major producers of marketable food crops, above all through large-scale irrigated rice farming backed by state credits, subsidized inputs, and other official support. Rather than advancing the fortunes of local farmers, however, the effort brought an influx of "stranger farmers"—military and police officers, senior civil servants, retired politicians, and businessmen, joined by some local traders and traditional chiefs. By the mid-1970s, there were eight hundred big rice farmers in the Northern Region alone. In Builsa and other localities, the arrival of these new operators provoked serious conflicts with local communities over access to land and water sources.[34] Ninsin termed it a "land grabbing spree."[35]

By itself, such conduct at the top might not have set off a national crisis. But the sheer rapaciousness of Acheampong and his fellow officers set an example that was widely emulated. In fact, the SMC abetted the spread for political reasons, to create new patronage networks loyal to the government and attract support among segments of a population suffering from severe inflation and economic decline. For leaders of market women's associations or trade unions, the ability to use personal or political connections with SMC members to acquire import licenses or "chits" for the purchase of scarce commodities at controlled prices through official state stores was a valuable resource to secure their own positions, followings, and fortunes. For those lower down the ladder, it could mean the difference between survival and complete destitution. Whether motivated at the top by politics or sheer greed—and many Ghanaian descriptions of that period emphasized the latter—the mid to late 1970s were marked by a frantic, chaotic scramble for individual gain and advantage.

In most other periods in Ghana, corruption could be seen as essentially a symptom of other political and social maladies. But during the later years of Acheampong's regime, graft and fraud became so extreme and prevalent that they seriously worsened many of the country's fundamental systemic problems. Social injustice, political mismanagement, and corruption all fed off each other.

This was known as the era of *kalabule*, a popular expression—apparently derived from the Hausa *kere kabure* (keep it quiet)—that encompassed a broad range of illicit activities from outright crime, smuggling, hoarding, and black marketeering to corruption and embezzlement. In its most intense expression, it lasted for about five years, from 1974 through the SMC's overthrow in June 1979, a period marked by "unbridled cheating meted out against the majority by the few."[36]

Vague and elastic in its meaning, kalabule was typified by four types of activity:

- 1. Corruption, embezzlement, and the abuse of public office, usually involving military personnel and state officials, alongside others with proximity to the government and its institutions. State enterprises were pilfered, equipment and other public goods were diverted to the black market, payments went to shoddy contractors, and young women traded sex with SMC officials to secure signatures for commercial licenses.

- 2. Smuggling, often with the collusion of customs officials, police officers, and border guards, across Ghana's borders and through its airports and harbors.
- 3. Hoarding and black-market trading. Sometimes linked with the smuggling networks, merchants routinely evaded official market restrictions by ignoring price controls and hoarding goods to drive up prices further.
- 4. Outright crime, with syndicates, sometimes including military and police personnel, stealing property or extorting payments from ordinary citizens, rich and poor alike.[37]

As the patterns of distribution within the patronage networks steadily narrowed, accumulation by the cliques at the top became so frenzied that it undermined the entire political system. Beyond kalabule's direct costs to the state and those Ghanaians immediately affected, its prevalence contributed to the overall crisis of the economy. The issuance of special import licenses to top army officers and their clients boosted profiteering in basic goods, while simultaneously choking off the supply of productive inputs for agriculture and industry. Between 1970 and 1978, agricultural production contracted by an annual average of 1.2 percent, while industrial output declined by 2.3 percent a year. By mid-decade, inflation had accelerated to an annual rate of around 100 percent. Teachers, lower-level civil servants, and most other employees could not survive on their salaries—by the end of the decade, workers' real incomes had fallen to 41 percent of their 1976 levels—forcing many into informal trading, hustling, and other petty economic activities. Cocoa farmers and other producers saw little recourse but to sell their crops to professional smugglers. Prostitution proliferated, and young Ghanaian women fanned out into neighboring countries in search of income. The existence of both official and unofficial markets turned "virtually everyone who was in any way associated with the system into a speculator, lawbreaker, corrupter, or corruptee."[38]

Contemporary accounts of the kalabule era recall other instances of extreme state predation elsewhere in the world. In James Scott's comparative study of corruption, he discussed Indonesia during the later years of the Sukarno regime in the mid-1960s: corruption so uncontrolled and widespread that it colored all areas of state functioning and undermined basic economic activities.[39] The case of Ghana under Acheampong was similar.

Broad Opposition

As Ghanaian living conditions worsened and the drive among senior officials for personal self-enrichment became ever more blatant, strong opposition emerged among both elites and ordinary citizens. Among those who had previously benefited from clientelism, the decline in patronage resources that actually trickled downward further undermined the SMC's already fragile bases of support and acquiescence. More generally, popular outrage was fueled by the sharp contrasts between the wealth of the officers and their cronies and the wretched circumstances facing most Ghanaians.

Along with everyone else, Ghana's middle and upper classes saw their savings eaten away by inflation and their business and professional prospects dry up. Even some chiefs publicly called for hikes in their state stipends. Most of the associations of manufacturers, merchants, timber cutters, and executives founded during the 1970s remained disorganized and often competed with each other. Other professionals, however, acquired greater unity, as groups of lawyers, doctors, accountants, and others came together in the Association of Recognized Professional Bodies (ARPB). Closely allied with the banned political parties, the ARPB soon became the foremost voice of "respectable society." In opposing the SMC and military rule more generally, it strove for reestablishment of the kind of civilian electoral system represented by the Busia government. As early as September 1976, the Ghana Bar Association, one of the leading components of the ARPB, began openly calling for a return to civilian rule.

Many ordinary Ghanaians, disgusted with the excesses of the SMC, appeared favorable to renewed civilian rule, although their grievances also reflected deeper concerns about social justice and the underlying foundations of the political system, not just whether those in power wore uniforms or civilian attire. Students protested at Cape Coast University and in secondary schools over food shortages and maladministration. From a low point in 1975, the number and duration of labor strikes began to mount the following year, usually over immediate economic grievances and often outside the control of union leaders. Petty traders started to agitate against the SMC's disastrous economic management.

Much of the dispersed agitation came together and acquired an overtly political direction after Acheampong, in October 1976, proposed as a solution to the crisis the establishment of a nonparty Union Government (Unigov) in which the military would continue to play an integral role. As labor unrest continued, students organized more protests, adding to their demands explicit opposition to high-level corruption and to Acheampong's proposed Unigov system. The ARPB backed the student protests, criticized corruption, and called several professional boycotts of its own, which were joined by individual unions. Meanwhile, local conflicts escalated outside the capital, sometimes taking a violent turn. Kumasi became a hotbed of antigovernment agitation, while in Koforidua market women organized a food boycott in 1977.[40]

Also that year, in the lead-up to a referendum on Union Government scheduled for early 1978, the Acheampong regime sought to manufacture a semblance of popular support for the proposal by setting up a committee to hear public opinions. Many of the groups that testified or submitted memoranda were newly created and often directly funded by the SMC itself. The leadership of the Trades Union Congress, which had benefited from some of Acheampong's favors, also supported Unigov. Only a few dissenting voices were permitted to formally present their views. Some of those recommended institutional checks against corruption, punishment of SMC members, and even establishment of a people's militia to counterbalance the regular armed forces.[41] The final committee report acknowledged that most of the hundreds of witnesses and memoranda examined by it had expressed "vehement criticism on bribery and corruption as well as the 'get-rich-quick' attitude of many people in the public service." But it also essentially backed Acheampong's proposal by claiming that the "preponderant political wish" of the witnesses was for a "national government without political parties" and with some form of military participation.[42] When Kofi Quantson, deputy director of the Special Branch, the police intelligence wing, submitted a report contradicting such claims of widespread support for Unigov, he was promptly demoted to a minor posting outside the capital.[43]

The refusal to seriously consider contrary views intensified opposition. The ARPB, National Union of Ghana Students, and new formations such as the People's Movement for Freedom and Justice (among whose leaders was General Afrifa from the ex-NLC) campaigned for a "no" vote in the referendum. Either in response to those groups' calls or independently, students and workers embarked on more strikes and protests of their own. The authorities sometimes responded with repression, leading to injuries and some deaths, further embittering public sentiment against the SMC. When the referendum was held in March 1978, most eligible voters stayed away. The government claimed a modest victory for the Unigov plan, with 54 percent for and 46 percent against. Given numerous irregularities in the vote-counting process, those results were widely seen as suspect. The claimed outcome thus spurred ever more unrest, as civil disobedience reached epidemic proportions and professional and labor strikes virtually paralyzed the country during May–July 1978.[44]

A few senior officers had an inkling of the deep anger sweeping Ghanaian society. One of the more prescient was General Afrifa, the last chairman of the NLC and a figure in the movement against Unigov. As early as December 1977, in a letter to Acheampong, he expressed his worries about the popular mood:

> My Dear General & Friend,
>
> I feel greatly disturbed about the future after your government. I have heard from certain quarters . . . threats which they will execute after 1979. In order to discourage the military from staging coups in the future, how about if they line all of us up and shoot us one by one? Then they would disband the Ghana Army, but I do not certainly want to be arrested, given some sort of trial and shot. These are my genuine fears.[45]

With Ghana seemingly on the edge of insurrection or complete chaos, Acheampong's military colleagues decided to sacrifice their chairman. On July 5, 1978, they forced Acheampong to abdicate, replacing him with General Fred Akuffo and a reconstituted military council, commonly known as the SMC-II. Rather than continuing its predecessor's stubborn insistence on maintaining military rule, the Akuffo regime presented itself as a caretaker government. It dropped the Unigov idea and sought to ease political tensions by releasing jailed protesters. Akuffo announced that the military council would eventually cede power to a "popularly elected government," going as far as to specify a target date of July 1, 1979. He lifted the ban on political parties in early November 1978 and authorized district council elections later that month, enabling local political patrons to rebuild their networks.[46]

For ex-politicians, professionals, business operators, and other "big men," it was a qualified victory. They accordingly ceased calling for strikes and demonstrations. And if Akuffo held to his promises, those social segments could look forward to regaining direct control over the reins of the state. The plan for a political transition thus appeared to have healed the previous split within Ghana's elites.

That rift, however, had already opened the door to widespread popular action. Considering Ghana's recent history, many were not sure that a return to government by elected civilian politicians would by itself solve the country's fundamental problems. Their anxieties were kept alive by continuing deterioration in economic and social conditions. Scores of labor strikes broke out under Akuffo's tenure, among workers in both the private and public sectors, including civil servants and militant railway workers. Student agitation also persisted, especially as it became clear that the members of Akuffo's SMC would try to shield themselves from future prosecution over graft and misdeeds. Only Acheampong himself was tried on charges of arbitrarily using import licenses and contributing to indiscipline in the armed forces. Though found guilty, he was given an astonishingly light punishment: loss of military rank and honors, loss of retirement benefits, and restriction to his hometown. Reflecting common sentiments for more thoroughgoing efforts to root out corruption and punish the worst offenders of the Acheampong years, the National Union of Ghana Students demanded probes of the wealth of all SMC members and appointees, so that all "state plunderers, looters and subversionists" would be brought to book.[47] The students' union warned the civilian politicians to not strike deals with the "zombie" regime and vowed to remain vigilant against "all those reactionary elements who identify with the rapacious interests of imperialism, neo-colonialism, semifeudalism, domestic khaki-clad armed robbers with [their] voracious civilian swindlers."[48]

Within the military barracks, noted an air force colonel who had served as a minister under Acheampong, the ordinary soldier was already upset at seeing "his senior officer running after material wealth and ignoring the welfare of the men under him."[49] So when the former president was simply stripped of his rank, a demand that he be retried swept through the barracks. Those barracks rumblings, which reflected the wider popular anger, soon erupted with unprecedented force.

5

From Mutiny to Revolution

In early May 1979, Ghana was in a state of social turmoil and political uncertainty. Doctors, nurses, and private transport drivers went on strike. Musicians marched against corruption in the recording industry. A group of students trying to clean up downtown Accra were fired upon by police, leaving one dead and two seriously wounded. Meanwhile, political parties and candidates were campaigning for the scheduled June 18 elections but finding little enthusiasm among potential voters. Many of the most tainted politicians had been barred from running, while their stand-ins struggled to overcome Ghanaians' deep distrust of the political process. "Ghana's problems," wrote one local commentator, "are obviously too serious for party politics to be considered as anything more than a formal improvement on military dictatorship."[1] Recognizing their uphill struggle, most parties pleaded with General Akuffo to postpone the Supreme Military Council's handover until January 1, 1980. Akuffo rejected the request: the officers of the SMC feared staying at the helm any longer. The government-owned daily newspaper hinted at the possible cost of delay when it ran a front-page report that another score of officials from the overthrown monarchy in Iran had been found guilty of torture and corruption by "secret revolutionary courts" and then executed.[2]

Yet for the SMC, it was already too late. At dawn on May 15, a hitherto unknown air force pilot, Flight Lieutenant Jerry John Rawlings Jr., led between fifty and sixty airmen equipped with armored personnel carriers and small arms in attacks on several military facilities in Accra. They took about forty hostages, including a dozen senior officers, but soon were overpowered by units loyal to the SMC. Many of the rebels were detained. Two weeks later, Rawlings and six others (a corporal, four airmen, and a captain) were charged with "conspiracy to cause mutiny and mutiny with violence" before a general court-martial at Burma Camp. When the trial began on May 28, it was open to the public and press, giving Ghanaians a glimpse of the rebel airmen's motives.

Rawlings did not have an opportunity to testify, but his views were relayed indirectly by the prosecutor, based on statements Rawlings and others had made to their military interrogators. The prosecutor said that Rawlings for some years had been growing disillusioned with the general situation in Ghana. According to a draft of a speech that Rawlings intended to give had his uprising succeeded, the basic issue in Ghana was "a question of THOSE WHO HAVE against those who HAVE NOT—a question of the vast majority of hungry people against a very tiny minority of greedy, inhuman, selfish senior officers, politicians, businessmen and their bank managers and a bunch of cowardly Lebanese [merchants]."[3] According to statements Rawlings made to his interrogators, he had initially welcomed Acheampong's takeover as an attempt to halt the rape of the nation's wealth and instill some dynamism and honesty into government. But when Colonel W. C. O. Acquaye-Nortey, a leading SMC member, was spared for hoarding large quantities of sugar, Rawlings lost hope. "The abuse of wealth and human dignity began," Rawlings said in a statement to investigators.[4] When Acheampong was removed from the SMC in 1978, Rawlings again thought things would improve. Once more he was disappointed. Among other concerns, he worried about the "tarnished image" of the armed forces. Sometime in 1978, the prosecutor charged, Rawlings began holding secret meetings with other air force personnel who thought as he did. They discussed ways to compel the SMC to create investigative committees, headed by junior officers, before the military handed over to civilians, to ensure that corrupt individuals did not escape punishment.[5]

From the testimony, the precise goal of Rawlings and his colleagues on May 15 was unclear: Was it to spark a general military revolt to overthrow the SMC or simply shock it into a sweeping purge and deep-going reforms before it left the scene? During negotiations that preceded the end of the rebellion, an officer asked Rawlings the objectives of his action. According to the prosecutor, Rawlings "started talking about widespread corruption in high places, and stated that this nasty state of affairs could be remedied only by going the Ethiopian way, and that there was need for bloodshed to clear up the country, and this should start from within the Armed Forces."[6] (The Ethiopia reference was to its revolution of 1974, during which many from the old aristocracy and officer corps were executed.)

The trial audience, numbering in the hundreds, burst into applause, prompting the judge to issue a stern warning. The proceedings and the prosecution's presentation received wide press coverage the next day, transforming Rawlings into an instant public hero. In subsequent sittings, on May 30 and May 31, large crowds gathered around the military courthouse. Chalked slogans appeared on the walls of the military camp proclaiming "Stop the trial or else . . ." and "Revolution or death." The judge had more and more difficulty maintaining order in the courtroom.[7] The trial was adjourned to Monday, June 4. It never reconvened.

The Armed Forces Revolutionary Council

Over the weekend, messages passed between Rawlings and other military personnel, with the active complicity of several of the guards assigned to watch him. Before dawn on June 4, soldiers burst into the facility where Rawlings was held and took him to Broadcasting House, nearby. Although Rawlings had prepared some notes, his first remarks over the radio were "disjointed, disorganized and mostly extemporaneous," according to one of his biographers.[8] Audibly agitated, and with sounds of gunshots in the background, Rawlings first addressed the military hierarchy:

> The ranks have just got me out of my cell. In other words the ranks have just taken over the destiny of this country. Fellow officers, if we are to avoid any bloodshed, I plead with you not to attempt to stand in their way because they are full of malice, hatred—hatred we have forced into them through all these years of suppression. They are ready to get it out—the venom we have created. So, for heaven's sake do not stand in their way. They are not fools.... The judgment will come.

Rawlings then proclaimed the abolition of the SMC, read out a list of army personnel and civilians ordered to report to Burma Camp, and urged all military units to elect representatives to a new Armed Forces Revolutionary Council (AFRC). Aware of the population's general desire for an end to military rule, he also pledged that elections would still be held. "But," he continued, "before the elections go on, justice which has been denied to the Ghanaian worker will have to take place, I promise you. Some of us have suffered for far too long. You are either a part of the problem or part of the solution. There is no middle way."[9]

At that moment, Rawlings and his colleagues were not yet firmly in control, nor had the AFRC been formally established. Confusion reigned the rest of the day. Twice, Major General A. Odartey-Wellington, the army commander, went to the same radio studios to urge an end to the rebellion. Fighting continued in various parts of Accra. Rawlings, unsure of what was happening and according to some accounts fearful that he might be killed by rebel soldiers along with other officers, took refuge at the University of Ghana campus in Legon, several miles from the city center. But late that afternoon Odartey-Wellington was killed during a clash at the Nima police station. Major General Joshua Hamidu, chief of defense staff and a member of the SMC, went on the air that evening to acknowledge the military council's overthrow.

The next day, in a message broadcast several times, an unidentified radio speaker said that the AFRC had been set up and that it would now conduct a "house-cleaning exercise." Although the original call had been for military units around the country to elect their representatives to the AFRC, that did not happen. According to Rawlings, a council of two hundred members would have been too unwieldy and would have taken the representatives away from their units to Accra, leaving the rest of Ghana more vulnerable to the AFRC's opponents. Thus, when the council's composition was announced, it comprised only a dozen military personnel, mostly junior officers but also a private, two corporals, and a sergeant, with Rawlings as its chairman.[10]

Though the AFRC was formally in power, the next months remained tumultuous. Many Ghanaians, even those sympathetic to the "June 4 Revolution," used the term *chaotic* to characterize the period. While the junior officers and rank-and-file soldiers holding the reins made clear what they did not like about the old order—corruption and cheating, social injustice and inequality, political exclusion, excessive deference to foreign interests—they presented few clear ideas of the political and social system they did want. Since the AFRC saw itself as a transitional regime, it never formulated a comprehensive program. Its leading spokesmen talked most often about injecting greater moral accountability into public service and social relations, placing community and societal interests above personal ones, and giving ordinary Ghanaians some voice in the decisions that affected them. Many in and around the AFRC seemed to believe this could be done by renovating Ghana's existing institutions, largely by removing and punishing the individuals who previously ran them.

Whatever the radical soldiers believed, they were not the only actors on the scene. The ouster of the SMC opened the floodgates of social protest, giving the furor of those months an aspect of a broader conflict "between the power of the haves in their entirety and the have-nots," as political scientist Naomi Chazan put it.[11] The AFRC leadership often appeared scarcely able to control the popular outpouring of grievance and anger. Many actions carried out in the council's name were never officially sanctioned.

The first dramatic expression of that anger came on June 16, when General Acheampong and a former Border Guard commander were shot by firing squad at the Teshie military range in Accra. Along with four others, two more former heads of state met the same fate ten days later: Generals Akuffo and Afrifa. Apart from Afrifa, who was from the National Liberation Council junta of the 1960s, all had been prominent in the SMC regimes. Supposedly, the eight were found guilty of corruption and abuse of office by a secret court, with details of their economic crimes published in the press. The executions were highly controversial and left a lasting stain on Rawlings's public image. Various foreign capitals, including Washington and London, denounced the shootings and threatened economic sanctions if more followed. Within the country, the National Catholic Secretariat, the Christian Council of Ghana, and the Ghana Bar Association called for an end to secret trials and summary executions.[12]

Yet the reaction in the streets was starkly different at the time, at least among a sector of the population. Drawing on Old Testament imagery, five hundred students in Takoradi demonstrated with placards proclaiming "No more kalabuleism," "Let the blood flow," "We need more bloodshed," and "The wages of sin is death."[13] University of Ghana students marched through central Accra, joined by market women, workers, and children, to protest the criticisms.[14] Slogans by students from the University of Science and Technology in Kumasi declared, "Lawyers do not pay taxes—away with them" and "For heaven's sake, kill." They adopted a resolution calling on the AFRC to institute the death penalty for all economic crimes and rejecting the denunciations of the Christian Council and Bar Association, accusing them of "defending only the propertied people because . . . all these groups are mainly afraid of the house-cleaning exercise for their own reason and have no concern whatsoever for the poor starving people."[15]

The Ghana Muslims Representative Council, while not endorsing further executions, nevertheless hailed the AFRC for "dispensing justice promptly and inflicting the just and due penalty without fear or favour."[16] Father Kwabena Damuah, then a Catholic priest and proponent of liberation theology, proclaimed, "This is the time to literally baptize the whole nation. . . . Of course, the executions are not the only solution, but they certainly form part of the solution."[17]

The strongest pressure for executions came from the barracks, the AFRC's immediate base of support. Soldiers, in the earliest days of the June 4 takeover, were the ones who popularized the slogan "Let the blood flow." Rumors circulated widely that rank-and-file soldiers had drawn up lists of many more officers who were to be shot, and some even called for executing all officers, along with some civilian personalities. Rawlings appears to have had a difficult time urging restraint. His early speeches repeatedly called on soldiers to avoid bloodshed, and he traveled to units around the country to persuade the ranks, first, to distinguish between honest and dishonest officers, and second, to opt for punishments other than execution, such as penal labor, property confiscation, and public shaming.[18] In fact, some senior officers had already been detained or subjected to public rituals of humiliation; for example, Brigadier Arnold Quainoo (who would subsequently be named army commander by the AFRC) had his head shaved.[19]

Although the executions ended, the actions of the firing squads at the Teshie range proved pivotal in fixing the identity of Rawlings's anticorruption crusade. To his opponents, they signified an ugly undercurrent of bloodlust and terror; to his supporters, a welcome determination to push ahead, regardless of what polite society might think. That popular reaction, in particular, made it politically harder for Rawlings and his colleagues to back down. They may have succeeded in momentarily deflecting the pressure for more executions but felt obliged to move forward with severe penal and monetary sanctions against other high offenders.

The same day as the last executions, the AFRC published a decree establishing new judicial entities it called "special courts."

Composed of panels of five persons appointed by the AFRC, their jurisdiction was to hear cases involving economic crimes committed by public officials and other persons, including bribery, abuse or exploitation of any official position, illegal or dishonest acquisition of property, conniving to overcharge for goods or services supplied to the state, smuggling, looting, hoarding, selling goods above the official control price, or any other act "with intent to sabotage the economy of Ghana." Possible sentences still included death by firing squad but also imprisonment with penal labor for not less than three years and confiscation by the state of assets found to have been illegally or dishonestly acquired. There was no appeal, but sentences were subject to review by the AFRC, which could reduce penalties deemed excessive.[20]

To determine how public officials had acquired their wealth, the AFRC decreed that all military officers who held political or administrative positions complete full disclosures of their assets. In July, the requirement was extended to nonmilitary officials of state corporations and enterprises. Once the details of the disclosures were published in the press, public suspicions of the extent of corruption during the Acheampong and Akuffo years were confirmed.

The special courts tried and sentenced dozens of former officers, as well as a handful of other public officials and businessmen, to terms ranging from a few years to life imprisonment, along with seizures of property and assets. The details published in the press painted a common picture: officers entered government service under Acheampong with modest if any wealth but then managed to acquire farms, houses, vehicles, businesses, and other assets. In one case, a businessman, with help from Acheampong and other high officials, overcharged the government for imported maize and other goods, ultimately defrauding the state of more than $2.5 million, for which he received a life sentence.[21]

Beyond such judicial measures, the AFRC also took administrative action to clean up the public service. Some senior civil service positions were abolished entirely, and many key officials and some lower-ranking personnel were dismissed from the bureaucracy and state corporations. The campaign, observed Chazan, "reflected the distaste with which critical fragments of the population regarded the machinery of government itself."[22]

Many Ghanaians also held private businesspeople and other wealthy Ghanaians in low regard, not only for questionable market dealings but also for prevalent tax evasion. Property owners alone were estimated to owe the state ₵320 million. In late June, the AFRC issued an ultimatum: tax defaulters had to pay their arrears or face investigation by the intelligence and security agencies. Many did make payments. A special account for seized assets, recovered customs duties, tax arrears, and other revenues collected by the AFRC in Accra alone ultimately reached nearly ₵24 million.[23]

Government contractors who had been paid but failed to fulfill their obligations were ordered to return their fees or face imprisonment. Market traders caught charging above the regulated price were detained and had their goods seized; sometimes they were publicly flogged by soldiers. In the capital alone, ninety-seven "ghost bakers"—who had official flour allocations but no actual baking facilities—were arrested. Some medium-sized businesses were seized for fraudulent dealings and violations of import and marketing regulations. The crackdown exhibited more than a taint of xenophobia. Some of the errant merchants were of Lebanese origin, leading to complaints by Lebanese that they were unfairly singled out. Rawlings denied the accusation, although his speeches soon after the takeover were peppered with negative references to Lebanese. In September, just before the handover to civilian rule, the AFRC revoked the citizenship of 107 naturalized Ghanaians, most of them with Arabic names.[24]

Women merchants also fared poorly. Because women dominated the retail trade in Accra and other cities and thus were in direct contact with consumers, they often were blamed for high prices and scarcities. There was a prevalent stereotype of market women as wealthy, although only the largest "market queens" active in the wholesale and textile trade actually were. Overall, market women were "stigmatized as exploitative parasites hoarding their wealth and essential goods while people starve."[25] Rank-and-file soldiers and some junior officers shared that perception. Many suspected of price gouging or hoarding had their goods seized, some were publicly flogged or stripped naked by soldiers, and a few were reported to have been shot.

The high point of the campaign against market women came on Saturday, August 18. After earlier radio warnings that all traders should vacate the large Makola market in Accra, troops and bulldozers moved in. Over the course of the day, they flattened the market. Crowds of excited young men harassed market women who had shown up, calling for the women's blood. Rawlings publicly sanctioned the destruction, saying that it should serve as a warning to all "hoarders and profiteers."[26] Some participants intended it as a warning to women in general. Visiting Makola two days after its demolition, a Ghanaian journalist noted that the act was "full of myths and scapegoats," including the old one of the market queens and "the even older scapegoat of women as the oppressors of men—Makola on that Monday was rank with misogyny; 'all women are evil,' said a corporal with conviction and another affirmed that destroying Makola would teach Ghanaian women to stop being wicked."[27]

The Makola action prompted some women's organizations, such as the Ghana Women's League for Social Advancement, to criticize the AFRC's house-cleaning campaigns.[28] Besides being an act of "madness," a Ghanaian women's rights activist told me years later, the razing of Makola was both naive and misdirected: "Kalabule, corruption existed in the market. Let us burn the market and then there will be no more corruption." That of course did not happen. Besides, "the market women were kind of the bottom line in the distribution chain; they were not the importers."[29]

Not only did Makola's destruction highlight the ugly side of the AFRC's populist mobilizations, it was also economically counterproductive: essential goods remained scarce and still sold at high prices.

Although marred by excesses and abuses, the crackdown on those deemed to be corrupt and dishonest was generally popular. Not content with passively applauding, some sectors of the public actively joined in the AFRC's housecleaning. Workers of the National Investment Bank and Agricultural Development Bank staged noisy demonstrations in Accra to demand removal of their managers and directors for corrupt and antilabor practices. A staff resolution called the Agricultural Development Bank "very, very dirty" and urged a review of its loan allocation system and a "scrubbing clean" of the bank.[30] Junior firemen demonstrated in Accra to demand removal of the chief fire officer and other senior officials and establishment of a committee of inquiry into their management. Public employees provided documentation of embezzlement and other misdeeds, leading to arrests of their bosses. The National Union of Ghana Students urged that workers be appointed to anticorruption inquiries, since it was "workers who live nearer to the dirt and filth" and could therefore do a better cleaning job.[31] In the Volta Region, workers in Hohoe demonstrated for setting up district revolutionary courts, with the death penalty for those found guilty of malpractices, while chiefs and other people in Golokwati urged the arrest of all road contractors who had abandoned their projects, along with the district and regional officials who had certified their work.[32] In Sekondi, the AFRC was urged by a local resident to probe traditional chiefs and elders who "by their positions as lords over their areas, have greatly amassed wealth to the detriment of their subjects."[33] In some regional capitals, rank-and-file police "arrested some of their senior officers on alleged charges of bribery, corruption, maladministration and nepotism."[34]

Evidently, many from the lower ranks of Ghanaian society saw an opportunity to press their own particular grievances—and sometimes act out their prejudices. In doing so, they bypassed the discredited and frayed patronage systems of the old order by appealing for direct support and action from the central government, for the first time perceived as sympathetic to their concerns.

That placed considerable public pressure on the AFRC to fulfill popular expectations. However, the AFRC's self-assumed mandate was a limited one: to clear out some of the worst excesses left by the previous military regimes and to do so within just a few months. Some Ghanaians regarded the AFRC's decision to hand power over to civilians as a compromise, one that "conceded plenty of ground and initiative to conservative forces"—a compromise also reflected in the reappointment of some commissioners from the previous regime and the naming of General Hamidu, the former chief of defense staff, as the AFRC's liaison with the other arms of government.[35]

The electoral process moved steadily forward, despite the general political chaos. Voters, however, displayed only limited interest in the election. In the first round of voting on June 18, only 35 percent of the electorate showed up at the polls, far below the 63.5 percent turnout during the previous election in 1969. The second round on July 9 had just a 36 percent turnout.[36]

The winner of the presidential race was Hilla Limann of the People's National Party (PNP), which also gained a majority of parliamentary seats. Although the party traced its political heritage to Nkrumah's former Convention People's Party, Limann was a relative political unknown, put forward as the PNP flag bearer after his uncle was barred from running because of corruption allegations. The PNP demonstrated a broad base of electoral support, both regionally and socially, incorporating trade-union leaders, student activists, and rural youths, as well as numerous wealthy patrons, especially in the north. The PNP's main competitor was Victor Owusu's Popular Front Party, a reincarnation of the old Progress Party of former president Busia.

With the machinery of transition under way, Rawlings warned the incoming administration to not attempt to "put out the flames of moral regeneration."[37] On September 24 the handover officially took place, amid chants of "J.J.!" from the large gathered crowd. Rawlings, in his farewell speech, reiterated many of the reasons for the June 4 uprising and pointedly indicated that the new government would remain under close observation: "Never before have the eyes of so many been focused on so few, Mr. President. The few are you, the illustrious members of our new civilian administration. The many are those in the factories and on the farms, in the dormitories and junior quarters, who will be watching you with eagles' eyes to see whether the change they are hoping for will actually materialize in their lifetime."[38]

The Limann Government

The conditions under which Limann took office were not propitious for any government. The economy was in difficult straits, following the debilitation of the SMC years and the further disruptions of the AFRC's housecleaning. Social tensions, which had become sharply polarized over the preceding months, remained volatile. The military was rife with agitation and confusion: no one knew who was actually in command, many in the ranks were unhappy that their turn at the helm had been truncated, and those most supportive of the AFRC were deeply suspicious of the new occupants of State House and the parliament chambers. Nevertheless, many Ghanaians, including those who had failed to vote, were willing to give the civilian politicians another chance. As a political newcomer, Limann was not personally tainted by the scandals of past administrations.

Before taking up the presidency, Limann promised to continue aspects of the housecleaning. Moreover, transitional provisions in the constitution made it legally difficult to roll back some of the AFRC's measures, such as a Special Tribunal mandated to continue investigating senior civil servants' sources of income and property. Around the country, autonomous vigilante groups arose to "check kalabule" in the marketplaces, that is, monitor prices; Limann initially gave his tacit approval to them.

The Limann government, however, was highly mistrustful of such societal mobilizations. The cabinet and other state institutions—composed of technocrats, professionals, and members of other social elites—preferred patronage connections to get things done. The PNP's particular patron-client networks were ethnically skewed toward northerners, westerners, and Ga, who attained many more high-level state positions than did Asante, Brong, or Ewe. The spoils did not go entirely to the PNP, however. Members of the parliament, including from the opposition, voted to give themselves hefty salary hikes and used their positions to secure business deals and personal advancement. Through such actions, commented Chazan, the government and its parliamentary allies "merely served to accentuate [their] image as elitist in derivation, patron-based in orientation, and exclusivist in thrust."[39]

Worried about the long shadow still cast by the AFRC's former members and supporters, Limann moved steadily to diminish their influence. All AFRC members but Rawlings soon accepted foreign scholarships or postings. In late November, the government forcibly retired Rawlings from the armed forces, along with five senior officers, including the army commander, Brigadier Quainoo, and the chief of defense staff, Brigadier Joseph Nunoo-Mensah. Under pressure, another two hundred officers eventually resigned their commissions. The campaign to reestablish control within and over the military had its limits: rank-and-file soldiers sometimes acted on their own, relations between junior and senior officers remained tense, and some senior officers simply resigned or fled abroad.[40] Two coup plots were discovered, in March 1980 and February 1981, the first with the avowed aim of restarting the AFRC's housecleaning.[41]

Meanwhile, the economy continued to deteriorate, and the government's policies were ineffective in halting the trend. As cocoa's world market price continued to decline, financial assistance from the International Monetary Fund remained out of reach in the absence of a politically difficult decision to devalue the cedi. Instead, the government sought to increase domestic revenue by introducing new taxes and raising water rates and petrol prices. It also tried to reduce spending by trimming staff costs, a highly unpopular measure. Within less than a year of the PNP's coming into office, the cost of a poor Ghanaian's breakfast had climbed to twice the minimum wage.[42]

Social discontent continued. University students staged strikes and demonstrations, leading to police clashes, the death of a student, and the universities' closure in early 1980. Workers, especially those in public corporations, mobilized against the austerity measures. In June 1980, workers of the Ghana Industrial Holding Corporation (GIHOC), the largest industrial establishment, struck to demand better conditions. In some factories they locked up management staff. From Accra and Tema, five hundred marched on Parliament House and disrupted the proceedings. They also invaded the Ministry of Industries, GIHOC's head office, and the Hall of Trade Unions. The government responded by ordering GIHOC to fire a thousand strikers.[43]

New political organizations emerged, including the People's Revolutionary League of Ghana (PRLG), which explicitly cited Rawlings's warning that Limann would be watched by "eagles' eyes."[44] In May 1980, the New Democratic Movement was launched, with an avowed Marxist orientation and a base on the campuses.[45] Then on the first anniversary of the AFRC takeover, at a rally of tens of thousands, Rawlings proclaimed the formation of the June Fourth Movement (JFM) to achieve honest government and "a just society in which the welfare of the majority of the people stands supreme."[46] At another rally on the second anniversary, Rawlings was even more pointed, referring to the prevailing system as an "empty democracy" that served to preserve "the exploiter class against the exploited." He endorsed the call of an earlier speaker for people to form "committees for the revolution." That revolution, he hoped, would be peaceful, but he quoted US president John F. Kennedy: "Those who make a peaceful revolution impossible make a violent revolution inevitable."[47]

Pushing back, the police harassed and sometimes detained members of the PRLG, JFM, and other groups. Retired captain Kojo Tsikata, a well-known radical who had by then become a close confidant of Rawlings, escaped a suspected assassination attempt. The Special Branch and Military Intelligence circulated pamphlets with anti-Ewe invective (Brigadier Quainoo and Captain Tsikata were Ewe, while Rawlings's mother was Ewe and his father, Scottish).[48]

In the eyes of Rawlings's new civilian allies and his old military supporters—who were still numerous in the barracks—the Limann regime had failed its probation period. Moreover, its wider public image was not only of elitism and incompetence but increasingly corruption as well, with allegations against several party leaders. In particular, former PNP chairman Nana Okutwer Bekoe was implicated in a bribery scandal involving money from South African sources.[49]

Few were surprised when sectors of the military once again intervened—and met almost no resistance. Early on the morning of December 31, 1981, a small group of soldiers of the Recce regiment, supported by air force personnel, moved on key installations in Accra. When word spread that Rawlings backed the action, the ranks and many officers rallied to the rebels. With minimal fuss, the Limann government fell.

The Provisional National Defence Council

From the beginning, Rawlings and his coconspirators declared that their December 31 intervention would be more than a simple replay of June 4: not a limited housecleaning but an attempt at fundamental structural change in the state, relations between state and society, and within society itself. As Rawlings proclaimed on the day of his seizure, "I ask for nothing less than a revolution. Something that would transform the social and economic order of this country."[50] Many supporters agreed wholeheartedly—although wide divergences later surfaced over what that meant.

Unlike the AFRC, the new government was presented not as transitional but as intent on remaining in power. And while Rawlings's earlier council was a strictly military affair, the new one was a military-civilian alliance from the start; it remained so throughout its various permutations, with a steadily diminishing military component over time.

The membership of the first Provisional National Defence Council (PNDC), the core decision-making body, included four military figures and three civilians. The military members covered the spectrum of ranks: Rawlings, its chairman and still a flight lieutenant; Sergeant Daniel Alolga Akata-Pore; Warrant Officer Class One Joseph Adjei Buadi; and Brigadier Joseph Nunoo-Mensah. The civilians symbolized different social constituencies: Joachim Amartey Kwei, a leader of the GIHOC workers; Chris Bukari Atim, a former student leader and prominent figure in the June Fourth Movement; and the Reverend Kwabena Damuah, the radical priest who had strongly supported the AFRC. The PNDC also named various cabinet secretaries; most were civilian and a few had been figures in the old political parties.

The PNDC soon demonstrated an impressive popular base, in part through large support rallies during the first weeks of 1982 across the country, a few numbering in the hundreds of thousands. While conservative organizations such as the Association of Recognized Professional Bodies urged a quick return to constitutional rule, many other societal groups proclaimed support for the PNDC's "Holy War," including student associations, rank-and-file workers and some union leaders, the national fishermen's organization, local youth and development associations, some chiefs, and nearly all the left-wing and nationalist political groups that had been critical of the Limann regime, including PNP dissidents in the Kwame Nkrumah Revolutionary Guards.

Although the PNDC, like AFRC, emphasized the initiative of the military's lower ranks, it tried from the start to build a wider base within the armed forces. Brigadier Nunoo-Mensah was not only incorporated into the PNDC but also reinstated as chief of defense staff, while Brigadier Quainoo was reappointed army commander. The December 31 takeover, Rawlings said, was a "joint officer-ranks action." He stressed the importance of maintaining military discipline and admonished soldiers to not "create fear amongst the civilian population by acts of looting, reckless show of force or wild behaviour," tacitly acknowledging some of the abuses in 1979.[51]

The AFRC's emphasis on promoting moral accountability and fighting corruption was still there. But more than previously, it was placed within a context of systemic change, both economic and political. Explained Rawlings shortly after retaking power,

> Our problems are economic. We are now making a comprehensive review of the domestic economy, initiating plans for the elimination of corruption and inefficiency, and building the basis of a sound and sustained economy. We have talked a lot about corruption. We are not claiming that corruption is the fundamental problem of the country but it has to be admitted that it is so pervasive and deep-seated in the country that its elimination has become a necessary precondition for the functioning of the system, let alone its change.[52]

Within a few days of its creation, the PNDC announced that it would establish new public tribunals alongside the old judicial apparatus, specifically to rapidly bring to justice those who had abused their office (see chapter 7). Many other initiatives sought to address ordinary Ghanaians' immediate economic problems: helping farmers get cocoa and other crops to market, providing tools and other agricultural inputs to boost food production, channeling scarce cement toward building cheap housing, reviewing labor contracts and working conditions, refurbishing the severely deteriorated road network, and directing essential commodities to those most in need. When dealing with market prices, Rawlings seemed to have learned from the AFRC's counterproductive assault against small-scale market women. The basic problem, he now emphasized, lay with big importers, who trapped ordinary market women in a "vicious circle ... not of their making."[53]

Repeatedly, Rawlings and other PNDC figures emphasized actively involving ordinary Ghanaians. In part, such pronouncements were intended to allay fears of arbitrary military action and bolster the legitimacy of a government that had taken power unconstitutionally. But there was also some real substance on the ground: student volunteers mobilized into task forces to help repair roads or transport cocoa to port, workers set up committees to expose corrupt managers and fight for better labor conditions, youths in villages along Ghana's frontiers reinforced the border guards to check smuggling. Throughout the country, popular bodies, known as People's Defence Committees (PDCs) and Workers Defence Committees (WDCs), were created with official sanction and mandated, according to Rawlings, "to defend the democratic rights of the people and expose corruption and any tendencies to undermine the Revolution."[54] The committees enjoyed widespread participation during the early 1980s and sometimes diverged from the PNDC's notions of reform (see chapter 6).

It was not uncommon to dismiss the PNDC's use of revolutionary language as a rhetorical gloss on a simple military coup, as did its domestic critics and numerous international media accounts. While many theorists of revolution would agree that the process in Ghana did not match the model of classic social revolutions that thoroughly transform society (France, Russia, China, and Cuba, among others), a case could be made that it did constitute a political revolution. According to a general definition advanced by Jack A. Goldstone, one of the field's leading scholars, a revolution is "an effort to transform the political institutions and the justifications for political authority in a society, accompanied by formal or informal mass mobilization."[55] To distinguish revolution from the many military takeovers in Africa and elsewhere that did not bring such change, he added that some "coups can lead to revolutions if the coup leaders or their followers present a vision for reshaping society on new principles of justice and social order, embark on a program of mass mobilization to build support for that vision, and then enact that vision by creating new institutions."[56] Beyond African revolutions stemming from successful anticolonial liberation movements and postcolonial insurgencies, there have been several radical military takeovers, from Gamal Abdel Nasser's 1952 seizure in Egypt and the Ethiopian revolution of 1974 to the 1983–87 revolution in Ghana's immediate neighbor to the north, Burkina Faso, led by Captain Thomas Sankara.[57]

Yet the revolutionary promise of the PNDC's first few years did not last. Weakened by rifts within its own alliance, unsettled by several coup attempts, beset by persistent opposition from Ghana's social elites, and driven to desperation by a severe economic crisis, the Rawlings government made an incremental retreat beginning in the middle of the 1980s. It first negotiated an agreement with the Western financial institutions and then reined in the PDCs and reached a tacit accommodation with components of Ghana's upper social strata. In the process, there were fundamental shifts in the PNDC's overall approach to both social transformation and state restructuring (see chapter 8).

Despite that shift, combating corruption remained a major element. Although inconsistent, the leadership often linked corruption issues to a range of desired political and social reforms. Whatever the PNDC's conceptions of those links, focusing on corruption had a practical benefit: it was an effective tool for mobilization, symbolizing the injustices of the existing system in a visceral fashion. Corruption usually had a face, while notions of class oppression or external economic dependence were less tangible. Because corruption was a complex and multisided phenomenon, the adoption of a strong anticorruption posture enabled the rallying of varied sectors of society with otherwise dissimilar interests and concerns. Moreover, in an initial atmosphere heady with notions of popular democracy and mobilization of the oppressed, the battle cry "Down with corruption!" could easily be taken up by nonstate actors—sometimes in ways not anticipated by those holding state power.

6

"We No Go Sit Down"

By echoing the various strands of social discontent prevalent in Ghana, Rawlings and his comrades were able to seize power with broad public acclaim. But that did not automatically provide them with a substantial, organized base of support. Their hold on power was tenuous. The political alliances they forged were new and untested, led by small groups with sometimes differing views, held together mostly by Rawlings's personal stature and following. Ranged against them were the old elites, still with substantial social and financial resources, as well as sectors of the state bureaucracy and military fearful of what the revolution might bring. Those conservative forces, moreover, received some backing from Western powers and several neighboring regimes.

The Provisional National Defence Council (PNDC) sought to strengthen its position by quickly organizing its diffuse followers and mobilizing new sources of support, initially among the lower rungs of society. Having rationalized the overthrow of the Limann regime with the argument that the old political institutions were bankrupt and unable to bring genuine democracy, they could not readily hold new elections or establish Western-style representative institutions. In the words of a leading Ghanaian scholar, the new authorities were inclined to instead establish "an alternative non-bourgeois political institution that would link the state to civil society."[1] They also developed fresh methods of mobilization and shifted the government's basis of social support to new strata.[2] The preamble to the PNDC's May 1982 policy guidelines—drafted by some of the left-wing intellectuals then influential within its inner circles—argued that the December takeover was a "national democratic revolution" that "must be anti-imperialist, anti-neocolonialist and must aim at instituting a popular democracy," with power "exercised by the people organised from the grassroots."[3]

At first, such views were encouraged from the summits of power. Beyond the small political and social groups that were already allied with the PNDC, new organizations also arose. Foremost among them were the People's Defence Committees (PDCs) and Workers Defence Committees (WDCs), organized respectively in residential locations and workplaces. Although encouraged by Rawlings's early pronouncements, the PDCs (as both variants were collectively known) were initiated mainly by local activists.

The committees were hybrid formations. From one direction, they functioned as semistate institutions to implement central directives at the local level, bypassing the patrons, chiefs, and other "big men" utilized by previous regimes. By linking local issues, conflicts, and grievances with a national agenda, they generated identification between ordinary citizens and the goals espoused by the central authorities in Accra. And when their efforts to win popular acceptance fell short, they also had behind them the power of the state—and its security services—to enforce compliance through more coercive means. From the other side, they provided new channels through which some members of local communities and marginalized sectors were able to advance their interests. Youths in particular rallied to the committees, along with workers, the unemployed, petty traders, artisans, fishermen, small farmers, students, and, to a limited extent, women.

The PDCs fulfilled several functions simultaneously. First, they sought to "defend the revolution" from internal and external antagonists, with limited powers of surveillance, investigation, arrest, and detention. Second, they helped, to a modest degree, to ease public discontent by addressing some of the immediate economic and social needs of local communities that the central state was unable to tackle. Finally, and most relevant to this study, they served as anticorruption watchdogs that actively investigated and exposed individuals suspected of embezzlement, theft, fraud, bribery, nepotism, and similar acts. Their bottom-up approach to fighting corruption brought to light many more cases than state agencies could have uncovered. Their emergence was one of the features that made Ghana's anticorruption experience so striking.

The PDCs' particular perspective on corruption differed from that of many state officials—and diverged considerably from the prevailing international anticorruption discourse. It tended to regard corruption not as a failing of errant individuals in high office but as a systemic problem rooted in Ghana's class-divided society. As K. Gyan-Apenteng, a national defense committee leader, commented during the PNDC's early weeks,

> Corruption . . . is the product of a social system and enriches a minority of the people whilst having the opposite effect on the majority. It ties in with the general economic and political enslavement of the toiling masses by their idle oppressors. Corruption has become the life-line of the system and the system symbiotically feeds it grease. . . .
>
> But how will the anti-corruption war be won? We will have to work towards the complete elimination of the system that allows a minority to exploit the majority of the people. On the way to achieving that end we must eradicate and abrogate all practices and regulations which without adding anything to either production or efficiency merely serve as avenues for extortion, bribery, graft, nepotism, etc. and encourage bureaucratic wastefulness.
>
> Then tough legislation must be enacted to deal with those found guilty of corrupt practices. The vigilance of the exploited

people is an essential feature in winning the war against corruption.[4]

The PDCs were launched with central state encouragement, and their members often functioned as if they had the full power of the state behind them. At least for a brief time, that link gave the committees political power rarely matched anywhere in Africa—or elsewhere in the world. But their activities soon acquired a life of their own, occasionally pushing beyond the government's direct control. Over time, especially as the PNDC's overall policy direction shifted, the authorities would repeatedly intervene, subtly or crudely, to rein them in.

Channeling Chaos

The creation of the PDCs, especially in their first months, was often rapid and disorderly. Their officers and executive committees were elected by general assemblies of residents or employees, but the sizes and structures of local leadership bodies varied greatly. There initially were no clear guidelines about how PDCs should be structured, how elections should be conducted, or who could or could not be a member. Overall, the committees were open to anyone who supported the goals of the revolution and was not of a social class or occupation deemed hostile to it. Executive members tended to be young, educated members of local communities, frequently students or recent graduates. But in some villages and smaller towns there were illiterate PDC leaders as well, a marker of the degree to which the committees were socially representative but also a shortcoming that made communications and coordination more difficult. The files of the Interim National Coordinating Committee (INCC) and the National Defence Committee, the appointed bodies in Accra that sought to bring some overall shape and direction to the local PDCs, were full of complaints about problems of transportation, communications, language differences, scarce funds, and numerous other organizational handicaps.

There were no accurate statistics on the number of PDCs and WDCs that existed, or of total defense committee membership. There probably were at least several thousand local committees, since practically every workplace and locality eventually had a WDC or PDC, or, as they were later called, a Committee for the Defence of the Revolution (CDR). Yaw Akrasi-Sarpong, at first a member of the National Defence Committee and later a liaison official between the PNDC and the defense committees, estimated in early 1985 that the committees had roughly "400,000 active, militant members. There are many more CDR members, but 400,000 militant members countrywide, the core."[5]

The defense committees were stronger in some areas than others, with the large towns and the eastern and northern parts demonstrating greater activity. In March 1982 an INCC staffer identified the areas of "low political activity" as the Ashanti, Brong Ahafo, Central, and Western regions.[6] Nearly a year later, problems still were evident in some areas, including the gold mining zone around Obuasi, in Ashanti, where many people were reported to be uninterested in the PDCs because they benefited either directly or indirectly from gold smuggling.[7]

Because of loose national supervision and confusion about membership and leadership criteria, some committees initially fell under the control of local elites: leaders of Limann's People's National Party, his former vigilante groups, criminals, chiefs' representatives, and "persons of no fixed address."[8] In Brong Ahafo, reported the PDC coordinator for the region, "Some of the members of the P.D.C. have questionable characters. Some of them are opportunists. Sometimes such PDC's are not taken serious and don't have confidence of the people. We have encouraged the people to weed out discreditable characters. It may take time before we get the quality we want."[9]

By March 1982, all PDCs had to be formally registered by the national coordinating committee, as a process of "vetting" local PDC leaderships began. In some cases, PDC executives were dissolved by the INCC or National Defence Committee or by regional and district government representatives. In others, PDC members took the initiative. At the Agricultural Development Bank, members voted out their WDC executive committee for incompetence and collusion with management, while in the small town of Kofi-Krom in Adansi district, the newly elected PDC chairman was publicly exposed as a black-market trader when the population's views about the executive members were solicited.[10] Occasionally local PDCs ousted higher-level PDC bodies. In the heavily working-class town of Sekondi, the Central Steering Committee of PDCs and WDCs voted to dissolve the Western Region Secretariat of the National Defence Committee, accusing its members of being opportunists, hangers-on, and job hunters. "Instead of the [National Defence Committee] upgrading the PDCs and WDCs to defend the revolution they have become power drunk,"[11] the resolution said. The National Defence Committee in Accra went along with the move but reminded the PDCs in Sekondi that only the national committee had the authority to remove a regional body.[12]

Despite such problems, the PDC leaderships were among the most socially representative of any institution Ghana had known. The executive committee in the small town of Agave-Afedume in the Volta Region was not untypical. Its chairman was a basket weaver, its secretary and financial secretary were teachers, its organizing secretary was a farmer, and the other members comprised two more farmers, three fishermen, two traders, a baker, and another teacher.[13]

Few women, however, were able to play significant roles. The patriarchal attitudes that prevailed in large parts of Ghanaian society threw up gender barriers, ensuring that few women stepped forward to run for positions in committee executives, even in cases such as the Ministry of Health where they were encouraged to do so.[14] Only a few PDCs had notable proportions of female members, as among storekeepers of the Ghana National Trading Corporation.[15] More typical were the PDCs in the Awutu Traditional Area, which had only 10 women among 425 executive members of the area's fifty-two PDCs.[16]

In an effort to introduce some uniformity, the INCC issued a first set of guidelines in March 1982. Reflecting the language of the June Fourth Movement and other left-wing groupings that predominated among committee leaders, the guidelines declared that the PDCs' first aim was to "guarantee that the working people of this country form the basis of power to carry out the December Revolution, under the PNDC." They also were to educate and mobilize working people to defend their democratic rights and economic and social needs, participate in decision-making, and counter all internal and external enemies, "especially imperialism." Their more specific tasks included acting as "watchdogs of the revolution" by checking corruption, waste, mismanagement, misuse of state property, smuggling, black-market dealing, hoarding, and other acts of "sabotage." They were to explain national issues and help implement PNDC decisions, with the perspective of eventually taking over local government administration. They also were to supervise the distribution of goods and services, organize self-help projects, ensure efficiency, productivity, and discipline in workplaces, and supervise the activities of local trade unions. Specifically excluded from membership were "class enemies," broadly understood to include enterprise managers, chiefs, landlords, absentee farmers, former leaders of banned political parties, and other sectors of the old elites. Officeholders were not to be accorded any special privileges, had to bring all major decisions before members for approval, and could hold leadership positions for only twelve-month, renewable terms.[17]

According to Emmanuel Hansen, an activist and academic, that perspective on social change made the PDCs "institutional mechanisms for the expression of class demands, instruments for class struggles and structures for the consolidation of class gains."[18] It also brought them into direct conflict not only with the vestiges of the old political and state system but also with virtually every sector of the social hierarchy: businessmen, importers, traders, company managers, multinational corporations, chiefs, church leaders, landlords, and large-scale cocoa farmers and fishermen.

In sweeping terms that left little room for discernment, anyone with some substantial degree of property was regarded as morally decadent, akin to smugglers, black-marketeers, thieves, corrupt bureaucrats, and embezzlers.

The symbolism utilized by the PDCs incorporated a range of ideological and cultural strands. "The political education must be based on the tenets of scientific socialism," wrote one PDC leader, and activists should allocate time to "the study of marxist literature."[19] Such views resonated with some urban workers, students and radical intellectuals but elicited incomprehension and distrust from members of the middle class, small-scale traders, rural folk, and even many workers and unemployed people. Local PDC activists therefore often reframed their declarations in more accessible language. In rural areas they included references to custom, frequently emphasizing commoner traditions but also enlisting the authority of chieftaincy when a local chief proved cooperative. In both countryside and cities, activists also employed religious symbols, borrowing heavily from liberation theology conceptions already popularized in Ghana by such individuals as Reverend Kwabena Damuah, a member of the PNDC. It was not unusual for PDC meetings, including those devoted to discussions of Marxist theory, to begin and end with prayers.

Many PDC leaders and members (and originally some PNDC officials) initially conceived of PDCs as the embryos of a new form of state power, or at least of local government. But as some committees exhibited a degree of autonomy or alarmed certain social sectors that the government hoped to placate, Rawlings and most government officials soon began to regard the committees with suspicion. As Akrasi-Sarpong was reported to have remarked, "If you give them too much power, they tend to misuse it; so you have to keep it and give it out in bits."[20] Radical activists in the PDCs certainly gave the authorities cause for concern, insofar as they regarded the committees as an alternative pole of political authority. That view was exemplified by Emmanuel Hansen, National Defence Committee secretary in 1982, who later wrote that the PDCs and other popular bodies "constituted the counter-institutions of state power."[21]

Cautiously at first, but later more forcefully, the PNDC began from around the middle of 1982 to try to constrict the PDCs' independent power and initiative without undercutting their ability to rally support for the government. That effort was reflected in a variety of disputes that on the surface seemed to revolve mainly around organizational squabbles. One source of contention came from a push by local PDCs to form higher-level coordinating committees, whether on a geographical basis or among WDCs in different branches of the same enterprise. The national INCC and National Defence Committee coordinators, under pressure from government representatives at various levels, tried to control that process, initially with mixed success. Another dispute was generated by the proposals of local PDCs to form their own irregular militia units to help counter attacks by domestic opponents, coup plotters, and external rebel groups. The PNDC, however, was not keen to build up the PDCs' power any further. What little militia training it did permit during the first year was intended less to strengthen military defense capacities than, as government representatives explicitly stated, to instill discipline and counter "laziness" in workplaces.[22] Not until after a nearly successful coup attempt in June 1983 was more systematic militia training initiated—but under the direct command of regular military officers, not the PDCs.

One of the most contentious issues during 1982–83 concerned the committees' then restrictive membership criteria. As early as April 1982, Sergeant Alolga Akata-Pore, a member of the PNDC and June Fourth Movement, counseled PDCs against automatically excluding senior managers. In August of that year, national PDC coordinators modified their guidelines to allow some management personnel to join PDCs, but only by exception, after vetting.[23] Sentiment within the PDCs remained hostile to allowing in the "cheap middle classes" and other conservative social strata, amid a battle cry of "Keep the rich out of the PDCs."[24]

The differences on membership did not fall neatly along the PDC-government divide. Some in local PDCs argued that the exclusion policy was too rigid and needlessly alienated potential supporters. A report to the INCC by a PDC activist in the Volta Region, who agreed with the PDCs' overall thrust, argued for greater diversity in committee membership:

> I suspect the reservation of PDC membership to just a section of the population at this stage of the revolution [is] a mistake, possibly culminating into friction and tension between members and non-members in view of the onerous social tasks before the PDCs. . . . The revolution has come to stay and we must be tactical about things.
>
> At this stage of their development they need be open to every citizen, regardless of his or her social stand unless there's obvious cause for elimination of an individual.[25]

The convergence of government pressure with a current of thinking already present in the PDCs resulted in a second set of guidelines in April 1983. They dropped the earlier exclusionary membership criteria and stipulated that PDCs were "open to all persons who are prepared to uphold and defend the basic objectives of the ongoing revolutionary process and who have a proven record of patriotism, integrity and democratic practice."[26]

The actual social composition of the PDCs and their leaderships did not greatly change at first. But as the government moved toward new alliances with some sectors of Ghana's middle and upper classes, the change in membership criteria opened the way for bringing more socially conservative individuals into the committees, in the process helping the authorities dampen their militancy.

Exposing Corruption and Kalabule

The PNDC's new monitoring, investigative, and judicial institutions brought many corrupt bureaucrats and other "big men" to account for their misdeeds (see chapter 7). But the evidence was often collected by PDCs, other organizations, and individuals. The brief flickers of popular anticorruption activity that started during the Armed Forces Revolutionary Council period flared into a full-blown national movement. Ordinary Ghanaians' determination to not remain passive victims was expressed in the popular slogan "We no go sit down make [let] them cheat us every day."

In the beginning they received encouragement from the authorities—not just those identified as radicals but also some more established figures. Along with other senior officers, Brigadier Arnold Quainoo, the army commander, addressed large rallies at which he urged people to root out corruption and inefficiency in their workplaces: "Workers should henceforth participate in the management of their organisations and make sure that all forms of corruption, dishonesty and indiscipline are eradicated from the Ghanaian society, especially the top hierarchy.... If you learn how to speak the truth, no power can prevail against you and you can have the moral authority to point your finger at corrupt officials."[27] Such approval from the top contributed to the extent of popular anticorruption action, but its intensity was mainly driven by Ghanaians' sense of injustice.

Municipal and district councils, which were responsible for local services, suddenly found themselves under scrutiny. Workers' committees of various divisions of the Accra City Council provided auditors with evidence of varied irregularities: revenue collectors who stole pension allowances, overpayments for shoddy equipment, fake leave and overtime claims, and landlord fees that went "to the pockets" of officials of the City Engineer's Department.[28] Two thousand taxi drivers marched on the Interior Ministry to protest city guards' brutalities, harassment, and illegal on-the-spot parking fines.[29] A former works overseer of the Ketu District Council sent to the INCC's investigation branch details of the misappropriation of a ₵1.3 million government sanitation grant, while the PDC in Togbloku accused the former chairman of the Ada District Council of using "for his own purposes" funds intended for building a middle school.[30] In Tamale, a WDC uncovered thirty-two "ghost employees" on the town's payroll, leading the regional treasury officer to flee. In Wawase, near the gold mining town of Obuasi, a former member of the Adansi District Council was forced by the PDC to refund money taken but never spent on roofing sheets for public toilets.[31] In Ajumako Besease, PDC members bearing placards declaring "Inspector thousand must go!" stormed the offices of the municipality's chief inspector, accused him of bribery, and physically ejected him.[32]

Public anger over corrupt education and health personnel was especially acute. A teachers' PDC in Ablekuma detained two officers of the Ministry of Education for diverting to the black-market government-supplied school exercise books, while defense committees at the National Vocational Training Institute and the Wa School for the Blind exposed similar malpractices.[33]

At Wenchi Secondary School in Brong Ahafo, students blamed the headmaster for the disappearance of supplies and questioned his claim that the school had to close early because funds had run out, asking that "military auditors" examine the accounts.[34] In October 1982, seven hundred pupils of St. John's Grammar School in Accra demonstrated for three hours to highlight claims that the headmaster, two bursars, and the storekeeper had stolen ten bags of rice and fifty-two bags of flour.[35]

In Adukrom, a PDC-supported Students' Task Force detained an assistant of the area's health center amid accusations of selling medicines that were supposed to be provided free and running the clinic as "a personal property to amass wealth at the expense of the suffering masses." A staff nurse was appointed to take over management of the center, which served a population of 90,000.[36] An "action unit" of a Students' Task Force in the Volta Region similarly held two senior Health Ministry officials and a regional treasury officer for pocketing the salaries of 120 fictitious health employees. "The days when people abused official positions to cheat workers are gone forever," declared a spokesman.[37] In August 1983, at a time when such detentions were no longer common, the WDC of Wa Hospital held two employees and a trader for diverting food intended for patients.[38]

Employees of Ghana's many state enterprises, sitting at the nexus of bureaucratic arbitrariness and economic opportunity, were uniquely positioned. Not only did they have information about corrupt managers but also they were especially angry over economic hardships.

With WDCs forming in nearly every enterprise and some trade unions shaken out of their earlier somnolence, hardly any state firm remained untouched. At a large workers' rally in Accra, an employee of the Produce Buying Division (PBD) of the Cocoa Marketing Board—the largest state enterprise—charged that the division was "plagued with corruption" and vowed that workers might have to take over the company if the government failed to act.[39] The PBD employees' interim defense committee then issued detailed accusations against numerous top officials, including Yiadom Ohene Boakye, the former chief manager. The committee claimed he had used his membership on the Central Committee of Limann's People's National Party (PNP) to gain the appointment in November 1979 and, in alliance with several "corrupt, dishonest" leaders of the local trade union, had turned the PBD into "a disgraceful, indisciplined, and inefficient dictatorship in which bribery and corruption, incompetence, persecution of qualified and experienced staff, punitive transfers and dismissals, unjustified and abnormal promotions, shortages and overstaffing were rife."[40] Before he could be officially charged, Boakye fled the country.[41]

Other state enterprise officials were not as fleet. The port of Tema, an industrial center just east of Accra, was brought to a standstill when workers of the Ghana Ports Authority detained twelve top management personnel, including the port's acting director, for various malpractices. The workers paraded them publicly before turning them over to military authorities. In Koforidua, members of the Nsawam district PDC arrested and handed to the police nine employees of the Ghana National

Trading Corporation for diverting essential goods to the black market.[42]

In the twin industrial cities of Sekondi and Takoradi, the WDC of the Ghana Railway Corporation accused management of corruption, inefficiency, and poor performance, demanding they be "probed."[43] In the same towns, the WDC of the State Insurance Corporation accused various officials of running a fraudulent insurance claims syndicate and placing their own relatives and friends on the payroll. "Surely, they have milked the corporation for too long and it is high time the PNDC check their wrecking-the-nation deals."[44] A Kwame Nkrumah Revolutionary Guards (KNRG) branch in Sekondi leveled similar charges against insurance company managers, providing inventories of the managers' luxurious houses and villas. But perhaps reflecting its national rivalry with the PDCs, the KNRG also accused the WDC at the State Insurance Corporation of having been "hijacked" by management.[45]

Individual employees of the State Fishing Corporation, headquartered in Tema, wrote letters to Rawlings, the corporation's PDC, and the National Investigations Committee (NIC) claiming malpractices by Managing Director Edmund Ocansey and other officials. Their alleged misdeeds included a scheme to store fish in the Canary Islands (for a company run by politically influential Ghanaians), supplying fish to favored traders in Tema (including the wife of the former PNP chairman) while ignoring markets elsewhere, accumulating wealth and property well beyond their official salaries, and victimizing employees who complained about such activities.[46] The workers' PDC investigated those and other charges, finding that the Canary Islands storage deal was "fishy, and detrimental to the corporation," that dismissed managers continued to collect funds or were sold corporation houses on credit, that corporate accounts were used to hide individuals' wealth, and that Ocansey had engaged in a "capricious use of power," dismissing, transferring, or redeploying employees who had crossed him. The PDC chairman cited some gross inequities: although the workers' canteen had closed the year before because of a supposed lack of funds, "the rich Board of Directors continued to enjoy their mouth-watering 4-course meals including sophisticated drinks, anytime they attended a meeting."[47] Ocansey was subsequently charged by the Citizens' Vetting Committee (which investigated the sources of individuals' wealth) when he was found to have paid for a Mercedes-Benz with corporation funds.[48]

Inequities also featured in the accusations against officials of the National Industrial Corporation's fabric manufacturing factory in Accra. The local WDC raised a variety of grievances, including misappropriation of funds and disrespectful conduct by the manufacturing director. A WDC leader explained, "We are not small boys to be treated in that way."[49] What seemed to have riled workers most was a management decision to give bolts of fabric as gifts to key managers and their political patrons just before Christmas 1981, although the vast majority of workers received nothing. A WDC letter to the government provided details of how company officials were able to serve both themselves and the political patronage networks with which they were connected. By noting that the recipients included President Limann, PNP Chairman Bekoe, and other top figures in the previous administration, the WDC leaders emphasized the affair's political undertones. "This is tantamount to stealing, and misuse of state property," the WDC leaders concluded. "Thanks to the PNDC that the worker has been given the power to talk."[50]

In some state firms, defense committees raised concerns that employees had also become corrupted. The WDC of the State Gold Mining Corporation at the Tarkwa goldfields in the Western Region coupled their complaints about management embezzlement with criticism of workers who took some of the gold powder and sold it illegally on the black market.[51] The WDC instead urged miners to fight for a "kind of power that can take over the re-allocation of the wealth of Society," since that wealth "is produced by the sweat and toil of the working people."[52]

Workers rarely singled out management officials simply for embezzlement or other fraudulent activities. They also raised standard labor grievances, from stagnant salaries and inadequate canteen facilities to unfair dismissals and arbitrary promotion practices, and frequently linked their own particular problems with society-wide injustices and inequities. Those employed in public firms also often displayed a strong sense of responsibility for the financial well-being and sound management of their enterprises and of the state more generally.

Virtually no organization with a public function of any sort escaped the drive for accountability. Some of the farmers' associations belonging to the Ghana National Farmers Council (GNFC), supported by the council's WDC, spearheaded the ouster of the secretary-general, whom they accused of diverting ₵3.5 million worth of textiles intended for sale to farmers, running the council as his "personal organization," and other malpractices.[53] "Oheneba Osei Yaw Akoto has exploited and cheated us illiterate farmer for long," declared a petition by thirty-one farmers and local GNFC leaders. "We shall not allow it any more."[54] In Kromantsi, fishermen leveled similar charges against their elected "chief fisherman," alleged to have profited from black-market sales of nets, buoys, ropes, and other equipment intended for the National Canoe Fishermen's Council.[55] Consumer cooperative societies, established in various trades and workplaces to enable their members to gain access to scarce commodities, appear to have been particularly vulnerable to diversion and generated many movements for the ouster of dishonest officers and recovery of embezzled funds.[56]

Churches also came under fire. In Keta-Ho, in the Volta Region, lay members of the Kpando Catholic Church accused the bishop and other officials of poor administration of the diocese, financial misdeeds at the Kpando Catholic Hospital, and generally ignoring the complaints of parishioners, some of whom attempted to take over the Kpando church as a "People's Church."[57] In Accra a group of "concerned members" of the Osu Presbyterian Church responded to the Christian Council's criticisms of the

Rawlings government by claiming the council was motivated by "self-aggrandisement and the fear of having corruption among the top echelon exposed."[58] Leaders of the Ghana Muslims Representative Council were removed from office for various infractions, including giving scholarships to unqualified students in exchange for bribes.[59]

Labor on Dual Tracks

In early government pronouncements and the rhetoric of many activists, wage and salary earners were portrayed as the most dynamic force for change. Yet while the WDCs were launched to help tap into that force, they were not the only organizations claiming to represent workers. Trade unions already existed in many enterprises, with more solid structures than the WDCs and more experience in bargaining around classic labor grievances.

Yet at the start of the PNDC era, union leaders' long record was less an advantage than a stigma. Members saw many union officials as little more than corrupt bureaucrats, detached from ordinary workers' daily concerns, overly friendly with management, and closely linked to the old political establishment. The head of the Trades Union Congress (TUC), Alhaji Issifu, had campaigned for General Acheampong's Union Government proposal in 1977, followed by the TUC's sponsorship of one of the political parties in the 1979 elections. Many union leaders were suspected of diverting or pocketing union funds, suspicions subsequently confirmed by probes into union corruption.

The national union leaders' lack of militancy had not prevented ordinary unionists, individual union chapters, or several national affiliates of the TUC from taking part in the struggles of the late 1970s and early 1980s. The actions of workers at the Ghana Industrial Holding Corporation (GIHOC) had helped undermine the Limann regime, while their best-known leader, Joachim Amartey Kwei, became a member of the PNDC. In the euphoric days immediately after the December 31 takeover, many unionists joined demonstrations and rallies around the country, and several unions issued statements backing Rawlings's calls for revolutionary change. The TUC itself issued a mildly supportive declaration.

However, as they denounced the corruption and oppression of Ghana's old elites, some workers simultaneously turned their anger against the heads of their unions. On January 8, 1982, as thousands of workers from the Accra-Tema industrial zones marched through the streets, some carried placards proclaiming "TUC must be scrapped" and "TUC, the workers are fed up." Issifu, the TUC secretary-general, was beaten with tree branches and had sand and stones thrown at him when he tried to address the marchers. At Nicholson Stadium; when he tried to climb on top of a van to again address the workers, he was blocked, amid shouts of "Issifu no way" and "Issifu kalabule."[60] Before the month was over, he resigned.

Soon the Association of Local Unions (ALU) was established to reform the TUC, including ousting other old-guard leaders. While not part of the ALU initiative, some affiliates of the TUC, such as the Industrial and Commercial Workers Union, similarly demanded an overhaul of the national federation's structures. Finally, on April 29, hundreds of workers mobilized by the ALU stormed the TUC Hall in Accra, despite an attempt by the PNDC's Reverend Damuah to calm them. They proclaimed the dismissal of the entire TUC leadership and establishment of interim management committees to run the federation and each of its seventeen affiliates.[61]

Meanwhile, the union reform initiative was complicated by the growth of the WDCs, which "creamed off the most militant and conscious workers" from the unions.[62] While some local unions participated in anticorruption and antimanagement mobilizations, the disarray of the national unions left the WDCs holding center stage in many enterprises during much of 1982. In part, some workers were also drawn to the committees because they addressed issues that transcended conventional union demands. As well, according to some analysts, the defense committees at the time "represented the independence, autonomy and militancy of labour."[63] Based solely on their official structures, which linked the WDCs directly to the government, that would not have seemed the case. Indeed, the tendency of some committee leaders to see themselves as local government representatives left them susceptible to pressures from above to institute greater workplace discipline.

In practice, however, as with many neighborhood PDCs, numerous WDCs displayed considerable initiative and independence of thought. Some were far to the left of the government and even some national PDC figures. The WDC of the Bank of Ghana identified with revolutionary struggles as far afield as Latin America, naming its newsletter *Venceremos*, which ran articles analyzing class relations in Ghana, denouncing the bank's management—as a "comprador bourgeoisie" and "remnants of the past corrupt political regimes"—and even criticizing several government secretaries by name.[64] Even far from Accra, in the Upper Region, WDC leaders went well beyond official rhetoric by urging that all land, foreign banks, and oil companies be nationalized, that a people's militia be established, and that the government stop being so "magnanimous and over-cautious," since "there can never be a half Revolution."[65]

There was confusion among WDC activists and union members alike about the appropriate relationship between the two. Official pronouncements and the earliest WDC guidelines said that the committees should cooperate with unions and not try to take over their functions, although a subsequent revision in the guidelines seemed to suggest that the WDCs "supervise" union activities.[66] On the ground, the relationships between unions and WDCs were fluid and ad hoc, depending on the history of conflict in a given workplace, the capacities and networks of influence of individual unionists and WDC leaders, and their links to political actors outside the enterprise. Sometimes either the WDC or the union took a clear lead. Sometimes they started out in tandem, but then one stumbled. At the Agricultural Development Bank, the union and WDC together campaigned hard for the release of a corruption probe report. But after the WDC arbitrarily blocked the broadcast of a union press conference, it was ousted by a workers assembly that accused the WDC executive of "conniving" with management.[67] In Sekondi-Takoradi, local defense committees clashed on several occasions with the railway unions over the composition of the area's National Defence Committee and efforts to oust certain railway managers.[68] At Ghana's electricity company, the leader of the Public Utility Workers Union (who also was chairman of the TUC's interim management committee) complained that the defense committee was "fabricating stories of misuse of funds" by union officials.[69]

Despite such tensions between WDCs and unions, they often were able to work together in coordinated corruption probes or joint campaigns to oust tainted managers. While the severe economic crisis then afflicting Ghana made it difficult to mount struggles for higher wages, both WDCs and unions generally agreed on the need to mobilize against job losses.

In early June 1982, the Volta Aluminum Company (Valco), a subsidiary of the US-based Kaiser empire, announced that it would close one of its production lines, threatening two hundred jobs. At a time when workers across Ghana were openly questioning management decisions, the announcement raised many suspicions, especially since serious economic constraints were not readily evident. Some saw political motives behind the move, which came shortly after the government deported three expatriate Valco employees for supposedly gathering intelligence to help PNDC opponents.[70] Defense committee leaders demanded that Valco inform Kaiser's home office that Ghana no longer had "a Government of slavery" and that "there is a shift of power base, now the power is with the people."[71] The Interim Coordinating Committee of WDCs in Tema—one of the few such WDC coordinating bodies in the country—spearheaded a national campaign against Valco's planned closure. On June 18, more than ten thousand workers rallied in Tema, then marched to Accra to present a petition to the US embassy and PNDC urging the government to renegotiate all agreements with foreign companies and consider nationalizing the recalcitrant ones.[72] Valco, realizing that the government was indeed putting together a team to renegotiate the company's original concession, later announced that it would not close the unit.[73]

Perhaps no workplace showdown was as dramatic as the one at Ghana Textile Printing (GTP) in Tema. Although majority government-owned, the company's management and largest minority shareholding were controlled by the United Africa Company (UAC), an old mainstay of British colonial capital. A relatively large enterprise, GTP normally employed about 1,200 workers. When management announced in early 1982 that low output and high debt would lead to the textile factory's closure, many distrusted the explanation. As one worker publicly complained, the managers were "all corrupt and . . . only think of their selfish ends."[74] The management subsequently offered a compromise that entailed giving the employees loans to go into farming, seriously dividing both the union and the WDC. That prompted radicals in the two organization, supported by Tema's Interim Coordinating Committee of WDCs (representing 41,000 workers in 127 establishments) to overturn their leaderships and embark on direct action. On November 5, 1982, workers occupied the GTP premises, placed the factory under workers' management, and demanded an end to UAC participation. Two weeks later, at a solidarity rally of thousands of workers, police beat a representative of the National Defence Committee (Yao Graham) and injured nearly two dozen others. Amid the furor provoked by the attack, Rawlings praised the GTP workers and the government announced the enterprise's nationalization.[75]

Less than a month later, workers also took over Juapong Textiles Ltd., which supplied the GTP with fabric and in which the UAC also held a minority share. The Juapong workers established an interim management committee that included WDC and union representatives. The two worker-run enterprises subsequently established a joint cotton farm to keep themselves supplied. Within a year the GTP registered a profit, after several years of losses.[76]

In April 1983, the PNDC adopted a severe austerity budget that marked the beginning of a gradual but major shift in overall economic orientation (see chapter 8). The budget followed a financing agreement with the International Monetary Fund (IMF) that brought devaluation of the national currency, sharply increased costs of many basic consumer goods, and threats to eliminate or reduce public enterprise workforces. The measures provoked outrage among many workers, who already were struggling with difficult living conditions and had expected the PNDC to maintain a pro-labor stance. While the TUC cautiously criticized the budget, some individual unions more sweepingly rejected it as "anti-people." In some areas, WDCs added their voices to the union protests, but the initial reaction of many was to simply come to the PNDC's defense. The WDCs in Accra's northern and western industrial zones were especially acquiescent, going as far as to describe the budget as a "perfect document."[77]

As even more austerity measures followed in subsequent years, the reactions of the defense committees and unions further diverged. The WDCs were in an awkward position: justify the new economic policies and risk losing worker support or directly challenge the policies of a government they were founded to defend. A handful did speak out and suffered retaliation as a result. But most did not. By contrast, the TUC and its affiliates took a forthright stance in defense of workers' immediate material interests and sought—with partial success—to negotiate compromises with the government. In the process, unions regained some stature and credibility with shop-floor activists.[78]

"Twin Evils"

Time and again, local activists and some national leaders referred to the corruption of public officials in the same breath with profiteering and fraud by private businessmen, merchants, and landlords. In the language of the time, corruption and exploitation were "twin evils" that had to be fought together.[79] Sometimes distinctions disappeared entirely. It was not unusual for Ghanaians to refer to businessmen not only as greedy but also as corrupt, giving the term a particularly broad meaning.[80] That tendency to blur the public-private divide was contrary to the distinctions that commonly underlay later international approaches to fighting corruption, which placed the heaviest emphasis on misdeeds in the public sector.

Like their comrades at Valco and GTP, Ghanaian workers in private firms accused managers of criminal behavior. Companies claiming financial difficulties often came under scrutiny from their WDCs, which combined typical labor grievances over lost jobs and unpaid salaries with demands to examine the companies' books. Defense committees at West African Mills in Takoradi, Saltpond Ceramics, Super Paper Products, Rockshell International, and other enterprises called on various government agencies to probe their companies' business practices and audit their books.[81] At M&K Engineering, Ghana's largest vehicle assembly plant, the WDC worried about the firm's large debt to the government and its failure to fulfill a contract to build railway cars. It accused the company of misusing an import license by diverting imported vehicle body materials to the local market and charged that the "Managing Directress, a Lebanese, changes and sends currency through the black market to abroad, whilst we are paid ₡323.00 a month."[82]

As in 1979, private traders again became common targets, whether they were small or large, officially registered or active on the black market. The latter were clearly engaged in illegal activity, most often in violation of import- or price-control laws.

Because some of the larger and better-organized smugglers were armed or had security personnel on their payroll, attempts to crack down prompted a "war" along Ghana's frontiers. It was especially intense on the eastern border with Togo, traversed by many unmarked roads and footpaths and closest to the large market of metropolitan Accra. Sometimes armed or unarmed PDC activists worked jointly with the military, border guards, and police.

But activists also ended up clashing with corrupt security forces in the pay of smugglers or themselves engaged in smuggling. In Dzindziso, PDC militants and border guards seized truckloads of fuel and timber being smuggled into Togo. However, the local PDC chairman and other militants were beaten by border guards when the activists tried to arrest a currency smuggler.[83] The PDC in Aflao, a major border post on the coastal road to the Togolese capital, appealed to the authorities to transfer out all Special Branch personnel "because their activities are not in line with the revolution," that is, they were colluding with smugglers.[84] In Anlo-Afiadenyigba, PDC members arrested a woman smuggling in sugar from Togo, but she was soon released by the nearby circuit court, the sugar was returned to her, and her husband, accompanied by a local police inspector, then sold it on the black market. "If our Peace Officers who are being paid for their work are behaving as such," asked the PDC leaders, "how can we carry on with our duties?"[85]

Following reports that PDC members and even the government's deputy regional secretary had been beaten on several occasions by border guards and police, the regional PDC coordinating committee called on public workers in Ho, the Volta regional capital, to march on police headquarters, precipitating a confrontation. The police fired warning shots and tried to prevent the deputy regional secretary from addressing the crowd. Demonstrators then ransacked several lodge houses frequented by police commanders and smugglers. Over the next weeks, several senior officials went into hiding or were dismissed by the PDCs, and the heads of many government departments, fearful of their unruly staffs, fled. Before the year's end, however, the central government sided with the regional hierarchy. It accused PDCs of taking the law into their own hands, dissolved the regional PDC coordinating committee, and dismissed the deputy regional secretary, a close ally of the PDCs.[86]

Ghana's domestic marketplaces also became battlefields. The PDCs in effect assumed the role of local market police, seeking to ensure enforcement of various regulations setting maximum prices, prohibiting hoarding, and channeling the allocation of scarce commodities to areas or sectors of the population. Often acting on information provided by dissatisfied consumers, activists sometimes warned traders to lower prices, sometimes handed them over to police or price-control tribunals, and sometimes simply seized their goods, which were then sold directly to the public at or below the control (official) price.

The national PDC coordinating committee authorized two representatives in Ada Foah to oversee the sale of sixty-nine bags of cement seized from a merchant.[87] In Ayirebi, local committee members confiscated commodities from a prominent businessman who lacked documentation of how he acquired the goods.[88] In Great Ningo, PDC members uncovered hoarded fish and compelled the merchant to sell them to the public, "persuaded" another trader to sell her fish at the official price through a PDC shop, and directly sold other fish left behind by a fleeing trader, with the proceeds deposited "into [the] government chest."[89]

At times, PDCs set their own prices. In Labadi, a coastal neighborhood of metropolitan Accra, the committee established prices for cassava cake, corn, dough, charcoal, and other food-related items. It warned, "Anyone who contravenes this directive challenges the people's popular power and will face the full wrath of the revolution."[90] Such initiatives resonated with the public, since even official government prices were often seen as too high by many poor Ghanaians. At a large rally in Tamale, a worker representative of the Central Defence Committee of the Northern Region announced that the committee was working out a new market pricing system, since prevailing prices were far beyond the pay packet of the ordinary worker.[91] In Mamprobi Sempe, six local PDCs formally protested to the government about the official price for a loaf of bread, which was almost as much as the daily minimum wage.[92]

In some places, PDCs were even more zealous than the norm. Three hundred members of various WDCs in Takoradi invaded the central marketplace, seized some goods, and ordered all traders (women) to close their stalls and leave. The market was shut for two weeks, with one WDC spokesman declaring that the workers had become "fed up" with high prices.[93] In Akatsi, in the Volta Region, the PDC took over management of the central market for a time, accusing the Ketu District Council of failing to use the market levies to improve its development.[94] Citing a similar justification, the PDC in Adabraka, a neighborhood of Accra, unsuccessfully tried to take over its local market. In that instance a physical confrontation nearly ensued between the Adabraka activists and members of the Accra City Council's Central WDC, which opposed the initiative as unplanned and arbitrary, threatening "disintegration and anarchy in the system."[95]

Flowing logically from PDC interventions in marketplaces, the notion of "People's Shops" was born.[96] They were retail outlets directly initiated by PDCs, intended as alternatives to both price-gouging merchants and inefficient and corrupt state outlets such as the Ghana National Trading Corporation. While a few government officials championed the People's Shops, the PNDC was ambivalent, at best. As a result, the shops never obtained enough goods or had sufficient political backing to significantly influence domestic markets, except in some poorer urban neighborhoods.

Nor was involvement with People's Shops good for the PDCs' long-term integrity. In effect, by placing them in control of distributing scarce commodities, the shops gave PDCs access to potential patronage resources. It was common for access to a People's Shop to be determined by someone's political sympathies. Some PDC marketing arrangements were reserved almost exclusively for PDC members and supporters. In a few instances, virtually the sole effective activity of a WDC was "the purchase of essential commodities for staff."[97] Such exclusionary practices contributed to conflicts. In the Mamponse neighborhood of Accra, a group of women retail sellers of *kenkey* (a maize dish) staged a protest at the house of the PDC distributing secretary because they were not given maize allocations. The PDC chairman justified their exclusion on the basis that they had failed to attend PDC meetings or join "voluntary" community work mobilizations.[98]

Some PDC leaders worried that a preoccupation with goods distribution would bring a regression to the methods of previous regimes, compromise the committees' commitment to the goals of revolution, and breed corruption within them.[99] Their fears were well founded. While not as widespread as right-wing critics of the PDCs claimed, corruption did develop within some leaderships. There were reports of PDC members accepting bribes, extorting money from merchants, and imposing arbitrary fines on ordinary citizens, sometimes for the flimsiest reasons, as in Kyebi, where a PDC executive committee was disbanded, among other reasons, for fining a woman ₵50 for not wearing sandals.[100] In the town of Damongo, people demonstrated to demand dissolution of the PDC executive committee for allegedly diverting kerosene, maize, and other goods intended for general distribution.[101] In the Odorkor zone of Accra, a bakers' association accused a PDC of being dominated by the relatives of bakers whose names had been stricken from the official flour allocation list and who were using the committee to regain access to flour supplies, to the extent of threatening distributors with execution if they did not comply.[102]

As market considerations, corruption, and self-serving behavior infected some PDCs, their political image became tarnished. In Dawa, a youth association appealed to the national PDC leadership to dissolve the local committee on the grounds that its activities were guided by self-interest:

> The nepotism being practised by the executives of the P.D.C. is highly abominable as far as distribution of goods is concerned. Whenever goods arrive, the secretary, apart from serving only moslems (who do not even join the queue), becomes a buying agent for several relatives thereby depriving many people of their chance to buy.... In fact the P.D.C. has become a commodity distribution syndicate and any challenger from any quarter loses his right to purchase goods whenever the goods arrive.[103]

The complaint about Muslims reflected another common taint to the antimerchant campaigns: a tendency among some activists to pick out scapegoats distinguished by religion, ethnicity, or gender. Statements by PDCs and other organizations were filled with derogatory references to "Alhajis," an honorific for Muslims who had completed the pilgrimage to Mecca, but signifying in the popular vernacular wealthy Muslim merchants, marked by greed, deviousness, and other negative traits. Sometimes the references were to "Zambramas," a name used in Ghana to refer to small-scale non-Ghanaian traders from countries to the north. Foreigners in general were believed to be heavily involved in smuggling and black marketeering, and in some rural areas of Ghana the term *alien* was even applied to traders from Ghanaian ethnic groups not indigenous to that locale. Such stereotypes did not go unchallenged. Just as women activists disputed simplistic representations of female traders, some Muslim organizations, including the National Muslim Task Force, sought to counter the image of Muslims as smugglers and cheats and urged Muslims to mobilize behind the revolution.[104]

Women traders continued to suffer abuse. While outright violence did not appear to be as intense as in 1979, nevertheless when PDC squads, Boy Scouts, and other groups swooped on marketplaces to enforce price controls and uncover hoarded goods, there still were beatings and humiliating head shavings. When activists of a PDC in Accra identified a woman retailer selling eggs above the official price, they proclaimed her "a counter-revolutionary" henceforth banned from the market, demolished her stall, and sold her seized goods to the public for a total of ₵417.90—hardly the value of a major profiteer's inventory.[105]

A handful of officials questioned the focus of the price-control campaigns. Secretary for Education Ama Ata Aidoo emphasized that most women who violated price controls were not profiteers but simply trying to make ends meet.[106] But such voices were rare. Takyiwaa Manuh, an activist of the Federation of Ghanaian Women, created shortly after the December 1981 takeover, attributed the prevalent attitudes among rank-and-file soldiers and young male activists to the PNDC's "military conception of women as the source of indiscipline, as a problem."[107] As Jeffrey Ahlman noted, such attitudes were not a preserve of military officers alone but deeply rooted in Ghanaian gender stereotypes, including among some of Nkrumah's closest ideological supporters.[108]

In the Villages

The political and social turbulence was not confined to the main cities and towns. Certain parts of the countryside saw considerable ferment, although without receiving as much attention as in urban areas. There was great variation. Rural conflicts often unfolded in complex ways. In some areas, chiefs saw their authority directly challenged by defense committees and youth associations; in others, they were able to work with the new organizations.

How activists intervened also differed. Those familiar with national political discourses sometimes tried to apply the language of their urban counterparts, with mixed results, since references to class struggle were sometimes met with puzzlement and even alarm. In the Central and Brong Ahafo regions, PDC cadres complained that "our urban and rural folks have not yet understood the revolution," that the people "are very much rooted in religion," that "certain cultural practices are still cherished by the people," and that "tribal tendencies are still rife."[109]

Other activists were more sensitive to local understandings and sought to adapt their messages. That included liberally employing religious images and the symbolism of anticolonialism. There were frequent references to the commoner-led *asafo* uprisings of the 1910s and 1920s, combining an identification with nationalist history and popular aspects of Ghanaian tradition. Allusions to asafo, argued Maxwell Owusu, meant that the process of political change was more adapted to local culture than the PDCs' leftist advocates thought.[110]

One facet of custom fit particularly well with the PDCs' emphasis on social solidarity and mobilization: the collective work party, known in Akan-speaking areas as *nnoboa*. Although nnoboa had gradually declined with the spread of market relations, notions of collective activity still survived sufficiently to elicit an echo. "Those who joined the nnoboa were supposed to have the highest qualities of voluntary service in the locality," a one-time PDC leader later recalled. Highly respected in the community, nnoboa members usually worked to clear, weed, and harvest each other's farms but also helped the elderly or sick. "That was the real communal spirit in our society."[111]

From early 1982, PDCs, youth associations, and other organizations organized frequent community mobilizations to clean up villages, dredge dams, clear rural roads, repair and rebuild schools and health clinics, set up day-care centers, and initiate local development projects. University students voted to suspend their studies and, through the new Students' Task Force, spent much of the rest of the year in the countryside helping cocoa farmers transport their crops to market collection points. In the Upper West Region, the National Youth Organizing Committee mobilized students and graduates to conduct an adult literacy drive.[112] With little expectation of government support, activists solicited public contributions and imposed monetary levies on local businesses, marketplaces, and well-to-do individuals.

Those early mobilizations helped pave the way for meeting the exceptional crises of 1983. At a time of continuing economic slowdown, Ghana was simultaneously hit by drought and widespread brush fires, seriously reducing food output. The Nigerian government, openly hostile to the PNDC, decided to abruptly expel nearly 1 million Ghanaian nationals. To keep their sudden return home from inflicting an enormous social and political shock, the government quickly adapted the mobilizational techniques of the PDCs to establish a special task force to immediately channel evacuees into productive activities.[113] The National Mobilization Programme (NMP) swiftly transported many returnees back to their home villages to set up farms on unused land, in part to keep large numbers of unemployed young men and women out of the cities but also to reinforce and expand rural self-help and development initiatives.

With national NMP support, some returnees formed Mobilization Volunteer Squads—Mobisquads—which by the end of 1985 had grown to about 200,000 members. The squads grew food and cash crops for income and their own sustenance and contributed volunteer labor to their communities: helping other farmers, digging wells, building schools and other facilities, and initiating small artisanal industries.[114] Although the Mobisquads were less politically engaged than the PDCs, their activities did bring some political benefits for the authorities in Accra. As Kofi Portuphy, a national NMP leader, put it, they "generated some enthusiasm for the revolution" in the countryside.[115]

In many cases, traditional chiefs supported mobilizations of the defense committees and Mobisquads, using their authority to summon villagers for collective labor campaigns, persuading prominent community members to contribute funds and goods, and giving permission for unutilized parcels of communal land to be cleared for cultivation.[116] Chiefs were generally more conservative than the young PDC cadres and probably went along with their initiatives to avoid confrontation. Some clearly resented the PDCs' usurpation of certain village functions that normally fell to the chiefs, such as summoning village assemblies, for which chiefs often had earned a small fee.[117]

Most village chiefs were not wealthy, shared common community concerns, and retained considerable respect. Recognizing the chiefs' social authority, PDC activists sometimes took disputes to chiefs' courts or otherwise welcomed identification with chieftaincy structures. In Todome Kpalime, the PDC chairman, a driver by profession, was proud to be named by traditional leaders as "youth chief" in recognition of his success in mobilizing communal labor participants.[118] Some chiefs even risked siding with PDCs that were in conflict with local patrons or corrupt officials. In Osenase, a small town in the Eastern Region, the head chief wrote to Rawlings urging "revolutionary action" against seven prominent PNP figures who had obstructed communal labor mobilizations and sought to disrupt the local PDC.[119] In Akatsi, in the Volta Region, five local chiefs joined a petition to the PNDC regional secretary defending local PDC members who had been attacked by border guards and supporting their campaign "against cheats and exploiters in our midst."[120]

Sometimes relations between chiefs and local PDCs became too cozy. In Ekumfi Edumafa, in the Central Region, visiting national PDC representatives accused the chief, who was also a teacher, of using his command of English, in a town of many illiterates, to establish a "palace PDC" that imposed heavy fines, excluded Ewe from all deliberations, and sided with the chief in his disputes with local fishermen. The INCC representatives from Accra called a public assembly and declared that the existing PDC should be dissolved and a new one elected, informing the assembly that "the PDCs are not for Chiefs but for the people."[121]

A conflict in Gomoa Dabenyin between PDC activists and local farmers over allocations of land for a communal farm became further complicated by the involvement of rival chiefs on each side of the dispute.[122] In Battor, in the Volta Region, the PDC was initially under the leadership of a local "chieftaincy contractor" representing one chiefly faction contesting the position of the paramount chief.[123] In Jachia Ashanti, the PDC fell into inactivity when members sided with different factions in yet another chieftaincy dispute.[124]

In Daboya, a town of one thousand in the Northern Region, PDC-chiefly relations shifted over time. The first PDC, formed in February 1982, was dominated by literate youths and included no chiefs; it lacked clear goals, failed to attract illiterates, and soon fell into inactivity. A second PDC, organized in November, won the involvement of illiterates, sons of chiefs, and members of all ethnic groups, including Gonja, Ewe, and Akan-speakers. The executive, however, was dominated by Gonja and effectively run by the sons of a provincial chief of the old Gonja kingdom. It had a broader base than its predecessor, but its chiefly links dampened initiatives that might challenge traditional authority. By 1984 the chief's family had lost its influence within the PDC. When the committee tried to revive a project to build a bridge across a river that would have threatened a subchief's traditional ferry tolls, chiefs called in a police detachment to stop the PDC's efforts to raise the necessary funds.[125]

Chiefs did not interact with defense committees only in their roles as guardians of "tradition" but often also on the basis of material interest. Over the years, chiefs had become embroiled in commercial undertakings, land speculation, patronage networks, and various schemes to divert state and royal funds. As a writer in Abrene-Kwahu commented, the chiefs there had long since lost their "unblemished character," and many were "using their positions to become Contractors, Business Executives, Transport owners etc to amass wealth for themselves. . . . They drink good wine and marry the beautiful girls in the town. Some of them have become exploiters." When communal lands were taken by the state for game reserves, resettlement schemes, or plantations, the chiefs pocketed the government's compensation payments, "while the poor farmers in these areas whose lands were taken from them cry for social amenities."[126]

Many PDCs and youth associations directly challenged the authority of particularly venal or oppressive chiefs. Some government officials, such as the regional secretary for the Upper Region, Abdulai Tinorgah, blamed the "temperament" of the activists for conflicts between PDCs and chiefs: where the PDCs showed more "respect," he told me, relations were more peaceful.[127] Yet many regional secretaries laid most responsibility on the chiefs. Government officials denounced chiefly malpractices; admonished chiefs to work with PDCs; ordered them to deposit market fees, tributes, land payments, and other stool funds into state accounts; and laid charges against those suspected of illegal acts.[128]

PDC cadres often reported that chiefs tried to obstruct them. In Old Ningo, forty miles east of Accra, a chief was alleged to have paid three military personnel to publicly drill and flog nine members of the local PDC executive who had dared "to call the people in town for communal labour without his permission."[129] Chiefs in the Volta and Eastern regions rejected requests from PDCs and other youth groups for uncultivated land to start farms, despite customary obligations to do so.[130] In Tomefa-Tease in the Eastern Region, two chiefs and several elders hired military personnel to strip and beat PDC members who tried to organize communal labor and acquire land for farming, with one of the chiefs admonishing the activists "that the land does not belong to Ft. Lt. Rawlings."[131]

Direct challenges to chiefs did not come only from PDCs. In the Sefwi Wiawso Traditional Area, hundreds of farmers appealed to the government to stop their chief from collecting one-third of their rice crop. People in Asante Akim petitioned to keep a chief from selling their farmland, while in Atigya Kwabre they refused to pay tribute to a chief. In the Adansi Traditional Area in Ashanti, the Dompoase Youth Association and local PDCs charged that the Dompoase chief had extorted money from farmers. After an investigative commission concluded that he and five other chiefs had pocketed funds that should have been deposited in Land Department accounts, the youths in the area declared him "destooled."[132]

Taming the Grassroots

As the Rawlings government moved beyond its preoccupation with immediate survival into a period of tenuous state consolidation, the defense functions of the PDCs and WDCs no longer seemed necessary. And as the PNDC's economic policies changed, so did its social perspectives. In workplaces the accent shifted from rooting out malpractices and injustice toward instilling greater discipline and productivity. "Fellow countrymen," Rawlings declared in August 1983 after the signing of the first IMF accord, "production and efficiency must be our watchwords. Populist nonsense must give way to popular sense. Many of us have spent too much time worrying about who owns what, but there can be no ownership without production first."[133] With that new emphasis came efforts to restore the power and authority of enterprise managers. At the same time, the PNDC began to send conciliatory signals to other sectors of the social elites, including chiefs, large-scale farmers, professionals, and businessmen. The PDCs' confrontational stance was now unwelcome.

The government, however, did not explicitly acknowledge those considerations as reasons for taming the defense committees. Instead, it pointed most often to the PDCs' many mistakes, abuses, instances of factionalism and corruption, and other shortcomings. In that, the authorities enjoyed support from many Ghanaians who had become disillusioned and fearful of the many excesses of the PDCs' undisciplined or exceedingly zealous activists (years later, after the transition to an electoral regime, public hearings attributed many cases of beatings, imprisonment, torture, and even killing to committee members).[134] However much the PDCs' abuses may have elicited official irritation or embarrassment, the government's clampdown was likely most motivated by the committees' direct challenges to its authority. The civil servants' WDC, for example, publicly derided the "flambouyant [sic] life-styles" of PNDC secretaries (ministers) and demanded the resignation of B. B. D. Assamoah after he declared that ideology was irrelevant.[135]

In the regions, government officials often took disciplinary action against defense committees and coordinating structures. PDC secretariat members in the Eastern, Central, and Greater Accra regions were detained or assaulted by troops sent from PNDC headquarters. The coordinating committee in the Tema industrial zone—the strongest WDC body in the country—was dissolved outright.[136]

Nationally, the PDCs' coordinating bodies were repeatedly restructured or purged. Finally, in December 1984 the National Defence Committee was scrapped and the PDCs and WDCs were redesignated Committees for the Defence of the Revolution (CDRs). According to Rawlings, the main reasons for the change were a need for reconciliation and to favor economic production over political struggle. Moreover, he added, the PDCs' national leadership had come to regard itself as a "parallel or alternative power structure."[137] The new-style CDRs came under a PNDC-designated "political counselor for the economic development of the CDRs," retired Lieutenant Colonel J. Y. Assasie.

A new set of guidelines set out a "chain of command" that clearly subordinated the CDRs to the state. There were still elections to local CDR executive committees, but district and regional committees were now headed by PNDC-appointed "organizing assistants." Although in principle the CDRs would continue to transmit ideas "to and from the grass-roots," most emphasis was on "the maintenance of discipline at all levels." CDR cadres would continue to expose "corrupt practices, exploitation in its various forms, as well as abuse of power," but their central mandate was now economic development: production and storage of food and other essential items, literacy classes, health and sanitation projects, reforestation, mobilization of building materials, and so on. In workplaces their "main function" was to "assist" managing directors and chief executives to ensure "maximum efficiency and productivity."[138]

In January 1985, the New Democratic Movement, Catholic Graduates for Action, and some prominent PDC advocates criticized the reorganization. Claiming that the change came at the behest of the IMF and World Bank, they charged that it was demoralizing activists and allowing committees to be infiltrated by "powerful social groups of the old order." The removal of the "instruments of control" provided by the committees, they predicted, would facilitate the return of autocratic management, corruption, and misappropriation.[139]

There was, however, little evidence of resistance among local committees. Many activists seemed ready to follow direction from the central authorities in Accra. The transition was also made easier by many elements of continuity on the ground, with day-to-day activities differing little from before. The CDRs, moreover, were accorded a high political profile, expressed symbolically by housing their national secretariat in the old Parliament House, the former seat of Ghana's legislature. Some CDR leaders promised smooth sailing ahead; among them was Grace Smith, a national secretariat member, who was thankful that the PDCs had been rescued "from the path of chaos and confusion."[140]

Gradually, however, it became increasingly evident that the CDRs were but pale reflections of their predecessors. There were declining reports of their activities in the Ghanaian media and even a marked downturn in community mobilizations for economic and social development, the CDRs' priority mandate. As well, they appeared less energetic in pursuing high officials suspected of corrupt practices. Worse, instances of corruption developed within the national CDR secretariat itself, according to Kofi Marrah, who worked there until 1986. Several staff members who were discovered to have taken bribes were quietly dismissed. But they were not prosecuted, said Marrah, because it was "not good to expose the dirty linen of the revolution to the public."[141]

7

Justice Fast and Rough

> There was a big problem with the legal system ... that people who were quite influential could get away with things in the ordinary courts.... There seemed to be a trend of one law for one group of people and one law for another group of people. The basic idea of this Tribunal system was to change that pattern.... The idea was for a swift kind of justice, but fair.
>
> —George Agyekum, Ghanaian public tribunal judge

For most Ghanaians, "justice" and "law" were elusive concepts. Daily life was arduous enough, but the constant depredations of local notables and corrupt functionaries made it still more difficult. When merchants used their connections to manipulate prices, officials absconded with funds from credit unions, or policemen extorted payoffs, ordinary people had little recourse through the established judicial machinery. They were far more likely to be its victims than its beneficiaries. And they watched with frustration and cynicism as the powerful kept plundering with impunity: few high-level perpetrators were ever brought to court, and fewer still were convicted and punished.

That began to change in the early 1980s. Some among the rich and mighty were summoned before new public tribunals to answer for suspected misdeeds and account for the origins of their wealth.

Before cameras, microphones, and packed galleries, they were obliged to listen to testimony of their victims, answer probing questions from prosecutors and judges, face ridicule and jeers from audiences, and submit to tough sentences that could include long prison terms and confiscation of property. Never before had the dominant elites faced such a concerted, overt challenge to one of their central methods of wealth accumulation—corruption. By "frying . . . big fish in public,"[1] the new authorities advanced their political agenda in several ways: by weakening a segment of the old opposition, demonstrating a clean break with past practices and the seriousness of their reform intentions, and bolstering their political legitimacy.

Although the new tribunals did not replace the regular courts, they did emerge out of widespread dissatisfaction with the established judiciary. For a long time that system was an amalgam of contemporary common law courts with the vestiges of precolonial customary tribunals adapted by the British authorities. Even after independence, when magistrates were appointed to head the former customary courts (by then renamed local courts), judicial bribery and corruption remained prevalent.[2] The state-run courts suffered from many other shortcomings as well. Upholding laws originally imported wholesale from Britain, they featured "esoteric symbolisms and rituals," including the wearing of robes and powdered wigs, mandatory attire for judges and lawyers—even in a tropical country.[3] Their trials were marked by an obscure formalism, stressed narrow rules and procedure over context, and relied extensively on arcane, technical, and ambiguous documentation, usually written in English, which was often not well understood by most villagers or poor urban residents.

For ordinary Ghanaians, judicial matters were not only excessively complex but also aggravatingly slow and costly. For the wealthy, however, it was usually possible to hire lawyers to navigate the intricacies of the law—or if necessary, pay off a judge. And because of the limited scope of existing legal statutes on economic crimes, few cases of corruption were ever brought to trial. According to a Ghanaian legal scholar, a prevalent view developed that "status and class had become important in deciding cases at the courts, with the result that different standards of justice had been created, one for the rich and one for the poor."[4]

There had been earlier efforts to bypass such obstacles through a variety of exceptional, "fast-track" courts. Those often had overt political agendas, most explicitly the special courts set up by Nkrumah in 1961 to try known government critics.[5] The military regimes of 1972–78 instituted similar courts, essentially military tribunals that also tried civilians. Although their jurisdiction included offenses of corruption, bribery, and theft of public funds, their main function was to repress political dissidents and labor activists.[6] The special courts of Rawlings's short-lived Armed Forces Revolutionary Council (AFRC) did, however, concentrate on cases of corruption, illegal enrichment, and other economic crimes, all the while enabling that regime to politically discredit and remove a segment of its conservative opposition.

It was thus logical that the new Provisional National Defence Council (PNDC) would also consider new court structures a high priority. Less than a week after seizing power, Rawlings announced in a national address that public tribunals would be set up to "democratize" justice and bring to trial those who had committed crimes against the people. Their sessions would be public, he explained, and they would "not be fettered in their procedures by technical rules which in the past have perverted the course of justice and enabled criminals to go free."[7]

As justification, some leading figures stressed social justice. According to Captain Tsikata, the PNDC member responsible for national security, one goal of the tribunals was "to straighten twisted justice, to shatter the chains of reactionary power with which the unjust shackle the just."[8] Others were more concerned about expediency. Said Brigadier Nunoo-Mensah, "What we don't like is that in the normal legal system there is too much procrastination. Things take too long."[9]

Still, there were delays in getting the new tribunals off the ground. In part, the new authorities were preoccupied with other pressing matters, such as beating back counterrevolutionary threats and consolidating their fragile, disorganized support base. But also, not everyone in or around the PNDC was enthusiastic about the concept of tribunals. Some of Rawlings's close advisers worried about the stigma of the AFRC-era "excesses," including executions and long prison terms that brought political backlash.[10] While some Ghanaian lawyers and legal scholars were attracted to notions of "popular justice" or the "jurisprudence of insurgency,"[11] others continued to hold more conventional perspectives. According to George Agyekum, proponents of the tribunals met "a lot of opposition . . . from leading members of the Government, especially those who are lawyers. . . . Their opposition was why it was difficult to set up the Tribunals in the first place."[12] In particular, Chief Justice F. K. Apaloo, a respected judge with close personal ties to Rawlings and several other PNDC figures, was highly critical of the tribunal idea.[13]

From the other direction, pressure came from the streets. In Agona Swedru, in the Central Region, a local People's Defence Committee (PDC) staged a large demonstration and occupation of the courthouse to demand removal of a magistrate who had acquitted several "profiteers" and a registrar who had extorted money from people seeking court services.[14] Individual defense committees organized ad hoc "people's courts" that fined or seized the properties of price-control violators or smugglers or sought to resolve community disputes.[15] The national PDC coordinating committee had a relatively large "investigations and complaints" department that often asserted jurisdiction over cases directly involving local PDC officials or more complex disputes referred to it by lower-level PDCs.[16]

Investigative and Quasi-Judicial Bodies

In advance of the tribunals, several structures with both investigative and judicial powers were launched during the PNDC's early months. The first two laws promulgated by the council, both in early February 1982, set up a couple such bodies, the Citizens' Vetting Committee (CVC) and the National Investigations Committee (NIC).

Of all the PNDC's early laws, the one establishing the CVC probably was the most explicitly class oriented. It gave the committee, comprising eleven appointed members, responsibility to "investigate persons whose life styles and expenditures substantially exceed their known or declared incomes," as well as anyone with bank balances above a specified amount (soon set at ₵50,000). If some of those assets were determined to have been amassed improperly, the committee was authorized to hand down monetary penalties or order the assets confiscated to the state. Finally, it could forward cases to a public tribunal or recommend dismissal of any public official for misconduct.[17] According to B. A. Sapati, a CVC investigator, the committee symbolized the belief that "there should be accountability in everything we do, whether you are in government or out of government."[18]

CVC officials usually denied that the committee was an instrument of social retribution against the rich. "It is not revenge against the wealthy, no," Sapati told me. "You can be wealthy. But you must pay what is due to the state by way of taxes."[19] Nevertheless, there was an inherent social slant in the CVC's work. Since most Ghanaians had few assets or did not earn enough to pay taxes and salaried workers often had their tax obligations directly withheld from their pay packets, tax evasion was most prevalent at the upper reaches of society.

The initial CVC law did not specifically mention taxes, but committee staff soon realized that focusing on tax evasion was an effective way to pursue illegally acquired wealth. Moreover, existing tax laws provided a handy schedule of penalties against defaulters. The basic instrument for gathering evidence was an asset declaration form, which required detailed information on all family members' bank accounts, salaries, business incomes, and ownership of houses, land, and vehicles, as well as how those properties were acquired. The form was then compared with properties and incomes previously declared to the tax authorities. Differences were considered evasion or underpayment of taxes and thus subject to sanctions.

The CVC also had other means for gathering evidence, including information provided by citizen-informants and collaboration with police, military, PDC, and other bodies. The names of prominent figures subject to vetting were frequently published in the press or announced on radio, with citizens invited to come forward with any details they might have. "We depended on the public for information, because we were not magicians," remarked Sapati. "We cannot know the background of everybody."[20] The CVC then sought to verify the information, to eliminate false or inaccurate allegations.

The first CVC sessions began within two weeks of the committee's establishment in Accra. Scores were found guilty of various infractions over the following months. Some were cleared of any wrongdoing. By April, a few regional CVCs had been set up, and the following month the national CVC toured regional capitals, holding sessions in Sunyani, Kumasi, Takoradi, Cape Coast, Koforidua, Ho, Tamale, and Bolgatanga. Those penalized spanned the spectrum of Ghana's middle and upper classes: businessmen, traders, senior civil servants, former politicians, lawyers, doctors. Lawyers were especially numerous, at rates higher than doctors, engineers, and other professionals: out of 260 registered lawyers in Accra, only 18 had paid taxes regularly. Those sessions had frequent political implications, because some lawyers had been former members of the parliament or political party leaders. Moreover, lawyers, through the Ghana Bar Association, were in the forefront of opposition to the PNDC and its public tribunals.

Although some cases were referred for further action to the NIC or the public tribunals, the CVC directly settled most. Its sanctions generally entailed financial penalties, orders to pay taxes due, and property seizures. Monetary payments went into a special PNDC bank account for later reallocation, while properties were temporarily vested in a Confiscated Assets Committee. The CVC's revenue collection was compared favorably to that of the Central Revenue Department, "a paper tiger which only roars but does not bite."[21] During the first ten months of its operation, the CVC imposed ₵277.2 million in total penalties and liabilities on 150 individuals and corporate bodies, of which ₵107.4 million had been collected by year's end.[22]

The NIC, unlike the high-profile CVC, worked behind the scenes, mainly to assist in investigations and help prepare case dockets for the public tribunals or regular courts. The NIC law gave it the authority to investigate "allegations of corruption, dishonesty, or abuse of office for private profit against any person or group of persons who held high office of State or any public office [and, among others] any person who may have willfully and corruptly acted in such a manner as to cause financial loss or damage to the State."[23] In practice, the NIC investigated serious economic crime, including bribery and embezzlement, over- and under-invoicing, evasion of customs duties, business fraud, and other malpractices. It had broad powers of detention for purposes of investigation and to prevent flight or the destruction of evidence.

According to Emmanuel Ohene, the first civilian lawyer to join the NIC staff in late 1982, one of the committee's unstated goals was to bring discipline and order to the "chaotic" situation prevailing during the early months of the PNDC, when some people were detained or even killed without due process. For the NIC investigators, he told me, "there was the need to sort out the innocent from the guilty," leading to freedom for the former and proper trials for the latter, based on solid, documented evidence. Like their comrades at the CVC, the NIC investigators solicited information from the public. "About 75 percent or 80 percent of the cases just came from ordinary people.... The ordinary Ghanaian doesn't like corruption. He hates it." To discourage false or self-serving allegations, there were stiff penalties for knowingly providing misleading information.[24]

Although NIC investigators claimed they were apolitical and professional, the overall political climate did influence their work. That was reflected in how the results of their investigations were directed. If a case were sent to the attorney general, it would likely end up in a regular court. But if it went to the special public prosecutor, it would go before a public tribunal. Thus, commented Ken Attafuah, "different persons charged with the identical offenses could be sent to radically different courts for trial, with the possibility of vastly different consequences. Predictably, 'enemies of the revolution' were typically processed by the public tribunals," which often handed down far stiffer sentences than the regular courts.[25]

Still, noted a Ghanaian academic, the vetting and investigation of incomes and assets "was a novelty in Ghanaian life, designed to infuse a sense of social responsibility and accountability, albeit through fear."[26]

Public Tribunals

By late July 1982, proponents of the public tribunals had finished drafting the initial legislation outlining their structures, scope, and jurisdiction and had convinced Rawlings to sign it into law. Some officials remained hesitant, but the increasingly polarized political atmosphere and insistence of the PDCs that those already in detention be tried finally overcame the resistance.

The public tribunals had wide jurisdiction to try virtually any case arising out of a commission of inquiry, NIC, or police investigation or put before it by the PNDC. Defendants could include any public official who "corruptly or dishonestly abuses or abused the office for private profit or benefit," dealt in foreign currency in a manner that could damage the economy, or acquired property "illegally or dishonestly." Various political crimes featured as well, such as inciting armed invasion, trying to forcibly alter government policies, or using "false information" to create disaffection against the government.[27] And because most offenses were retroactive, even acts that had not been previously defined as crimes could be punished.[28]

In contrast with the regular courts, which were composed of legal professionals, public tribunals of between three and five panelists each were appointed from among "members of the public." The Board of Public Tribunals, which oversaw the system, had to include at least one lawyer.[29] Originally there was no right of appeal, except directly to the PNDC. The absence of a right to appeal brought condemnations from the Ghana Bar Association and international human rights groups, such as Amnesty International. Many Ghanaians also questioned its absence, especially considering the tribunals' severe penalties and the fact that they were not infallible. The controversy

Justice Fast and Rough

eventually led to an amendment in 1984 that allowed judgments to be appealed to a higher tribunal, although not to any regular court.[30]

The participation of people who were neither magistrates nor lawyers was one of the tribunals' most notable features. The Board of Public Tribunals was socially diverse, including non-legal professionals, policemen, soldiers, a farmer, and at one point a traditional "queen mother."[31] Regional and district tribunals were often even more plebeian. Because of their unfamiliarity with the law or court procedures, lay members usually received several months of training and served as "understudies" on tribunals before sitting as full panelists. Still there were problems, as some lay judges tended to uncritically follow their law-trained colleagues or succumbed to political pressures.[32] However, commented Agyekum, with nearly a decade of experience as a tribunal judge, "Most of the lay people I worked with had very broad insight into issues, since most cases are based on facts, cumulating into legal issues.... They had a very sharp perception of honesty and dishonesty."[33]

Although their jurisdictions and structures were different, the tribunals still applied laws that were drawn from the existing legal code. "We knew that even though we wanted justice, it had to be justice according to the law," explained Kwamena Ahwoi, the overall coordinator for the public tribunals, CVC, and NIC. He contrasted that with the approach of the PDCs, whose conception of justice was "very arbitrary... not regulated by any rules or laws." For the tribunals, however, bridging "the need for law against the demand for justice" was like walking a "tightrope." At times, the drive to achieve speedy and resolute justice did considerable violence to the law and to the rights of defendants, he admitted to me. At other times, concern for legality or the interests of the state tended to extinguish the more popular features of the tribunals.[34]

The tribunals, however, sought to avoid lengthy trials by giving less weight to standard judicial rules of testimony and evidence, instead following "a kind of intermediate procedure... a relaxed procedure," as Agyekum put it.[35] Tribunal panelists readily admitted any document or testimony that appeared pertinent to clarifying the facts of a case. They also had the authority to question witnesses directly or ask nonscheduled witnesses to shed light on specific points. And while the basic principles of "natural justice" that had long been applied in Ghana included a defendant's right to be present and confront witnesses, the tribunal law specifically provided that individuals could be tried in absentia if they had fled the country or were in hiding. The guiding principle on procedures was "common sense," stated J. C. Amonoo-Monney, one of the special public prosecutors who argued cases before the tribunals. "You don't let the rules get in the way of the truth."[36]

When the tribunal panelists finished hearing evidence and considering the arguments, they decided verdicts by vote. Usually, a majority vote was sufficient to convict, except in death penalty cases, which required unanimity.

The tribunals' avoidance of arcane and obscure legal language made it easier for members of the public to follow court proceedings. Despite their evident shortcomings, the tribunals appeared quite popular with poorer Ghanaians, who flocked to tribunal sessions in large numbers. Still, the often very harsh sentences spread fear and alarm—and not only among the elites.

Economic and Social Cases

Many Ghanaians later recalled the trials of the 1980s for their political dynamics, etched in memory because of the long prison terms meted out to prominent figures of the old regime or the death sentences swiftly carried out against armed criminals or rebellious soldiers. Yet the bulk of the cases before the public tribunals involved economic and social infractions, chiefly corruption, embezzlement, fraud, smuggling, and violations of various trade and currency regulations, as well as theft, murder, and similar "hard crimes."

Of 1,417 individual tribunal defendants between 1982 and 1987 identified by this author, specific charges could be determined for 1,409. Of those, 93 percent were charged with economic and social crimes.[37] Among the 300 defendants accused specifically of corruption, many once held high state positions, including with the cotton and timber boards, the ports and harbors authority, the regional development corporations, and even the offices of the comptroller and accountant general. Although some infractions were quite small, such as misusing school funds, many entailed significant sums, especially in institutions that were engaged directly in economic affairs, such as commodity marketing, contracting, external trade, or revenue collection.

Typifying the latter, five senior accounts officers at the Ghana Ports Authority were charged with embezzling ₵11 million, while three accountants at the Ghana Oil Corporation were accused of making off with ₵1.7 million.[38] Other cases involved the Cocoa Marketing Board, responsible for purchasing and exporting Ghana's most important cash crop. In August–September 1983, a former chief manager of the board's Produce Buying Division was sentenced to twelve years of hard labor for illegally acquiring ₵119,400, while a purchasing officer in Abuakwa was sentenced to death (in absentia) for masterminding a diversion of 528 bags of cocoa, worth ₵405,000, and several accomplices received prison terms ranging from fifteen years to life.[39]

Closely related were crimes of fraud, which sometimes overlapped with or were facilitated by public sector corruption and incompetence. Six directors of two private companies were found guilty in late 1985 of "dishonest misappropriation" by defrauding a Ghana Commercial Bank branch at Tema harbor of ₵145 million by cashing bad checks, with the bank manager convicted of negligence.[40] Other instances of fraud involved the sale of fake medicines, road contractors who failed to do the work, misuse of land compensation payments, bus conductors who altered tickets to charge passengers higher prices, and a series of false insurance claims to the state insurance company (some of which featured police, lawyers, and insurance investigators as accomplices).

Initially there were so many cases involving violations of official price, trading, and currency regulations that separate price-control tribunals were established in January 1983 to manage the minor ones, leaving only more serious cases to the regular tribunals. By

1985, however, such infractions had virtually disappeared as new economic liberalization policies gradually legalized such activities. That shift, commented tribunal coordinator Kwamena Ahwoi, was "a very good example of economics leading the law."[41]

Export and import restrictions remained, however, and the public tribunals continued to hear smuggling cases, most often involving attempts to avoid Ghana's marketing boards and sell cocoa or timber directly in neighboring Côte d'Ivoire or Togo. Although the leaders of some large-scale smuggling rings were hauled before tribunals, many ordinary farmers were tried as well, even for attempting to carry a single bag of cocoa across the border by foot. Illicit small-scale gold mining, called *galamsey*, was also periodically tried before the tribunals.

Over time, the tribunals' focus on economic infractions became blurred, as more crimes of violence were shifted from the regular courts to the tribunals. The first murder trial before a tribunal was in 1983, but thereafter such cases occurred regularly. Home break-ins, armed robberies, and other holdups of individuals mounted, averaging about forty-five a year during 1984–87. By the latter year, about half of all defendants in the sample were charged with traditional hard crimes: murder, robbery, narcotics dealing and possession, kidnapping, arson, and illicit gambling.

Defendants in Social Profile

To both proponents and critics of the public tribunals, it was evident that they did not function as neutral enforcers of the law. Beyond their obvious political implications, the trials reflected the shifting social agendas of the new state leadership and its supporters, who initially held a more equitable vision of society. In the judicial realm, that meant redressing old imbalances that had punished the poor almost exclusively and let wealthy and powerful perpetrators escape with impunity. It appeared to many Ghanaians that one purpose of the tribunals was specifically to target the rich and well connected, to carry out a "retributive" form of justice.[42] Many judges, prosecutors, and other tribunal personnel, sensitive to accusations of social or political bias, claimed they were merely applying the law "without fear or favor," a phrase heard repeatedly in courtroom arguments or judgments. Yet some more radical PNDC supporters did profess an explicit social agenda, portraying the tribunals as a step toward a new system of "class justice" that would unselfconsciously protect and promote the interests of working people and other poor Ghanaians.

The news reports used to compile this author's tribunal dataset frequently cited the defendants' occupations, enabling a broad assessment of such claims. Out of the total sample of 1,417 accused, occupations were specifically cited or could be confidently determined for an even 1,000 defendants, as shown in table 7.1.

Table 7.1. Occupations of defendants before Ghana's public tribunals

State (middle & high)	211	Labor	282
public officer	96	worker (unspecified)	87
accountant, auditor	53	clerk	51
storekeeper	23	driver	45
bursar, cashier	14	miner	34
PDC	11	worker, skilled	15
customs agent	10	other labor	30
foreman	4	unemployed	20
Security, law enforcement	**201**	**Rural**	**68**
military	104	farmer	42
police	65	chief	16
other uniformed	30	fisherman	3
judge	2	other rural	7
Private business	**144**	**Other**	**27**
trader	69	student	22
executive	38	party leader	5
other businessman	37		
Professionals	**67**		
craftsperson	25		
lawyer	11		
teacher	6		
doctor	3		
other professional	22	Total	1,000

Note: From the author's dataset of public tribunal cases (described in endnotes). According to the occupation descriptions, some defendants could have been placed in more than one category. To simplify tabulation, here they were counted only in the category that seemed primary or most relevant to the particular case.

Consistent with the tribunals' emphasis on combating corruption, state personnel in middle-to-high positions constituted a large portion of defendants, more than a fifth of the total sample. Many were directors, supervisors, or other management staff of state enterprises and other public institutions (labeled "public officers" in table 7.1). They had enough discretionary authority to arrange corrupt dealings of one kind or another and rarely functioned alone—most had networks (small or large) of active collaborators. Some accomplices included accountants, auditors, paymasters, customs agents, storekeepers, and others who directly handled money and goods or at least managed the financial records and thus were in a position to implement or cover up the misdeeds of their superiors. The eleven defendants who were identified as primarily leaders or members of PDCs—and for that reason enjoyed high political status in the early years of the PNDC—were accused of small-scale infractions, such as extortion and abuse of office, or, in one case, sexual coercion. Uniformed security personnel (soldiers, police, sailors, militiamen, border guards, etc.) also constituted a notable group of defendants, sometimes charged in connection with corruption or extortion cases but also with coup attempts, murder, and armed robbery.

Private businesspeople and professionals accounted for another substantial bloc of defendants. The private business category included executives from banks and private companies, construction contractors, and various others, but nearly half were traders, who were hit particularly hard by the government's initial attempts to enforce price controls and other market regulations. Some were large-scale merchants, yet many were petty traders and market vendors. Similarly, among those labeled "farmer" or "fisherman" in the rural category, a few were well off, but many were relatively poor. Chiefs, by contrast, were usually relatively well-to-do and had considerable political and social influence. Of the sixteen chiefs charged before the tribunals, one was also a lawyer; one, a construction contractor; one, a security officer at the Cocoa Marketing Board; and one, a former national chairman of the People's National Party. Four were charged with fraudulent land deals; five, with various corruption, smuggling, and other economic charges; and the remainder, in connection with fatal clashes resulting from chieftaincy disputes.

While individuals from Ghana's old political and social elites were well represented among the tribunal defendants, that did not mean that the "toiling masses" received any breaks. According to a rough and somewhat arbitrary classification of 976 defendants according to whether their socioeconomic status seemed likely to have been high, medium, or low, 173 (17.7 percent) were from the upper levels of society, 320 (32.8 percent) from the middle, and 483 (49.5 percent) from the lower strata. The "labor" designation constituted the largest occupational category of tribunal defendants, comprising unspecified "workers" and low-level employees in the public and private sectors: clerks, drivers, mine workers, unemployed workers, skilled workers, and others. Tellingly, as a share of total defendants, they increased over time, from an annual average of 19 percent during the tribunals' first two years to nearly 31 percent over the next four.

Amonoo-Monney, the prosecutor, attributed the large number of ordinary Ghanaians charged before the tribunals to the legal and logistical difficulties of preparing solid cases against those higher up the social ladder. "It's hard to get evidence against big fish," he argued.[43] Others pointed more toward the government's economic and social priorities. Attafuah noted that the PNDC, as part of its drive to instill a sense of discipline in Ghanaian society, criminalized "labor slacking" and cracked down particularly hard on workers who tried to supplement their meager incomes by pilfering goods from their enterprises.[44] Whatever the reasons, Ghanaians from the popular strata of society apparently were not exempt from "popular justice."

Political Agendas and Contexts

While all tribunal cases were linked to charges stemming from laws on the statute books, the system itself had profound political implications, providing a mechanism for the PNDC to advance its political goals and repress those who might oppose it. Those motivations were not always explicit but were nevertheless evident, especially during the highly charged political atmosphere of the early 1980s.

The Ghana Bar Association, a core component of the political opposition, denounced the tribunals as representing "a misguided attempt to supplant the ordinary criminal courts" and called on its members to boycott them.[45] In reaction, PDC activists staged raucous demonstrations outside regular courthouses. In the Accra-Tema region, a June 1983 general assembly of Workers Defence Committees and community PDCs called for replacing "the old judicial system once and for all with a more dynamic, humane and egalitarian people's judicial system and a people's court of justice," run by workers, farmers, fishermen, and community activists.[46]

Some proponents readily acknowledged the tribunals' political implications. As Agyekum put it, the tribunals were established to advance the PNDC's anticorruption "crusade" and counter a culture of political practice that was primarily self-serving. "The idea was to let people know that going into politics to look for money will not pay, and that service to the country should be foremost in terms of political office, and not to fill one's pockets."[47] Others were more reticent, especially in the face of criticisms by external human rights organizations that the tribunals were not sufficiently independent or accusations by domestic opponents that the PNDC was using the tribunals for partisan purposes. "We will always resist that argument," said Ahwoi when asked about such criticisms: cases were brought before the tribunals to punish people not for their political activities but for their criminal acts, according to "very clear guidelines." Yet even he admitted that "you can't run away from an argument that such things are usually politically motivated."[48]

There were different ways through which political influences could be brought to bear: the PNDC's power to appoint and remove tribunal judges, its authority to revise verdicts and sentences, and judgments by politically savvy investigative and prosecutorial officials over which cases to bring before tribunals. The overall climate also influenced deliberations; in their rulings, panelists sometimes cited specific government campaigns against certain kinds of misconduct. In this, the tribunals were comparable to other organs of "revolutionary justice" elsewhere in the world, in which notions about a separation of powers between the judiciary and executive hardly mattered.

Among cases heard by public tribunals, some were overtly political. The defendants included former party leaders, opposition figures, or student activists brought up on charges that were themselves political, such as "spreading false information" about the government or demonstrating illegally, or only ostensibly relating to criminal infractions, including corruption and drug possession.

Trials involving former party leaders were a small fraction of the total. But during the tribunals' initial months they took the limelight, contributing to a lasting impression that one of the main purposes of the trials was to deal directly with the old political guard. In fact, the first case, starting in mid-September 1982, was of several top leaders of former president Limann's People's National Party. They included Krobo Edusei, the PNP's Ashanti regional chair and already infamous in Ghana as one of Nkrumah's more corrupt ministers, and Nana Okutwer Bekoe III, the party's former national chair. They were accused of taking a $1 million loan from an Italian businessman for PNP activities, in violation of laws prohibiting foreign funding of political parties. In introducing the case, Amonoo-Monney, the prosecutor, emphasized that it was politically symbolic, in that for many years offenses by high officials and their "non-Ghanaian collaborators . . . went unpunished either because the perpetrators had powerful connections with officialdom, or could buy off their freedom thus creating the impression that officers of state to whom the welfare of the people had been entrusted freely collaborated with criminals to gradually install lawlessness in the country."[49] Both Bekoe and Edusei were found guilty and sentenced to eleven years each, while four other PNP leaders received prison terms, fines, and other penalties.[50]

Also explicitly political were trials stemming from antigovernment coup attempts or plots by military personnel, sometimes with civilian accomplices. Scores of defendants were charged, with several killed during escape attempts, a dozen acquitted, twenty-six given prison sentences ranging from several years to life, and thirty-four sentenced to death. A few of the latter later had their sentences commuted to life or were amnestied, but most were executed.

The most spectacular case before a public tribunal was the "judges murder trial." Held in August 1983, around the same time as the first two coup cases, it stemmed from the kidnapping and murder of three politically conservative high court judges and a retired military officer in June 1982. The crime shocked the country and immediately aroused widespread suspicions that the government was behind the killings. Those suspicions were partly borne out when it emerged that the main perpetrator was a former member of the PNDC, Joachim Amartey Kwei, once a workers' leader at the Ghana Industrial Holding Corporation (GIHOC). Kwei soon came under suspicion because the slain ex-officer had been GIHOC's personnel director and one of the three judges had rejected a suit for reinstatement by dismissed GIHOC workers. Kwei and four soldiers acting under his command were found guilty of murder and conspiracy. All five were sentenced to death and executed by firing squad. In its ruling, the tribunal underscored what it saw as the political lessons of the case: "Political terrorism should never be encouraged, be it from the left or right. A revolution is not anarchy and senseless taking away of lives and destruction. The end of this case should be a lesson to misguided revolutionaries who see terror and destruction as revolution. A revolution is to build, develop and create and consolidate and not to create political terror and revenge by settling old scores."[51]

Many Ghanaians drew different lessons, however. The original murders and strong suspicions that other PNDC figures may have been implicated, followed by the swift executions, left a lasting impression in many minds associating the Rawlings government with extreme violence. The taint hung over Rawlings and his comrades for many years.

As for the experience of the public tribunals, even Mike Oquaye, in an otherwise highly critical assessment of their work, admitted that they were popular among many: "The ordinary citizen visibly rejoiced as the privileged were drilled, exposed and made to confess in public various 'crimes against the State.'" But, he added, "the harsh sentences, including instant death sentences, ultimately aroused mixed feelings."[52]

Tribunals Moderated

As the PNDC gradually consolidated its position and modified significant aspects of its overall approach, the dynamics of the public tribunals also changed. From as early as 1984, the tribunals steadily adopted more of the procedures and practices of the established court system. The erosion of the Ghana Bar Association's boycott contributed, in turn, to greater numbers of lawyers taking part not only in the trials but also as members of tribunal panels, which they frequently tended to dominate because of their legal knowledge. Delays and postponements became more frequent, in contrast to the rapid pace of the first few years, leading to backlogs in case dockets. One result, noted a researcher, was to make the tribunals "increasingly like the regular courts that they were supposed to replace."[53]

Some changes were generally welcomed, including the introduction of a right of appeal. In a related development, by 1984 the authorities started to more systematically review verdicts originally handed down in 1979 by the special courts of the Armed Forces Revolutionary Council. That brought numerous pardons, frequent vacating of sentences, and often a return of confiscated properties.[54] The average length of tribunal prison sentences declined from their most severe period in 1982–83, while fines and other forms of monetary penalties increased in frequency.

According to Attafuah, there were several reasons for such shifts. The draconian sentences often imposed during the tribunals' first years had elicited sharp denunciations from domestic opposition and international human rights groups, eventually prompting the authorities to try to placate the critics. The propensity toward long and frequent prison sentences also had contributed to prison congestion and an expensive drain on limited state resources. Finally, commented Attafuah, the tribunals' greater use of fines or monetary penalties sought to "raise much-needed revenue for the state."[55]

Running against that trend, however, was an increase in the use of the death penalty. From 1983 (the first year the tribunals were authorized to impose death sentences) through 1987, 184 death sentences were cited in the data sample. Although there was a pronounced tendency by the PNDC to grant pardons from 1986 onward, about 60 tribunal death sentences were actually carried out by mid-1987.[56] Initially, many such sentences stemmed from coup-plot charges. Twenty-five resulted from serious corruption accusations, especially in 1985 and 1986. By 1987, the year of the greatest number of death penalties (57), all stemmed from either murder or robbery charges. While death sentences continued to be handed down for a while longer, actual executions ceased. Arguing that the political fallout of the killings "was threatening the survival of the revolution," nine of Rawlings's closest collaborators successfully pleaded with him to halt executions.[57]

In the name of getting tribunals to function in a more predictable, rule-bound fashion, the authorities sought to impose stricter discipline over the entire system. Although a few informal or ad hoc local revolutionary courts continued to function into the mid-1980s, the gradual reduction in the defense committees' autonomy led to their eventual disappearance. As a justification for tightening its control, the PNDC usually cited the need to counter abuses and corruption. According to Ahwoi, however honest and motivated most tribunal members initially were, some eventually "succumbed to temptations."[58] The most prominent instance involved the first chairman of the Ashanti regional tribunal, Kwame Arhin, a lawyer. After several proceedings in 1984 and 1985, he was sentenced to six months for misuse of tribunal funds.[59] Also significant was the 1986 conviction of Major Kwabena Adutu, an army officer and a lawyer who had served for several years as national chairman of the Citizens' Vetting Committee. He received a ten-year sentence for involvement in a diversion of ₵35.4 million worth of goods seized from tax defaulters.[60]

By that point, the CVC had been transformed into a new Office of Revenue Commissioners (ORC). Although many of the CVC staff were carried over into the new body, more changed than just the name. In effect, the ORC was primarily a tax court, and its rulings could be appealed.[61] According to Attafuah, the transformation was one consequence of the PNDC's economic agreements with the International Monetary Fund and World Bank. In the new climate, the government was keen to distance itself from the "manifestly pro-socialist, anti-capitalist and anti-western posture" of the original CVC. "The ORC was not nearly half as radical in outlook and far-reaching in its functions as its defunct ancestor."[62]

The National Investigations Committee, which worked closely with the CVC and ORC, came under pressures of a different sort. By the mid-1980s, after most of the cases involving crimes prior to 1982 had been thoroughly examined, some NIC investigators probed corruption allegations against current officeholders, including several government secretaries. Although some cases were successfully pursued, they often confronted high-level resistance. "The attitude was, 'Let's cover our own people,'" remarked Ohene. "It became a cat and mouse game for us to survive. At every opportunity, the government wanted a way of dissolving this investigative organ."[63]

As for the tribunals, the PNDC demonstrated less and less interest in maintaining their work. As early as 1984, provisions were adopted to create tribunals at the district and community levels, but only in 1989 were the first ones officially inaugurated in Accra.[64]

The Board of Public Tribunals complained that the concerns of the tribunals were "not sufficiently heard or not heard at all at the levels of government." In terms of material resources, the board observed with bitterness that since 1982 "not one single structure" had been newly built as a tribunal courtroom. The Ashanti Regional Public Tribunal had no regular facilities, while that in the Western Region occupied "a precariously dangerous wooden shack constructed as a railway workers' social centre in the 1920s."[65]

The government seemed to be rethinking the judicial system as a whole. In 1986 the Board of Public Tribunals and many national and regional tribunals were significantly reorganized, with many original members removed or "reassigned" to other responsibilities and a circuit court judge, S. A. Brobbey, brought in to chair the board.[66] Simultaneously, the regular courts came back into favor. Rather than denigrating or simply ignoring them, the authorities talked more frequently about reforming the old judiciary to make it more expeditious and effective. In July 1986, the government named ten new members of the high court, among them Brobbey, a few days after his appointment to the tribunals board.[67]

If the pendulum's swing back toward the regular courts was not already clear enough, the attorney general, G. E. K. Aikins, spelled it out in July 1987. The public tribunals, he affirmed, should be allowed to continue functioning independently of other courts—until they were "assimilated" into the regular judicial system.[68] The tribunals limped along for a few years more, but in 1992, with the adoption of a new constitution and multiparty political system, they were abolished at the national and district levels. Only the regional tribunals were retained, as integral components of the regular court system.

8

Shifting State Agendas

According to leading figures and supporters of the Provisional National Defence Council (PNDC), "house cleaning" meant considerably more than simply sweeping out and bringing to justice the corrupt bureaucrats, brokers, profiteers, and other undesirables of the old political system. It also entailed structural changes that included rebuilding major elements of the state apparatus, from the central bureaucracy and main government institutions down to the most remote district offices and border posts. Yet while there were many sharp critiques of what was wrong with the established structures during the first months in particular, the precise shape of what should replace them was not well defined. Nor was the nature of governmental authority specified. The PNDC projected an image of being transitional—thus the "provisional" in its name—but left open what might follow. At times, there were suggestions that the People's Defence Committees (PDCs) would eventually select or coalesce into a "people's assembly," with at least some legislative power.[1] That notion soon disappeared, however. For the moment, it was understood that all legal authority would flow directly from the PNDC.

After trying to hold fast during its first two chaotic years, the ruling council eventually reacted to conflicting pressures from both a right-wing opposition and its own radical components. In response, it pursued a complex and gradual course adjustment that brought a partial accommodation with elite opponents, at the cost of purging some of its members and reining in the defense committees. One of the most dramatic elements of that shift was the introduction of a new program of promarket economic reforms under the supervision of the International Monetary Fund (IMF) and World Bank. The substantial financing that came with the agreement helped the PNDC not merely survive but consolidate its hold on power. Yet despite that turnaround in economic policy, an underlying set of common concerns and goals remained: to build up the Ghanaian state's capacities and authority. That still meant trying to reduce corruption, which in previous years had done much to undermine the state.

From Transformation to Adjustment

Within the literature on economic reform and development, Ghana's experience with economic liberalization in the 1980s was among the most intensely studied anywhere. Labeled by World Bank and IMF officials as an outstanding adjustment success story, Ghana's policy changes and economic performance received detailed scrutiny. Some hoped to see its example replicated elsewhere. Critics sought to highlight its limits.

Everyone agreed that Ghana's economy had previously been in deep crisis. Between 1970 and 1982, gross domestic product declined an average of 0.5 percent annually, one of the most prolonged contractions anywhere in Africa. Per capita income fell by nearly a third, and infant mortality rose sharply. To make matters worse, 1983 brought a string of catastrophes. A serious drought and widespread brush fires destroyed much of the grain harvest. Nigeria expelled an estimated one million Ghanaian migrant workers and petty traders, bringing a sudden influx of returnees at a time when they could not be easily absorbed.[2]

The government's initial responses reflected the ideological notions of the radical intellectuals in and around the PNDC. They believed that the fundamental weakness of the economy lay in its relations of dependency with the industrialized West and argued that the immediate crisis could be weathered with sufficient popular mobilization and a reorientation of existing resources toward the most productive sectors. As Rawlings maintained, "Ghana's engagement in the international capitalist system has contributed in no small measure toward the country's present predicament."[3] Yet the perverse effects of earlier government interventions in the economy made it difficult to generate enthusiasm for more efforts to administratively regulate economic activity. Even the left-wing intellectuals who drafted the May 1982 "preamble" to the PNDC's first policy guidelines recognized that the bureaucracy had become so bloated by past political patronage practices that the public service "must be dismantled, pruned or abolished."[4] That idea, it would soon become apparent, could be readily adapted to economic liberalization policies.

The PNDC initially tried to combine attempts to directly administer market prices with relatively orthodox fiscal management measures to control public spending. Those included ordering all public enterprises to weed out "ghost workers"—fictitious employees whose salaries were pocketed by corrupt management or accounting personnel.[5] Real employees were also targeted, however. Addressing a farmers' rally, Rawlings demagogically declared that the staff of the Cocoa Marketing Board, numbering 105,800, would be reduced to end a system "whereby officials live off the sweat of farmers."[6]

A May 1982 budget speech by Secretary for Finance and Economic Planning Kwesi Botchwey featured a peculiar mix. Echoing the classes on Marxist economics that he had previously taught at the University of Ghana, Botchwey railed against multinational corporations and transnational banks. Ghana, he hoped, would eventually pursue institutional changes to reduce "external dependency and local parasitism." But in the meantime, the crisis dictated immediate measures to contain the deficit through "financial discipline," overcome "bureaucratic inertia," and ensure that public corporations were not "grossly mismanaged."[7] By the end of 1982, the budget deficit was indeed reduced by 35 percent from the year before.[8]

Belt tightening alone would not work, and the PNDC desperately sought external financing as well. A series of diplomatic missions to the Soviet Union, Libya, and other non-Western countries secured some verbal expressions of solidarity but little cash.[9] Meanwhile most Western governments and banks continued to withhold financing in the absence of an accommodation with the IMF. Caught in a bind, the PNDC finally decided in September 1982 to send Botchwey to Washington for "exploratory talks" with the IMF.[10] That set off a fierce national debate in which radical commentators saw the choice as "the revolution or the IMF"[11] and contributed to the political tensions surrounding an abortive October 1982 coup attempt. But the PNDC stayed the course, including among its justifications the notion that austerity measures and easing price controls would deny "windfall gains" to "corrupt company officials and profiteering middlemen," as Botchwey put it.[12]

By February 1983, the IMF had agreed to let Ghana draw some $300 million in credits and the World Bank announced it would provide $110 million for projects in transport, agriculture, timber, cocoa, and mining.[13] That year brought several notable policy changes, including substantially higher hospital fees and a sharp devaluation of the national currency, the cedi, from ₵2.75 to ₵30 to the dollar.[14] Numerous other policy reforms followed in two successive Economic Recovery Programmes (ERPs), extending from 1984 through 1988. As late as 1985, some of the regime's radicals, such as PNDC special adviser Kojo Tsikata, were still portraying the agreement as an unavoidable concession, made with misgivings and reluctance. "It is true that we have taken a lot of measures which, as revolutionaries, we cannot describe as popular measures," Tsikata told me. "These are very, very hard decisions that we have had to make. These are not decisions which a revolutionary regime should take."[15]

Yet what at first was described by Ghanaian officials as a necessary tactical compromise soon evolved into a fairly faithful approximation of the kind of prescriptions usually favored by the IMF and World Bank, known at the time as "structural adjustment." They included a heavy emphasis on market mechanisms, repeated currency devaluations, tight fiscal management, restrictive credit policies, all-out promotion of exports, trimming state marketing boards, and, toward the end of the 1980s, significant cuts in public employment and moves to begin privatizing state-owned enterprises. "To put it vulgarly," commented a Ghanaian scholar, "having secured one foot in the door in the 1983 agreement, the [World] Bank used the subsequent process of 'rationalisation' to push its whole body inside."[16]

Still, Ghana's program was not a carbon copy of what the IMF and World Bank imposed on other African economies. The two institutions did not immediately get everything they wanted, such as a total end to price controls, a wage freeze, or dissolution of the Cocoa Marketing Board.[17] Ghanaian officials also managed to secure a few departures from the standard formula, such as an explicitly expansionary budgetary approach, instead of simply cutting back spending on all fronts.[18]

Judged strictly from macroeconomic figures—the most important indicators in the eyes of the Washington financial institutions—the PNDC's economic reforms were a resounding success. From 1984 through the end of the decade, real economic growth averaged 5.7 percent annually, the highest sustained rate anywhere in sub-Saharan Africa. Levels of exports and imports, production, government revenue and expenditures, inflation, and most other macroeconomic indicators showed significant improvements.[19]

While the statistics enabled officials of the IMF and World Bank to present Ghana as an adjustment model, critics nevertheless asked probing questions: Did Ghana's high growth rates result from the policy changes, or were they simply a mechanical outcome of the massive injection of foreign financing, reaching $2.8 billion between 1983 and 1989? How viable was an economic recovery program that led to a sharp buildup in foreign debt—doubling from $1.7 billion in 1983 to $3.4 billion in 1989?[20] Would market-led growth improve living and social conditions for Ghanaians generally, or would it foster greater poverty and social inequities?[21] Did the preoccupation with promoting a handful of raw material exports (cocoa, timber, gold) promote long-term development or lock the economy deeper into a system of international exchange that operated to the detriment of primary commodity-producing countries?[22] Did trade liberalization, followed by the removal of protectionist tariffs in the late 1980s, help stimulate more efficient and competitive manufacturing industries, or did they contribute to an ongoing process of de-industrialization?[23]

Social Repercussions

Whatever the implications of the economic changes of the 1980s for Ghana's long-term development, they both directly and indirectly reshaped the PNDC's possibilities for building social alliances and reforming the basic institutions of the Ghanaian state. Although some key economic indicators trended upward, living conditions did not improve significantly and, for certain sectors of the population, remained stagnant or deteriorated.

Some PNDC supporters had feared as much as soon as the 1983 budget was unveiled. PNDC officials attending a May Day rally were hit with catcalls and shouts of "We are hungry," while an attempt by Botchwey to explain the budget was met with a large workers' demonstration in Kumasi, complete with protest barricades, hooting, warning shots from police, and tear gas.[24] Such dissatisfaction, one of Rawlings's leading advisers later acknowledged, "threatened the very stability of the government."[25]

The World Bank acknowledged the danger when it praised the PNDC for its "great political courage" in devaluing the currency, a move that had provoked serious political instability in the past.[26] That was probably one reason why the Bank and IMF gave the government some slack by letting it increase state spending, permit occasional wage increases, and allow economic liberalization to be phased in over several years, rather than through a "shock therapy" approach often applied elsewhere.

The PNDC's continued anticorruption efforts also helped it ride out the storm. One reason previous governments had difficulty selling devaluation or liberalizing the economy was a common perception that only the poor would suffer, while those with black-market and political connections would continue to prosper. As one British development expert observed, Rawlings's crackdowns on corrupt schemes and perks "created an image of honesty, concern and energy" that generated a measure of public acceptance for the policy changes.[27] Similarly, Huudu Yahaya, the PNDC's secretary for mobilization and social welfare, told me, "When you are telling the ordinary man to sacrifice, then he appreciates that even the top man is sacrificing to a point. A lot of privileges had to go."[28]

The immediate impact on ordinary Ghanaians differed notably. One survey found that while many wage earners in the formal sector were highly critical of the ERP programs, other urban respondents were favorable, judging that their conditions might have gotten worse without it.[29] Moreover, some sectors of labor directly benefited. Rehabilitation of the dilapidated road system, for example, improved job security for transport workers, making the Ghana Private Road Transport Union one of the PNDC's staunchest defenders.[30]

Yet for many Ghanaians, times were hard. A study by the United Nations Children's Fund reported "very severe deterioration in incomes among most households in both rural and urban areas" during the first half of the 1980s, with more than half of all households falling below the absolute poverty line and child labor becoming more prevalent in poor families.[31] As food prices rose, hardly any worker's salary could buy enough food for a single individual, let alone for an entire family and other necessities. In 1987 it took two-thirds of the minimum wage to buy a kilogram of rice.[32]

Ghana's education system suffered lasting effects. Higher book fees for primary school students and other strains on teachers and institutions seriously eroded the quality of primary education, while charges for residential secondary schools and universities sparked student protests.[33] Overall enrollments rose over the years, especially in the lower grades, as donors placed greater emphasis on increasing the number of students in primary education. The quality of learning remained poor, however, contributing to high dropout rates. The immediate impact on Ghana's universities was less evident but became more obvious in later decades. Given an apparent bias in donor-driven educational policy against higher learning, funding for universities remained limited, despite an increase in enrollments to fifty thousand, according to a minister for higher education.[34] Baffour Agyeman-Duah of the Center for Democratic Development pointed out that simply "cramming in teeming numbers of students," without enough funding, had created a "real crisis."[35] Responding to the policy distortions that starved the universities of adequate resources, George Benneh, a former vice-chancellor of the University of Ghana, remarked, "Unless you have well-trained, skilled people from our universities and science and technology institutes, Africa will continue to depend on outsiders. Do you want Africa to remain backward?"[36]

As the initial shift in economic policies in the 1980s took hold, the political dynamics facing the PNDC also changed. The authorities were less able to count on the backing of increasingly disillusioned urban workers and intensified their efforts to secure other bases of social support. In particular, they devoted more attention to the countryside.[37] In 1984 the PNDC issued a "Rural Manifesto" that professed concern for Ghanaian villagers while simultaneously justifying austerity measures in the cities, with the argument that Ghana had a system of "urbanteid" (akin to apartheid in South Africa) that discriminated in favor of city dwellers. The vast majority of Ghanaians, claimed the manifesto, suffered from exploitation by a "parasitic minority" in the towns.[38]

Cocoa farmers were the most immediate beneficiaries of that rural shift. The price paid by the Cocoa Marketing Board was raised regularly, bringing real producer prices back to the levels of a decade earlier and encouraging increased production from 179,000 tons to 228,000 tons between 1983 and 1987.[39] Meanwhile, there also were sharp increases in food output, with cereals rising from 388,000 tons in 1983 to 1.1 million tons in 1987, and roots and tubers from 3.1 million to 6 million tons over the same period.[40] But that had little to do with the new policies: after the disastrous drought of 1983, when harvests were exceptionally poor, the rains returned. Unfortunately, food farmers' higher sales were practically wiped out by higher prices for the consumer goods and services they had to buy. Between 1982 and 1987, the terms of trade for food producers—what they received for their crops against the cost of manufactured goods—fell by half, while for cocoa farmers they rose dramatically, by about 80 percent.[41] When I pressed Ibrahim Adam, an agriculture minister, about whether the government's monetary policies had hurt food farmers, he admitted, "Perhaps in relative terms that may be so. If the costs of goods and services go up faster than the rate of growth of the farmers' income, then naturally they'll be worse off."[42]

Differences in income between those at the lower and upper reaches of rural society widened appreciably. The strong bias in market prices and state assistance toward cocoa tended to widen the gap between the country's 265,000 cocoa farmers (plus their families) and the rest of the farming population. That in turn had geographical and gender implications. Most cocoa was grown in the already better-off western and central regions, compared with poorer rural areas in the east and especially the highly impoverished north.

Northern Ghana, historically neglected since the colonial era, suffered especially severely. Since independence, successive governments had conducted various initiatives to promote economic development in the north, including widespread irrigated rice-farming projects, noted John Nabila, paramount chief of the West

Mamprusi district and the Northern Region's representative to the advisory Council of State when I spoke with him in 2008. "Then came the World Bank," Nabila explained. Economic liberalization brought the removal of subsidies for agricultural inputs, irrigation schemes, and farm extension services. Meanwhile an end to tariffs on imported rice flooded the domestic market with cheaper Asian rice, driving nearly half a million rice farmers out of business and drastically reducing domestic rice production. Only about 100,000 rice farmers survived. "The rice industry collapsed. Because of that change in policies, the whole country has suffered."[43]

There also were inequalities within rural sectors. A 1987 survey of farming households in the cocoa-rich Ashanti Region found that the top 11 percent of landholders (thirty acres or more) controlled 48 percent of total cocoa income, while the 70 percent of households with less than twenty acres accounted for just a third of cocoa income.[44] Similar processes were evident elsewhere. A Ghanaian researcher who conducted two surveys in the predominantly food-growing town of Ayirebi in the southeastern forest zone, one in 1982–83 and the other in 1989–90, found notable social changes. Initially, most households had little involvement in the national market and community and self-help initiatives were common. Yet at the end of the decade, more farming households were engaged in market production, community self-help initiatives had declined, and more youths were selling their labor to wealthy farming households.[45]

The process of social differentiation extended throughout society. In the countryside, women were hit hard by the difficulties facing food production, in which they were most active, while the bulk of cocoa producers were men, who fared better. Differences were accentuated in urban areas as well. Among the biggest beneficiaries of liberalization, Kwame Ninsin noted, were "those members of the middle classes who occupied executive positions in multinational enterprises[;] . . . those who had access to foreign currency and could invest such money in the lucrative imports trade; those who were local agents of foreign exporters of fashionable middle class consumer items; and those in the rapidly expanding service sector."[46] After the previous emphasis on social equity and advancing the poor, the introduction of the ERP removed much of the stigma attached to wealth acquisition. Under the new ethic, individual accumulation was once again officially acceptable—provided, of course, that it was by legal means.

Political Adjustment(s)

At the time, the Washington-based international financial institutions were not yet pushing any particular model of political and state reform to accompany their economic liberalization programs. Not until the late 1980s did the World Bank and some donor agencies begin talking about "good governance," and not until the next decade did they start imposing political conditions, such as multi-party elections. In fact, the IMF and World Bank still appeared comfortable financing authoritarian regimes, as long as those regimes accepted neoliberal reforms. In Ghana's case, the government's ability to push through unpopular policies was admired in Washington; few publicly questioned the absence of elections. The only political concern the World Bank expressed was that the continued influence of the defense committees might cause "unintended harm" to the implementation of the new policies.[47]

The PNDC, of course, had its own reasons for bringing the defense committees under stricter control. But it saw little need to "attempt to develop an ideological perspective based on its economic reforms.... Rather, the PNDC tried to retain its old radicalism while implementing economic orthodoxy."[48]

Although some aspects of the PNDC's political discourse were clearly out of alignment with the new economic approach, many were not. The campaign against corruption was one part of the original vision that could be easily adapted to the ERP. The ways in which corruption was officially discussed in 1979 and the early 1980s were sufficiently vague and elastic to enable the PNDC to tailor its anticorruption message to fit the new contours. All it had to do was drop references linking corruption with social inequality and class exploitation and redefine it primarily as an issue of morals or economic management. On the moral front, government officials tended to portray corruption as a blight on Ghanaian society as a whole, affecting not only those at the top but also at "the working base," as Rawlings's wife, Nana Konadu Agyeman-Rawlings, put it.[49] Meanwhile, Rawlings and other officials increasingly used the term *rent seeking*, a label preferred by economists to describe corruption, black-market dealings, and similar practices.[50] In that way, corruption could be presented as a distortion of market mechanisms and opposition to it as a technocratic "correction."

Parallel to the policy alterations, the composition of the PNDC became more reflective of society's middle to upper reaches. The first council, constituted in January 1982, represented a symbolic double alliance: first, across the military's lower (sergeant and warrant officer), middle (lieutenant), and upper ranks (brigadier general); and second, between the military and radical civilians (a unionist, former student leader, and radical priest). That August, the unionist and the radical priest resigned and were replaced by another unionist and a manager of the State Fishing Corporation (also the PNDC's first woman). Around the time of the successive coup attempts of October and November 1982, the brigadier general resigned, the sergeant was arrested, and the former student leader fled the country. Then in January 1983, Rawlings named to the PNDC a traditional chief from the Northern Region. In July 1984, both a retired judge and a former Nkrumah-era cabinet minister (another woman) were appointed. Upon the chief's death from an illness the following month, another former minister was named to replace him. In July 1985, the PNDC was expanded with the addition of a captain (who had been in charge of internal security) and a former director of a group of companies. At the end of 1985, two more senior officers (both generals) were added as well.[51] Thus, as the radicals departed, more moderate enterprise executives, senior officers, and ministers entered.

Such symbolic changes, combined with the ERP's new pro-business measures, made the government somewhat more acceptable to the higher reaches of Ghanaian society and contributed to an evident slackening of outright conservative political opposition during the mid-1980s. Yet few among the elites rushed to embrace the PNDC. They still held fresh memories of their treatment at the hands of the defense committees and remained skeptical of Rawlings's intentions, especially as the tribunals continued to jail prominent figures and the PNDC refused to permit the formation of political parties. While certain business sectors benefited from economic liberalization, others did not. Finally, the government's concerted drive to collect more taxes from wealthy individuals and companies was unwelcome to those accustomed to shirking their fiscal obligations.

Disciplining the State Bureaucracy

If there was any one point upon which most Ghanaians could agree, whatever their other views, it was that the state bureaucracy was bloated, incompetent, self-serving, and undisciplined. The PNDC, even before its agreement with the IMF and World Bank, had regarded the bureaucracy as overstaffed, largely because the patronage policies of previous governments had rewarded political supporters with jobs in the civil service and state firms. Early on, the civil service's own central workers defense committee argued for structural changes, as many bureaucrats continued to function as the colonialists did, in ways that "do not benefit the majority of our people."[52] Rawlings denounced the "waste, red tape and inertia" of state institutions and went on to warn, "We have already started to weed out those who cannot meet the new standards of efficiency and responsibility. This process will continue."[53]

Besides the hundreds sanctioned by the public tribunals, many others were subjected to administrative dismissal for infractions ranging from improper travel and housing claims to incompetence or negligence. Yet the PNDC's goal was not to shrink the state as such. To the contrary, strengthening the state administration remained a high priority. In that respect, Ghana's experience was different from other cases of structural adjustment in Africa during the 1980s, when many such programs brought massive dismissals of state employees, drastic cuts in public services, and severe contractions of state institutions. Ghana's exceptional "expansionary" ERP aimed foremost to increase the efficiency of the state.

That did entail streamlining state institutions where necessary. But the government set limits, resisting dismantlement of the large Cocoa Marketing Board (CMB) or privatization of many state enterprises, as the IMF and World Bank demanded. It instead moved carefully, initially focusing on an easy target: fictitious employees. At the CMB alone, about 30,000 ghost workers were eventually stricken from the rolls. Other state enterprises reduced their staffs by not replacing workers when they retired or left. By the end of the decade, however, thousands of real employees had fallen under the ax. At the CMB, for instance, as the board "divested" several large cocoa farms and withdrew from various transport, supply, and storage activities, the number of actual jobs that were cut climbed to 17,000.[54]

In general, official policy toward the government's more than two hundred state enterprises was to improve their efficiency, profitability, and productivity. Only in 1987 was an initial list of thirty enterprises approved for divestment. Most were either inactive or running at a loss, while a few were small agricultural or industrial enterprises slated for takeover by existing management or Ghanaian businesspeople.[55]

In the PNDC's view, the state continued to bear the major responsibility for economic development, since private businesses were not capable of stepping into the breach—or could not be trusted to uphold national interests. The problem with most state firms, Rawlings said, was not that they were state owned but that they had ceased to function as genuinely public institutions. Their executives, by pocketing the firms' profits rather than reinvesting them, had in effect "already privatised the state enterprises."[56] To reinforce an ethos of public service, the government tightened guidelines on the conduct of civil servants, such as requiring employees to make official asset declarations.

High bureaucrats, meanwhile, came under decreasing pressure from the waning defense committees. And it was often easy for them to evade the scrutiny of auditors and other investigative agencies. As a 1985 report of the auditor general's office lamented, millions of cedis continued to be lost annually through corruption and financial irregularities in virtually all government institutions.[57] The latter half of the 1980s brought even more signs that corruption was making at least a partial comeback. The state media carried more reports about corruption and abuse of office, while Rawlings complained that graft had "crept back" into some public institutions.[58] In 1988 a member of the PNDC Secretariat publicly accused senior military officers of diverting cement supplies for their own purposes—but was then detained in retaliation. The following year, a secretary of trade and four other officials were named in a commission of inquiry for arranging financing to companies in which they were directors, while the Volta regional secretary was indicted for collecting bribes from contractors.[59]

Yet government officials failed to acknowledge that their anticorruption efforts had slackened or become less effective. They instead shifted blame by pointing to declining morality throughout society. Rawlings, in a national address, admonished the Ghanaian "underdog" for being "baptised with corruption." In the past, corrupt governments presided over an uncorrupted, angry populace. But now, he claimed, "we have a government that is suffering under the weight of a corrupted people."[60]

"The Tax Man Cometh"

The PNDC's support for economic liberalization included an implicit bargain with Ghanaians holding significant property and assets: they could enjoy improved market prospects and opportunities but in return had to pick up a bigger share of the tax burden. As Huudu Yahaya, then PNDC secretary for the

Northern Region, remarked in 1986, "Civilisation demands that richer people pay more taxes towards the cost of government than the poor."[61] Beyond giving tax policy a populist accent, such declarations also expressed a more fundamental reality—that the state could not rely excessively on external financing but had to improve its mobilization of domestic resources.

The first step entailed overhauling the revenue agencies. A National Revenue Secretariat was established in 1984 to place individual tax offices under more central direction. Revenue officers who were found to have been corrupt were dismissed. Added the author of one World Bank study, "Those considered somewhat less corrupt—including many who had thrived on giving unauthorized credit, aiding and abetting smugglers, and accepting postdated checks that were subsequently dishonored, as well as known heavy drinkers—were retired."[62] Ultimately, a tenth of all tax personnel were dismissed or retired.

The Customs and Excise Department, responsible for collecting import and export duties, came under scrutiny. Corrupt customs officials and agents had been well known for soliciting payoffs in exchange for exempting or lowering rates on goods. In one case in 1986 alone, eleven customs officials were detained for suspected undervaluation of goods that resulted in losses of ₵120 million.[63]

New levies were imposed, such as a 1984 "wealth tax" on land, buildings, noncommercial vehicles, ships, and aircraft owned by anyone with a net worth of ₵500,000 or above.[64] Most of all, there were increased efforts to collect existing taxes from those who had previously evaded them. "The Tax Man Cometh" proclaimed the headline of an editorial in the state-owned daily newspaper.[65] The revenue agencies mounted a succession of intense tax-collection campaigns in 1985–86. In one, nearly 1,000 students were mobilized to interview more than 100,000 potential taxpayers—the bulk of whom had never previously paid taxes.[66] Collections rose among all categories, with companies' share generally increasing and that of salaried employees and self-employed professionals and businesspeople declining appreciably.

As a result of improving efficiency, plugging leaks, and tapping a wider array of payers, tax collection rose significantly. The ratio of total tax revenue to GDP increased from a pitiful 4.6 percent in 1983 to a level consistently above 12 percent during 1986–89.[67] For Ghana, like every other country, the ability to extract domestic resources was a notable indicator of state power.

Military "Purification"

In many news reports and some scholarly works, the PNDC was often referred to simply as a "military regime." That characterization missed two essential points. First, although the 1981 takeover was led by Rawlings and some of his military colleagues against a civilian regime, the PNDC and the government it established were hybrid formations that included many civilian members and were supported by an array of civilian groups. Second, as in 1979, the PNDC's seizure of power in part reflected a serious divide within the armed forces, pitting younger, junior ranks against the corrupt old guard of senior officers.

Over time, the government's visage became increasingly civilian. Already by the middle of the 1980s, as Ghanaian scholar Eboe Hutchful observed, there had been a "deliberate 'demilitarisation' of the regime itself, with increasing emphasis on its 'civilian' character and insulation of the policy process from both the military and popular forces." Except for one brief episode, the secretary for defense was a civilian throughout the PNDC period, while military and security policies helped successfully "subordinate the Armed Forces to ministerial authority."[68] Unlike previous military regimes in Ghana, officers were largely kept out of the bureaucracy and management of ministries, state-owned enterprises, and other institutions, which were left in civilian hands.[69] The effective subordination of the armed forces, as an institution, to political authority received scant recognition in most accounts of the PNDC's reform process, however.

Ghana's experience of repeated bouts of military rule was one factor aiding that subordination. Ghanaians—including many in uniform—had become tired of the succession of generals and colonels who tried to dominate the political process, hand out scarce patronage favors to their loyal followers, and bleed the state dry. Anger among ordinary soldiers worsened as their material conditions deteriorated. As General Arnold Quainoo, one of the few senior officers to retain some rapport with the rank and file, later recalled,

> The soldiers saw them [senior officers] leave to become ministers.... He's got a plot [of land] there, he's building a house here, he's got a farm there. That kind of thing became a source of great envy. Those who stayed in the military began to wonder why they should stay in the military at all.... They just sat down and sulked and they felt a sense of bitterness against those who were their colleagues and who were now politicians, with the privileges, the powers of state being used to further their own ends.[70]

Rawlings's two takeovers rode on such anger and resentment. The revolt of the ranks and resulting political turbulence effectively destroyed the authority of the old officer corps. Some were detained, dismissed, or forced into early retirement, while the survivors had great difficulty getting anyone to follow their orders. In many camps and units, junior officers and rank-and-file soldiers took the lead and wielded considerable authority. In place of the previous form of military "politics"—oriented toward the abuse of public office—a new, more ideologically driven wave of politicization swept through the barracks. Many among the lower ranks came to identify themselves as among the oppressed, along with workers, students, farmers, and the unemployed.

Organizationally, that dynamic was reflected in the formation of Armed Forces Defence Committees (AFDCs), comparable to the civilian PDCs. Their members participated with other defense committee activists in promoting community self-help projects—repairing sanitation systems, digging wells, and so on—projecting a more cooperative form of interaction with civilian society.[71] The leaderships of the AFDCs were elected by general assemblies of soldiers, sailors, and air force personnel. That served to further isolate the discredited senior officers and provided an alternative pole of authority to the regular chain of command. Some in the AFDCs agitated for even more radical changes, including the outright election of senior officers, control by the ranks over promotions and discipline, and abolition of the practice by which senior officers used the lower ranks to perform menial personal services.[72]

While many officers resented the AFDCs, the committees nevertheless contributed a measure of short-term stability within the armed forces at a critical juncture when the government was under intense pressure from domestic and external opponents. Yet they simultaneously introduced elements of instability by openly challenging officers' ability to command. The alleged involvement in an October 1982 coup plot by Sergeant Daniel Alolga Akata-Pore—then a member of the PNDC as well as national secretary of the AFDCs—only amplified the concern.

In 1984, when the authorities sought to reestablish some political order and dampen the exuberance of the defense committees, policy toward the military underwent a parallel shift. There was a renewed emphasis on restoring discipline and hierarchy, while units considered too rebellious were purged or, in a few cases, disbanded entirely. The AFDCs too were transformed at the same time that the PDCs were converted into the tamer CDRs. The new Armed Forces Committees for the Defence of the Revolution, as they were called, were depoliticized in two important ways: they were insulated from the influence of civilian activists and their membership was opened to officers.[73] According to Quainoo, who drafted the instructions for the new version of the armed forces' committees, they reported to the commander of a given unit, company, or battalion, while any suggestions raised in general assemblies (known as "durbars") were passed upward through the regular chain of command.[74] "A counterrevolution was thus carried out within the armed forces, so as to restore the former command structure," commented a scholar of military affairs.[75]

That shift did not mean that Ghana's armed forces had reverted to the past, however; in many respects, the structures and functioning became more professional. Greater attention was devoted to the training and living conditions of ordinary soldiers. Junior ranks were permitted to sit on armed forces' internal disciplinary boards.[76] Officers, meanwhile, were expected to be more accountable, and those judged to be corrupt, ineffective, or poor leaders continued to be dismissed.

Throughout the 1980s, however, the process of professionalization was hampered by tight limits on military spending. As a review commission reported in 1988, virtually all operations of the army, navy, and air force were beset with severe problems, including deterioration of aging vehicles, barracks, and other facilities. Service commanders had little to spend on upkeep, in part because funding decisions were centralized within the general headquarters—ostensibly to deter corruption and embezzlement at lower levels—but mostly because financing was scarce.[77] As a share of total government spending, military outlays fell from 7.4 percent to 3 percent from 1985 to 1989. In the early 1990s, military spending started to recover, but by then the number of uniformed personnel had declined. Between 1989 and 1990 alone, the total complement of troops was cut from 16,000 to 9,000; two years later, troop numbers fell to 7,000, a level maintained throughout the rest of that decade.[78]

For military professionals, the government's success in streamlining the armed forces and taking the military out of direct state administration was a notable and lasting accomplishment. General Carl Coleman regarded it as a shift from a politicized military that served "as a tool of oppression" to one that had been "moved away from being part of the political order" and could thus devote itself more toward protecting the Ghanaian people and nation.[79] For Quainoo, in giving up management of state enterprises and other nonmilitary institutions, officers became more insulated from the opportunities for corruption that had undermined the credibility and integrity of their predecessors. "We saw the revolution as a way of purification," he explained, "a chance to reverse things, to reestablish the armed forces as we think it should be in Ghanaian society, dedicated to the defense of this country." Having restrained the military from "interfering in the political process," he added, the PNDC helped establish a principle that "soldiers will just do soldiering."[80]

Those assessments were retrospective, after Ghana had transitioned to a system of elected government. The actual process of military professionalization was far from smooth. Throughout the 1980s, military involvement in political life—even beyond Rawlings's obvious role—remained prominent. Whether it was by troops, national police, or other wings of the security apparatus, repression persisted as long as the PNDC held power, directed against both politically conservative critics and disillusioned former supporters. In 1987 the authorities responded to student demonstrations by closing the universities and detaining several left-wing intellectuals accused of inciting the students. Labor unrest reemerged in the late 1980s with a series of strikes by miners, media workers, and others, some of which were suppressed by police interventions and the banning of union activities.[81]

Local Reform

While consolidating and building up central institutions in Accra and other cities, the PNDC also sought to extend the state's presence deeper into the villages, towns, and districts, or as the Ministry of Local Government entitled a collection of decentralization documents, *From the Centre to the Grassroots*.[82]

The first step, as in other areas of reform, was to sweep out the old. In March 1982, all sixty-five of Ghana's district councils were dissolved and replaced with "interim management committees" chaired by PNDC-appointed district secretaries. These secretaries named other committee members, a few of whom were respected local figures, but initially many of them were "revolutionary cadres" from the defense committees.[83] The process soon reached larger municipalities, including the Accra City Council.

The PNDC's first official policy on decentralization, released in December 1982, sharply criticized the "highly centralised apparatus" Ghana inherited from colonial rule, which created administrative bottlenecks, "killed initiative," and "encouraged corruption and illegal transactions." Besides proposing that all central ministries establish decentralized district offices, the policy recommended a three-tier structure, with area, town, and village councils at the lowest level, district councils just above, and regional councils capping the system. The defense committees were "to take full charge" of the area, town, and village councils, while the district councils would initially be appointed and later elected.[84]

The authorities later clarified that the new structures would have limited powers, entailing "the *devolution* of central *administration (Not Political)* authority to the local level."[85] Yet they also claimed that the councils would "create a new kind of democracy."[86] No timetable was set for creating the councils, and for several years attention shifted toward less political aspects of administrative reform.

Those reforms included mandating nineteen central ministries to establish local offices and transfer about 15,000 civil servants to the regions and districts.[87] Financial audits of virtually all district and regional administrations uncovered numerous irregularities and identified some 1,800 local government employees as responsible, with most simply dismissed and those suspected of more serious crimes turned over to the tribunals.[88] By plugging financial leaks, the authorities sought to conserve limited funds. They also pushed district officials to raise more local revenue. However, revenue sources were limited: a minimal flat tax (called the "basic rate") paid by every adult resident in a locality, property taxes, market fees, development levies, and various license charges. In Ghana's poorer districts, the amounts that could be collected were especially low. Overall, the government's inability to provide more financing to the districts hampered their functioning, effectively stalling the decentralization process.[89]

The district councils were not the only intermediaries between the central government and residents of small towns and rural areas. For a few more years at least, the defense committees retained a measure of authority and influence. But with their overall role increasingly in question, the government gradually accorded more importance to customary chiefs. Despite the disdain that many of the PNDC's youthful followers expressed toward "backward" chiefs, the central authorities never seriously questioned the chieftaincy structures inherited from the suspended 1979 constitution, including 130 traditional councils and ten regional councils of chiefs.[90] In December 1982, the PNDC permitted the reconstitution of the National House of Chiefs, with Asantehene Otumfuo Opoku-Ware II, the highest-ranking Ashanti chief, as president.[91] The following year the government restored to power sixteen chiefs who had been arbitrarily ousted from office in 1966, under the National Liberation Council junta.[92]

There nevertheless were some efforts to "modernize" chieftaincy and make its practices and structures more institutionalized and professional. Some chiefs identified as corrupt or particularly oppressive were tried before tribunals and regular courts. The government's secretary for chieftaincy affairs urged traditional elders and other "kingmakers" to cease supporting unpopular chiefs "who have lost the support of their people, but yet hang on to the patronage of a few elders to the annoyance of their people."[93] Partly in response to such pressure, the National House of Chiefs widened the grounds for deposing a chief to include stealing, selling royal property, and misappropriating state funds. The regional houses drew up lists of chiefs who had been convicted or accused of serious allegations. If the houses did not remove them, the PNDC warned, the state authorities would do so. The state authorities did in fact withdraw official recognition from four chiefs in December 1987, in effect deposing them.[94]

For their part, rural defense committees only rarely challenged chiefs and most often sought to use chiefs' authority to secure land and mobilize community labor for development projects. After the CDR statutes were modified to allow anyone to join, some chiefs became formal or honorary members—including the Asantehene. In late 1985, a first CDR of chiefs was launched, in the Aowin Traditional Area.[95]

Nationally, some chiefs acquired high political office. Naa Polkuu Konkuu Chiiri's appointment to the PNDC in early 1983 was only the most prominent. Another became PNDC secretary for the Central Region; another, secretary for health; and yet another, secretary for chieftaincy affairs and acting attorney general. According to P. V. Obeng, a PNDC member and chairman of the Committee of Secretaries (the Ghanaian cabinet), "We have coopted the traditional authorities some way into the structure."[96] Rawlings used his personal authority to bolster chiefs' standing, declaring in 1987 that the PNDC recognized the institution of chieftaincy as a "focal point" for local development.[97] The following year, in a highly symbolic gesture, the Asantehene called Rawlings—whose wife was a member of the Asante royal family—"my son" and then publicly embraced him.[98]

There were other links between the central state and local communities, from town development committees formed by local notables to a variety of civic associations that received some degree of government encouragement and support. The National Mobilization Programme (NMP), originally established to help resettle Ghanaian returnees from Nigeria, eventually grew to some 200,000 volunteers in its Mobisquads. But as foreign donations declined, observed Kofi Portuphy, the NMP's chief coordinator, "we realized we couldn't sustain the Mobisquads as strictly voluntary." As a result, they turned increasing toward farming, crafts, and other income-generating activities, with some Mobisquad farms eventually registering as formal cooperatives.[99] As a matter of policy, Mobisquads often sought close relations with chiefs, mostly to secure land allocations but also sometimes to encourage them to serve as Mobisquad "patrons."[100] Many rural Ghanaians saw the Mobisquads as a means to access scarce goods and important institutional and market connections. Few people took part in NMP-organized activities unless they were given food, textiles, or other commodities.[101] The relationship echoed the prevalent patronage practices of the past and helped the central authorities in Accra win political favor in the countryside.

The 31st December Women's Movement played a comparable role. From about 50,000 members in 1983, it grew to well over a million by the end of the decade, with branches in all ten regions and more than two dozen affiliates, from market associations and bakers' unions to the Achimota Brewery Ladies Club and the Police Wives Association. The women's movement was the largest organization in the country by far.[102] Its influence, like that of the NMP, owed much to its state connections. Not only did Rawlings frequently appear at its meetings, but in 1984 his wife, Nana Konadu Agyeman-Rawlings, became the movement's national president. It worked closely with PNDC-appointed regional and district secretaries, and its staff included personnel seconded from government departments.[103] Such connections enabled the movement to deliver services and other benefits to many Ghanaian women, including help in organizing income-earning projects, establishing day-care facilities for professional and working women, and passing legislation to improve women's marriage, divorce, and inheritance rights. In rural areas, women were able to use such official leverage to counter some of the customary practices they regarded as particularly oppressive.

The 31st December Women's Movement actively sought out prosperous and influential patrons, including traditional queen mothers.[104] Customarily in Ghana, queen mothers hold traditional office, often independently from regular chiefs, with advisory powers and specific responsibility for women's and domestic affairs, although their roles and status had long gone unrecognized.[105] According to Cecelia Johnson, the movement's acting general secretary, the direct engagement of queen mothers sometimes facilitated getting almost all women in a village to join. "The queen mothers normally would not engage in these kinds of activities," she told me, "but for the moment they are the focal point of organization in the communities."[106]

Despite its mass membership, remarked one analyst, the movement's leadership tended to "become the preserve of urban middle-class women" and exhibited little concern "about the deteriorating conditions of working class, peasant and petty-trader women."[107]

As useful as such informal channels were for strengthening central state influence outside the main cities, they were not enough to clearly establish its political authority in the absence of some institution for local representation. The earlier discussions about developing an electoral mechanism for the district councils thus began to gain new traction.

Those discussions were led by the National Commission for Democracy (NCD). It was originally established in 1983 to formulate a program for "true democracy" in Ghana.[108] But it remained largely dormant and was only able to step out of the shadows with the decline of the defense committees. In 1984, the NCD came under the chairmanship of D. F. Annan, a politically moderate former judge who had been named to the PNDC that same year. It was time for "shifting away from the blood and thunder politics of earlier years," Annan affirmed, and to begin thinking about political structures that would be acceptable to all sectors of society.[109] He invited Ghanaians to submit proposals, although initially these proposals were only in relation to local government structures.[110]

In August 1986, the NCD initiated a series of public meetings to air various ideas. Since most participants favored the government, the commission was able to steer the discussions away from politically sensitive issues such as the nature of national political institutions. It simultaneously affirmed that the "principle of grassroots participation" was no longer limited to the defense committees and other "revolutionary organs" but had to incorporate "the cardinal area of local government as the foundation in the construction of a more democratic nation."[111]

Meanwhile, regarding 65 existing districts as too large, the authorities demarcated 45 new ones in 1987 to create a total of

110 districts. One justification was that smaller districts could better promote more geographically equitable economic and social development.[112]

Very soon, the government announced preparations for elections to new district assemblies, to replace the interim district councils. Their outlines were delineated in a pamphlet known as the "Blue Book," for the color of its cover. They reflected a cautious balance between encouraging local development initiatives and maintaining central political control. The district assemblies were to support productive activities, ensure construction of infrastructure, provide services, raise revenues, and prepare district budgets—all "within the framework of policies determined by the national political authority." Only two-thirds of assembly members were to be directly elected, with the national government appointing the remaining third from among traditional chiefs, economic associations, and other groups. Given the PNDC's continued opposition to political parties, no candidate could be nominated by or campaign for an organization. Otherwise, anyone eighteen years old or above could run, provided they had met their tax obligations and not been convicted or named in a commission of inquiry for involvement in fraud, dishonesty, violence, or electoral offenses.[113]

Unlike earlier elections, there were no property ownership or educational criteria. According to Kwamena Ahwoi, later a minister of local government, that allowed poorer Ghanaians to become assembly members. Nor were candidates required to be proficient in English, as long as they knew the predominant local language. "That immediately opened the doors wide."[114]

Despite the assemblies' limited authority, many Ghanaians responded to the electoral opening. During the last three months of 1987, 5.8 million Ghanaians—87 percent of all those estimated to be eligible—registered to vote.[115] The elections were held in three phases between December 1988 and March 1989, with an overall turnout of 59 percent, far higher than for either the 1978 local council polls (18 percent) or the 1979 general election (35 percent).[116]

The voting, which went relatively smoothly, demonstrated the PNDC's success in building up a support base in the countryside. For some sectors of rural society, the efforts to make the assemblies more open to ordinary Ghanaians provided new opportunities for political participation. As one analyst noted, "An unprecedented number of women were represented among district candidates even in northern areas, and nationally around 100 women were elected."[117] Yet since there were nearly 6,600 assembly members nationally, the percentage of women elected to the assemblies was still small. Overall, most successful candidates were not from the rural poor but consisted of small property owners, lawyers, teachers, prosperous farmers, skilled employees, and local bureaucrats.[118]

Most significantly, the district assembly elections revived debates over the country's wider political future. The NCD later commented that the regional discussions it had initiated set off an "organic process" of institutional change. With many participants expressing hopes for a return to constitutional rule—a move not yet envisaged by the PNDC—the commission cautioned that the dynamic unleashed by the local elections could not be reversed without triggering a "serious threat."[119]

9

Elections and Money

The turn of the decade was a politically turbulent time across Africa, as powerful movements for democratic change swept country after country. The era of military regimes and one-party states that had predominated for more than two decades abruptly faced unprecedented challenges and within several years gave way to a succession of new or restored multiparty electoral systems. From 1990 to 1994, the number of sub-Saharan countries with competitive elections increased from five to thirty-eight, or 80 percent of all states in the region.[1]

Ghana was one of them. But in important respects, its transition was different from most others. Prior to the decision by the Provisional National Defence Council (PNDC) to draft a new constitution permitting competitive party elections, there was less public agitation for reform than in many other countries. Rawlings and his comrades succeeded in retaining overall control of the process, contributing to their initial electoral victories in 1992 and 1996, unlike the dozen or so African countries where incumbents were ousted, but like those in which sitting presidents managed to ride out the storm, at least for a time. In 2000, Rawlings was barred by constitutional term limits from running again; the party he founded, the National Democratic Congress (NDC), lost to the opposition New Patriotic Party (NPP). For political analysts, that changeover represented a major step toward democratic consolidation, as liberal constitutionalists defined it. Two more handovers between the NPP and NDC followed, in 2008 and 2016, marking the emergence of a de facto two-party system.

Unlike many other nations in Africa in which democratic transitions yielded unstable parliamentary regimes—if not new military coups or debilitating civil wars—Ghana was acknowledged to have built one of the continent's most stable electoral systems. It was quite a turnaround from the political turmoil, breakdown, and insecurity of the 1960s–80s. The change reduced the level of political violence, brought more legally recognized freedoms, and entrenched citizens' right to vote—no small improvement. Yet for many ordinary Ghanaians, the practical benefits were mixed. Their electoral choices were in practice limited to one elite faction or another, while living conditions remained difficult and social inequalities widened visibly.

Corruption was not a major issue in Ghana's initial political transition. As the years passed, however, it would again become a central element in political discourse, as journalists and civil society activists brought to light more scandals involving figures from both major parties and politicians running for office found it expedient to advance their prospects with shady financing, all the while leveling graft accusations against their rivals.

In fact, the switch to a multiparty political system provided a new framework for the revival of corrupt practices. The dynamics of partisan electoral competition, fueled by poorly regulated campaign financing and politicians' links to business interests, gave the political process a strong scent of profiteering, with the winners using their control of office to recoup their investments through accepting bribes, embezzlement, cronyism, and other illegal or dubious means. Yet the system had a built-in check: incumbents could at some point be voted out. More significantly, the restoration of constitutional rule was not limited to elections. It also came with a range of citizen rights and oversight institutions designed, in theory, to promote accountability: a more independent judiciary; a variety of investigative, auditing, and prosecutorial mechanisms; a media better able to expose abuses; and varied avenues through which activists and ordinary citizens could demand transparency and justice.

When the prior era of Rawlings's unconstitutional regime is compared with the new democratic framework, two observations stand out: First, the previous period, unfettered by legal restraints, appeared more effective in combating corruption, while the subsequent elected governments, with their constitutional checks but numerous scandals, seemed more prone to patronage and graft. Second, although the anticorruption initiatives of the electoral era were more lethargic and less dramatic, they had the advantage of featuring fewer abuses and provided new avenues for a more open and democratic struggle against corruption. Yet contrary to simplistic notions equating democratization with steady advancement in institutional reform, the actual process was messy, uneven, and full of contradictions, as contending political and social interests battled to shape the direction, nature—and often, limits—of those reforms. Such problems were not unique to Ghana, of course, and have afflicted electoral democracies across the globe. The struggles of Ghanaians to improve their own system showed not only the difficulties but also the possibilities for progress, however halting and uneven those were.

Controlled Democratization

In a 1991 New Year's address, Rawlings maintained that his government had initiated a process of democratization and restructuring years before the fall of the Berlin Wall helped encourage pro-democracy movements globally.[2] Insofar as he was referring to the district assembly elections and the wider political debates they unleashed, that was true. But how far he and his supporters were initially willing to go and what form of democracy they had in mind were questionable. At various regional consultations organized by the government-appointed National Commission for Democracy (NCD), they often cited the corruption and other failures of Ghana's previous electoral systems and spoke instead of ushering in a new form of "true democracy," variously described as either building on the popular mobilizations of the early 1980s or, less ambitiously, extending the no-party district assembly model to the national level.

Other Ghanaians countered with different notions. They most often drew on the dominant international discourses of liberal democracy that emphasized multiparty, pluralist elections. The leaders of the Ghana Bar Association, among the foremost elite critics of the PNDC, had long advanced such ideas, as did the Catholic Bishops Conference and the Christian Council of Ghana. More notable were the decisions of the trade unions and national students' association, with their many thousands of members, to make similar calls. As early as 1986, a commission of the Trades Union Congress recommended establishing a "democratically constituted People's Assembly."[3] Over the next two years congress leaders and delegates' assemblies became increasingly explicit in rejecting the government's no-party proposals and demanding instead the free election of both a national legislature and president. Unionists, beyond desiring an end to state repression and respect for the right to strike and assemble, also wanted greater space to promote policy alternatives to the PNDC's severe austerity measures, which brought job losses and worsened living conditions.[4]

Also significant was the formation in August 1990 of a new alliance, the Movement for Freedom and Justice (MFJ), which spanned the ideological spectrum, from Adu Boahen, a well-known and politically moderate historian, to the journalist Kwesi Pratt Jr. and two radical former PNDC secretaries who had broken with the government after its shift in economic policy. The MFJ forthrightly denounced the PNDC's attempts to constrain debate on Ghana's political future and vowed to campaign for democracy, basic rights, and an end to press censorship.[5] Yet like most other government critics at the time, the MFJ refrained from making any corruption allegations, despite revelations of misdeeds by some high officials—anticorruption discourse was still largely seen as part of the Rawlings brand. The group did, however, contest the authorities' claim that party politics were inherently corrupt, and for that reason should be avoided. In its first public statement, the MFJ declared that "though the multi-party system of government can breed corruption because of the demands of those who finance them, the way out is surely not the retention of military dictatorships, nor no-party or one-party systems."[6]

No sooner had the MFJ openly challenged the PNDC than the group was harassed by security agents, threatened with violence, barred from holding rallies, and denounced in the state media.[7] The authorities' repressive response, coming on top of repeated crackdowns on strikes and other protests, accounted in part for the absence of the kind of large pro-democracy mobilizations then sweeping some of Ghana's neighbors. Another factor was the continued domination of the political space by the varied pro-PNDC "mass organizations." Those included the remnants of the defense committees, the 31st December Women's Movement (with 1.5 million members), and many newly elected officers of the district assemblies—all of whom provided the authorities a substantial base of support throughout the country. As the PNDC came to feel more secure, it increasingly permitted dissenting views in public political discussions.

Rawlings denied he was bending to external pressures to democratize, as happened to other African regimes facing increased Western demands for the introduction of multiparty systems. Indeed, during the 1980s, Ghana's main foreign financiers expressed no public criticisms of the PNDC's tight hold—and may in fact have regarded that as essential for the effective adoption of structural adjustment policies. But the collapse of the Soviet bloc and the global wave of democratization changed their calculations. And even if the International Monetary Fund, World Bank, and other Western institutions still did not explicitly urge the PNDC to open up politically, they did exert some pressure through "quiet" diplomatic channels.[8] They also hinted that if a regime proved recalcitrant, they might shift more funding toward Africa's "new democracies" instead. The Ghanaian government was sensitive to such subtle warnings. Foreign grants had risen from 4.2 percent of total budgetary revenue in 1984 to 11.5 percent by 1990. "With this level of dependence on external donors," two Ghanaian scholars observed, "political conditionality was difficult to resist."[9]

Whatever the precise mix of foreign and domestic considerations, the government demonstrated a clear capacity to seize the initiative and outmaneuver its critics by unexpectedly altering the parameters of the debate. In his 1991 New Year's address, Rawlings surprised everyone by announcing that the NCD would complete its report by that March, to be quickly followed by a constitutional consultative body.[10]

While much of the opposition expected that the PNDC-appointed NCD would simply endorse the authorities' "pet theories," one analyst commented, "Its report actually provided some further surprises of its own."[11] Despite many abuses under previous electoral regimes, the NCD reported, the consultations revealed a broad public view that "a multi-party system is inherently good."[12] Any residual worries about whether the PNDC would continue to resist the central demand of democracy advocates were further allayed when Rawlings announced that the drafters of the new constitution would pursue the multiparty option, effectively abandoning the alternatives. "I have my reservations and doubts," he added, "but I am bound by the collective decision of my colleagues."[13]

That did not mean that the political gates were thrown wide open. The way the authorities constituted the Consultative Assembly demonstrated little intention to fully loosen the reins. Of the 260 assembly members, 117 were selected by the district assemblies, 22 named directly by the government, and 121 allotted to sixty-two professional and occupational groups; many of the latter were small and unrepresentative or previously supportive of the PNDC. Fearing that the constitutional process would thus be stage-managed in the government's favor, the Ghana Bar

Association and National Union of Ghana Students boycotted the sessions.

In one respect their fears were justified. Tacked onto the end of the draft constitution were several "transitional provisions" that explicitly indemnified any member or appointee of the PNDC, the Armed Forces Revolutionary Council, or previous unelected governments for anything they did or did not do and prohibited the courts from acting against them—in other words, a proclamation of blanket immunity for Rawlings and his comrades. Commented the National Union of Ghana Students, "It is most incongruous that after a decade of probity and accountability slogan chanting[,] those who coined the slogan and enforced it with the gun should now attempt to escape the litmus test."[14] The Ghana Bar Association similarly declared that "it is manifest hypocrisy and humbug for the people of this country to be told of the need to avoid corrupt and self-seeking 'politicians' in civilian administrations if the same yardstick is not going to be applied to politicians in military garb."[15]

Those shortcomings notwithstanding, the core clauses of the draft constitution met with wide acclaim, including from the PNDC's fiercest critics, the Ghana Bar Association among them. The document incorporated selected features of previous constitutions, providing for both a strong elected executive limited to two four-year terms and a national parliament, also elected every four years. It included clauses to ensure independence of the judiciary and incorporation of the public tribunals into the regular court system. Various investigative and watchdog bodies were mandated, including the Commission on Human Rights and Administrative Justice to look into allegations of corruption and other abuses. Media freedom was guaranteed, along with a range of other individual rights—some going beyond prevailing international norms. One of the constitution's opening clauses even empowered all Ghanaian citizens to "do all in their power" to restore the constitution if it were suspended or overthrown,[16] in other words, to rise up against any future coup attempt or other illegal usurpation of power.

The PNDC promptly accepted the draft without alteration and set in motion a tight schedule to move forward. At the end of April 1992, the draft constitution was put to voters in a national referendum. With major religious bodies and both government supporters and opponents calling for its approval, it received a massive "yes" vote. About 93 percent of voters cast their ballots for the constitution and only 7 percent against.[17] Ghana's Fourth Republic, following the three previous periods of constitutional rule (under Nkrumah, Busia, and Limann), was thus born.

Less than three weeks later, the formation of political parties was authorized. Though some objected to cumbersome procedures for securing official registration, many of the small informal "clubs" that had begun to emerge quickly reorganized themselves into full-fledged parties to contest elections at the end of the year.

From Contention to Consensus

In launching their own party, Rawlings and his comrades consciously sought to retain an identification with their decade in power. They called their formation the National Democratic Congress, its acronym, NDC, lacking only the "P." With parties again legal, a dozen others also emerged, although several left hardly any electoral imprint. Two aligned themselves with the NDC; while they ran parliamentary candidates, they did not field presidential aspirants, backing Rawlings instead. Of those in opposition, three came out of the Nkrumahist tradition (as did one of the NDC's allies). The most substantial opposition formation, the New Patriotic Party (NPP), positioned itself within the old conservative tradition that opposed Nkrumah, vigorously promoted private business interests, and had a strong base in the heartlands of the old Asante empire.

In the first race to lead Ghana's Fourth Republic, Rawlings and his NDC held a clear advantage. Although newly minted, the party inherited many foot soldiers from the PNDC era, including recently elected district assembly councillors, former defense committee cadres, and supportive "civil" associations such as the

31st December Women's Movement, all seasoned in the art of political mobilization. Rawlings, moreover, remained personally popular, able to draw huge crowds to campaign rallies. And while some of his associates were suspected of corruption, Rawlings himself still had "a formidable reputation for personal honesty," something that could not be said of some opposition candidates.[18] Many Ghanaians grumbled about the hardships of Rawlings's liberalization policies, but the NPP could not offer a credible alternative, since its outlook was even more neoliberal and unabashedly elitist: NPP leaders often boasted of their wealth or high social status and described themselves as "property owning democrats."[19] Nor could the fragmented Nkrumahist parties gain much traction against the NDC, which had appropriated some of that tradition's rhetoric and symbols. Finally, the campaign playing field was uneven. Not only did Rawlings and his comrades control the election's timing and practical arrangements, but they already held state office and employed it in their favor. As one Ghanaian political scientist observed, "Rawlings used state resources at his disposal for his campaign—money, government vehicles, helicopters, the press—while the other parties, starved of funds and resources, could only complain bitterly."[20]

The outcome of the November 1992 presidential election may not have been preordained but was hardly surprising. Rawlings won nationally with 58 percent of the vote, against 30 percent for his nearest rival, Adu Boahen of the NPP. The geographical sweep of the victory reflected the NDC's broad roots. Rawlings won majorities in nine of the ten regions, with a poor showing only in Ashanti, the historic stronghold of the NPP hierarchy. Rawlings also consistently polled more strongly in rural areas, while Boahen did better in most cities—except in poorer neighborhoods, where Rawlings also did well.[21]

International observers endorsed the election as "free and fair," despite scattered evidence of fraud in certain constituencies. But the opposition parties angrily rejected the observers' judgment, claiming a "stolen verdict." Rioting rocked Kumasi, the Ashanti capital, while the NPP and other opposition parties protested by boycotting the parliamentary elections the following month. That gesture failed to embarrass the authorities, instead clearing the way for the NDC to easily sweep up 189 of the 200 National Assembly seats, with two allied parties and two independents taking the remainder.[22] To all intents and purposes, the first government of the Fourth Republic was thus a one-party affair, albeit with the opposition absent through its own doing.

Some skeptics, with an eye on authoritarian-dominated transitions to multiparty systems elsewhere in Africa, anticipated little more than a facade of democracy. But the actual experience of Rawlings's first elected term revealed some adherence to the new "rules of the game" and an unexpected degree of openness. The NDC and NPP leaderships soon agreed "to do business" with each other, including through a new Inter-Party Advisory Committee formed under the electoral commission's auspices to negotiate acceptable procedures for updating the voters' roll and issuing new voter identity cards before the next elections in 1996. As early as 1993, the NPP was permitted to submit comments on the budget, even though it had no National Assembly deputies. The NDC's dominance appeared to facilitate, rather than hinder, passage of legislation to establish new institutions designed to hold officeholders to account, including the Commission on Human Rights and Administrative Justice and the Serious Fraud Office. Meanwhile, dissent by some deputies, including from the NDC, obliged the government to alter legislation and even drop plans to raise fuel prices. The judiciary also asserted its independence on several occasions, with the Supreme Court overturning a government requirement that demonstrations needed prior police approval and obliging the state-owned media to give equal coverage to opposition parties.[23]

The 1996 elections were a rerun but with fully committed opposition participation and electoral procedures that made it easier for opposition candidates to campaign. Again, two small parties allied with the NDC and backed Rawlings's reelection. The

NPP's presidential candidate was John Kufuor, who had briefly been a minister in the early PNDC days. The broad issues were also essentially similar, with both main parties in accord on basic economic policies. But opposition candidates had become more vocal about suspicions of high-level corruption among NDC and government figures. Once more, ruling party candidates enjoyed access to state resources off-limits to the opposition: "Each [NDC] headquarters was provided with brand new vehicles for electioneering campaign purposes. Rawlings himself used a Ghana Air Force helicopter to reach inaccessible areas during the campaign."[24] The election outcome was somewhat different, however. In the presidential race, which Rawlings won with 57 percent of the vote, only slightly below his score in 1992, Kufuor pulled in nearly 40 percent of the vote, ten percentage points better than his NPP predecessor. And because this time the opposition ran for the National Assembly, the new parliament was decidedly more diverse: 133 for the NDC, 61 for the NPP, and the remaining 6 for two oppositional Nkrumahist parties.[25]

There was another difference as well: The 1996 elections were seen as more credible than the previous round. First, popular confidence was reflected in a relatively high turnout, 78.2 percent, significantly above the level in 1992, when 50.2 percent of registered voters participated in the presidential poll and only 29 percent in the legislative election.[26] Second, although the opposition parties had some grievances, they promptly congratulated the winners, conferring the outcome with a degree of legitimacy. Rawlings responded with a conciliatory acceptance speech, commending the opposition candidates for their "competitive spirit" and concluding, "Together we have established the tradition of orderly democratic procedure."[27]

It was easy for Rawlings to be magnanimous—he had just won. It was not clear, however, whether Ghana was on track toward an orderly democratic process. That would entail not just regular elections but also the real possibility of a political turnover. Was the NDC's hold so strong that it could forestall any real chance of opposition victory? Would Rawlings step aside once he ran out his last term permitted under the constitution—or would he try to amend the term limit to run again? Numerous examples elsewhere in Africa suggested that political elites coming out of previous authoritarian systems could prolong their grip, with just enough electoral trappings to mollify their Western allies and financiers.

Sometime after the 1996 election, an NDC figure informally floated the idea of prolonging the president's term. While that raised some initial alarm, Rawlings silenced the concern in 1998 when he said his preferred candidate for the next election was his vice-president, John Atta Mills.[28]

Indeed, when the 2000 race commenced, the NDC put Mills forward as its standard-bearer, with Rawlings active on the campaign trail. That time, internal dissension led some sidelined NDC figures to form a splinter party or run as independents, weakening the party in several key constituencies. The NPP, meanwhile, was better structured and could run on its record in the parliament, enabling it to wage a more effective campaign. As well, a sizable army of independent poll watchers was on the scene to try to minimize outright fraud, of which both the NDC and NPP were guilty to some extent. And the state-owned media, while still biased toward the NDC, did a better job of reporting opposition activities.[29]

Another notable difference was that the NDC had lost its monopoly on anticorruption rhetoric, especially since several top figures were suspected of questionable dealings. Moreover, the party faced an array of opposition candidates who had no recent connection to state power and thus could credibly claim clean hands. Early in the campaign, Kufuor excoriated the Rawlings era as "the most arrogant, cruel, wasteful, incompetent and corrupt government this country has ever seen" and pledged to eradicate corruption if he were elected.[30] To what extent that theme resonated with voters was unclear, but it was one which Kufuor and other NPP candidates sounded throughout the campaign.

By December 2000, those cumulative changes were enough to yield a different outcome. When the votes were tallied after the December 7 election, neither Mills nor Kufuor obtained the majority required for an outright victory, with Mills trailing 44.9 percent to Kufuor's 48.4 percent. That balance was also reflected in the parliamentary results, as the NPP took 101 seats against 92 for the NDC (the remainder went to two small parties and several independents). The lack of a clear presidential winner triggered a second round three weeks later. With all opposition parties throwing their weight behind the NPP candidate and the NDC unable to mobilize enough voters to shift the tide, Kufuor was able to win the runoff with a handy 57 percent.[31]

NPP supporters poured into the streets to celebrate. Many independents, rights activists, and even some NDCers also welcomed the outcome as a signal that Ghana's democracy had begun to sink deeper roots. Among theorists of democratic transitions, an actual turnover in leadership—as opposed to elections that simply returned to office figures from the same political circle—signaled that an electoral system was on the way toward consolidation.[32] But Ghana was not quite there. Other democratic transitions in Africa showed the pitfalls that could still lie ahead: political polarization could spiral out of control and trigger violence, popular unrest could make it impossible for an elected regime to govern, some faction could try to seize power, or severe ethnic clashes could descend into civil war. While partisan competition between the NPP and NDC did bring occasional violence, none of the other dangers raised serious alarms in Ghana.

In any case, the next few elections put most concerns to rest. Kufuor and his NPP won a second term in 2004. Then, in the 2008 elections, Mills and the NDC came back into office. Analysts, both Ghanaian and foreign, saw that second turnover as solidifying Ghana's credentials as a "shining democratic star" and "model democracy" in Africa and beyond.[33] Among international political scientists, the outcome of the 2008 election meant that Ghana had passed the "two turnover test," considered by some as a benchmark of democratic consolidation.[34] The pattern continued. Mills died in office in 2012, a few months before the next elections. He was succeeded by his vice-president, John Mahama, who then won his own presidential term. But in 2016 Mahama lost to the NPP's Nana Akufo-Addo and lost again four years later (albeit by only a razor-thin margin), giving the NPP two more turns at the helm.

Ghana had thus developed a relatively stable two-party system. While smaller parties were effectively crowded out—limiting voters' choices at the polls and more critical voices in the parliament—the arrangement had benefits in many eyes. The relative political calm that came with orderly handovers made it easier for ordinary citizens to deal with their daily concerns and, if sufficiently organized, to defend their constitutional rights. Ghana's recent past and the examples of authoritarianism or serious armed conflict in some regional neighbors were reminders of how much devastation political turmoil could bring.

Yet Ghana's particular version of stability had its drawbacks. In theory, periodic alternations in power should have served as a check on corruption and self-serving by those in office, since voters could throw out errant leaders at the next election. But the tacit understanding that developed between the two main parties limited the real impact of electoral change. Since at least 1996, according to Kwame Ninsin, the NDC and NPP maintained an "elite consensus" to settle election disputes amicably, with the loser conceding defeat (when the vote margin was wide) or challenging the results in court (when the tally was close). But otherwise the parties remained highly competitive, to an extent that weakened Ghana's overall state system. Despite glowing characterizations of Ghanaian democracy, Ninsin wrote, "there is mounting evidence that governance institutions are not working according to global standards," with the parliament "unable to exercise its oversight functions due to extreme partisanship" and the parties becoming "instruments for sectarian, ethnic and money politics." Those partisan confrontations, moreover, were sharpened by the parties' common view that elections were a "means to control the state for private accumulation."[35] In other words, the contention between the NPP and NDC was not about alternate policy visions. It was essentially about which party controlled the spoils of office and for how long. To the extent there was consensus, it centered on taking turns at the trough.

The main parties often sought to obscure that reality by presenting a public image of commitment to peaceful and orderly electoral competition. Thus, in 2012, the NDC, NPP, and six smaller parties reiterated their support for a "code of conduct" that was originally negotiated four years earlier. The code prohibited the signatory parties from "all forms of intimidation and political violence," derogatory or insulting attacks on individuals or "ethnic and religious groups," and any offer of bribes or other forms of "gratification" to candidates or voters.[36] The NPP and NDC in particular had already displayed numerous instances of such misconduct. And they would continue to do so, despite pledges to run cleaner campaigns in future.

Reign of the "Macho Men"

According to Ghanaian analysts, every election featured some form of violence, with incidents worsening during particularly tight races, reflecting a recurring pattern of "low intensity electoral violence."[37] Much of the violence could be attributed directly to partisan jostling. Some, however, had roots in Ghana's diverse local economic and social conflicts, whether community disputes over land, chieftaincy succession fights, ethnic rivalry, or competition for scarce resources of various kinds. Frequently, such struggles were colored—and made more combustible—by the intervention of national politics, as party activists took advantage of fractures to win electoral support and local actors sought external leverage to advance their positions. In Asutsuare, in the Eastern Region, villagers faithful to the then-ruling NDC received favored access to irrigation permits, while NPP supporters were physically assaulted by police and NDC thugs. When the 2000 election brought the NPP to power in Accra, the tables turned in Asutsuare as well, bringing more clashes that this time drove out NDC supporters.[38] Similarly, in the northern town of Tamale, a feud between competing factions of butchers descended into armed confrontation when the rivals lined up behind opposing parties.[39]

Local disputes were often worsened when national politicians stirred their supporters with inflammatory rhetoric and insults. Unfounded accusations of fraud—and occasionally real instances of partisan bias by police or election personnel—were used to demonize rivals and justify countermobilizations that could end in confrontation. In some instances, hundreds of party activists armed with clubs, stones, cutlasses, and guns prevented campaigning by opposing candidates, intimidated potential voters, and disrupted vote counting.

The most feared purveyors of violence were informal militias organized by both main parties. Commonly known as "macho men," the partisan vigilantes often adopted names intended to intimidate. The NPP had the Delta Force, Kandahar Boys, Alidu Mafia, and similar outfits. Those affiliated with the NDC included the Aluta Boys, Cyborg Killers, Hawks, and others.[40] Some were ad hoc and operated only in specific localities. Others were more established and ranged over wider areas. A handful, often associated with body-building gyms, were not wedded to any party but offered their services to the highest bidder. Most members were young unemployed men, although in some places young women provided intelligence and support. The more than two dozen identified vigilante groups were not necessarily paid outright but frequently acted on promises of future jobs (including in the security forces) should their party win. The NPP and NDC leaderships usually claimed the groups were simply providing security for candidates and campaign events. Yet their activities often went beyond defense to include outright intimidation: terrorizing voters, beating up—and occasionally killing—opposition campaigners, tearing down posters, snatching ballot boxes, and the like.

The vigilantes were not always inactive between election cycles. When factional conflicts erupted within parties—usually

Elections and Money

during candidate-selection primaries or when nominating local government officials—the militias were sometimes mobilized against rivals. In Kumasi, about fifty NDC vigilantes mounted on motorbikes threatened a party nominee for metropolitan chief executive, while in Tema West two hundred NDC "macho men" stormed a party constituency office to support their favored candidate in the primaries.[41] During the two years before its 2016 election victory, the NPP was stricken by especially dramatic bouts of factional violence, often pitting supporters of Akufo-Addo against those of then national party chairman Paul Afoko. The latter was ultimately ousted after his brother was arrested for a gruesome acid-attack murder of an NPP regional party chairman in the northern town of Bolgatanga.[42]

After the NPP was back in power, members of its Delta Force attacked a Kumasi circuit court to free thirteen comrades facing charges for assaulting a regional security coordinator nominated by President Akufo-Addo.[43] The incident dramatized the extent to which such groups had become powerful enough to escape control and even pose a direct threat to state authorities. It also prompted wide condemnation, including from the Ghana Bar Association, which denounced the attack as a "glorification of violence" and called for disbandment of the Delta Force and other vigilante groups.[44] The authorities instead dropped charges against eight people accused in the court attack, while the thirteen Delta Force members involved in the original assault were sentenced to only modest fines.[45] Even more, in 2018 the Delta Force commander for the Ashanti Region rose to become a deputy director in the NPP's youth wing—paralleling the ascension that same year of the leader of the pro-NDC Azorka Boys to become first vice-president of that party.[46]

Such reluctance to rein in partisan militias fueled mounting public anger. In January 2019, a by-election in a constituency on the outskirts of Accra resulted in the wounding by gunfire of five NDC supporters near a polling station. While vigilantes from both parties were apparently on the scene, most of the violence that time came from masked members of a government security unit known as the SWAT team, who also assaulted an NDC member of parliament acting as a poll watcher. The fact that the confrontation was in the capital, and video of the assault quickly circulated, stirred enough outrage, including street demonstrations, to compel the government to permit an independent inquiry. The commission sharply criticized the conduct of the SWAT team and the tendency of successive governments to absorb former vigilantes into the official security forces. It called the vigilantes "a threat to the very stability of Ghana's constitutional democracy."[47] By that point, the legislature had already adopted a law ordering the disbandment of vigilante groups and providing stiff sentences for those found guilty of vigilante activities.[48] Since other laws covering similar offenses were only poorly enforced, many were skeptical that the new one would end the problem.[49] Indeed, while there were few reported activities by armed party groups during the 2020 election cycle, seven Ghanaians were nevertheless killed and many others injured in more than a score of violent confrontations.[50]

Playing the Ethnic Card

Like most African countries, Ghana is composed of a mosaic of ethnic groups, languages, and cultures. Disputes within and among communities over land, access to resources, chieftaincy succession, and other issues sometimes followed or were colored by ethnic cleavages, contributing to sporadic bouts of violence. Unlike some states, however, those tensions were driven largely by local dynamics and never threatened the stability of the central state.[51] In part, the limited impact of ethnic conflict on national politics reflected the success of nationalist efforts since the first decades of independence to forge an overarching identity. While many Ghanaians continued to maintain strong links to their home areas or with others of their particular culture, in the political sphere they most of all viewed themselves as Ghanaians and acted on that basis.

Trying to keep it that way, Ghana's constitution explicitly prohibited any party from having an ethnic, religious, or regional basis and required it to draw national committee members from multiple regions. In practice, that legal stipulation only put limits on the way party leaders and members utilized ethnic identities to advance their fortunes. In an environment of tight competition between the two main parties, there often were implicit—and sometimes explicit—attempts to mobilize voters on the basis of ethnicity. The NDC and NPP both built perceived strongholds in different regions and among different ethnic constituencies. Elections were not decided on that basis alone, and voter preferences were usually influenced by multiple factors, including ideology, social difference, assessments of parties' past performance, and promises of access to future jobs or other patronage. But during the heat of campaigns in particular, some candidates projected messages aimed at voters of specific groups—and at least a fraction of the electorate was swayed. According to a University of Ghana survey, 8.3 percent of nearly 12,000 respondents who voted in 2016 admitted that they cast ballots for a party because it was "the party of my tribesmen/women."[52] The real figure was likely higher, since some would be reluctant to identify themselves as "tribalist," with its pejorative connotations.

During the first two elections of the Fourth Republic, the ethnic dimensions of the NDC's base were not so apparent, since the victories of Rawlings and his party were easily explainable by their access to state resources, popularity among poorer social strata, and other factors. But its less successful performance in 2000, when the NPP won, revealed more clearly the party's ethnic strongholds: among various communities in the ethnically diverse north and most starkly among the Ewe of the Volta Region (later split into the Volta and Oti regions). That pattern held in subsequent elections. The NDC generally dominated in the Volta/Oti regions, often regarded as the party's electoral "World Bank," regardless of whether its presidential candidate was Ewe (Rawlings), Fante (Mills), or northern (Mahama). The party's support base in the north was more uneven and variable but still strong, especially in the Upper West Region.[53] Because of the poverty and paucity of opportunities in the north, many individuals have historically migrated southward, creating notable northern enclaves in Accra, Kumasi, and elsewhere, there too providing strong support bases for the NDC.[54] In effect, the NDC's diverse voting blocs represented peoples who historically were either dominated by the precolonial Asante empire or on its margins. At times, that image of what the NDC was against (rather than for) was voiced openly, as during the 2000 elections when Rawlings, campaigning on behalf of his chosen successor, Mills, warned voters in Accra that an NPP victory could bring Asante domination.[55] Amid other ethnically tinged remarks by prominent NDC leaders over the years, Mahama during his 2020 presidential bid made disparaging remarks about Akyem, an Akan group, provoking public protests.[56]

Leaders of the NPP often bristled at accusations of being a party of the Asante, the core of the old Asante empire. But there was ample evidence to fuel that perception. In the 1992 elections, the Ashanti Region was the only one carried by the NPP, which remained the region's overwhelmingly dominant force in every subsequent poll, assisted not only by ethnic identification but also by explicit political endorsements by traditional chiefs. The party later performed much better as it expanded its vote totals among related Akan peoples (Fante, Brong, Akyem, Akwapim, Nzema, and others), helping it carry the Central, Eastern, and former Brong Ahafo regions (the latter subdivided in 2018 into the Ahafo, Bono, and Bono East regions). Although Ghana's Akan peoples together account for 44 percent of the total population, the largest bloc of ethnic affinities, the NPP still had to secure enough support in Greater Accra, parts of the north, and elsewhere to win nationally. Voters clearly did not choose candidates solely because of ethnicity; the NPP's emphasis on policies favoring the private sector also appealed to businesspeople, prosperous cocoa farmers, and others in the better-off Akan regions. Still, NPP leaders often acted as if their role was to represent Akans. Kufuor, the NPP's first presidential winner, packed his cabinet with Akan ministers; when asked about the absence of anyone from the Upper West Region, he insultingly responded that he could not find "any qualified or suitable" person from there—despite the fact that several individuals from the Upper West had played major roles in the previous Rawlings governments.[57] From time to time, other NPP leaders also made intemperate remarks. Those included a former finance minister who, according to a leaked recording, appeared to suggest to party colleagues that it was unthinkable for Akans, who supposedly control most of Ghana's resources, to allow any other ethnic group to rule.[58]

Most leaders and candidates of the NPP and NDC tempered their public declarations and at times chastised party colleagues for remarks that could be taken as ethnic incitement. The parties also took care to field candidates of diverse backgrounds. In most campaigns, the NPP nominated someone from the north as its vice-presidential candidate, part of a broader strategy to make electoral inroads in the northern regions. While serving to blur any ethnic image it projected nationally, those efforts at the same time heightened competition with the NDC in an especially volatile region.

By any measure—income, employment, school-attendance rates, access to health care, infrastructure—residents of the north have fared much worse than non-northerners.[59] The north's ethnic patchwork made the resulting social tensions more explosive. In the former Northern Region alone (divided in 2018 into the Northern, Savannah, and North East regions), there were some fifteen ethnic groups with different histories, customs, and traditions. Most generally got along well, but disputes flared sporadically. Ghanaian scholar Cletus Dordunoo judged that some northern groups felt they had received an "unfair deal" in access to resources or chieftaincy positions.[60] Several of those conflicts were long-standing and erupted into periodic violence. After the reestablishment of electoral politics, the two main parties sometimes sought to mediate tensions but at other times worsened them by lining up with opposing sides. The deadliest conflict was a dispute over land rights in the Northern Region between the Konkomba and Nanumba, which spread to draw in other ethnic groups on each side and ultimately claimed thousands of lives during a February 1994 war.[61] Subsequently, the NPP made political inroads by siding with the Konkomba against the Nanumba, who generally voted for the NDC, contributing to fighting between party militants in 2002.[62] In Bawku in the Upper East Region, some fifty people died in election violence in 2000 that pitted Kusasi supporters of the NDC against the NPP's Mamprusi backers.[63] Two years later, a conflict between competing royal families of the Dagbon kingdom in the Northern Region led to the assassination of the reigning monarch, with serious tensions festering for years after, again with the NPP and NDC on opposing sides.[64]

In the north, as elsewhere, partisan and ethnic conflicts have often been defused before reaching the stage of mass violence. More sober heads within the two parties often weighed in to cool tensions. Civil society organizations also played important roles in trying to depoliticize and mediate local disputes.[65] The Trades Union Congress, for example, called on politicians "to refrain from inflaming passions" and "avoid any action or utterances that give an opportunity for extremist elements."[66]

Dynamics of "Moneycracy"

When campaigning, Ghana's parties and candidates relied on words: lofty rhetoric to capture media headlines, slogans to inspire activists, promises to address voters' immediate needs and future aspirations. Following a long tradition in Ghana, parties always launched official campaign manifestos, combining criticisms of their competitors' records, broader societal visions, and long lists of "knife and fork" promises pitched to voters' immediate material interests.[67] On their face, those promises were directed to all citizens. But the NDC and NPP in fact mostly addressed their own followers or those who might be swayed. Both parties functioned as patronage machines, with the benefits of victory intended first and foremost for party supporters and the resources of office distributed on a noninclusive basis through partisan, ethnic, and kinship channels.

The NPP, always more open about its elitism and reliance on "big men," had little difficulty developing extensive patron-client networks, especially after it first won power in the 2000 elections and thus had access to state resources, jobs, and contracts for its members and followers. However, the NDC, which came in with the progressive heritage of Rawlings's revolutionary era, had to adapt to the new context. In the process, the technocrats and managers who had played a central role in the previous PNDC regime gave way, according to Eboe Hutchful, to "political brokers more concerned with patronage" and "carpetbaggers" comfortable operating amid increasing "cronyism and corruption," as the NDC forged alliances with chiefs, cocoa farmers, and new and old business classes.[68] The 1996 elections were an important marker of the NDC's starker shift toward patronage methods, as about eighty of its sitting legislators were dropped during the party primaries and replaced with "big men" better able to construct clientelist networks and compete with their NPP counterparts. Those who were bumped from the NDC ticket then received compensation in the form of cash, end-of-service gratuities, favorable house loans, and promises of future jobs.[69]

Overall, Ghanaian electoral politics could not be reduced simply to patronage considerations. Some candidates ran to serve the public interest and when elected sought to fulfill the duties of office as best they could. Yet some—many Ghanaians would say, far too many—entered politics in a quest for social advancement and material gain. In that way, the country's democratic system was corrupted by money, making it at least in part a "moneycracy," as Ghanaians often called it. Despite codes of conduct and ethics, financial concerns tainted virtually every phase of the electoral process: candidate selection, campaigning, voting, and the postelection distribution of spoils.

With the avowed aim of fielding candidates who enjoyed some credibility among party ranks, the NPP and NDC chose most of their nominees through systems of primaries. Those were selective processes, in which electoral colleges of party executives, constituency leaders, officeholders, and other authoritative figures chose those candidates deemed most likely to win. Often, however, primary delegates succumbed to bribery, especially in the absence of laws criminalizing vote buying within parties. Although the NDC's primary campaigns were also marred, NPP primaries appeared particularly tainted, judging by the number of losing candidates who publicly blamed their defeats on bribery by the winners. No less than party chairman Jake Obetsebi-Lamptey seemed to condone vote buying when he declared that potential candidates should maximize whatever advantage they had, including "if you have money, then use the money."[70]

During active campaigning, the governing party often used the powers of office to support its candidates in ways unavailable to the opposition, such as using state vehicles, doling out gifts to potential voters, and timing the inauguration of official development projects to influence the electorate. Sometimes ruling party officials threatened to withhold development funding from communities favoring the opposition, as when the NPP's northern regional minister, Abubakar Saddique Boniface, warned voters in NDC strongholds that if they craved "development and you don't want to join the government of the day, then you are deceiving yourself.... If you are an NDC this is not your time, so why don't you join NPP and enjoy the national cake?"[71] Independent civil society groups, including the Ghana Center for Democratic Development, monitored the conduct of campaigns during the 2004 and 2008 elections and discovered numerous instances of "abuse of incumbency" by the NPP, then in power. The monitoring groups also did so in 2012, when President Mahama's NDC sought reelection. They cited six verified instances in which official government ceremonies were used as campaign events, as well as other cases of incumbency abuse, including a diversion of funds from the Ghana Investment Promotion Centre to support Mahama's campaign.[72] Party conduct was little better in subsequent elections. In 2020, when the NPP was back in power and campaigning for reelection, observers from the European Union, while generally positive, nevertheless found that the incumbents' misuse of state resources had created an "unlevel playing field."[73]

Since overt cash payments to voters were illegal, the practice was conducted surreptitiously. The NPP and NDC, whether in power or opposition, were both accused of giving out "gifts" of textiles, bicycles, sewing machines, cutlasses, cornmills, and other consumer goods. Civil society groups that monitored the 2012 election confirmed instances of vote buying by each of the two parties.[74] In 2020, an NDC parliamentary candidate in the Greater Accra Region denied that he gave cash to voters but admitted that he used funds from "benevolent" friends to purchase "essential needs" for people in his constituency.[75] That same year, 9 percent of respondents to a pre-election survey reported that they had been offered money, food, or gifts, and 24 percent said they knew people who benefited from inducements. Of those who were offered something for their votes, 74 percent said the offers came from the NPP and 43 percent, from the NDC.[76]

Even if candidates or party leaders did not take the initiative to offer inducements, pressures to do so sometimes came from local election brokers who solicited promises in exchange for blocs of voters. In a parliamentary debate in 2019 on money politics, the NDC's minority whip said pressure often came from traditional chiefs, clergy, imams, and other opinion leaders: "When you go to campaign in their territories, they keep pointing to things that you must do for them before their village or town will vote for you, and most of the demands are personal in nature and have nothing to [do] with the development of their villages and towns."[77]

After elections came the spoils. With each turnover between the NDC and NPP, there was a large-scale alternation in who filled executive, legislative, administrative, and other posts, from the executive down to local government. For some newcomers, the changeover provided a chance to implement new policies, shake up bureaucratic lethargy, or advance their party standing.

For those more inclined toward social and material advancement, their new positions offered access to state resources; an ability to assign contracts to relatives, friends, and business associates; and opportunities to hand out jobs to selected hangers-on.

Some of those openings for corruption played out at the summits of political power, over the duration of a party's tenure in office. Some, however, came immediately after an election, as party foot soldiers battled for control of local moneymaking ventures, occasionally with violence. After the NPP's first victory, local party loyalists took over a lorry park and several other projects that generated fees in the Ashaiman constituency east of Accra. When the NDC came back eight years later, young NDC militants chased away the NPP supporters but also clashed with another NDC faction and the police, culminating in injuries and one death.[78] As similar incidents played out across the country, the Ashanti regional representative on the Council of State openly condoned such takeovers, stating, "If NDC supporters are taking over public offices, it is right, because that is exactly what happened in 2001 when former President Kufuor took over office."[79]

Winner Takes All

Scrambles for lucrative rents extended across many institutions, all the way to the summit of executive power. While some instances clearly skirted or violated the law, many were sanctioned by Ghana's constitution. Unlike countries that accorded greater powers to the parliament or where systems of proportional or decentralized representation tended to spread out some share of political authority among multiple actors, elections in Ghana were decided by simple majority. In such a first-past-the-post election marked by two dominant and sharply competitive parties, the candidate or party with just over 50 percent of the vote inevitably emerged fully victorious and those with less—even just a percentage point less—were effectively shut out.

Ghana's reliance on a strong executive also set the stage for a "winner takes all" system. The 1992 constitution not only established the presidency as paramount—over and above the legislature—but also gave the chief executive authority to directly appoint people to a wide range of state and administrative positions. In addition to cabinet ministers and a large presidential staff, those included the heads of departments and agencies, chief executives of state-owned enterprises, board members of all state institutions, and 30 percent of the members of district assemblies—nearly four thousand posts.[80]

While not necessarily the intention of the constitutional framers, that vast power of appointment had detrimental consequences for Ghana's democracy. It gave the winner of the presidency a large pool of positions to dole out as rewards to loyal political supporters and, if there was also a change in governing party, to dismiss many of the previous occupants. First, the expectation of a sweeping changeover—with all the attendant shifts in future opportunities to acquire or lose wealth—injected greater urgency into the electoral process, heightening its monetization, partisanship, and risk of violence. Second, the wholesale and politically motivated dismissal of so many sitting personnel not only deprived the state of experienced administrators but also opened the doors to newcomers chosen on the basis of political loyalty, not competence. Third, a further constitutional stipulation that the president appoint a majority of his cabinet ministers from among sitting members of the parliament tended to make the legislature even more politically subservient to the executive. The powers of parliamentary members to exercise oversight of presidential decisions were thus diminished. With limited scrutiny, several ill-considered external aid and investment agreements were adopted, leading in some cases to huge financial losses to the state.[81]

The constitution did not mandate the size of the cabinet, but Ghana's number of ministers has been high. Moreover, during the first three decades following the restoration of electoral rule there was a strong inflationary tendency as each succeeding president created yet more patronage positions for party colleagues. Rawlings set the pace, naming 83 full and deputy ministers in his first term and 82 in his second. Kufuor started with 88 ministers and ended with 93.[82] In 2005 the African Peer Review Mechanism, in which African experts evaluated countries' governance performance, cited the large size of Kufuor's cabinet as a shortcoming.[83] When the NDC's Mills was elected, the number of ministers dipped slightly to 75 but then bounced back up to 84 under his successor, Mahama. Although the NPP chided Mahama for making too many ministerial appointments, when its own leader, Akufo-Addo, named his first cabinet in January 2017, there was an expansion to 110 full and deputy ministers, and then 113 in 2021.[84] The Ghana Center for Democratic Development criticized not only the large cabinet but also Akufo-Addo's "super-sized presidential staff and retinue," numbering 998 individuals.[85]

There were many calls over the years for constitutional amendments and other reforms to limit the system's "winner takes all" nature and thus reduce the influence of money politics. The NPP and NDC, when in opposition, sometimes added their voices to those calls, but when in power tended to forget them. Finally, in 2010 the Mills administration appointed a Constitutional Review Commission to consider amendments. While recommending a variety of measures, including to depoliticize the national development planning process, the commission treaded cautiously when dealing with presidential appointment powers. It acknowledged that they were "too huge" and urged unspecified steps to "reduce political patronage in the choice of appointments" but otherwise proposed leaving much of that authority intact. Regarding the local district assemblies, the commission suggested retaining presidential authority to nominate 30 percent of members, but on the recommendation of traditional chiefs, and to grant the parliament the authority to permit political parties to openly contest the elected assembly seats at some unspecified future time.[86] Those modest proposals were too much for the government, which rejected any changes in the district assemblies and only accepted a few minor reforms.[87] Not even those were implemented before the NDC was voted out of office in 2016, and the next NPP administration expressed little interest in pursuing them.

Against the authorities' stubborn resistance to substantive electoral and institutional reform, there was a drumbeat of criticism from leading voices in Ghana's universities, think tanks, and civil society groups. Until his death (in November 2020), Rawlings decried the "cancerous growth" of corruption and electoral malfeasance under both the NPP and NDC:

> Right from constituency primaries for party executives to regional and national executives and even the election of presidential candidates, huge monetary and material inducements of offensive proportions are employed to sway elections in favour of the highest bidder. . . . If we look on as our political process is abused with monetary and material inducement as the basis of determining who wins elections at even the grassroots level, wherein lies the basis for the sacrifices many made with their lives to guarantee decent political development for Ghana?[88]

A handful of NDC and NPP leaders made similar criticisms from time to time. On a rare occasion in 2020, a bipartisan forum of legislators acknowledged that the "opulent and shameful monetisation" of the parties' candidate selection process had contributed to turning the parliament into a "preserve of the elite and wealthy."[89] Ordinary Ghanaians expressed far more scathing opinions, reflecting widespread cynicism about politics and politicians. Samuel Ofori Bekoe, president of the University Teachers Association of Ghana, commented, "People enter politics not to contribute their quota to national development, but rather to amass wealth."[90]

10

Corruption the Democratic Way

With Ghana's robust legacy of anticorruption discourse, each newly elected administration deemed it politically expedient to reiterate a strong commitment to combatting the problem. President John Kufuor of the New Patriotic Party (NPP), the first opposition figure to win against an incumbent, set the tone during his swearing-in: "We pledge to cut waste and corruption from public life. There will be, under this administration, ZERO TOLERANCE for corruption and I make a solemn pledge to you my compatriots and fellow citizens, that I shall set a personal example."[1] Nearly eight years later, while presidential candidate John Atta Mills was campaigning to return the National Democratic Congress (NDC) to power, he proclaimed during an election debate, "As President I will lead the fight against corruption. I will not allow any of my ministers, my party faithfuls or cronies who are involved in corruption to go scot-free. . . . You know with corruption you must be seen to be biting and not only barking."[2] After Mills's death and ascension to the presidency of his second-in-command, John Mahama also emphasized the importance of cleaning house within one's own ranks: "This is the first government that is actually investigating corruption under its tenure and sanctioning people who hold public positions," even claiming that he had done more to counter graft than any other president.[3] Mahama's successor, Nana Akufo-Addo of the NPP, touted not only his administration's various anticorruption measures but also his personal integrity: "I did not come into public life to make money out of public service and members of my family know fully well that they have to behave and are not involved in anything untoward. . . . Public service is just that—service and not an avenue for making money."[4]

No one expected presidential affirmations to do much more than encourage greater action within the administration, in the judicial sphere, and among anticorruption campaigners. In the absence of verifiable ways to measure corruption, assessing the real impact of high-level initiatives has been impossible. Nor has the transition to multiparty elections clearly improved the situation. Scholars of corruption have noted that democratic transitions elsewhere have been plagued by problems. According to Susan Rose-Ackerman, some forms of corruption might actually increase in periods of democratic transition, given the persistence of patronage politics, vote buying, influence peddling, and other types of fraud.[5]

Seasoned Ghanaian experts cited another factor: a slackening of anticorruption controls, especially in comparison with the rigors of the pre-electoral era. During the early years of the transition, noted former investigator B. A. Sapati, things "got out of hand by way of people thinking they could do anything and get away with it. . . . Everything got relaxed. The criminals sharpened their tools and started all over."[6] Nearly a decade later, at the end of the Kufuor presidency, Vitus Azeem, then executive secretary of the Ghana Integrity Initiative, made a similar observation. The Provisional National Defence Council (PNDC) period, he remarked, "scared everyone," and corruption went dormant for a time. But then it gradually came back. With the restoration of electoral rule in 1992, corruption only "worsened" further.[7]

A "Zig-Zag" Score

How bad was the corruption? From time to time, estimates based on annual reports by the auditor general's office pointed to staggering numbers. In the three-year period 2012–14, losses of public moneys averaged about $3 billion a year, or three times the total aid Ghana then received. While some losses undoubtedly resulted from bureaucratic mismanagement and incompetence, some disappeared through apparent embezzlement or by being intentionally siphoned off through improper public procurement practices, with officials inflating contract prices paid to vendors for the provision of goods or services and pocketing the difference. As an example, Reverend Richard Quayson, a deputy commissioner for the constitutionally mandated Commission on Human Rights and Administrative Justice, asked, "How is it possible that the African Development Bank can construct a 150-bed hospital in Accra at the cost of less than $3 million, and yet when the Ghana government constructs a 60-bed hospital in the district, it costs the nation more than $25 million. How?"[8]

Each year since the return of elections, under the administrations of both main parties, a variety of scandals surfaced, whether involving a former public official caught embezzling funds, a procurement officer who solicited bribes from contractors, or a businessman who used his state connections to arrange favorable trade or investment deals. When exposed in the media or brought to trial, such cases gave a glimpse of the problem in specific parts of the administration or sectors of the economy. But as in other nations around the world, formal accusations or trials could only give a blurry picture of corruption's scope. Unlike assault, robbery, or similar crimes, most parties to a corrupt arrangement are complicit to some extent and thus have no incentive to alert the authorities. Without dependable police or court records, the closest approximation of the extent and shape of corruption in Ghana generally came from "perception" surveys, when available.

The best known were those of Transparency International, the global nongovernmental organization founded in 1993 with notable corporate financing. Two years later it began compiling a Corruption Perceptions Index (CPI) by which to rank countries around the world, beginning initially with 41 states and reaching 180 by 2020. Ghana joined the list for the first time in 1998 and

Corruption the Democratic Way

was assigned a CPI score every year after, essentially a composite of the results of a dozen international business and risk assessment surveys. Figure 10.1 shows two side-by-side series; because Transparency International changed not only the scale of its indices in 2012 (from 0–10 to 0–100) but also the methodology for calculating the CPIs, the scores before and after that year are not directly comparable. For reference, which of the two parties was in power during those years is also indicated, with no claim that the policies of either party necessarily influenced the CPI changes. That qualification aside, a few observations are in order. With some ups and downs, there was an overall improvement in Ghana's CPI score during the 1998–2011 period, under both NPP and NDC administrations. In the second series for 2012–21, the CPI's upward swing initially continued under the NDC but then dropped during that party's final two years in office. It resumed increasing when the NPP took over but still lagged behind the NDC's 2014 peak. Observed Mary Addah, program manager of the Ghana Integrity Initiative, Ghana's overall CPI score reflected a "zig-zag" pattern.[9]

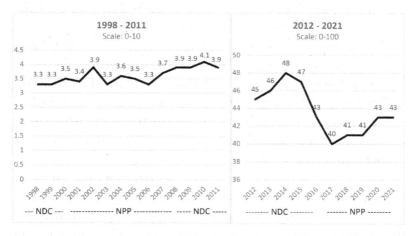

FIGURE 10.1. Corruption Perceptions Index for Ghana. Because of different scales and methodologies, the two CPI series are not directly comparable. Data from Transparency International, www.transparency.org.

Transparency International acknowledged that the CPI, whatever the year or methodology, was not designed to capture all aspects of corruption, including private sector corruption, tax fraud, money laundering, or illicit financial flows. The absence of citizens' perceptions was a particular limitation, failing to capture aspects that lay outside the preoccupations of international business and financial agencies. Fortunately, the Afrobarometer research project, which has conducted periodic (but not annual) public opinion surveys in many African countries, began polling Ghanaians' views in 1999. Its surveys, administered locally by the Ghana Center for Democratic Development (CDD-Ghana), have sampled 2,400 people, both urban and rural, in all regions; to ensure that the respondents were not only from among the more educated (and better-off) populations, the interviews were conducted in English as well as local African languages.[10]

Figure 10.2 gives an overview of responses over the years to one question: How well or poorly is the government fighting corruption? In half the surveys a majority of respondents thought the government performed "fairly well" or "very well," but in half only a minority thought so. With respect to which party was in office at the time, the NPP appeared to perform better than the NDC, although in the 2019 survey the NPP had the second lowest score overall.

As summarized by two researchers from the CDD-Ghana, the survey conducted in 2019 provided considerable detail on other aspects of Ghanaians' views about corruption. That year, just over half the respondents, 53 percent, believed that corruption had worsened "somewhat" or "a lot" during the preceding year. To try to capture Ghana's economic disparities and corruption's uneven impact across social class, the survey categorized respondents according to a "lived poverty" scale (experiencing deprivation of food, water, cash income, health care, and other necessities). More Ghanaians in the "high lived poverty" category, 67 percent, believed that corruption had worsened, compared to 47 percent with "no lived poverty." In other words, poorer Ghanaians felt negative impacts from corruption more than those who were better off. The

Corruption the Democratic Way

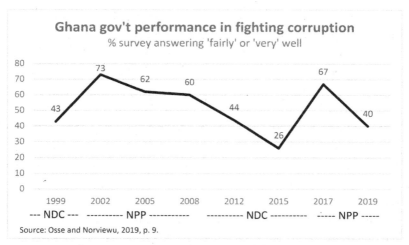

FIGURE 10.2. Ghana government performance in fighting corruption, 1999–2019, measured by percentage of surveyed respondents rating that performance as "fairly" or "very" well. Data from Lionel Osse and Newton Norviewu, "Ghanaians Perceive Increase in Corruption Level, Give Government Low Marks on Fighting Graft," Afrobarometer and Ghana Center for Democratic Development, news release AD333, December 4, 2019, 9.

survey also looked at interactions between citizens and specific sectors of the state. Asked whether they had to pay a bribe, give a gift, or provide some other favor in exchange for access to a public service, 42 percent said they had to do so to avoid a problem with the police and 39 percent to receive police assistance. To obtain an identity document, which is supposedly freely available to all citizens, 28 percent had to pay a bribe. For access to medical and public school services, the results were 17 percent and 15 percent, respectively.[11] After the NPP's reelection in 2020, another survey conducted by the CDD reported that 62 percent of respondents were "not at all or not very confident" about the Akufo-Addo government's capacity to curb corruption and high-level impunity.[12]

Scandals Galore

As in earlier periods of Ghanaian history, governments' efforts to curb corruption had two main aspects: institutional mechanisms (new laws, regulations, and bodies) to prevent, dissuade, or expose corrupt practices; and punitive action to clean house, that is, root out the "bad apples." Many lawmakers, experts, and activists agreed that institutional measures would have the greatest long-term benefit. Yet progress on that front was painfully slow, sporadic, and limited, its impact evident only in time. By contrast, exposing and sanctioning corrupt individuals was more immediate and visible. It made for dramatic media copy—which in turn influenced public perceptions of both corruption and governments' anticorruption commitment. Above all, in Ghana's highly partisan atmosphere, corruption trials and accusations provided rich political fodder for the leaders and foot soldiers of both main parties.

During President Rawlings's first two elected NDC governments, many suspected corruption cases came to light, through both media exposés and the work of the Commission on Human Rights and Administrative Justice (CHRAJ), an independent body established under the constitution. In 1996 an interior minister, agriculture minister, and presidential aide were forced to resign after a public uproar sparked by a CHRAJ investigation. Most other cases, however, only implicated lowly officials: police officers who used their authority to extort a foreign businessman, district officials who embezzled funds from development projects in the Afram Plains near Lake Volta, a housing official who defrauded staff, and irregular procurement contracts signed by a customs commissioner, among other instances.[13] A probe was opened into one high official, the chief executive of the then-state-owned Ashanti Goldfields Corporation. Many believed he was targeted in retaliation for a political falling out with Rawlings.[14] Nothing came of that investigation by the time the NDC was voted out of office.

The ascension of President Kufuor's NPP in 2000 came with high expectations, not least in going after officials suspected of misusing state resources. With one exception, most former cabinet ministers swept up by anticorruption proceedings under Kufuor belonged to the NDC. The accused complained they were victims of a political witch-hunt. The NPP government replied that it was just seeking justice. The fact that most defendants were NDCers was at least partly a reflection of the circumstances: they had been in power for years and thus had access to corrupt opportunities, while the NPP had not. Still, the trials certainly held political benefits for the NPP. They simultaneously bolstered the Kufuor government's credibility and delegitimized its political rivals.

The first high figure brought to court, Mallam Yusif Issah, while not an NPP member, was Kufuor's appointee as youth and sports minister. After promising to use "a big broom to sweep out all the rot" left in the ministry by the previous administration, Issah was soon tried and sentenced in 2001 to four years in prison for causing the state a financial loss of $46,000.[15] Several other former ministers were also imprisoned that decade, all of them from the NDC. In a prosecution initiated by the attorney general (and future president) Nana Akufo-Addo, Victor Selormey, an ex–deputy finance minister, received eight years for authorizing the transfer of $1.2 million to a Texas-based company owned by a personal friend that failed to deliver computers to Ghana's court system.[16] In another case, Selormey and Dan Abodakpi, a former minister of trade and industry, were jointly charged with conspiracy, fraud, and causing a $400,000 financial loss. After five years—and the death of Selormey from a cardiac condition—Abodakpi was sentenced to an exceptionally stiff term of ten years.[17]

Meanwhile, the biggest and most complicated case wound its way through the courts in 2001–3. It stemmed from the Quality Grain scandal, named after a US company that in the late 1990s was supposed to develop a massive 20,000-acre rice project in Ghana. The Rawlings government saw it as a potential boon that, if successful, could reduce dependence on imported rice. Officials therefore extended assistance to the Quality Grain Company, including by guaranteeing sizable loans. The company, however, went bankrupt after the owner squandered much of its resources on lavish personal spending in the United States. Unable to try the owner, the authorities went after five Ghanaian officials instead, including Kwame Peprah, the finance minister who signed the deal; Ibrahim Adam, the agriculture minister; and George Yankey, the Finance Ministry's legal director. All were charged with causing $20 million in losses. The three were found guilty, with Peprah drawing a four-year sentence and Adam and Yankey sentenced to two years each.[18] The law on causing financial loss to the state (which the prosecution used in other cases as well) generated considerable controversy. As the judge noted "with sadness," the charges against the defendants related primarily to how they implemented "orders from above."[19] He also remarked, "This is not a case of stealing or corruption."[20]

The case of Tsatsu Tsikata, a former chief executive of the Ghana National Petroleum Corporation (GNPC), also revolved around losses incurred under his management. As part of a scheme to use high-end cocoa earnings to offset the cost of oil imports, the GNPC guaranteed a loan that a private cocoa company received in 1991 from a French aid agency. Five years later the company defaulted on the loan, obliging the GNPC to pay it off instead, for a loss of GH₵230,000 ($37,000 at the new exchange rate). In 2008 an Accra court ruled that Tsikata was criminally liable for the loss and sentenced him to five years. Leaders of the NDC and activist groups allied with the party condemned the case as politically motivated.[21] That was a view shared beyond the party's partisan supporters, given the clear pattern of prosecutions of other former NDC officials, as well as the filing of charges against Nana Konadu Agyeman-Rawlings, wife of the ex-president, in connection with the acquisition of a privatized cannery by the 31st December Women's Movement, which she headed.[22]

The lopsided nature of the Kufuor government's judicial action was evident in the absence of any notable NPP defendants. Even Kufuor's former youth and sports minister, Mallam Yusif Issah, had belonged to another party (the People's National Convention); he later accused the then–attorney general,

Akufo-Addo, of sacrificing him so that his ministerial post could be given to an NPP member.[23] During the eight years of the Kufuor administration, there nevertheless were at least four notable scandals implicating NPP figures, most driven by media exposés. None ever reached the courts. The "Bamba-gate" affair involved a deputy minister of presidential affairs, Moctar Bamba, suspected of fraudulent visa dealings, forgery, and abuse of office to incorporate a private company. Although the attorney general declined to prosecute, claiming he did not believe there was criminal intent, Bamba nevertheless was compelled to resign.[24] Kofi Asante, a former diplomat and executive secretary of the government's Energy Commission, similarly stepped down after a leaked investigation by the auditor general detailed malfeasance in acquiring vehicles, spending significant funds on a building renovation, and arbitrarily raising the salaries of favored staff members.[25] Other affairs were investigated by the CHRAJ, including one involving Richard Anane, a prominent NPP legislator and minister of roads and transport. Although the commission absolved him of outright corruption, it found that he had abused his office and lied to the parliament, prompting his resignation.[26]

Finally, the purchase of a hotel by one of Kufuor's sons raised questions about whether the president had used his influence to facilitate the deal. A CHRAJ inquiry found no evidence that Kufuor had personally engaged in corruption or conflict of interest.[27] Not everyone was convinced the transaction was entirely aboveboard, however. A subsequent examination by the independent newspaper *Palaver* highlighted lapses in the CHRAJ report, including a failure to thoroughly probe how a consortium of banks approved the deal's $3.5 million funding. The consortium included not only two wholly or partially state-owned Ghanaian banks but also the regional investment bank of the Economic Community of West African States (ECOWAS); at the time the loan was approved, the ECOWAS bank was headed by a member of Kufuor's Council of State and Kufuor chaired the regional body. In its usual sensationalist style, the newspaper affirmed, "'Hotel

Kufuor' is about corruption; it is about conflict of interest; it is about abuse of office."[28]

The evident political bias in judicial undertakings was not condemned only by the NDC. A secret document sent to Washington in January 2009 by US ambassador Donald Teitelbaum—and later publicly exposed by the hacker activists of Wikileaks—referred to the Ghanaian authorities' "use of the judicial process to persecute political opponents." The diplomat also noted Kufuor's decision at the end of his presidency to grant full pardons to all convicted NDC ministers, interpreting those acts as a tacit admission there had been judicial abuses.[29] The pardons—granted literally during Kufuor's last hours in office—may also have had an immediate political calculation: to dissuade Mills's incoming NDC administration from retaliating in kind.

Before taking office, Mills had signaled his intention to pursue anticorruption efforts in a more nonpartisan fashion, a clear critique of the NPP's focus on targeting party rivals. The decision caused some controversy within the NDC, with insiders indicating that Rawlings in particular was incensed that Mills did not go after former NPP ministers.[30] Instead, the first major instances of housecleaning under the new NDC administration involved officials of the president's own party. Just a few months into his term, allegations of financial malpractices involving Minister of Youth and Sports Mohammed Muntaka were investigated by the national security service. The probe found evidence of financial irregularities against two lower-ranking officials but not the minister himself—although it did conclude that he had misused his position to arrange a visa and flight to a sporting event for a secretary of the NDC parliamentary majority leader. For that, Muntaka was pressured into resigning.[31] A few months later, several former and current NDC ministers were alleged to have received bribes from a British bridge construction firm. During a trial in London in which the company was found guilty of illegally bribing officials in several countries to secure contracts, there was testimony that £470,792 had been paid out to five Ghanaian officials between 1994 and 1999, that is, under Rawlings. Although Mills instructed his attorney general, Betty Mould-Iddrisu, to investigate, no cases were brought. Nevertheless, two individuals serving in the Mills government, Health Minister Sipa Yankey and Minister of State at the Presidency Ahmadu Seidu, were obliged to resign; a third, who had been slated to become Ghana's high commissioner to Nigeria, lost that appointment. While welcoming the resignations, NPP supporters lamented the authorities' failure to pursue legal action.[32]

The Mills government did file formal charges against several officials of the previous administration. Even before the NPP was voted out, there was notable public controversy over excessive spending to commemorate Ghana's fiftieth anniversary of independence in 2007, but no action was taken to clarify matters. Upon taking office, Mills appointed a commission to examine the "Ghana@50" scandal. Among other irregularities, the commission found that officials had spent more than twice the amount originally approved by the parliament, took out unauthorized loans, and were slow in reimbursing contractors, leading to unplanned interest payments and late fees. The commission recommended that two officials who testified before it, the chairman of the NPP government's National Planning Committee and the chief executive officer of the Ghana@50 Secretariat, be prosecuted, a recommendation upheld by Mills.[33] But the charges of causing financial loss to the state eventually had to be dismissed because Ghanaian law exempted witnesses appearing before presidential commissions of inquiry from subsequent prosecution.[34] There was a prevalent perception within the NDC that the minister of justice and attorney general, Mould-Iddrisu, had bungled the case, contributing to her subsequent removal from that post.

"Judgment Debt"

By that point, another affair had already started to fester, one that would eventually balloon into the biggest—and most politicized—scandal of the NDC administration. In 2006 Alfred Woyome, a businessman and key NDC fundraiser, bid on a contract to build several sports stadiums. After failing to secure the deal, he sued for damages stemming from unpaid consultancy fees. Based on settlement negotiations between Woyome and the attorney general's office, the court awarded Woyome the equivalent of nearly $30 million. Upon realizing that Woyome lacked adequate proof to support his claim, the government tried to block the settlement but the efforts came too late to stop the funds' disbursement. The new minister of justice and attorney general, Martin Amidu, then went to court to try to overturn the deal and recover the funds. Suspecting some NDC figures of facilitating the payment to Woyome, NPP supporters mounted street demonstrations claiming a government cover-up. Independent newspapers, anticorruption associations, and the Trades Union Congress called for an independent inquiry. Adding fuel to the controversy, the outspoken Amidu publicly lashed out against criticisms of him by pro-NDC media and accused both major parties of harboring "hard core criminals" in their ranks. That, plus other tensions within the government, contributed to Amidu's dismissal. Finally, in 2014, the Supreme Court ruled that Woyome's original contract claims were invalid and ordered that he repay the settlement funds, although a subsequent criminal case against him found insufficient evidence to prove intentional fraud.[35]

The furor over the Woyome scandal popularized the phenomenon of "judgment debt," that is, court-ordered settlements paid to contractors or individuals who claimed breach of contract or some other form of injury by the government. Although many such judgments were legitimate, arising from government lapses or violations of domestic or international commercial law, the fact that some resulted from fraud by politically connected businessmen or corrupt conduct by public officials left a strong "stink" to them, to use Justice Yaw Appau's term.[36]

In response to the clamor—and to dispel any notion that the problem occurred only under the NDC—President Mahama (who succeeded Mills upon the latter's death) appointed a commission in late 2012 to conduct hearings. Two and a half years later, the commission, consisting solely of Justice Appau, released a 501-page report implicating thirteen state institutions—under all political regimes. It detailed more than three dozen instances. The commission placed much of the blame for the Woyome case on the original—and "wrong"—court ruling. But overall, the shortcomings were wide-ranging: the inattention or ignorance of "lackadaisical" officials, poor record-keeping or understanding of contract law, political interference in the work of state agencies, and disruptions caused by personnel changes during transitions from one administration to another. Sometimes relatively manageable debts swelled into "outrageous" ones when successive governments stalled on paying and then incurred inordinate interest charges and penalties, as in a 1983 construction debt of less than $9,000 that mushroomed into $35 million by the time it was finally paid in 2009, more than a quarter century later.[37]

Political partisanship was sometimes a factor, the Appau commission found. A foreign company, Construction Pioneers, was contracted to pave several roads in 1996, but the Rawlings government did not pay the bill. The company later won an International Chamber of Commerce arbitration ruling in London for the equivalent of €27.5 million. The subsequent Kufuor administration refused to pay the judgment, citing suspicions of corruption. "Meanwhile," said the commission report, "the bills kept swelling up higher and higher on account of compounding interests and penalties," so that by 2009 the company's claim had grown to €163 million. "The cost to the country of this pettiness is too high."[38] The attorney general at the time, Mould-Iddrisu, ultimately negotiated the sum down to €94 million.

While the Appau commission laid plenty of blame on the governments of both parties, its report contained enough "dirt" against the NPP to suit the Mahama administration's political needs in advance of the next elections. Mahama's official "white paper" on the report emphasized those aspects. The report's findings on one case involving a dispute between the Ghana National Petroleum Corporation (GNPC) and a French commodities bank was especially useful in throwing suspicion on the integrity of Nana Akufo-Addo, the NPP presidential candidate. Akufo-Addo had been the attorney general when a London high court ruled in 2001 that the GNPC owed the French bank $47 million for the Kufuor government's decision to break the contract. Although negotiations later brought that amount down to $19.5 million, the commission accused Akufo-Addo of contributing to the size of Ghana's financial loss.[39] Those details were leaked to the press four months before the report was released.[40] The NPP denied the allegations, but Arthur Kobina Kennedy, a veteran party leader, admitted that the report's political damage was "gargantuan." He added, "That report, in the hands of the NDC propaganda apparatus, would blow a very wide hole in Nana Addo's pretensions to incorruptibility. Every villager and street urchin in Ghana would hear of how Nana Addo willfully colluded with others to make Ghana pay $19.5 million."[41]

While the political flak may have tarnished Akufo-Addo, it did not keep him and the NPP from winning the 2016 elections. But judgment debts, as a political issue, persisted. Among other instances, in 2018 the Akufo-Addo administration terminated an electricity supply contract with a private company, leading an arbitration court in London to order the Ghanaian government to pay $170 million. The NDC demanded legal action against any officials responsible for the "wrongful" and costly termination.[42] None came.

The most explosive scandal during Akufo-Addo's first term involved bribery and corruption within the world of football, a strong passion of many Ghanaians. The resulting outrage led the country's top football official, Kwesi Nyantakyi, to resign his posts in various national, African, and international football associations. The government, however, could claim no credit for resolving that affair, since the original exposé came from an investigative journalist and the attorney general's office failed to prosecute Nyantakyi or his colleagues.

There were numerous other cases. Many further highlighted shortcomings in regulating procurement contracts, in which public officials—often in connivance with private businesspeople—inflated the cost of goods or services purchased by state institutions. In 2018, the chairwoman of the nonpartisan Electoral Commission, Charlotte Osei, and two deputies were fired after a judicial inquiry uncovered procurement abuses during the 2016 election campaign. Another affair, also dating from the end of the previous NDC administration, involved collusion between officials of the National Communications Agency and the National Security Council Secretariat to order antiterrorism surveillance equipment from an Israeli company, at a purported cost of $4 million. While $1 million of that went to a Ghanaian businessman who brokered the Israeli deal, the remainder simply disappeared. After a trial that lasted two years, a deputy national security coordinator and two leading officials of the communications agency were sentenced to five or six years in prison on charges of violating the Public Procurement Act and causing financial loss to the state. In 2021, a court acquitted a prominent NDC member of parliament, Mahama Ayariga, and six others who had been charged with improperly procuring an ambulance.[43]

In a break from the earlier pattern of NPP governments just going after NDC appointees, Akufo-Addo suspended the chief executive officer of the Public Procurement Authority, Agyenim Boateng Adjei, in 2019. The move followed an independent media revelation that he had formed a private company to basically "sell" procurement contracts. When investigations the following year confirmed Adjei's misconduct, the president fired him outright. A coalition of ten anticorruption, media, and civil rights associations welcomed Akufo-Addo's move but argued that he should have gone "the full nine yards" by dismissing the procurement agency's entire board, bringing to court all those who abused the procurement process, and pursuing other high officials suspected of corruption.[44]

No Sector Untouched

Sanctions against political luminaries made for good media copy and provided governments with symbolic trophies to highlight their anticorruption credentials. But for every case of large-scale graft by a senior politician or civil servant, there were scores of less spectacular instances, in various corners of Ghanaian life: a policeman extorting bribes from motorists, a contractor smuggling timber across the border to evade customs, a district administrator pocketing funds earmarked for a local development project, a village chief illegally selling community land, or a school bursar stealing classroom supplies.

In the 2019 Afrobarometer survey, fully 57 percent of respondents said they regarded "most or all" police as corrupt, and another 32 percent said "some" police were. In the eyes of Ghanaians, the police thus belonged to the most corrupt profession in the country.[45] Police corruption was both petty and grand, from street-level bribery and extortion to major criminal enterprises.[46] As the chief law enforcers, police were especially well positioned to cover up their crimes. Some instances nevertheless came to light. But if the errant officers were sanctioned at all, they were most likely to be reprimanded, transferred, or occasionally fired. Rarely were they tried in court. A few dramatic cases implicating commanding officers could not be swept under the rug, however. In 2008, after cocaine seized from a drug trafficker went missing from a police evidence room, an investigating committee reported lapses in police procedure and held some officials responsible but could not pinpoint who actually took the drugs.[47] There were recurrent media reports of police extorting money from illegal timber cutters or soldiers working with illicit gold miners. An especially dramatic scandal involved a police recruitment scam in 2015, in which hundreds of young people paid modest sums to fictitious enlistment agents. Implicated were several policemen, a pastor, and other civilians—as well as a commissioner of the police service's human resources department. Two years later the commissioner was fired.[48]

Next behind the police came judges and magistrates. According to the Afrobarometer survey, 40 percent of respondents believed that "most or all" high court officials were corrupt, and another 45 percent thought that some were.[49] That negative view was fed by repeated exposures of judges taking bribes to influence rulings. As early as the "zero tolerance" campaign of President Kufuor's first term, a chairman of an Accra circuit tribunal was fired for accepting a bribe in a murder case.[50] The subsequent NDC administration dealt with several instances involving judges, most dramatically in 2015 when an investigative journalist surreptitiously filmed scores of judges and lower-ranking judicial staff taking bribes or trying to extort money from litigants. No named judge or magistrate was officially charged, but investigations by the Judicial Council eventually led to the dismissal of five high court judges and twenty-three circuit judges and district magistrates.[51]

Although judicial graft generally did not entail the kind of financial losses associated with embezzlement or other types of corruption and fraud, it was particularly harmful to Ghana's overall system. Commented Kenneth Attafuah, a director of the Commission on Human Rights and Administrative Justice (CHRAJ), "Corruption and inefficiency within the justice system, both civil and criminal, probably constitute the single most serious threat to lawfulness and rule of law in the nation."[52]

Despite common images associating corruption with the public sector, "the private sector is part of the problem," noted Emile Short, head of the CHRAJ. "We are so quick to point to one public officer or the other receiving a bribe, but we are less enthusiastic to condemn the private person or business company that offers the bribe.... The reality is that both the giver and the taker conspire to defraud the public."[53] According to Ghana's National Anti-Corruption Action Plan, nearly two-thirds of private companies paid gifts of some kind to obtain government contracts.[54] Internationally, experts working on corporate governance have also pointed to the role of private businesses. "Often there is a blame game," remarked Georg Kell, executive director of the UN Global Compact, which works to improve business ethics. "The private sector blames the public sector. The public sector retorts that it is the private sector which is the initiator. The truth is that there is supply and demand and both are complicit."[55]

In the early 2000s, revelations emerged that the market for supplying engine fuel to fisherfolk was rife with diversion, black-market dealings, and outright fraud. The government had established a committee to oversee the distribution of a standardized "pre-mix" fuel (a mixture of petrol and lubricant) to ensure that enough quality fuel was available where it was needed. Some committee members discovered missing shipments, orders by fictitious companies or cooperatives, and other abuses. But when they tried to alert the authorities, nothing was done, prompting them to take their revelations directly to the media. One of the whistleblowers, Kojo Mbir, who was a member of the then-ruling NPP, came under party pressure to drop the matter. He refused and went further to self-publish a book that included many incriminating documents. "For me," Mbir explained, "the interest of the state was paramount to the parochial party interest."[56] Eventually the exposures contributed to reforms in the fuel distribution system.

Other media investigations revealed that different economic sectors, from road construction to timber marketing, suffered from various forms of fraud, tax evasion, and smuggling, sometimes with the collusion of public officials, sometimes not.[57] Banks were also afflicted by fraud—and at an increasing rate. According to a banking sector report, the value of all reported cases of fraud in Ghanaian public and private banks reached GH₵115.5 million in 2019. That sum shot up by nearly ten times the following year, to an estimated GH₵1 billion. More than three-quarters of the instances involved bank staff accused of diverting customers' cash deposits.[58]

Customary chiefs were not immune to the temptations arising from Ghana's changing state forms and market relationships. The 1992 constitution officially recognized their role in allocating land held under customary tenure (80 percent of the total), thus giving them considerable power at the local level.[59] In theory, chiefs were supposed to manage land to aid their communities' development. But all too often they sought to advance their own interests. They were aided by the ambiguities, complexities, and changing dynamics of "customary" traditions and norms. Those

Corruption the Democratic Way

not only varied from one region or ethnic group to another but also were constantly reshaped to suit new circumstances and possibilities. Moreover, many chiefs did not function only according to customary roles but had other occupations and sidelines. Some were lawyers or other professionals. Many engaged in business. A few were especially wealthy. Otumfuo Osei Tutu II, who in 1999 became the Asantehene, the highest Asante chief, was ranked as the fifth richest monarch in Africa, with an estimated net worth of $10 million, mainly from selling mining equipment.[60]

Many chiefs continued to abide by expectations that they assign land to legitimate farmers or consult with communities to lease land for businesses and other projects that could generate local jobs and other benefits—a key factor in the chieftaincy's lasting legitimacy. Some, however, abused their custodial duties and treated land under their authority as if it were private property. The practice of chiefs illegally selling land was so widespread that the Asantehene and other high-ranking paramount chiefs periodically warned local chiefs that if they did so, they would be dethroned; some were in fact ousted.[61]

Chiefs often functioned as brokers with foreign companies, signing leases on behalf of their communities with little or no consultation. A paramount chief in Asante Akyem North in Ashanti leased land to a Norwegian company in the late 2000s to produce corn for poultry producers and breweries. However, farmers who lost access to farmland received little compensation and the project brought few wider benefits. The paramount chief, meanwhile, pocketed an undisclosed amount of "drink money," traditionally a small gratuity that in contemporary times can disguise sizable payoffs.[62] In Donkro Nkwanta, a farming community in the Brong Ahafo Region, an attempt by a paramount chief to promote land acquisition by a gold mining company provoked angry youth demonstrations. A protest petition calling on the government to deny the company an exploration permit explained, "If we lose our ancestral lands, which we inherited from generations before us, to mining, no amount of compensation, whether cash or in kind, can adequately replace the loss of the land."[63] There were many other instances of chiefs accused of profiting from deals with illegal timber cutters, embezzling money intended as community royalties, or stealing aid funds provided by donor agencies. The ability of chiefs to monetize their strategic positions in society was one factor in Ghana's proliferation of chieftaincy disputes and succession struggles, bringing serious violence and loss of lives and property in rural (and urban) communities across the country.

Despite constitutional prohibitions against chiefs' involvement in politics, some maintained strong political connections. One of the most glaring examples during the early days of Ghana's democratic transition was Nana Akwasi Agyemang, a wealthy businessman and member of the Asante royal family who served as Kumasi's mayor and then metropolitan chief executive for more than two decades. After forging close ties with Rawlings's PNDC regime, he became a leading member of the NDC when it was founded. That political alignment shielded him from any official sanction over accusations of favoritism in awarding municipal contracts to friends and cronies. It also provided leverage in his ultimately unsuccessful campaign to become Asantehene. Agyemang was removed from office only after the NDC lost power in Accra.[64] More widely, many chiefs operated as de facto political brokers during national and local elections. Candidates often asked chiefs to mobilize voters on their behalf, and "in return for their endorsements," chiefs were "rewarded with money, cars and houses."[65]

Notwithstanding chiefs' informal political influence, the main official political arena at the local level was the district, each with a predominantly elected assembly and a centrally nominated chief executive. At the time of the 1992 transition, there were 110 districts and 10 regions. Through further subdivision, by 2021 their number had grown to 146 districts and 16 regions, along with 109 municipalities and 6 metropolitan areas.[66] The official motivation for expanding the decentralization process echoed that put forward at their creation: to shift some public functions and resources from Accra to local entities and thus bring government closer to ordinary citizens. That, it was argued, would improve decision-making, allow more popular involvement in development projects, and, in the government's words, unleash "local energies, enthusiasm, initiative and organization."[67]

Yet the actual record of Ghana's local government bodies was very mixed. Some scholars, even among skeptics, saw signs of progress across many districts, with more social and economic projects and programs coming to previously neglected areas, rural youths finding opportunities to forge new careers, and people in general acquiring greater interest in local affairs. But since Ghana is marked by sharp economic and social inequalities—within communities and across geographical regions—not all were able to take equal advantage of the benefits and openings. Almost everywhere, elites were those who wielded real power locally, not people from the lower social strata who were supposed to be decentralization's main beneficiaries. The devolution of some political authority and resources to local governments enhanced those elites' dominance even more.

Certain structural defects also hindered the districts' functioning. Although 70 percent of district assembly members were elected on an ostensibly nonpartisan basis, in reality political parties promoted favorites. The remaining 30 percent were appointed directly by the central government. The original motivation for that was to name people with particular skills or improve the representation of women or members of minorities who might not be chosen by electorates. In practice, however, many appointed members were simply stand-ins for whichever party held power in Accra. And they were replaced whenever that power changed. As a result, the often-sharp partisan divisions that plagued Ghanaian politics at the national level were replicated locally. Competition was also fierce within parties because of frequent rivalry between the appointed district chief executives and those members of the national legislature who participated in district affairs.[68]

The financial resources of the districts (coming from central government transfers, local taxes, fees, and levies) were usually limited. But they were still enough to feed graft. The absence of media scrutiny outside the main towns, minimal auditing and supervisory capacities, and the dynamics of electoral money politics combined to provide plentiful incentives and opportunities for corruption. Commented one close analyst of Ghana's district assembly system, "If, as is likely, corruption is more widespread at the local level than at the national level, then decentralization automatically increases the overall level of corruption."[69]

Local corruption was a source of endless complaints—from ordinary citizens, members of district assemblies, and top national officials in the governments of both major parties. In 1997, during Rawlings's final administration, 25 district chief executives—nearly a quarter of the total at the time—were dismissed for "rent seeking." Mills, then vice-president, warned, "Severe sanctions, not excluding criminal prosecutions, would be imposed on any district chief executive caught dipping his hands" into district coffers.[70] None, however, were prosecuted before the NDC left office. In 2001, the new NPP government ordered an audit of all 110 districts. Thirty-seven emerged with a clean bill of health, but the cases of former chief executives from the remaining 73 districts were forwarded to the attorney general's office. The minister of local government warned that those culpable of misappropriating resources would lose their end-of-service bonuses and have to pay back any embezzled funds.[71] Media investigations subsequently revealed further accusations of corruption and improper contracting deals involving several NPP-appointed district executives, but none of those cases appeared to result in anything more than punitive transfers.

The aftermath of the 2008 elections and the NDC's return to office brought another spate of investigations, often into the financial dealings of former NPP appointees, but also landing several NDCers in hot water. The latter included two party constituency chairmen in the Ashanti Region suspected of extorting money from district sanitation workers, a vice-chairman in the western region of Bono arrested for selling insecticides to private businessmen instead of to the cocoa farmers for whom they were earmarked, and the head of security for the Kumasi Metropolitan Assembly fired for shaking down merchants.[72] In 2015, the auditor general's office issued yet another report highlighting poor financial disclosure and possible misuse of funds in 43 district assemblies.[73] The subsequent NPP government conducted further investigations in districts ranging from Kumasi to Sunyani to Ga West. In late 2021, the special prosecutor opened an investigation into bribery in an election for municipal chief executive in Juaben, in the Ashanti Region. The president's favored nominee struggled to win the support of the two-thirds of assembly members required to confirm the appointment. He fell far short in two separate votes, despite allegedly handing out bribes to assembly members. The most dramatic evidence against him was a video circulating on social media showing him openly soliciting repayment of the bribes. "Unhappy with the turn of events," explained a newspaper, "he started pacing the room where the election was conducted, wagging his fingers at some of the assembly members and demanding his money back."[74]

11

Vigilance from Above and Below

> [Fighting corruption] is not a responsibility that just falls on the government or other official bodies. Each of us has a role to play in combating corruption and none of us should be under any illusion, as it is a Herculean task that lies ahead of us.
>
> —Alfred Tuah-Yeboah, deputy minister of justice

As in earlier periods of Ghanaian history, anticorruption efforts continued to entail initiatives by government officials and citizens across the board, including those lower in the social hierarchy. And as before, action by the authorities was not consistent or energetic: some powerholders, after all, were involved in graft, nepotism, and other abuses, while some went through anticorruption motions simply to please Western donors. The National Anti-Corruption Action Plan, drafted in 2011 following consultations with an array of governmental, judicial, professional, media, and civil participants, strongly emphasized the need for an approach "designed with the active participation of the citizenry and their full and sustained involvement in its implementation."[1]

The transition to elections in the early 1990s altered the kinds of anticorruption measures undertaken and the means available to ordinary Ghanaians to press for enforcement. Unlike the loose and sometimes arbitrary methods of Rawlings's public tribunals, the court system emphasized rule-of-law safeguards of defendants' rights and enabled appeals. Those protections reduced abuses and yielded more balanced verdicts and sentences. Yet they also reintroduced lengthy judicial proceedings and gave defendants able to afford lawyers an advantage in stalling or evading justice. Nor was the justice system above partisan political influences, from the appointment of judges to who was targeted by investigators and prosecutors. Parliamentary bickering, moreover, slowed the adoption of necessary legislation and creation of more effective oversight mechanisms.

Constitutionally, Ghanaian citizens had more scope than before to question, speak out, and organize against venal bureaucrats. In a few instances, as in Ghana's nascent oil industry, civil associations were able to win new safeguards to counter the "resource curse" of rampant corruption and fraud that often afflicted other African oil producers. Yet Ghana's wide inequalities in power and wealth still seriously hindered ordinary people's ability to mobilize and influence policy.

A Mountain of Laws

One argument for legalistic approaches to combating corruption was their ability to draw on Ghana's rich tradition of judicial practice and case law. Beyond the customary codes of the precolonial era, Britain introduced its own "common law" courts in 1844, which, as in England, took direction from state legislation and largely followed the precedence of past rulings. Well after colonialism's end, the common law tradition continued to inform the Ghanaian judiciary. Much was imitative. As one Ghanaian legal scholar noted, "Lawyers and judges in Ghana dress like their British counterparts and cases are presented in the same manner as the English courts," to the extent of drawing on English case law.[2] Some Ghanaians, including legal practitioners, believed that the system was too wedded to the formal and sometimes archaic language of the law, contributing to dubious rulings and failing to deliver substantive justice. The innovations of the public tribunal system under the Provisional National Defence Council (PNDC) had attempted to circumvent such cumbersome procedures, although in ways that were sometimes arbitrary and violated defendants' protections.

The 1992 constitution then sought to ground Ghana's legal institutions and practices in liberal democratic approaches to justice. While it left Ghana's common law tradition in place, the document superimposed a "jurisprudence of constitutionalism" that empowered the Supreme Court to overrule precedents that failed to protect constitutional guarantees.[3] Those guarantees explicitly included a range of political and media freedoms, citizens' rights, and formal checks on arbitrary authority. The constitution emphasized the accountability of public officials and asserted that "the state shall take steps to eradicate corrupt practices and abuse of power."[4] Yet it simultaneously undercut its own anticorruption ideals by giving excessively wide discretionary powers to the executive. And however lofty the constitution's language, it was still just language. It failed to challenge many of Ghana's underlying informal political realities: the dominance of money in elections, the role of patronage in party and government functioning, and the inordinate influence of wealthy individuals over the entire state system. In combating corruption, the constitution left a wide gap between aspiration and enforcement.[5]

Ghana's laws against corruption nevertheless continued to evolve, as new ones were adopted to cover specific features or old laws were amended to plug gaps or stiffen punishments. For most of Ghana's existence as an independent state, the Criminal Offences Act of 1960—which covered all manner of crimes from murder, theft, and rape to vandalism and public disorder—was the main tool for prosecuting suspected graft. As originally defined, the act limited the definition of corruption to bribery of public officers and considered it no more serious than a misdemeanor.[6] Only sixty years later, in 2020, did the parliament finally make bribery a felony, subject to penalties between twelve and twenty-five years in prison.[7] Before then, the act was amended to sharpen ambiguous language or outlaw offenses such as human trafficking or child abuse. Certain infractions sometimes associated with corruption were also incorporated. Early in the first (Rawlings) administration of the Fourth Republic, an amendment inserted the crime of causing financial loss to the state, designed to make public officials accountable for improper decisions. Ironically, though introduced by a National Democratic Congress (NDC) regime, the financial loss law was first wielded under a New Patriotic Party (NPP) government to convict several former NDC ministers. There was some debate about whether the law should be repealed—spurred mainly by NDC leaders claiming it was a tool for partisan witch-hunting. But Dan Abodakpi, one of the ministers convicted (and later pardoned), argued for the law's retention, maintaining that the only problem was its interpretation.[8] That view was echoed by a Ghanaian legal scholar who found that courts tended to interpret the financial loss law too broadly.[9]

A variety of other laws further widened the anticorruption net. Four were adopted by the parliament between 2003 and 2008, providing for audits of all national and local state bodies, regulation of all central state funds (with punishments for anyone guilty of mismanagement, bribery, or fraud), transparent public procurement procedures, and prohibition of money laundering.[10] The laundering of corrupt proceeds then became even more difficult with the Companies Act of 2019, which required regular, verifiable financial reporting by private companies. "The phenomenon of the creation of shell companies and opaque financial systems that provide opportunities for the laundering and concealment of illicit wealth is being drastically reduced," maintained Godfred Yeboah Dame, then attorney general.[11]

The most controversial legislation involved officials' wealth declarations, designed to hinder using public office for enrichment. Asset declarations were not a new idea, having featured in earlier constitutions and during Rawlings's unelected and elected regimes. Under the PNDC, the requirement was extended beyond public officers and their families, while undocumented assets were presumed to have been acquired illegally. A scaled-back version survived in the 1992 constitution, requiring high officials to declare assets upon taking office, every four years, and after leaving their posts. The declarations were not public, however, but kept in sealed envelopes at the auditor general's office. As previously, any assets more than known salaries or other income sources were presumed to have been acquired illegally.[12]

The asset declaration system came under intense criticism by anticorruption activists, independent experts, and even some government and party figures. Critics noted that the declarations did not apply to spouses or other family members, allowing corrupt officials to hide ill-gotten property under someone else's name. They also cited the declarations' secrecy and absence of any means to systematically verify the information's accuracy. Even with those shortcomings, many officials failed to file declarations, and higher authorities made little effort to enforce compliance. Shortly after his appointment in 2017 as auditor general, Daniel Yao Domelevo called the asset declaration system a "complete joke." When he learned that his duties included holding onto the declarations, he stated, "I took the constitution, I read it, I took the Act, I read it. And I concluded this is not asset declaration, this is asset concealment."[13]

Two further bills sought to promote transparency in public administration: one to protect whistleblowers, the other to strengthen the constitutional right to information. The Whistleblowers Act, passed in 2006, provided legal protection to public employees who exposed illicit acts and even awarded them compensation if their information led to convictions.[14] It was later amended to extend the same guarantees to private employees.[15]

While the whistleblowers' measure took five years to make it through the lethargic parliamentary process to the president's final signature, the journey of the Right to Information bill was yet more tortuous. The idea was first raised in 1999, but various drafts hit repeated snags, postponements, and delays, despite promises by successive NPP and NDC parliamentary majorities to pass it. Only in 2019 was it finally signed into law. There appeared to be two main reasons for the drawn-out process. Most seriously, in a country where officialdom was accustomed to operating beyond the public eye, there was great reluctance to make it easier for Ghanaians to scrutinize the state's inner workings. As an editorial in the independent *Ghanaian Chronicle* commented, the lags in adopting the legislation were likely because "members of the two major political parties . . . have corruptive tendencies which they are unwilling to curb, and at the same time, do not want exposed."[16] Beyond simply stalling, legislators sought to encumber the bill with multiple restrictions to make it harder for people to obtain information.

That led to the second reason for the delays: a stubborn struggle by activists to minimize the restrictions. The main umbrella body pushing for passage of a strong bill was the Coalition on the Right to Information, which included media, anticorruption, democratic rights, and trade union organizations. Among other shortcomings, the coalition objected to excessive "exemptions" to exclude certain types of information, long deadlines for responding to requests, high processing fees, and an initial proposal for the Ministry of Justice to oversee implementation. Most (though not all) of the objections were addressed in the final act, including creation of an independent Right to Information Commission to manage requests.[17] Even then, getting officials to respond was not easy. In 2020, the coalition submitted information requests to eighteen state institutions in Accra and Kumasi to test the new system. All but two ignored the requests.[18]

Courts' Struggle for Independence

Under the 1992 constitution, the regular state courts constituted the centerpiece of Ghana's judicial system. Except for a few instances heard by traditional councils, crimes of corruption, bribery, and similar offenses fell overwhelmingly under the jurisdictions of those state courts. There were 379 of them in 2018, ranging from the Supreme Court and appeals and high courts across the regions down to local circuit and district courts. About a quarter of the total were in Accra, with the next highest concentration in the Ashanti Region; the northern regions had the fewest courts. While most courts heard a variety of cases, not all judges were sufficiently trained to deal with the often-complex features of financial crimes and disputes. Consequently, two dozen specialized high courts were established in seven regions to hear cases involving commercial conflicts, including major fraud cases.[19] In 2014, five financial administration courts were also authorized to try public officials accused of mismanaging state assets and liabilities.[20] The bulk of the corruption cases involving ex-ministers or other high officials were heard before one of Accra's high courts, except when rulings were appealed to a superior court.

In an effort to ensure the courts' political impartiality, the constitution explicitly excluded any interference by other branches of state power: "Neither the President nor parliament nor any organ or agency of the President or parliament shall have or be given final judicial power." Moreover, the constitution called on the courts to protect the civil and human rights of Ghanaian citizens, prevent the executive and legislature from exceeding their authority, and function as the ultimate referee when laws appeared to violate the constitution or conflicted with each other.[21]

In practice, however, the courts' independence was not unqualified, especially given Ghana's polarized patronage system and executive dominance. From decisions about which cases were prosecuted to how the trials were conducted, partisan considerations often left a clear imprint, eroding public confidence in the integrity of legal institutions.

Officially, all state prosecutions were initiated in the name of the attorney general. In practice, the police service conducted investigations and prosecutions of all but the most serious crimes. Yet police prosecutors were plagued by poor training, limited funds, and "allegations and perceptions of engaging in bribery and corruption," including instances of collusion between prosecutors and judges to extort money from defendants.[22] Major crimes—such as murder, drug trafficking, rape, or misdeeds by current or former officials—were generally referred directly to the attorney general's office. And because the attorney general and minister of justice were the same individual since the democratic transition, the government's interests would weigh heavily on whether or not to prosecute a case. There were several instances in the mid-2000s when parliamentary vetting of nominated ministers exposed possible corruption but those revelations were never investigated.

The vaunted independence of the courts was compromised by various factors. At least initially, most judges had been trained mainly in the common law tradition, which deferred to state authority, a tendency reinforced by Ghana's long succession of authoritarian regimes. As a Ghanaian legal scholar pointed out, grafting new notions of constitutional law that emphasized citizens' rights onto that system could only go so far: "Ghanaians have entrusted a fairly progressive constitution to the care of a rather 'conservative' judiciary . . . that has a trained and long-cultivated inclination to favor the State over the citizen, the public official over the public, power over freedom and, of course, the familiar over the unfamiliar."[23] If the problem of judicial deference to state authority lay mainly in the ingrained attitudes of individual judges, then further education in constitutional rights and the recruitment of new generations of younger court personnel would eventually overcome the problem.

However, the most fundamental obstacles to judicial independence were rooted in the constitution itself, above all the prerogatives it accorded the executive. The president was given authority to appoint all judges to the Supreme Court, the appeals and high courts, and regional tribunals. He was obliged to consult with the Judicial Council, but that was a relatively weak body that generally rubber-stamped presidential nominations. The president could also name whoever he wanted as chief justice of the Supreme Court, provided he consult the Council of State and parliament (the former filled largely with presidential appointees and the latter usually dominated by the president's own party).[24] The position of chief justice was especially powerful. He or she not only appointed judges to fill vacancies in the lower courts (with the president's approval) but also, by convention, could influence proceedings before the Supreme Court by cherry-picking which justices sat on the panels for particular cases.[25]

Not since the Rawlings years had nominated judges been closely identified with a particular party, and over time professional qualifications came to carry increasing weight in their selection. Still, the political authorities had considerable latitude in picking at least some judges deemed favorable to the government. One particularly egregious example came in 2002. During the trial of Tsatsu Tsikata, the NDC's former petroleum corporation head, the defendant initially won Supreme Court support for disqualifying the court hearing the case. The NPP government, taking advantage of the constitution's silence on the maximum number of Supreme Court justices, named another one just before the ruling was reviewed. His presence was decisive in the Supreme Court's reversal of its earlier decision, paving the way for Tsikata's ultimate conviction. That led critics to claim the authorities had packed the court to achieve the desired result. A few years later, a high court judge who quashed a case of corruption and conflict of interest against a former NPP minister was soon promoted, first to the appeals court and then to the Supreme Court, in what appeared to many as a reward from the ruling party.[26]

Against the thousands of cases heard annually by Ghanaian courts, such instances of questionable conduct by judges and government officials were exceptional. Overall, judicial staff appeared to pursue their roles with political impartiality and professionalism, despite limited training, insufficient funds, and severely overcrowded caseloads. Most donor institutions, in fact, regarded Ghana's justice system as a model on a continent plagued by widespread judicial corruption and overt state interference. According to the Open Society Initiative of West Africa, Ghana's commitment to the rule of law increased steadily after the democratic transition, while its "judiciary has enjoyed a considerable level of independence and the law is generally obeyed by representatives of the executive branch."[27] The degree of Ghanaians' trust in their judicial system has fluctuated, however. According to the Afrobarometer surveys, those respondents who said they had "somewhat" or "a lot" of trust in the courts reached a high of 68 percent in 2005. That level dipped to 44 percent in 2014, before bouncing back up slightly to 48 percent in 2019.[28]

Institution upon Institution

Out of all judicial and investigative bodies, the Commission on Human Rights and Administrative Justice (CHRAJ) won the greatest public credibility. It was created from the constitution's human rights clauses, with a triple mandate to protect human rights, combat corruption, and resolve citizens' complaints about administrative services. The latter role in effect incorporated the functions of earlier ombudsman offices. The CHRAJ was afforded judicial powers to subpoena witnesses and documents. However, if its inquiries uncovered criminal conduct, it could not try anyone, only recommend that the government, attorney general, or courts take action. While the commissioner and deputy commissioners were presidential appointees, their tenures could not be easily revoked, giving them some ability to resist political pressures.[29]

With offices around the country, the CHRAJ not only established a national presence accessible to many citizens outside Accra but also was extremely active. Even from the beginning it handled several thousand cases annually, and in some years its caseload exceeded 10,000. Most addressed rights violations (including domestic custody disputes and abuses against women and children), followed by citizens' grievances against public institutions, and finally a few dozen instances of corruption each year.[30]

Anticorruption cases were only a tiny fraction of the CHRAJ's total, but several early ones cemented its reputation. Under its initial commissioner, Emile Short, the CHRAJ became the first institution to investigate sitting government ministers in 1996. After a series of exposés by the private *Ghanaian Chronicle* newspaper, the CHRAJ examined accusations of corruption, illicit enrichment, and abuse of office against two ministers, Ibrahim Adam (trade and industry) and Colonel Osei Owusum (interior), and two senior presidential advisers, Isaac Adjei Marfo and P. V. Obeng. Following public hearings, the commission exonerated Obeng but affirmed misdeeds by the three others.[31] "The government did not take kindly to our report," Short later recalled.[32] Rawlings rejected the findings and publicly castigated Short by name. Yet Short and his colleagues stood their ground. With only a few months before general elections and public sentiment mounting against the accused NDC officials, the three were ultimately obliged to resign. Commented an analyst, "These cases represented the first time in Ghanaian history that an incumbent government faced investigations, earning CHRAJ a reputation for independence among the Ghanaian public, media and civil society."[33] Other investigations followed, prompting an occasional high-level resignation and even probing accusations against Presidents Kufuor and Mahama, both of whom were cleared.

The CHRAJ, however, confronted many obstacles. Its rulings and recommendations were sometimes rejected by various state institutions—or simply ignored. Some officials subjected to adverse findings went to court to negate the rulings. Two of Short's successors were not confirmed by the government and had to function for years in an acting capacity, with weakened standing. One commissioner was dismissed for unauthorized spending, a serious breach since the CHRAJ suffered from chronic budgetary shortfalls. Insufficient state support combined with a large caseload contributed to significant staff turnover. The commission sought to narrow the financing gaps by accepting funds from the United Nations and the Danish, US, and British aid agencies. It also built close ties with domestic associations devoted to strengthening democracy and combating corruption. The commission, in fact, played a key role in establishing two of the most influential civil society anticorruption groups, the Ghana Integrity Initiative and the Ghana Anti-Corruption Coalition.[34]

The Serious Fraud Office (SFO), created in 1993, was preoccupied with offenses involving major financial losses to the state. Some saw an element of continuity with the PNDC's anticorruption efforts. An executive director, B. A. Sapati (who had been an investigator in the 1980s), attributed the need for such institutions in part to the rise in fraud and corruption that accompanied the democratic transition's loosened restrictions. "Everybody is saying it's all over," he said in an interview at the SFO headquarters, "maybe even on a larger scale than it was before, because now you open up every sector of the economy."[35]

Initially there appeared to be little difference in the SFO and CHRAJ anticorruption mandates. The SFO, however, had more powers than the commission, including to directly prosecute cases, freeze suspects' assets and accounts, conduct searches, and seize property deemed to have been acquired illegally. In 2010 the SFO was reorganized as the Economic and Organized Crime Office (EOCO), with an expanded mandate that included money laundering, human trafficking, terrorism financing, cyber-crimes, and computer-related fraud. That expansion more clearly distinguished it from the CHRAJ. Not only did the EOCO tend to deal with more complex forms of financial crime but also its cases more frequently included fraud by private individuals and companies, while the CHRAJ focused mainly on public officials and institutions.[36]

Overall, the SFO/EOCO handled far fewer cases than the CHRAJ, given the former's narrower focus on major financial crimes, averaging about seventy-five annually in 1999–2000, for example.[37] The defendants included local government officials, school administrators, judicial staff, officials of the Ghana Broadcasting Corporation, a few political candidates, and many bank and company executives. Some critics, including a former SFO director, accused the EOCO of not pushing harder to prosecute suspects in the face of reluctance from the attorney general's office.[38] Nevertheless, President Mahama (NDC) specifically referred a case of financial misdeeds at a youth employment scheme to the EOCO for investigation and prosecution. President Akufo-Addo (NPP) subsequently sent a case of conflict of interest by the director of the Public Procurement Authority to the CHRAJ. As a result of the commission findings, the director was subsequently sacked and disqualified from holding any public office for five years, and further charges of money laundering were passed along to the EOCO for investigation.[39]

The auditor general's office was likewise established under the constitution, to monitor use of public funds by various state institutions. It was best known for submitting annual reports to the parliament that in some years enumerated staggering losses resulting from shoddy bookkeeping, embezzlement, public procurement violations, and illicit enrichment. Sometimes the parliament did little but file the reports. But even when the parliament's Public Accounts Committee proposed sanctioning or prosecuting corrupt officials, the attorney general's office often ignored the recommendations.[40]

Generally, the auditor general's office did not itself pursue cases against high-ranking officials. That changed under Daniel Domelevo, a financial management specialist appointed by President Mahama in early January 2017 during the final days of Mahama's administration. Later that year, reinforced by a Supreme Court ruling ordering the recovery of misused state funds, Domelevo issued "certificates of indebtedness" to implicated individuals. The certificates, he explained, sent a message "that you have used government money wrongly, pay it back."[41] He also scrutinized procurement contracts, including one signed by Finance Minister Yaw Osafo-Maafo awarding more than $1 million to a British consulting firm. Domelevo determined that the firm had not done any actual work. In an unprecedented move against a sitting minister, he disqualified the contract and ordered Osafo-Maafo to repay the money.[42] While the minister was challenging the ruling in the courts, President Akufo-Addo removed Domelevo from his position.[43] A coalition of five hundred civil society organizations condemned the dismissal. Emmanuel Gyimah-Boadi, the former executive director of the Center for Democratic Development, commented that while Akufo-Addo's anticorruption credibility was already "in tatters," the auditor general's removal put it "in the coffin."[44]

Close on the heels of the auditor general's abrupt replacement came another embarrassing disagreement, involving the Office of the Special Prosecutor. The office was first created in 2017, after years of agitation by anticorruption activists who hoped that an autonomous prosecutor dedicated specifically to combating graft and not directly under the attorney general would be more effective. Akufo-Addo's first pick promised to shake things up. Contrary to expectations of a partisan choice, he selected Martin Amidu, a jurist who had served as deputy attorney general under both the PNDC and the first elected NDC government, ran for vice-president in the NDC's unsuccessful 2000 election campaign, and served as interior minister and minister of justice in 2010–12 under President Mills. The latter then sacked Amidu for publicly accusing NDC officials of "gargantuan crimes" of corruption.[45] Given Amidu's combative reputation and rift with the NDC, the Akufo-Addo administration may have judged that he would be keen to go after his former comrades. Indeed, several of his initial investigations were directed against ex-members of the Mahama government.

Amidu, however, soon widened his sights. He issued a scathing report against a deal that the NPP government was promoting with a British firm to leverage investment funds from gold mine earnings. Upon examining the Agyapa deal, as it was known, Amidu cited significant risks of bribery, money laundering, and other problems, concerns that were soon echoed by Transparency International and other groups. According to Amidu, the president tried to pressure him into shelving his report. Rather than comply, he dramatically resigned, charging both "political interference" and the authorities' failure to provide his office with adequate staff and resources.[46] Civil society groups and opposition parties cited Amidu's resignation as further evidence that the government was unwilling to give its anticorruption agencies and officers a truly free hand. The authorities, stung by the backlash over the Amidu resignation, promptly named a new special prosecutor, Kissi Agyebeng. He subsequently opened investigations into numerous cases of corruption and fraud, including against public procurement officers, bank executives, police recruiters, and high officials, including a minister of sanitation and water.[47]

Over the years, civil society activists had worked with several of the state's anticorruption agencies, especially the CHRAJ. And they advocated for others, such as the special prosecutor's office. But overall, anticorruption campaigners were not particularly impressed. Nana Oye Lithur, a social rights activist and former gender minister, cited the long list of government bodies and offices responsible for combating graft. "We have institutions and they have not made any meaningful impact," she declared in 2019. "To what extent have they actually reduced corruption in Ghana?"[48] Some added that when violators were brought to account, that was at least partly because of pressure from nonstate actors, including the press, civil society, and ordinary citizens.

Media Watchdogs

From colonial times, Ghana had a long history of robust, independent journalism, although the postindependence era featured many years of censorship and control. The constitution of 1992 was thus notable for ushering in a renewed epoch of press freedoms. It regarded an unfettered press as essential for promoting open democratic debate, providing alternative sources of information, and ensuring that the actions of high officials, prominent businessmen, and other dignitaries could be questioned. Through print newspapers and radio and television stations, a wide range of nonstate viewpoints had new avenues for expression.

A series of legal and institutional reforms followed to make the constitution's provisions a practical reality. First, a PNDC-era press licensing law—mainly to bar critical media—was scrapped, opening the way for private newspapers and FM radio stations. Then in 1993 the parliament established a National Media Commission (NMC) to ensure press freedom and independence, "insulate the state-owned media from government control," and promote professional journalistic standards. Although two members of the commission were appointed by the president and three by the parliament, the majority came from nongovernmental groups, such as the journalists' association, teachers' union, legal bar, religious organizations of various denominations, and media and communications training institutes. The NMC's chairperson was selected by the commission members.[49] One lever of government control over media remained for nearly a decade longer, however: a criminal libel law, under which journalists, editors, and publishers had been fined or imprisoned for stories deemed libelous by public authorities. Only after the opposition NPP came to power was the libel law finally repealed. While libelous stories could still bring civil suits or reprimands from the NMC, they no longer incurred criminal penalties. "People are free to write about anything," commented Paul Adu-Gyamfi, an NMC chairman.[50]

The elimination of most press restrictions opened the way for an explosion of new media outlets. According to the Media Foundation of West Africa, as of 2019 there were 136 newspapers and nearly 400 radio stations.[51] By 2017, a total of 128 television stations had been registered, although only 53 were then on the air.[52] The state-owned Ghana Broadcasting Corporation (GBC) long operated a national network of television and radio stations, covering much of the country, in English and several indigenous languages. Several private television networks also developed a national presence, while private radio stations emerged in most cities and towns. Two state-owned daily newspapers, *Daily Graphic* and *Ghanaian Times*, still had the largest circulations by far (100,000 and 80,000 daily copies, respectively), followed by the *Ghanaian Chronicle* as the most-circulated private newspaper (45,000 copies).[53] While broadcasters reached far more Ghanaians than did the print media, the latter had an impact beyond their raw circulation numbers: most newspapers maintained websites, their print editions were often passed around among multiple readers, and the lead stories of the largest publications provided discussion topics for popular radio talk shows. In the more remote regions of the north, the internet reigned, with 46 percent of people preferring that source, compared to radio (27 percent), television (18 percent), and newspapers (9 percent).[54]

The constitution did not merely proclaim press freedom but went further to encourage media to actively contribute to state transparency and accountability, in the public interest. Only a small minority of outlets did so, however. Most—state-owned or private—followed market dynamics to boost advertising revenue by maximizing newspaper sales or broadcast audiences. Reporting hard news was part of that, but so was covering entertainment, sports, and other affairs, along with heavy doses of rumor and gossip about the personal lives of celebrities and other prominent Ghanaians.

A handful of private newspapers began crusading against corruption during Rawlings's NDC governments. Both the *Ghanaian Chronicle* and the *Independent* ran articles naming government officials suspected of profiting from their positions. Since the authorities were openly hostile to critical media outlets and readily employed the criminal libel law against them, analysts viewed such muckraking forays as a form of "guerrilla journalism."[55] The newspapers eventually were vindicated when the exposures forced several officials to resign in 1996.

For the *Ghanaian Chronicle*, that outcome also signaled commercial success and committed the newspaper to further specialize in investigative reporting. As one of its journalists, Arthur Adjei, told a researcher, "Political scandals, corruption in official circles. Politicians and their outrageous remarks sell."[56] That drive for headlines impelled the *Chronicle*, *Statesman*, *Guide*, and other private newspapers to sometimes let professional standards slip by running articles based largely on rumors and speculation, failing to corroborate sources, and paying for inside information or documents. In the worst cases, journalists accepted payments from wealthy figures, either to kill incriminating articles or to promote damaging stories against political or business rivals.[57] A handful of reporters thus mirrored the kind of corrupt behavior they claimed to oppose.

The private media's combative style was in some measure a reaction to the Rawlings government's continuing (though increasingly ineffective) efforts to intimidate journalists. A 1999 libel case against the editors of the *Statesman* and *Guide*, stemming from articles about the president's wife and culminating in fines and thirty-day prison sentences, was but one dramatic example.[58] After the opposition NPP took office and scrapped the criminal libel law, tensions between the press and authorities eased significantly. But intemperate language and unprofessional conduct were persistent shortcomings. The problem was particularly evident with Ghana's many FM radio stations, prompting George Sarpong, the NMC executive secretary, to condemn the "inflammatory language, hate speech and obscene content" often broadcast over the airwaves.[59]

Initially much of Ghana's private media was staunchly pro-NPP. And when that party took power, the newspapers that specialized in exposing high-level misdeeds relished covering the government's numerous corruption cases against former NDC ministers. But while newspapers like the *Ghanaian Chronicle* often reported positively about the Kufuor government's pronouncements and policies, they also sometimes covered NPP scandals, such as allegations in 2005 that a newly designated deputy interior minister may have engaged in a visa racket and other dubious deals.[60] The *Chronicle* and Joy FM, an independent radio station, broke a series of corruption stories under both NDC and NPP governments. In 2011, the newspaper and station publicized allegations of corruption at a national youth employment scheme, leading the Mahama administration two years later to order a major overhaul and prosecution of the culprits. In 2013, the same two outlets raised serious questions about $35 million in payments by the Ghana Revenue Authority to a Ghanaian-owned information technology company, Subah Infosolutions, to analyze telecommunications traffic although the company did little actual work. The exposure prompted the authorities to suspend the deal.[61] Under Akufo-Addo's subsequent NPP government, Joy FM also played a major role in uncovering corruption by the head of the procurement authority, leading to his dismissal.[62]

Among Ghana's investigative reporters, a few engaged in what became known as "undercover journalism," usually involving disguises, secret recordings, eavesdropping, or other stealthy means of acquiring information. Several worked for private newspapers or radio stations. The best known were the reporting team of Tiger Eye, headed by Anas Aremeyaw Anas, formerly of the *Crusading Guide* newspaper. Anas often disguised himself to acquire surreptitiously filmed abuses of patients at a psychiatric hospital or customs officials taking bribes from cocoa smugglers. Some footage was aired by television stations, and some was edited into documentary films shown in public theaters. Several Tiger Eye documentaries stirred wide outrage. Particularly shocking was one that captured football referees and officials accepting bribes from reporters disguised as fictitious sponsors. When it was first shown at the Accra International Conference Center, the main auditorium was packed.[63] In November 2022, Charles Adu Boahen, a minister of state in the Finance Ministry, was fired and referred for prosecution after a Tiger Eye exposé of fraud in the artisan gold mining sector cited evidence that he may have solicited payoffs from potential investors.[64] Tiger Eye's popularity was evident in the appearance of automobile bumper stickers and painted slogans on walls proclaiming "Anas is watching."[65]

Anas cited the seriousness of the abuses to justify Tiger Eye's use of devious methods. "I see what is happening in my country as an extreme disease and we in the media must be the extreme remedy. We ought to ensure that we make public officials accountable."[66] Some critics disagreed with such deceptive tactics, arguing that they were sensationalistic, verged on entrapment, and therefore were not true journalism.[67] However, the president of the Ghana Journalists Association, Roland Affail Monney, endorsed Anas's style. Ghana's security agencies should have conducted similar investigations, he said, but did not. "Therefore, we should commend those who have risked their lives to do so."[68]

That risk was real, as dramatically highlighted by the murder a few months later of Tiger Eye reporter Ahmed Hussein-Suale. Among the team's most vociferous critics was Kennedy Agyapong, an NPP member of parliament. Agyapong was so incensed that he sought to unmask Hussein-Suale and several other team members by broadcasting on his television station their photos and home addresses—and then urged viewers to beat them. Agyapong denied any role in Hussein-Suale's shooting but added that he had no regrets about his broadcast, since the journalists were "evil."[69]

In contrast to independent media outlets, the state-owned press was far less active in trying to ferret out misdeeds, especially those involving high officials. The *Daily Graphic* and GBC did cover some major scandals, but usually only after the stories were already broken by others or were officially acknowledged by government inquiries, reports, or sanctions. The creation of the NMC, which took over the government's role in hiring and dismissing state media directors and staff, was in principle supposed to insulate them from direct government pressure and give them a freer hand in pursuing worthwhile stories. But old habits died hard. Professor Kwame Karikari, a former director of the University of Ghana's School of Communication Studies, noted that it took the GBC a long time to report on the scandal involving Alfred Woyome, a key NDC financier. The staff avoided the story not because of any government pressure but because of "their own timidity. . . . They are independent, but they are not yet awakened from the slumber of all the decades of state control." Karikari, a longtime journalist and activist, described the journalism practiced by the state media as "civil service journalism."[70] In a sign of possible change, in 2017 the NMC appointed Karikari chairman of the board overseeing the *Daily Graphic* and its related publications.[71]

While most outlets that sought to expose corruption did so to sell newspapers or attract listeners, from time to time their articles also prompted investigations, dismissals, resignations, and even prosecutions. For Anas, who sometimes provided his videotaped footage directly to the police, such outcomes were an explicit goal.[72] Far too often, sensationalist treatments of corrupt officials focused attention mainly on implicated individuals and did little to advance public understanding of corruption's underlying political and social factors, let alone long-term solutions. Some media, however, also contributed to wider discussions by running analytical essays, declarations of civil society associations, and reforms proposed by anticorruption groups. Two FM stations, Adom and Joy, partnered with the Center for Democratic Development and the Ghana Anti-Corruption Coalition to regularly air a program called *Corruption Watch*.[73]

"We Want Change Now!"

As with media liberties, the constitution enshrined ordinary citizens' rights to freely organize, assemble, march, and demonstrate. The first practical advance came in 1993 when a suit by the NPP against the inspector general of police won a Supreme Court ruling declaring unconstitutional a requirement of a police permit before demonstrators could assemble.[74] Organizers still had to notify local police of the details of their event, ostensibly to identify any security concerns and arrange for an orderly action.

Two years later came a dramatic test, at a time of political tensions and labor unrest. In March 1995, further liberalization demanded by Ghana's external financiers brought the introduction of a 17.5 percent value added tax (VAT) to replace the previous sales tax. The measure was poorly explained and badly implemented, and merchants sharply raised prices across the board, even on "exempt" goods such as food. Public outrage swept the country. A new opposition coalition, the Alliance for Change, called mass demonstrations to demand withdrawal of the VAT and accelerated democratic reform. The protest was named *Kume preko* ("You may as well kill me now" in Akan), to dramatize the economic pain. The first action, in Accra on May 11, drew crowds estimated at between 50,000 and 100,000, the largest antigovernment outpouring in many years. Signs reflected the demonstrators' dual political and economic grievances: "VAT is the killer, not AIDS," "We want a change now," and "Rawlings give way to a better man." The march was initially peaceful, following negotiations between police and organizers. But then protesters were violently confronted by a proregime group, bringing four deaths and numerous injuries. Another demonstration on May 25 in Kumasi was as large, if not larger, but remained peaceful. Under such pressure, the authorities eventually withdrew the VAT law. (They reintroduced it a couple of years later but with greater tact and at a lower rate.)[75]

The violence of the Kume preko encounter carried lessons for both authorities and protesters. To minimize confrontation, leading police and state officials more often sought some form of accommodation with demonstrators. In turn, organizers of larger national protests mostly sought to avoid clashes that could distract from their message or alienate potential supporters. Hundreds of demonstrations unfolded across Ghana over the years, the bulk of them orderly and peaceful. But police brutality still occurred far too often, and some protesters in both major urban centers and more remote locales turned unruly, disruptive, or violent, leading to occasional deaths.

A two-day protest at the end of June 2022 illustrated the risks that persisted decades after Kume preko. A new group, Arise Ghana, called for action to highlight economic and corruption grievances against the NPP government, with plans to march on Jubilee House, the seat of the presidency. The police objected to plans to picket into the night in such a security zone. When Arise Ghana persisted, the police secured a court ruling ordering changes in the timing, march route, and end point. On the first day, June 28, marchers deviated from that route, leading to chaotic clashes with police. Scores of demonstrators were wounded by police tear gas, rubber bullets, and water cannon; a dozen police officers were injured when protesters responded with stones; and nearly thirty protesters were arrested. The government's information minister tried to justify the crackdown by accusing the organizers of intentionally seeking to "create instability." Arise Ghana in turn denounced police brutality.[76]

Arise Ghana's demands were a familiar mix of grievances. They featured complaints about the economic burdens of high fuel prices and a new digital tax system but were also combined with several corruption-related issues: a call for a probe into the suspected misuse of expenditures for combating the COVID-19 pandemic, an end to illegal seizures of state lands by high officials, and abandonment of the controversial Agyapa royalties deal, which the government was still considering.[77]

Overall, however, corruption was not an issue in most protests: The bulk of mobilizations were dominated by economic and social concerns. During the twenty-five-year span from 1998 through 2022, there were at least 675 distinct protest marches, rallies, marches, labor strikes, and other forms of popular mobilization, as tabulated by this writer from available print media outlets.[78] Of that total, 63—less than 1 in 10—included demands related to corruption, either as a central focus or, more often, as one concern among others. (Those tallies were certainly an undercount. Some forms of protest were so routine that journalists or editors had minimal interest in covering them, and the national media had only a few reporters outside major towns, thus missing actions that occurred in smaller or more remote locales.)

The mobilizations surveyed by this author included both national demonstrations and strikes organized in multiple locations as well as local protests in a single town or village. Their participation ranged from several dozen people to tens of thousands. Some scholars of social movements in Ghana have characterized them as largely "middle class," or at least consisting of educated urban activists.[79] There were some protests in this study's sample that resembled that image. In July 2014, about 300 people joined a protest dubbed "Occupy Flagstaff House" (the old name of the presidential palace) to denounce poor governance and corruption. The participants included lecturers, lawyers, information technology experts, business executives, and members of several recognized civil society groups. Local newspapers referred to them as "middle class," a label some of the protesters may have embraced.[80] But many other actions also included Ghanaians of more humble social origins: urban workers, rural farmers, women market traders, artisans, fisherfolk, village youths, residents of poor neighborhoods, and so on.

Ghana's labor strikes and demonstrations (275 of the total sample) were prompted overwhelmingly by classic worker concerns over salaries, benefits, and job conditions. Yet a handful also incorporated corruption-related demands. At the large Obuasi gold mine owned by the multinational Ashanti Goldfields Corporation, miners staged a wildcat strike in 1999 for higher pay and removal of the managing director.[81] A researcher who interviewed many strikers found considerable animosity toward the director, whom they blamed for mass retrenchments as well as "self-aggrandizement" and "rapacious avarice."[82] Several years later, striking diamond miners demanded the ouster of two managers accused of financial improprieties, while striking gold miners in the Western Region accused the company of bribing local police and Environmental Protection Agency inspectors. They declared, "If you could pay huge bribes to the EPA and police, then pay us our bonus."[83] Bank and cocoa workers in Accra and bus drivers in Kumasi also accused management of corruption, teachers in Wa demanded removal of a polytechnical college rector over financial irregularities, and private transport drivers in the Volta Region called for investigation of their chairman for illicit enrichment and mismanagement of union finances. Sometimes, as during a large demonstration by industrial workers in Tema, protesters directly linked Ghana's economic difficulties to corruption's waste of state resources.

Youths were often in the lead of the numerous community protests across the country. In Bolgatanga, youths demonstrated against police for extorting money from residents. In Ho, the Volta regional capital, they protested a suspected diversion of toll funds by a local executive. In the northern district of Gonja, youths demanded removal of a health insurance manager and an audit into suspected embezzlement from the insurance accounts; the manager happened to be a constituency secretary of the ruling NPP. Elsewhere, youths in the Ave Traditional Area protested a reelection bid by an NDC member of parliament they suspected of corruption. In Kenyasi in the Brong Ahafo Region, similar allegations prompted a march against a district chief executive, also from the NDC—as were most of the young marchers. But youths did not hold a monopoly. In Kumasi, an estimated one hundred "old men and women" marched to protest high prices, power cuts, the collapse of businesses, and high-level corruption. They called the action *Mmrewa re su* (The aged are crying). The route became challenging at an uphill stretch: "They moved [a] few steps and stopped, moved and stopped and requested for water before continuing the march."[84]

Apart from a few protests called by anticorruption civil society groups, corruption featured most often in demonstrations and marches organized by political parties—usually led by the NDC against an NPP government or the NPP against an NDC government. In a slight departure from that pattern, in 2013–14 the People's Progressive Party (PPP), a small Nkrumahist formation, organized three protest marches, in Accra, Kumasi, and Cape Coast, explicitly advocating "Say no to corruption!" According to PPP leader Kwesi Ndoum, the action was not aimed against the government (then run by the NDC) but to press for stronger anticorruption laws and institutions generally.[85]

More consistently, the partisan rivalry between the two main parties drove them to try to drum up active opposition to their competitor by highlighting the corrupt failings of the prevailing government. They did so not merely in their own names but often as part of broader coalitions with other parties, civil society groups, prominent intellectuals, student activists, and various seemingly nonpolitical organizations.

The first example was the 1995 Kume preko protests, called by the Alliance for Change, in which NPP leaders played a major role. Then came a series of protests in Accra and most regional capitals in 2005–6, named *Wahala* (pidgin English for "trouble" or "hardship") and organized by the NDC-led Committee for Joint Action. Tapping into widespread anger over high fuel prices and other economic difficulties under Kufuor's NPP government, they often drew tens of thousands of participants, who chanted slogans against fuel costs, school fees, and government deregulation of public services. Many ridiculed Kufuor's proclaimed "zero tolerance" against corruption. Protesters sang songs, setting new words to popular tunes, as during the fifth *Wahala* action in the Brong Ahafo capital, Techiman, referencing suspicions of corruption in Kufuor's son's acquisition of an Accra hotel:

- Kufuor no no.
- Wagye waa, waa.
- Wagye dollar.
- Wakoto hotel.
- [That's Kufuor. / He has taken it, waa, waa. / He's taken dollars. / He's gone and bought a hotel.][86]

After the 2008 election put the NDC back in power, the NPP followed the established playbook by organizing a new coalition, the Alliance for Accountable Governance. It held a few large demonstrations against the Mahama government in 2014–15, headlining popular anger over power outages (known as *dumsor*). Among the placards were the following: "Buy one Mahama and get dumsor free," "National Dumsor Committee (NDC)," and "Mahama + Corruption = Stealing."[87] When the NPP returned to office after the 2016 polls, the cycle repeated, with the NDC promoting yet another protest movement, called Fix the Country. It organized demonstrations in Accra and Sekondi-Takoradi to denounce widespread youth unemployment, corruption, and nepotism.[88]

Civil Society

While a few joined party-led alliances, many of Ghana's established civil society groups tried to maintain a nonpartisan stance. Those dedicated to combating corruption generally focused on the systemic shortcomings of Ghana's state, institutions, and laws, regardless of which party was in office, and did not want to be used by party politicians.

They did not always succeed. Some organizers of the 2014 Occupy Flagstaff House protest later that year registered a new group, OccupyGhana. It was led mainly by young professionals of diverse outlooks, some "with a class-based agenda focusing on the fate of the working classes" and some leaning toward "the neo-conservative, market-oriented NPP" against the then-governing NDC. When a founding member openly campaigned for the NPP in 2016 (and after the NPP's victory was appointed chief executive of the Ghana Investment Promotion Centre), that alignment provoked a crisis, prompting some activists to leave.[89] OccupyGhana survived the rift, subsequently emphasizing its character as a "non-partisan pressure group" hoping to serve "as a watch-dog to hold all elected governments accountable."[90] It organized street actions and successfully petitioned the Supreme Court to demand that the offices of the attorney general and auditor general recover funds stolen by previous (NDC) government officials. Yet it also pressured the NPP authorities to enforce the asset declaration law, questioned the NPP government's hasty adoption of a military defense agreement with the United States, and demanded the resignation of the NPP health minister for mishandling COVID-19 vaccine funds.[91]

Several older, established advocacy organizations functioned in a more consistently nonpartisan manner. The Center for Democratic Development (CDD-Ghana) was formed in 1998 as a pro-democracy (and anticorruption) think tank and research center. It became part of the Afrobarometer project, not only running Afrobarometer opinion surveys in Ghana but also assisting the project's activities across the continent. The CDD-Ghana collaborated with a variety of Ghanaian and African civil society networks involved in election monitoring, combating corruption, and other activities.[92] It focused in particular on educating Ghanaians about democratic rights and promoted electoral integrity, an area that overlapped its anticorruption work. Some months before the December 2020 elections, for instance, the center publicly criticized the conduct of NPP candidates who used bribery to secure nominations. Certain politicians, it said, "buy their way through to office, and then tend to recoup their investments through corrupt deals."[93]

The Ghana Integrity Initiative (GII) was founded in 1999, a year after the CDD, as the national chapter of Transparency International. From the start, its main focus and motivation was fighting corruption, through opinion surveys, publicizing Transparency International's annual reports, conducting education activities, training activists, promoting anticorruption reforms, and networking with like-minded organizations and institutions.[94] GII's collaborative work with other groups was highlighted in particular by its participation in the Ghana Anti-Corruption Coalition (GACC), registered in 2001 and encompassing various businesses, religious groups, research centers, the journalists' association, and even several state institutions (CHRAJ, EOCO, and the auditor general's office).[95]

That period marked a veritable explosion of independent civil associations, from around 450 officially registered in 1999 to more than 3,000 just three years later.[96] Given the extent of corruption in other spheres, it was inevitable that a few civil organizations would also succumb to the malady or at least face accusations of poor use of their funding.[97] But with limited financing or access to lucrative markets, the opportunities for graft were minimal.

Most civil society groups focused on particular communities or specific economic or social issues. Some, however, were concerned more generally with democratic rights, governance, and corruption. Besides the GACC, they included coalitions to promote passage of the Right to Information bill and to block the controversial Agyapa royalties deal. Among organizations focused on corruption, the Center for Freedom and Accuracy, in collaboration with the journalists of Anas's Tiger Eye team, exposed tax evasion by commercial importers in collusion with customs officials.[98] The Citizen Ghana Movement campaigned to enforce the provisions of the Political Parties Act obliging parties to publicly reveal their financing.[99]

Several of Ghana's most prominent anticorruption organizations benefited from external funding. The GII, through its affiliation with Transparency International, had corporate sponsorship, foundation support, and financing from bilateral and multilateral donor agencies. So did the GACC, which in addition featured a leading role by four of Ghana's private business associations. Much of the language, approach, and activities of such groups reflected the dominant donor perspectives on corruption, which focused on public sector shortcomings and incremental reform, an approach largely shared by Ghana's business community and other social elites. While their research and surveys also captured some of the concerns of individuals lower down the social hierarchy, the latter had less input in shaping their agendas. The groups' anticorruption discourse rarely featured calls for stronger social welfare programs, protection of land and natural resources from the ravages of neoliberal economic policies, or reducing income and wealth inequalities.

One problem was the weakness of the labor movement, which for decades had been a prominent voice for Ghana's working classes and injected some of the concerns of poor Ghanaians into wider governance debates. The Trades Union Congress, which had 750,000 members in 1987, was reduced to 351,000 by 1991, following the privatizations, public enterprise restructurings, and other retrenchments of the 1980s.[100] Although TUC representatives occasionally joined others' anticorruption activities or criticized high-level graft and financial improprieties during their annual May Day parades, CDD Executive Director Henry Kwasi Prempeh accurately noted that the congress no longer played the role it once did.[101]

There were, however, some new groups concerned with Ghana's poor. They often confronted the different ways corruption, fraud, and related ills disproportionately hurt their constituents. A coalition campaigning for improved public schooling noted that corruption diverted funds from essential educational programs and projects. Another coalition, the People's Action Against Corruption, denounced illicit charges by public health practitioners, arguing that it "denies poor people access to basic health care."[102] Some associations were local. In Tamale, an activist of the Northern Regional Anti-Corruption Committee exposed theft of pension allowances. In Kumawu, near Kumasi, a community group grilled members of the town council about their handling of funds. In the eastern town of Ho, an association working with disabled women campaigned against corruption in local government bodies, in part because graft and opaque financial practices made it harder to access available benefits.[103]

For decades, the exploitation of Ghana's natural resources provided ample occasion for high-level profiteering and conflict between local communities and the Ghanaian and foreign businesses extracting that wealth. Poor state regulation, worsened by market liberalization, permitted all sorts of abuses. In some instances, as in the mining of salt by a British conglomerate around the Keta lagoon in eastern Ghana, local residents—without any evident support from civil society organizations—directly confronted efforts to exclude them from access, leading to violent clashes and deaths.[104] Elsewhere, civil associations were able to play a role. Among other groups, the Third World Network–Africa and its newspaper, *Public Agenda*, regularly criticized laws and policies favoring mining companies and ignoring the needs of surrounding communities.[105] Forest Watch Ghana, a civil society coalition, accused the government of "massive corruption" that enabled unlicensed operators to illegally cut and export timber.[106]

After the first discovery of oil in commercial quantities off Ghana's coast in 2007, there was considerable interest among activists in avoiding the immense graft that afflicted Nigeria and other African oil producers. Actual production began in 2011, from the Jubilee oil field just off Ghana's far western coastline; that site had total estimated reserves of 2 billion barrels, not counting associated natural gas. Operations later began at two smaller fields, and preliminary work was initiated at yet another. After some initial ups and downs, total output grew sufficiently by the start of 2022 (173,000 barrels a day) to make Ghana Africa's eighth largest oil producer.[107] While modest by global standards, oil's earnings were a major addition to Ghana's economy. Sales of oil and natural gas reached (and some years exceeded) those of the long-dominant exports, cocoa and gold. Government income from taxes, royalties, and other oil and gas revenues amounted to about $1 billion in 2022.[108]

While government officials and politicians hailed the dawn of a new era for economic and social development in Ghana, many ordinary citizens wondered "whether Ghana would be able to break the 'curse' that has often marked Africa's oil and mining industries: decades of extraction that often saw only a few getting richer but the majority getting poorer, economic distortions caused by improperly managed resource wealth and hardly any money set aside for times when commodity prices dip or the wells dry up."[109]

The Petroleum Revenue Management Act of 2011 intended to guard against some of those potential pitfalls. It mandated that fixed percentages of oil and gas income be allotted for specific purposes: to support the Ghana National Petroleum Corporation, to fund special set-aside accounts to stabilize income against oil price fluctuations or for future needs, and, through dedicated state budget funds, to finance road and other development projects, including in communities affected by oil operations, such as the loss of coastal fishing grounds. In theory, such binding allocations would prevent officials from squandering oil revenues. In what many industry analysts regarded as a particularly innovative step, the law also authorized a multistakeholder Public Interest and Accountability Committee (PIAC) to monitor compliance. Because the committee was dominated by civil society groups, professional associations, and other nonstate bodies, it cast a critical eye on the authorities' handling of oil funds.[110]

After a decade, there were indications that oil funds were being managed more transparently than in other sectors. Yet shortcomings also appeared. Some lay outside the scope of the petroleum law. Contrary to promises, the authorities were slow in publicizing the terms of the contracts with foreign oil companies, fueling nationalist criticisms that Ghana was being shortchanged.[111] And while the law ensured that oil revenues were allocated for development projects, those suffered the same ills as other expenditures: inflated costs, shoddy contracting, and, in a few cases, completely fictitious projects. While some communities did get new infrastructure, more local taxes, or new jobs and economic activities, many saw nothing tangible, contributing to unrest. As a coastal fish seller commented, "It is the big men in the city that enjoy the money but we fishmongers and fishermen we do not get anything from this oil."[112]

Although the civil society–led PIAC had a mandate to monitor and report on the government's oil revenue use, the committee's powers were limited. During the initial parliamentary debates on the petroleum bill, many legislators hampered efforts to make the PIAC truly independent. It was given no enforcement powers and could only make periodic public reports—often ignored by both the government and the parliament. In 2019, for example, the PIAC highlighted fictitious projects. But, said its chair, Steve Manteaw, "we have not seen a single person who has been brought to book for investigation and prosecution for misuse of oil revenue." The committee, he added, "does not have power to prosecute or enforce its recommendation[s]. PIAC produces a report, highlights abuses of petroleum revenue and that's all it can do, so the abuses continue."[113] Still, the committee's ability to throw a spotlight on discrepancies helped pressure the authorities to be more diligent. Even a severe critic of Ghana's political system, Kwame Ninsin, acknowledged the PIAC's limited success as an example of what could be accomplished by independent, nonpartisan institutions.[114]

Despite the continuing flaws in Ghana's oil sector, there did seem to be some improvement. According to the Revenue Watch Institute, a US nonprofit monitoring natural resource projects, Ghana's oil and gas revenue management was relatively satisfactory. The group's index of transparency and accountability ranked Ghana's oil and gas performance in 2014–17 far higher than its mining industry—and thirteenth out of eighty-nine countries worldwide.[115]

That experience encouraged Ghanaian anticorruption activists and natural resource experts to turn greater attention toward other extractive industries, in particular lithium, a major "green mineral" in high demand worldwide to produce electric vehicles. Its discovery in commercial quantities in Ghana's Central Region in 2022 was expected to set the stage for West Africa's first active lithium mine.[116]

Greater transparency in one part of the Ghanaian economy could not, of course, transform the authorities' economic management overall. Buoyed by unrealistic expectations of future oil revenues, they borrowed heavily to finance ambitious infrastructure and social projects designed to appeal to voters, but they neglected critical investments to boost agriculture and other productive sectors. Those missteps were compounded by unexpected external shocks: the COVID-19 pandemic hit the economy especially hard, while Russia's invasion of Ukraine disrupted global grain markets, stoking inflation. By the end of 2022, Ghana's ratio of foreign debt to gross domestic product had climbed to 80 percent, food prices were the highest in Africa, and the currency, the cedi, was the worst performing in the world.[117] "We have gold, oil, and cocoa, yet we're still foundering as a nation," commented an activist of Arise Ghana. "Government officials are looting state funds and assets, so how do we develop?"[118]

12

For a Society Just and Fair

Despite corruption's seeming persistence, officials often sounded an upbeat note. "We have not lost the fight against corruption," Minister of Justice Marrieta Brew Appiah Oppong said. "There is hope in Ghana."[1] Over the arc of Ghanaian history, there has been ample evidence to justify a more skeptical outlook. From an isolated phenomenon among a handful of powerful individuals during the early days, corruption not only changed forms but also became more generalized. Yet there were also grounds for optimism. The social and political forces for countering corruption simultaneously strengthened and matured over time. Citizens and campaigners alike learned from the missteps of the past. Crowds clamoring for the execution of tainted officers gave way to a greater appreciation for the rule of law and more deliberative focus on institutional reforms to narrow the opportunities for graft and strengthen investigative and judicial mechanisms to identity and punish transgressors—even if those reform efforts did not receive all the resources and space needed to do an adequate job.

For Ghana—and many other countries as well—the ultimate lesson is a positive one: progress against corruption and its related ills is possible. That progress will not come in a linear fashion but will experience reverses and twists as segments of the elites try to block accountability and meaningful change. It will not result from simplistic "zero tolerance" campaigns or as a natural by-product of democratization. The fight against corruption—and for social justice more widely—is usually very muddled, as various social and political actors pursue goals that sometimes align—but often diverge. Yet, Ghana's experience shows, persistence and mobilized public engagement can make headway over time.

Political Contexts and Consequences

Throughout its history, Ghana has had a variety of regime types: precolonial and colonial, a single dominant party system, repeated military takeovers interspersed with unstable electoral interludes, Rawlings's revolutionary era, and finally a more stable period of multiparty electoral rule. Each type of political system in Ghana left its own mark on the forms of abuse and the reactions they elicited. That variety of systems and consequences makes Ghana a good comparative case study. Most other African countries can find some feature or features in common with Ghana, giving its experiences and lessons wider relevance.

While indigenous precolonial polities ranged from weak and decentralized entities to the central, hierarchical Asante empire, most had some means of keeping chiefs and other powerful figures at least partly in check, exemplified most dramatically by the commoner *asafo* companies that could depose chiefs who engaged in especially odious conduct. The colonial conquest imposed new bureaucratic structures on top of those societies and transformed the chieftaincies into local "indirect rule" vehicles subordinate to British authorities. As with any administrative apparatus, employees of the state—both British and African—found opportunities to use their offices to advance their own interests. So did some of Ghana's customary chiefs, who took advantage of their intermediate position to exploit their subjects—but without the popular checks that restrained them in the past.

The First Republic of Kwame Nkrumah was an exemplar of the single-party regimes that prevailed across much of newly independent Africa soon after independence, albeit with a more radical thrust than most. Initially, Nkrumah's Convention People's Party (CPP) had a strongly nationalist dynamic that aimed to mobilize Ghana's resources and masses to build the foundations of an independent state and economy. That revolutionary energy weakened as the party adopted classic patronage methods, in which favored access to jobs, resources, and markets played an increasing role in cementing loyalty. Despite the narratives of rampant corruption and greed later spun by Nkrumah's opponents, the CPP's efforts to mobilize supporters on the basis of patronage did not at the time raise widespread popular concern, even if it did sap commitment and confidence among its followers.

The subsequent decade demonstrated to Ghanaians that military officers and elected civilian politicians alike could be inept, oppressive, and greedy. The rule of the generals who overthrew Nkrumah and the conservative politicians allied with them may have placed a greater emphasis on acquiring wealth through the marketplace but revealed that they were also capable of profiting from state funds and positions. Lieutenant Colonel Acheampong and his fellow officers subsequently pulled out all stops to pursue a reign of pillage that virtually destroyed the economy and society. Public protests forced Acheampong's comrades to ditch him but failed to reverse the rot.

With the established elites seriously discredited and popular sectors not well organized, the initiative for sweeping change came from the lower ranks of the military. Rawlings's brief and turbulent takeover in 1979 sent shockwaves through society. The summary executions of former military heads of state and other prominent individuals could not bring real change. But that "housecleaning" did strike fear in those who had engaged in illicit practices—or simply were better off than the majority of ordinary people. For Ghanaians, Rawlings's military council signaled that drastic alternatives were available, even though there was limited follow-through. When the Limann government that was soon elected failed to build on the momentum of the junior officers' revolt, the stage was set for Rawlings's second takeover on the last day of 1981.

That change came with a more ambitious agenda. While Rawlings's pledge to conduct a far-reaching revolution ultimately fell short, it did bring a serious shake-up of Ghana's state system and balance of social relations. Beyond plentiful rhetoric about eliminating corruption, the Provisional National Defence Council (PNDC) touched on broader issues, from trimming the powers and privileges of Ghana's elites to instilling in civil servants a stronger sense of public service, overhauling the judicial system, professionalizing the army, decentralizing government and state, and shifting at least some attention and resources from urban centers to the countryside. In the process, the early years of the PNDC gave young people, the marginalized, and those from the lower classes an opportunity to mobilize in their own interests—however brief that opening.

For Ghana and much of the rest of Africa, the shift toward multiparty political systems changed the framework for the behavior of state and political authorities, as well as the legal and practical options for holding them to account. With the major donor powers generally opposing most forms of military intervention, robust reform efforts by radical officers were largely precluded. Still, in Ghana, the PNDC's anticorruption discourse imprinted such notions on political life for years after the council gave way to electoral politics. Some of the PNDC's structural, policy, and judicial legacies continued to make it difficult for corrupt officials to escape detection. The professionalization of the military helped shield that institution from the worst temptations of power and better protected the state as a whole from coup threats. Other changes had more mixed results. Although government and administrative decentralization was beneficial overall, by bringing services closer to ordinary citizens and making it easier for them to influence local decision-making, it also inadvertently created many new avenues for illicit dealings by local powerholders, farther from the eyes of the central state and its agencies. The turn toward a more open embrace of market policies in the latter half of the 1980s gave those interested in accumulating wealth avenues other than simply pilfering state coffers. But that shift simultaneously brought weaker state regulation of unfair business practices, including the use of bribery and insider connections to secure contracts and other advantages.

The persistence of those deficiencies left a mark on Ghana's democracy. While a distinct improvement over the arbitrary and often repressive features of previous systems, the actual performance of the new democratic order did not meet public expectations. The National Democratic Congress (NDC) and New Patriotic Party (NPP) managed to pragmatically take turns leading the executive and parliament, contributing to a degree of political stability rare among African electoral systems. But that arrangement entrenched the role of patronage, as party leaders traded access to jobs, contracts, and promises of future benefits for the delivery of ballots on election day. The label of "moneyocracy" probably overstated things but nevertheless conveyed one of the central blemishes: the excessive influence of financial considerations on electoral campaigns—and then on how the victors governed. According to one embittered former NPP member of parliament, who blamed his failure to secure renomination on bribery by his party rivals, vote buying meant that election winners would later have to provide corrupt favors to the financiers who "invested" in them.[2] Those corrupting influences had far-reaching consequences. They distorted the legislative process, tainted judicial appointments and the conduct of courts and prosecutors, encouraged civil servants to ignore ethical standards, and hampered delivery of public services to those who most needed them.

Nevertheless, the same constitution that seemed blind to such defects also entrenched press freedoms, the right to assemble and protest, and other liberties. Those rights made it easier for citizens to express grievances, including against high-level corruption and abuses. Popular action and accusations in turn impelled Ghana's elites to engage with the politics of corruption in their own ways, perhaps to deflect responsibility, direct public discontent against rivals and competitors, or, somewhat rarely, harness the power of citizens' anger for reform, whether genuine or cosmetic.

Across Ghana's different historical periods and regime types, the politics of corruption were evident in several recurrent ways. Principally, those included

- political challengers wielding charges of graft to diminish the legitimacy of sitting officeholders and showcase their own worthiness;
- governing officials tapping into public concerns about corruption to deflect from other major problems, secure greater public following, or justify the elimination of rivals; and
- ordinary citizens, on occasion, combining anticorruption grievances with other demands to advance their struggles for political, economic, and social change.

State and Market

The nature of the political system set the context within which corruption and struggles against it played out. However, matters that affected citizens' daily lives were not determined by the character of the regime alone. Different leaders and parties pursued different policies, across a range of issues. Some of the most consequential were associated with the relationship between state and market.

In broad terms, the prevailing approaches veered back and forth between the state-centered development ambitions of Nkrumah's era and the laissez-faire liberalism of Busia, Kufuor, and Akufo-Addo—with Rawlings's PNDC shifting from one to the other and the elected NDC regimes mixing liberalism with elements of social welfarism. The different sets of policies had implications for not only the forms of corruption that developed but also the language and methods of anticorruption campaigners. Those favoring liberalism—which has become ubiquitous across much of the African continent—saw corruption as mainly a malady of the public sector. They generally regarded wealth acquisition in the marketplace as laudable (even if competition was not entirely fair or some players had the advantage of high state connections). For them, the most effective solution to corruption was to reduce the size of the state and thus the opportunities for graft that came with it. Their pursuit of policies to check corruption on the surface appeared to be technical or nonpolitical. But as corruption scholar Michael Johnston pointed out, the business interests and international aid and lending agencies that promoted the standard approach to fighting corruption tended to view the problem as both "a cause and consequence of incomplete or uneven economic liberalization." In that framework, he added, anticorruption reform tethered to further liberalization "masks agendas that benefit very few."[3]

Ghana also has had a robust body of thought that placed a stronger emphasis on state action than market mechanisms. Historically, it could trace its lineage to the Nkrumahist tradition, which saw the state as central to nation building and collective social advancement, while the market, whatever its benefits for innovation and initiative, was also considered a source of individualistic greed and avarice. As the seasoned social anthropologist Maxwell Owusu remarked, "The common obsession with status and wealth, with the power, prestige and high status that wealth possession and its conspicuous consumption confer, partly explain the vicious cycle of corruption and absence of effective institutional and structural restraint or checks against corruption. Ironically, neo-liberalism and globalization, with emphasis on private enterprise, building the middle class, with little concern for the social cost of capitalism, seem to have contributed to the worsening of corruption, rather than its reduction."[4]

Even some conservative political figures agreed. J. H. Mensah, a longtime member of parliament for the NPP, warned an international anticorruption conference of the "ethical implications of the capitalist paradigm," in which profit is paramount and "the moral aspect of how the bottom line is realized becomes secondary."[5]

Many supporters of Transparency International and similar groups might well have shared such concerns about the negative consequences of unchecked market forces. But their options for striking out in different directions were limited. Promarket responses to Ghana's myriad problems—including corruption—became so embedded that only a few radical academics or activists raised questions or pointed to possible alternatives. The Ghanaian authorities' approach to combatting graft tried to incorporate some wider social and political concerns but also bore a distinct neoliberal imprint. The government's first national action plan against corruption, drafted in 2000, was partly funded by the World Bank, while the Bank and US and UK aid agencies, among others, helped draft or support specific anticorruption laws and measures. The Danish aid agency helped finance the second national plan, covering the period 2015–24, which cited in its first paragraph a recitation of corruption's "corrosive effects," including that it "distorts markets" and "diminishes the country's attractiveness for investment."[6] Those consequences were undoubtedly real. But they resonated most with businesspeople and their foreign partners.

The View from Below

Ordinary Ghanaians were preoccupied with quite different problems: jobs and incomes, the cost of daily necessities, the ability to educate their children and keep them healthy, the quality of public services, and so on. As far as corruption made those things more costly or difficult to obtain, it was clearly an acute concern. Fortunately, Ghana's relative political stability and its comparatively vibrant economy facilitated incremental improvements in many Ghanaians' daily lives from the 1990s onward. The national poverty rate fell by nearly half, from 47.4 percent in 1991 to 25.2 percent in 2005, and then even further over the next decade.[7]

Those advances were uneven, however. They could not hide a striking paradox: even amid strong growth, social and economic inequalities increased. While the average consumption of the poorest tenth of rural Ghanaians rose by 19 percent between

2005–6 and 2012–13, that of the wealthiest tenth of the total population increased more sharply, by 27 percent, thus widening the gap. Overall, inequalities grew between urban and rural Ghanaians, between southern and northern regions, and within communities, including between genders.[8] While some sub-Saharan countries registered declines in income inequality, "in Ghana," the United Nations reported in 2017, "it has risen without interruption for the past three decades."[9]

Ghanaian society was never equitable. Yet in precolonial times, the rudimentary development of local productive capacities limited the possibilities for extreme wealth accumulation, while traditional practices provided some checks against abuses and ensured collective support for community members who fell on hard times. With Ghana's progressive incorporation into the global economy and the generalization of market relations, many of those customary norms eroded, and excessive acquisition of money and property no longer elicited the same popular antipathy. At least at the summit of society, cultural norms evolved to the point at which wealth came to be celebrated—even if some still questioned how it might have been acquired. One reflection of the obsession with moneymaking was the proliferation since the 1990s of hundreds of new evangelical and charismatic churches that preached the "gospel of prosperity," the belief that devotion—and generous tithes—would bring the faithful blessings of cash, cars, houses, and other material goods.[10] More widely, social relations became increasingly monetized across the spectrum of practices, from lavish displays of wealth at weddings and funerals to giving envelopes of cash to civil servants for performing routine duties. For many Ghanaians, the links between corruption and crass materialism were evident. When Ghana's Institute of Economic Affairs asked survey respondents in 2015 what they considered the leading causes of corruption in the country, 28 percent cited "greed and selfishness" as their first choice, with another 24 percent naming "get rich quick" attitudes.[11]

Throughout Ghanaian history, ordinary citizens demonstrated repeatedly that they abhorred the theft of public goods and funds by high officials and civil servants, along with fraud, cheating, and profiteering by private business owners and managers. But most did not oppose those ills simply because they saw them as personally harmful. Like people across the globe, they also did so out of a broader sense of justice, a vision of society in which ordinary citizens could pursue their political aspirations and economic well-being free from elite abuses and exploitation.[12]

The chaotic year of 1982, when popular hopes were openly and repeatedly expressed across different sectors of Ghanaian society, brought many such affirmations. Workers of the national social security agency declared that they were speaking out against the mismanagement of senior administrators "to ensure that justice, fair play and equity was done."[13] A landowner in Dansoman, near Accra, appealed to activists to help him stop illegal encroachments, stating, "Revolutionary justice does not support people who are cheats in the society, who are strong and take advantage over the weak, who are rich and take advantage over the poor, who are lawless and take advantage over the law-abiding citizens."[14]

The aspirations of that time remained largely unmet. But over the more than four decades that followed, there was little evidence that Ghanaians had abandoned their hopes. They still imagined a society free of corruption and injustice.

Notes

Chapter 1: Local Realities, Global Narratives

1. *Daily Graphic*, January 17, 2019; Joel Gunter, "Murder in Accra: The Life and Death of Ahmed Hussein-Suale," BBC Africa Eye, January 30, 2019, www.bbc.com/.
2. *Daily Graphic*, March 1, 2019.
3. Lionel Osse and Newton Norviewu, "Ghanaians Perceive Increase in Corruption Level, Give Government Low Marks on Fighting Graft," Afrobarometer and Ghana Center for Democratic Development, news release AD333, December 4, 2019.
4. Republic of Ghana, *Final Report of the Commission of Enquiry on Bribery and Corruption* (Accra: Ghana Publishing Corporation, 1975), 45.
5. Giorgio Blundo and Jean-Pierre Olivier de Sardan, eds., *Etat et corruption en Afrique: Une anthropologie comparative des relations entre fonctionnaires et usagers (Bénin, Niger, Sénégal)* (Paris: Karthala, 2007).
6. "Petition for Investigations," typed letter signed by thirty-one employees of the Ghana National Farmers Council to the Chairman, Interim National Coordinating Committee, State House, Accra, August 5, 1982, PDC Collection.
7. *Ghanaian Chronicle*, November 26, 1999.
8. Global Integrity Report, "Global Integrity Scorecard: Ghana 2008," accessed October 16, 2011, http://report.globalintegrity.org/Ghana/2008.
9. Afrobarometer / Ghana Center for Democratic Development, *Summary of Results: Afrobarometer Round 7, Survey in Ghana, 2017* (Ghana: Afrobarometer / Ghana Center for Democratic Development, n.d.), 27–30, https://www.afrobarometer.org/publication/ghana-summary-results-2017/.
10. Irving Leonard Markovitz, *Power and Class in Africa* (Englewood Cliffs, NJ: Prentice-Hall, 1977); Richard Sandbrook and Robin Cohen, eds., *The Development of an African Working Class* (Toronto: University of Toronto Press, 1975); Eme Ekekwe, *Class and State in Nigeria* (London: Longman, 1986); Larry Diamond, "Class Formation in the Swollen African State," *Journal of Modern African Studies* 25, no. 4 (December 1987): 567–96; Nelson

Kasfir, "State, Magendo, and Class Formation in Uganda," *Journal of Commonwealth and Comparative Politics* 21, no. 3 (November 1983): 84–103.

11. Transparency International, Corruption Perceptions Index, 1998–2018, accessed March 12, 2019, http://www.transparency.org/policy_research/surveys_indices/cpi.

12. Kivutha Kibwana, Smokin Wanjala, and Okech-Owiti, *The Anatomy of Corruption in Kenya: Legal, Political and Socio-economic Perspectives* (Nairobi: Claripress, 1996); Daniel Jordan Smith, *A Culture of Corruption: Everyday Deception and Popular Discontent in Nigeria* (Princeton, NJ: Princeton University Press, 2007); Sahr John Kpundeh, *Politics and Corruption in Africa: A Case Study of Sierra Leone* (Lanham, MD: University Press of America, 1995).

13. Ernest Harsch, "Accumulators and Democrats: Challenging State Corruption in Africa," *Journal of Modern African Studies* 31, no. 1 (March 1993): 31–48; Ernest Harsch, "Corruption and State Reform in Africa: Perspectives from Above and Below." In *Good Governance and Economic Development*, vol. 6 of *African Development Perspectives Yearbook 1997/98*, ed. Karl Wohlmuth, Hans H. Bass, and Frank Messner (Munich: LIT, 1999), 65–87.

14. Ernest Harsch, "Africans Taking Action on Corruption," *Africa Recovery* 11, no. 1 (July 1997): 26.

15. Jean-François Médard, "L'Etat patrimonialisé," *Politique africaine*, no. 39 (1990): 25–36.

16. World Bank, *Sub-Saharan Africa: From Crisis to Sustainable Growth* (Washington, DC: 1989), 55–56, 61.

17. Pierre Landell-Mills and Ismail Serageldin, "Governance and the Development Process," *Finance and Development* 28, no. 3 (1991): 14.

18. Peter Eigen, author's interview, Durban, South Africa, October 15, 1999.

19. World Bank, *World Development Report: The State in a Changing World* (New York: Oxford University Press, 1997), 24–25.

20. World Bank, 99–107, 150.

21. World Bank, 154.

22. International Monetary Fund, "Corruption Must Be Fought on Global Scale," *IMF Survey* 26, no. 18 (1997): 303.

23. Thandika Mkandawire and Adebayo Olukoshi, eds., *Between Liberalisation and Oppression: The Politics of Structural Adjustment in Africa* (Dakar: CODESRIA, 1995).

24. Michael Johnston, *Syndromes of Corruption: Wealth, Power, and Democracy* (Cambridge: Cambridge University Press, 2005), 195.

25. J. S. Nye, "Corruption and Political Development: A Cost-Benefit Analysis," *American Political Science Review* 61, no. 2 (1967): 417–27; Robin Theobald, *Corruption, Development and Underdevelopment* (London: MacMillan, 1990); Nathaniel H. Leff, "Economic Development through

Corruption," in *Bureaucratic Corruption in Sub-Saharan Africa: Toward a Search for Causes and Consequences*, ed. Monday O. Ekpo (Washington, DC: University Press of America): 325–40; J. P. Olivier de Sardan, "A Moral Economy of Corruption in Africa?" *Journal of Modern African Studies* 37, no. 1 (1999): 25–52.

26. Joseph A. Ayee, *The Roots of Corruption: The Ghanaian Inquiry Revisited* (Accra: Institute of Economic Affairs, 2016), 15.
27. Republic of Ghana, *National Anti-Corruption Action Plan (2015–2024)* (Accra, 2011), 23.
28. Michael Johnston, "Corruption, Inequality, and Change," in *Corruption, Development and Inequality: Soft Touch or Hard Graft?*, ed. Peter M. Ward (London: Routledge, 1989), 14.
29. Gerald E. Caiden, O. P. Dwivedi, and Joseph Jabbra, eds., *Where Corruption Lives* (Bloomfield, CT: Kumarian Press, 2001), 6.
30. "Your Class—'Partners Not Wage-Workers,'" *Venceremos*, Official Organ of the Workers Defence Committee of the Bank of Ghana, 1, no. 3 (April 1982): 3, PDC Collection.
31. Republic of Ghana, *Final Report . . . on Bribery and Corruption*, 38.
32. Steven Pierce, *Moral Economies of Corruption: State Formation and Political Culture in Nigeria* (Durham, NC: Duke University Press, 2016), 21.
33. Jean-François Médard, "Public Corruption in Africa: A Comparative Perspective," *Corruption and Reform* 1, no. 2 (1986): 127–28.
34. Sidney Tarrow, *Power in Movement: Social Movements, Collective Action and Politics* (Cambridge: Cambridge University Press, 1994), 224.
35. Kwame Akon Ninsin, *The Corrupt Elites: Anatomy of Power and Wealth in Ghana* (Accra: Gavoss Education, 2018), 79.
36. "State Gold Mining Corporation, Workers Defence Committees Seminar, Sat. 3rd–Sun. 4th July 1982, Report, 5th July 1982," signed by Steve Ocansey, Secretary, Organising Committee, Tarkwa Goldfields Limited, PDC Collection.
37. Ninsin, *Corrupt Elites*, 78.
38. Jean-François Bayart, *The State in Africa: The Politics of the Belly* (London: Longman, 1993); Mbongiseni Buthelezi and Peter Vale, eds., *State Capture in South Africa: How and Why It Happened* (Johannesburg: Wits University Press, 2023).

Chapter 2: Chiefs and Colonial Bureaucrats

1. Charles Tilly, *Coercion, Capital, and European States, AD 990–1992* (Cambridge, MA: Blackwell, 1992).
2. Jack Goody, *The Social Organisation of the LoWiili* (Oxford: Oxford University Press, 1967); Georges Savonnet, *Les Birifor de Diépla et sa région insulaires du rameau lobi (Haute-Volta)* (Paris: ORSTOM, 1976), 100–107.

3. Michel Verdon, "Political Sovereignty, Village Reproduction and Legends of Origin: A Comparative Hypothesis," *Africa* 51, no. 1 (1981): 471–72.
4. Michel Verdon, "Re-defining Pre-colonial Ewe Polities: The Case of Abutia," *Africa* 50, no. 3 (1980): 289.
5. Sandra E. Greene, "Social Change in Eighteenth-Century Anlo: The Role of Technology, Markets and Military Conflict," *Africa* 58, no. 1 (1988): 70–85.
6. Louis E. Wilson, "The Evolution of Paramount Chiefs among the Adangme to the End of the Nineteenth Century: The Case of the Krobo (Ghana)," *Genève-Afrique* 24, no. 2 (1986): 73–100.
7. Jack Goody, "The Over-Kingdom of Gonja," in *West African Kingdoms in the Nineteenth Century*, ed. Daryll Forde and P. M. Kaberry (London: Oxford University Press, 1967), 179–205.
8. T. C. McCaskie, *State and Society in Pre-colonial Asante* (Cambridge: Cambridge University Press, 1995), 25, 37, 42, 47, 77.
9. J. C. De Graft Johnson, "The Fante Asafu," *Africa* 15, no. 3 (1932): 308.
10. Maxwell Owusu, "Rebellion, Revolution, and Tradition: Reinterpreting Coups in Ghana," *Comparative Studies in Society and History* 31, no. 2 (1989): 382.
11. Ivor Wilks, *Asante in the Nineteenth Century: The Structure and Evolution of a Political Order* (Cambridge: Cambridge University Press, 1975), 692–95.
12. Catherine Coquery-Vidrovitch, "The Political Economy of the African Peasantry and Modes of Production," in *The Political Economy of Contemporary Africa*, ed. Peter C. W. Gutkind and Immanuel Wallerstein (Beverly Hills, CA: Sage Publications, 1976), 92. Emphasis in original.
13. McCaskie, *State and Society*, 33.
14. McCaskie, 38.
15. McCaskie, 48–57.
16. Wilks, *Asante in the Nineteenth Century*, 387–431.
17. The term *proto-corruption* has been suggested for the misuse of resources in situations where state treasuries have not been clearly removed from monarchs' discretionary whims, as in early Stuart England. See James C. Scott, *Comparative Political Corruption* (Englewood Cliffs, NJ: Prentice-Hall, 1972).
18. Wilks, *Asante in the Nineteenth Century*, 396, 423–29.
19. McCaskie, *State and Society*, 68–70; Wilks, *Asante in the Nineteenth Century*, 512, 527–39; George P. Hagan, *Destoolment: The Pattern of Tenurial Instability of Kumasi Stools* (Legon: Institute of African Studies, University of Ghana, 1972), 18.
20. McCaskie, *State and Society*, 133.
21. Wilks, *Asante in the Nineteenth Century*, 535–37.

Notes to Pages 23–36

22. Hagan, *Destoolment*, 26.
23. Kwame Arhin and Joseph Ki-Zerbo, "States and Peoples of the Niger Bend and the Volta," in *General History of Africa*, vol. 6, *Africa in the Nineteenth Century until the 1880s*, ed. J. F. Ade Ajayi (Paris: UNESCO, 1989), 666.
24. Frances Agbodeka, *African Politics and British Policy in the Gold Coast, 1868–1900* (London: Longman, 1971), 26.
25. Agbodeka, 15–33.
26. Agbodeka, 55.
27. Agbodeka, 104–46.
28. H. L. Wesseling, *Divide and Rule: The Partition of Africa, 1880–1914* (Westport, CT: Praeger, 1996), 182.
29. Henceforth in this book, the official name "Ashanti" is used to refer to the geographical and political region as designated in the colonial and postcolonial periods, while "Asante" is used for the people, as well as in references to the precolonial state.
30. Agbodeka, *African Politics*, 114.
31. Mahmood Mamdani, *Citizen and Subject: Contemporary Africa and the Legacy of Late Colonialism* (Princeton, NJ: Princeton University Press, 1996).
32. Catherine Boone, "States and Ruling Classes in Postcolonial Africa: The Enduring Contradictions of Power," in *State Power and Social Forces: Domination and Transformation in the Third World*, ed. Joel S. Migdal, Atul Kohli, and Vivienne Shue (Cambridge: Cambridge University Press, 1994), 117–18.
33. Agbodeka, *African Politics*, 22–23.
34. Martin Staniland, *The Lions of Dagbon: Political Change in Northern Ghana* (Cambridge: Cambridge University Press, 1975), 46.
35. R. F. Betts, "Methods and Institutions of European Domination," in *General History of Africa*, vol. 7, *Africa under Colonial Domination, 1880–1935*, ed. A. Adu Boahen (Paris: UNESCO, 1985), 318.
36. David Kimble, *A Political History of Ghana: The Rise of Gold Coast Nationalism, 1850–1928* (Oxford: Oxford University Press, 1963), 461.
37. Agbodeka, *African Politics*, 113–15.
38. Kimble, *Political History of Ghana*, 475, 503–4.
39. Wilks, *Asante in the Nineteenth Century*, 308.
40. Staniland, *Lions of Dagbon*, 60–61.
41. Staniland, 86.
42. Kimble, *Political History of Ghana*, 474.
43. W. E. F. Ward, *A History of the Gold Coast* (London: George Allen & Unwin, 1948), 326.
44. Staniland, *Lions of Dagbon*, 78, 81.

45. Staniland, 105–09.
46. Roger G. Thomas, "The 1916 Bongo 'Riots' and Their Background: Aspects of the Early Colonial Administration of Eastern Upper Ghana," *Journal of African History* 24, no. 1 (1983): 74.
47. Hagan, *Destoolment*, 26–29.
48. David E. Apter, *Ghana in Transition* (Princeton, NJ: Princeton University Press, 1972), 114.
49. Kimble, *Political History of Ghana*, 471.
50. Maxwell Owusu, "Custom and Coups: A Juridical Interpretation of Civil Order and Disorder in Ghana," *Journal of Modern African Studies* 24, no. 1 (1986): 96–97; Kimble, *Political History of Ghana*, 470–71.
51. F. M. Bourret, *Ghana: The Road to Independence, 1919–1957* (Stanford: Stanford University Press, 1960), 46.
52. Kimble, *Political History of Ghana*, 490.
53. Peter P. Ekeh, "Colonialism and the Two Publics in Africa: A Theoretical Statement," *Comparative Studies in Society and History* 17, no. 1 (1975): 91–112; Stanislav Andreski, *The African Predicament* (New York: Atherton Press, 1968); Alice Nicole Sindzingre, *Etat, développement et rationalité en Afrique: Contribution à une analyse de la corruption*, Travaux et documents 43 (Bordeaux: Centre d'étude d'Afrique noire, 1994).
54. Republic of Ghana, *Final Report of the Commission of Enquiry on Bribery and Corruption* (Accra: Ghana Publishing Corporation, 1975), 7.
55. C. A. Ackah, *Akan Ethics* (Accra: Ghana Universities Press, 1988), 51.
56. Kwame Arhin, "The Economic and Social Significance of Rubber Production and Exchange on the Gold and Ivory Coasts, 1880–1900," *Cahiers d'études africaines* 20, nos. 1–2 (1980): 49–62.
57. Kwame Arhin, "Trade, Accumulation and the State in Asante in the Nineteenth Century," *Africa* 60, no. 4 (1990): 533.
58. Rhoda Howard, *Colonialism and Underdevelopment in Ghana* (New York: Holmes & Meier, 1978), 18, 113, 152, 182–83.
59. Goody, *Social Organisation*, 110.
60. Bourret, *Ghana: Road to Independence*, 122–23.
61. Keith Hart, "Swindler or Public Benefactor?—The Entrepreneur in His Community," in *Changing Social Structure in Ghana: Essays in the Comparative Sociology of a New State and an Old Tradition*, ed. Jack Goody (London: International Affairs Institute, 1975), 27.
62. M. M. Huq, *The Economy of Ghana: The First 25 Years since Independence* (London: MacMillan, 1989), 37–43.
63. Jeff Crisp, *The Story of an African Working Class: Ghanaian Miners' Struggles, 1870–1980* (London: Zed Books, 1984), 58, 61, 85–86, 118, 127.

Chapter 3: Nationalism and Patronage

1. Benedict Anderson, *Imagined Communities: Reflections on the Origin and Spread of Nationalism* (London: Verso, 1991).
2. Bolanle Awe, "Empires of the Western Sudan: Ghana, Mali, Songhai," in *A Thousand Years of West African History*, ed. J. F. Ade Ajayi and Ian Espie (New York: Humanities Press, 1972), 55–71; Nehemia Levtzion, "The Early States of the Western Sudan to 1500," in *History of West Africa*, vol. 1, ed. J. F. A. Ajayi and Michael Crowder (New York: Columbia University Press, 1976), 114–51.
3. Thomas Hodgkin, *Nationalism in Colonial Africa* (New York: New York University Press, 1957).
4. William Burnett Harvey, *Law and Social Change in Ghana* (Princeton, NJ: Princeton University Press, 1966), 210–11.
5. *Ghanaian Chronicle*, August 4, 2022.
6. Dennis Austin, *Politics in Ghana, 1946–1960* (London: Oxford University Press, 1970), 52–58.
7. David Killingray, "Soldiers, Ex-servicemen, and Politics in the Gold Coast, 1939–50," *Journal of Modern African Studies* 21, no. 3 (1983): 523–34; Austin, *Politics in Ghana*, 70–74; C. L. R. James, *Nkrumah and the Ghana Revolution* (London: Allison & Busby, 1977), 42–45; Jeffrey S. Ahlman, *Living with Nkrumahism: Nation, State, and Pan-Africanism in Ghana* (Athens: Ohio University Press, 2017), 8–10.
8. Jeffrey S. Ahlman, *Kwame Nkrumah: Visions of Liberation* (Athens: Ohio University Press, 2021), 96.
9. Austin, *Politics in Ghana*, 56, 66.
10. Kwame Nkrumah, *Revolutionary Path* (New York: International Publishers, 1973), 58.
11. Austin, *Politics in Ghana*, 87–90.
12. John Waterbury, "An Attempt to Put Patrons and Clients in Their Place," in *Patrons and Clients in Mediterranean Societies*, ed. Ernest Gellner and John Waterbury (London: Duckworth, 1977), 329–42.
13. René Lemarchand, "The State, the Parallel Economy, and the Changing Structure of Patronage Systems," in *The Precarious Balance: State and Society in Africa*, ed. Donald Rothchild and Naomi Chazan (Boulder, CO: Westview, 1988), 149–70; Christopher Clapham, "Clientelism and the State," in *Private Patronage and Public Power: Political Clientelism in the Modern State*, ed. Christopher Clapham (New York: St. Martin's, 1982), 1–35.
14. Joel S. Migdal, *Strong Societies and Weak States: State-Society Relations and State Capabilities in the Third World* (Princeton, NJ: Princeton University Press, 1988).

15. René Lemarchand, "Political Clientelism and Ethnicity in Tropical Africa: Competing Solidarities in Nation-Building," in *Friends, Followers, and Factions: A Reader in Political Clientelism*, ed. Steffen W. Schmidt, Laura Guasti, Carl H. Landé, and James C. Scott (Berkeley: University of California Press, 1977), 107.
16. Lemarchand, "Political Clientelism," 103.
17. Maxwell Owusu, *Uses and Abuses of Political Power: A Case Study of Continuity and Change in the Politics of Ghana* (Chicago: University of Chicago Press, 1970), 248.
18. Austin, *Politics in Ghana*, 211.
19. *West Africa*, December 10, 1984.
20. David E. Apter, *Ghana in Transition* (Princeton, NJ: Princeton University Press, 1972), 210.
21. Basil Davidson, *Black Star: A View of the Life and Times of Kwame Nkrumah* (Boulder, CO: Westview, 1989), 127.
22. Gold Coast, *Report of the Commission of Enquiry in Mr. Braimah's Resignation and Allegations Arising Therefrom* (Accra: Government Printing Department, 1954), 42.
23. Republic of Ghana, *Report of the Commission Appointed to Enquire into the Circumstances which Led to the Payment of £28,545 to James Colledge (Cocoa) Limited as Compensation for Land Acquired for the Achiasi-Kotoku Railway* (Accra: Government Printing Department, 1962), 33.
24. Gold Coast, *Report of the Commission of Enquiry into the Affairs of the Cocoa Purchasing Company Limited* (Accra, 1956), 28, 43.
25. Austin, *Politics in Ghana*, 351.
26. Jean Marie Allman, *The Quills of the Porcupine: Asante Nationalism in an Emergent Ghana* (Madison: University of Wisconsin Press, 1993), 156.
27. Austin, *Politics in Ghana*, 325, 332.
28. Allman, *Quills of the Porcupine*, 59, 140–41.
29. Convention People's Party, *Manifesto for the General Election, 1954* (London: National Labour Press, 1954), 9.
30. Austin, *Politics in Ghana*, 347–54.
31. Allman, *Quills of the Porcupine*, 168–73.
32. Richard Rathbone, *Nkrumah and the Chiefs: The Politics of Chieftaincy in Ghana, 1951–60* (Oxford, UK: James Currey, 2000), 98.
33. David Birmingham, *Kwame Nkrumah: The Father of African Nationalism* (Athens: Ohio University Press, 1999).
34. Austin, *Politics in Ghana*, 430–46.
35. Bob Fitch and Mary Oppenheimer, *Ghana: End of an Illusion* (New York: Monthly Review Press, 1966), 68–71, 83, 123.
36. Austin, *Politics in Ghana*, 373–76.

Notes to Pages 57–63

37. Kwame Arhin, "The Search for 'Constitutional Chieftaincy,'" in *The Life and Work of Kwame Nkrumah*, ed. Kwame Arhin (Trenton, NJ: Africa World Press, 1993), 27–51.
38. Harvey, *Law and Social Change*, 86–87.
39. Rathbone, *Nkrumah and the Chiefs*, 143.
40. Owusu, *Uses and Abuses*, 285–93, 321, 328.
41. Jonathan H. Frimpong-Ansah, *The Vampire State in Africa: The Political Economy of Decline in Ghana* (Trenton, NJ: Africa World Press, 1992), 97–99.
42. James C. Scott, *Comparative Political Corruption* (Englewood Cliffs, NJ: Prentice-Hall, 1972), 123–31.
43. Republic of Ghana, *Report of Commission of Enquiry into Alleged Irregularities and Malpractices in Connection with the Issue of Import Licences* (Accra: Ministry of Information and Broadcasting, 1964); Republic of Ghana, *Report of the Commission of Inquiry into Trade Malpractices in Ghana* (Accra: Ministry of Information and Broadcasting, 1965).
44. Nkrumah, *Revolutionary Path*, 154–55.
45. Austin, *Politics in Ghana*, 404–6.
46. Republic of Ghana, *White Paper on the Report of the Commission of Enquiry into Alleged Irregularities and Malpractices in Connection with the Grant of Import Licences*, W.P. no. 4/67 (Accra: State Publishing Corporation, 1967), 2.
47. Republic of Ghana, *Report of the Commission Appointed to Enquire into the Affairs of the Ghana Timber Marketing Board and the Ghana Timber Co-operative Union* (Accra: Tema State Publishing Corporation, 1968).
48. Republic of Ghana, *Report of the Commission to Enquire into the Affairs of NADECO Limited* (Accra: State Publishing Corporation, 1966), 8.
49. Republic of Ghana, *Report . . . into the Affairs of NADECO*, 28, 36.
50. Republic of Ghana, *White Paper on the Report of the Commission of Enquiry into Kwame Nkrumah Properties*, W.P. no. 1/67 (Accra: State Publishing Corporation, 1967).
51. Republic of Ghana, *White Paper on the Interim Report of Sowah Commission of Enquiry into the Assets of Specified Persons*, W.P. no. 13/68 (Accra: State Publishing Corporation, 1968); *White Paper on the Report of the Jiagge Commission of Enquiry into the Assets of Specified Persons*, W.P. no. 3/69 (Accra: Ghana Publishing Corporation, 1969); *White Paper on the Report of the Manyo-Plange Commission of Enquiry into the Assets of Specified Persons*, W.P. no. 11/69 (Accra: Ghana Publishing Corporation, 1969).
52. Republic of Ghana, *Report of the Commission Appointed to Enquire into the Functions, Operations and Administration of the Workers Brigade* (Accra: State Publishing Corporation, 1967).

53. Victor T. Le Vine, *Political Corruption: The Ghana Case* (Stanford, CA: Hoover Institution Press, 1975), 23.
54. Republic of Ghana, *Report of the Commission of Enquiry on the Local Purchasing of Cocoa* (Accra: State Publishing Corporation, 1966).
55. Björn Beckman, *Organising the Farmers: Cocoa Politics and National Development in Ghana* (Uppsala: Scandinavian Institute of African Studies, 1976), 144.
56. Republic of Ghana, *White Paper on the Report of the Commission of Enquiry into the Ghana Trades Union Congress Funds*, W.P. no. 7/69 (Accra: Ghana Publishing Corporation, 1969), 2.
57. Fitch and Oppenheimer, *Ghana*, 101–2.
58. Paul S. Gray, *Unions and Leaders in Ghana: A Model of Labor and Development* (Owerri, Nigeria: Conch Magazine, 1981), 139.
59. Jeff Crisp, *The Story of an African Working Class: Ghanaian Miners' Struggles, 1870–1980* (London: Zed Books, 1984), 135, 141.
60. Richard D. Jeffries, "Populist Tendencies in the Ghanaian Trade Union Movement," in *The Development of an African Working Class: Studies in Class Formation and Action*, ed. Richard Sandbrook and Robin Cohen (Toronto: University of Toronto Press, 1975), 272.
61. Jeffries, "Populist Tendencies," 264, 268–72; Fitch and Oppenheimer, *Ghana*, 103.
62. Le Vine, *Political Corruption*, 14.
63. Herbert H. Werlin, "The Roots of Corruption—the Ghanaian Enquiry," *Journal of Modern African Studies* 10, no. 2 (1972): 261.
64. Simon Baynham, *The Military and Politics in Nkrumah's Ghana* (Boulder, CO: Westview, 1988).

Chapter 4: Path to Plunder

1. Robert Dowse, "Military and Police Rule," in *Politicians and Soldiers in Ghana, 1966–1972*, ed. Dennis Austin and Robin Luckham (London: Frank Cass, 1975), 21–22.
2. Republic of Ghana, *Report of the Commission of Enquiry into the Affairs of the Anlo Traditional Area* (Accra: Ghana Publishing Corporation, 1969); Republic of Ghana, *White Paper on the Report of the Commission of Enquiry into the Affairs of the Anlo Traditional Area*, W.P. no. 12/69 (Accra: Ghana Publishing Corporation, 1969); Republic of Ghana, *Report of the Committee of Enquiry into the Yendi Skin Affairs* (Accra: Ghana Publishing Corporation, 1969); Republic of Ghana, *White Paper on the Report of the Committee of Enquiry into the Yendi Skin Affairs*, W.P. no. 14/69 (Accra: Ghana Publishing Corporation, 1969).
3. Naomi Chazan, *An Anatomy of Ghanaian Politics: Managing Political Recession, 1969–1982* (Boulder, CO: Westview, 1983), 53–54.

4. Republic of Ghana, *Report of the Committee of Enquiry into Ejura Affairs* (Accra: Ghana Publishing House, 1973), 10, 30, 42.
5. Robin Luckham and Stephen Nkrumah, "The Constituent Assembly—A Social and Political Portrait," in Austin and Luckham, *Politicians and Soldiers*, 121.
6. Eboe Hutchful, ed., *The IMF and Ghana: The Confidential Record* (London: Zed Books, 1987).
7. Republic of Ghana, *Report of the Committee of Enquiry into Alleged Irregularities and Malpractices in the Affairs of the Tema Development Corporation* (Accra: Ghana Publishing Corporation, 1970).
8. Dowse, "Military and Police Rule," 22.
9. Hutchful, *IMF and Ghana*, 24.
10. Victor T. Le Vine, *Political Corruption: The Ghana Case* (Stanford, CA: Hoover Institution Press, 1975), 35–37.
11. S. A. Amoa, *University Students' Political Action in Ghana* (Accra: Ghana Publishing Corporation, 1979), 39–42.
12. Kwame A. Ninsin, *Political Struggles in Ghana, 1967–1981* (Accra: Tornado Publishers, 1985), 24; Jeff Crisp, *The Story of an African Working Class: Ghanaian Miners' Struggles, 1870–1980* (London: Zed Books, 1984), 151–67.
13. Republic of Ghana, *White Paper on the Committee Appointed to Enquire into Recent Disturbances at Prestea*, W.P. no. 8/69 (Accra, 1969).
14. Yaw Twumasi, "1969 Election," in Austin and Luckham, *Politicians and Soldiers*, 140–63.
15. Chazan, *Anatomy of Ghanaian Politics*, 53.
16. Kwamena Bentsi-Enchill, *A Blueprint for the Party Game in Ghana* (Accra: Graphic Press, 1968), 10.
17. Ray Kakrabah-Quarshie, *Achievements of the Progress Party, 1969–1971* (Accra: Bekumah Agencies, 1971), 40; Fred M. Hayward, "Ghana Experiments with Civic Education," *Africa Report* 16, no. 5 (May 1971): 24–27.
18. Republic of Ghana, *First [Second and Third] Interim Report of the Commission of Inquiry into Bribery and Corruption* (Accra: Ghana Publishing Corporation, 1972).
19. Chazan, *Anatomy of Ghanaian Politics*, 102.
20. Republic of Ghana, *White Paper on the Report of the Taylor Assets Committee*, W.P. no. 1/76 (Accra: Ghana Publishing Corporation, 1976).
21. Chazan, *Anatomy of Ghanaian Politics*, 46–49, 222–27.
22. Ninsin, *Political Struggles in Ghana*, 30–35; Chazan, *Anatomy of Ghanaian Politics*, 159, 161, 225–29; Amoa, *University Students' Political Action*, 42, 82.
23. Valerie Plave Bennett, "Malcontents in Uniform—The 1972 Coup d'Etat," in Austin and Luckham, *Politicians and Soldiers*, 308.
24. Bennett, 308.

25. Bennett, 309.
26. Bennett, 310.
27. Chazan, *Anatomy of Ghanaian Politics*, 162–64, 235–36; Jon Kraus, "The Political Economy of Food in Ghana," in *Coping with Africa's Food Crisis*, ed. Naomi Chazan and Timothy M. Shaw (Boulder, CO: Lynne Rienner, 1988), 90–91.
28. Michael Johnston, "The Political Consequences of Corruption: A Reassessment," *Comparative Politics* 18, no. 4 (July 1986): 459–77.
29. Chazan, *Anatomy of Ghanaian Politics*, 46–51, 238–42; Kofi Awoonor, *The Ghana Revolution: Background Account from a Personal Perspective* (New York: Oasis Publishers, 1984), 37–73.
30. Mike Oquaye, *Politics in Ghana, 1972–1979* (Accra: Tornado Publications, 1980), 31–32, 46–49.
31. *Daily Graphic*, June 16, 26, 27, 28, and 29, 1979.
32. Eboe Hutchful, "A Tale of Two Regimes: Imperialism, the Military and Class in Ghana," *Review of African Political Economy*, no. 14 (January–April 1979): 50; emphasis in original.
33. Kwame Akon Ninsin, *The Corrupt Elites: Anatomy of Power and Wealth in Ghana* (Accra: Gavoss Education, 2018), 68, 98, 115.
34. Piet Konings, *The State and Rural Class Formation in Ghana: A Comparative Analysis* (London: KPI, 1986), 141–96, 221–32; Piet Konings, "Rizculteurs capitalistes et petits paysans: La naissance d'un conflit de classe au Ghana," *Politique africaine*, no. 11 (September 1983): 77–94.
35. Ninsin, *Corrupt Elites*, 27.
36. Oquaye, *Politics in Ghana*, 17.
37. Chazan, *Anatomy of Ghanaian Politics*, 194–96; Oquaye, *Politics in Ghana*, 17–45.
38. Chazan, *Anatomy of Ghanaian Politics*, 197.
39. James C. Scott, *Comparative Political Corruption* (Englewood Cliffs, NJ: Prentice-Hall, 1972), 80–84.
40. Chazan, *Anatomy of Ghanaian Politics*, 242–46; Gwendolyn Mikell, *Cocoa and Chaos in Ghana* (New York: Paragon House, 1989), 207.
41. Oquaye, *Politics in Ghana*, 94.
42. Republic of Ghana, *Report of the Ad Hoc Committee on Union Government* (Accra: State Publishing Corporation, 1977), 66–69, 113.
43. Kofi B. Quantson, *Ghana: Peace and Stability; Chapters from the Intelligence Sector* (Accra: Napascom, 2000), 155–56.
44. Chazan, *Anatomy of Ghanaian Politics*, 261–68.
45. Oquaye, *Politics in Ghana*, 225–26.
46. Oquaye, 111–16; Chazan, *Anatomy of Ghanaian Politics*, 269–77.
47. Oquaye, *Politics in Ghana*, 121.
48. Ninsin, *Political Struggles in Ghana*, 56.

Notes to Pages 87–98

49. Kofi Abaka Jackson, *When Gun Rules: A Soldier's Testimony* (Accra: Woeli Publishing Services, 1999), 63.

Chapter 5: From Mutiny to Revolution

1. *West Africa*, March 12, 1979.
2. *Daily Graphic*, May 9, 1979.
3. Kojo Yankah, *The Trial of JJ Rawlings: Echoes of the 31st December Revolution* (Accra: Ghana Publishing Corporation, 1986), 17–18; emphasis in original.
4. Yankah, 13.
5. Yankah, 12–13.
6. Barbara E. Okeke, *4 June: A Revolution Betrayed* (Enugu, Nigeria: Ikenga Publishers, 1982), 130.
7. Yankah, *Trial of JJ Rawlings*, 16–19.
8. Yankah, 22.
9. Okeke, *4 June*, 133.
10. Okeke, 44–45; Yankah, *Trial of JJ Rawlings*, 28.
11. Naomi Chazan, *An Anatomy of Ghanaian Politics: Managing Political Recession, 1969–1982* (Boulder, CO: Westview, 1983), 281.
12. *Daily Graphic*, June 28 and 29, 1979.
13. *Daily Graphic*, June 18, 1979.
14. *Daily Graphic*, July 4, 1979.
15. *Daily Graphic*, July 3, 1979.
16. Yankah, *Trial of JJ Rawlings*, 33–34.
17. *Catholic Standard*, July 29, 1979.
18. Yankah, *Trial of JJ Rawlings*, 31–33.
19. Arnold Quainoo, author's interview, Accra, February 15, 1999.
20. *Daily Graphic*, June 26, 1979.
21. *Daily Graphic*, July 20, 1979.
22. Chazan, *Anatomy of Ghanaian Politics*, 282.
23. *Daily Graphic*, June 23 and July 10, 1979; Okeke, *4 June*, 93.
24. Armed Forces Revolutionary Council, Ghana Nationality (Amendment) Decree, 1979, AFRCD 42, September 17, 1979.
25. Claire Robertson, "The Death of Makola and Other Tragedies," *Canadian Journal of African Studies* 17, no. 3 (1983): 472.
26. *Daily Graphic*, August 20, 1979.
27. Nii K. Bentsi-Enchill, "Losing Illusions at Makola Market," *West Africa*, September 3, 1979, 1591–92.
28. *Daily Graphic*, August 18, 1979.
29. Takyiwaa Manuh, author's interview, Accra, January 20, 1999.
30. *Daily Graphic*, July 13, 1979.
31. *Daily Graphic*, August 10, 1979.
32. *Daily Graphic*, June 22, 1979.

33. *Daily Graphic*, August 4, 1979.
34. Joseph G. Amamoo, *The Ghanaian Revolution* (London: Jafint Publishers, 1988), 199.
35. *West Africa*, June 25, 1979.
36. Chazan, *Anatomy of Ghanaian Politics*, 299.
37. Yankah, *Trial of JJ Rawlings*, 50.
38. Okeke, *4 June*, 93.
39. Chazan, *Anatomy of Ghanaian Politics*, 307–9.
40. Eboe Hutchful, "Reconstructing Civil-Military Relations and the Collapse of Democracy in Ghana, 1979–81," *African Affairs* 96 (1997): 535–60.
41. *West Africa*, April 14 and May 19, 1980.
42. *Daily Graphic*, July 10, 1980.
43. *West Africa*, June 16, 1980.
44. Yankah, *Trial of JJ Rawlings*, 58–59.
45. *West Africa*, May 19, 1980; Donald Ray, *Ghana: Politics, Economics and Society* (London: Francis Pinter, 1986), 27–28.
46. Yankah, *Trial of JJ Rawlings*, 60–61.
47. *West Africa*, June 15, 1981; Yankah, *Trial of JJ Rawlings*, 61–62.
48. Simon Baynham, "Divide et Impera: Civilian Control of the Military in Ghana's Second and Third Republics," *Journal of Modern African Studies* 23, no. 4 (December 1985): 639–40.
49. *West Africa*, December 7 and 14, 1981.
50. Radio broadcast to the nation, December 31, 1981, in Jerry John Rawlings Jr., *A Revolutionary Journey: Selected Speeches of Flt.-Lt. Jerry John Rawlings, Chairman of the PNDC*, vol. 1, *Dec. 31st 1981–Dec. 31st 1982* (Accra: Information Services Department, n.d.), 1.
51. Rawlings, *Revolutionary Journey*, 1, 5.
52. Rawlings, 14.
53. Rawlings, 8.
54. Rawlings, 6.
55. Jack A. Goldstone, "Toward a Fourth Generation of Revolutionary Theory," *Annual Review of Political Science* 4 (2001): 142.
56. Jack A. Goldstone, *Revolutions: A Very Short History* (Oxford: Oxford University Press, 2014), 7.
57. Ernest Harsch, *Thomas Sankara: An African Revolutionary* (Athens: Ohio University Press, 2014); Ernest Harsch, *Burkina Faso: A History of Power, Protest and Revolution* (London: Zed Press, 2017).

Chapter 6: "We No Go Sit Down"

1. Kwame A. Ninsin, "Strategies of Mobilisation under the PNDC Government," in *Ghana under PNDC Rule*, ed. Emmanuel Gyimah-Boadi (Oxford: CODESRIA, 1993), 100.

Notes to Pages 109–117

2. Ninsin, 100–102.
3. Provisional National Defence Council, *Preamble to Policy Guidelines of the Provisional National Defence Council* (Accra: Ghana Information Services Department, 1982), 7–8.
4. *Daily Graphic*, February 11, 1982.
5. Yaw Akrasi-Sarpong, author's interview, Accra, March 8, 1985.
6. "Re-organisation of the M/C Sub-Committee—Proposals," typed memorandum by Kofi Gafatsi Normanyo, INCC, Accra, March 1982, PDC Collection.
7. *People's Daily Graphic*, January 31, 1983.
8. *Daily Graphic*, February 27, 1982.
9. "Report on PDC/WDC Activities in the Brong-Ahafo Region since the Launching of the Revolution on 31st December, 1981," by Kwabena Anane-Adjei, Regional Interim Coordinator of Brong Ahafo PDCs, May 20, 1982, PDC Collection.
10. *Daily Graphic*, June 25 and September 22, 1982.
11. *Daily Graphic*, October 12, 1982.
12. *Daily Graphic*, October 14, 1982.
13. Letter from D. M. A. Afianu, secretary, Agave-Afedume PDC, Volta Region, to the INCC, Accra, June 18, 1982, PDC Collection.
14. "Minutes of a General Staff Meeting Held at the Conference Room on 11th June, 1982," Ministry of Health, Accra, June 29, 1982, PDC Collection.
15. Letter from Seth W. Senahey, Secretary, PDC, GNTC Storekeepers Association Branch, Accra, to INCC, Accra, February 24, 1982, PDC Collection.
16. Report from A. K. Provinseh, Registrar, Awutu Traditional Council, to National Coordinator PDCs, Accra, March 12, 1982, PDC Collection.
17. Paul Nugent, *Big Men, Small Boys and Politics in Ghana: Power, Ideology and the Burden of History, 1982–1994* (London: Pinter, 1995), 58.
18. Emmanuel Hansen, "The State and Popular Struggles in Ghana, 1982–86," in *Popular Struggles for Democracy in Africa*, ed. Peter Anyang' Nyong'o (London: United Nations University and Zed Books, 1987), 179.
19. Ampofo Kwesi Emmanuel, "Programme of Political Work among Broad Groups of People's Defence Committees," duplicated paper, 1982, PDC Collection.
20. Piet Konings, "The State and the Defence Committees in the Ghanaian Revolution, 1981–1984" (unpublished manuscript, n.d.), 8.
21. Hansen, "State and Popular Struggles," 178.
22. *Daily Graphic*, April 28, 1982.
23. *Daily Graphic*, April 5 and August 3, 1982.
24. *Daily Graphic*, June 16, 1982.
25. C. Adablah, "PDC Membership," report from Keta, Volta Region, to INCC, Accra, March 10, 1982, PDC Collection.

26. Provisional National Defence Council, *The New Guidelines for the National Defence Committee and People's Defence Committees* (Accra: Information Services Department, 1983), 5.
27. *Daily Graphic*, January 8, 1982.
28. "Joint Workers' Defence Committee Meeting Held at the Conference Room of the Ministry of Local Government on the 16th July, 1982," report signed by B. A. Tagoe, WDC Chairman, PDC Collection.
29. *Daily Graphic*, September 28, 1982.
30. Letter from H. K. Gaddah to INCC Investigation Branch, Accra, May 12, 1982; letter from T. D. Sewu for the Chairman, Togbloku Towns PDC, to the Secretary, Citizens Vetting Committee, Accra, March 16, 1982, PDC Collection.
31. *Daily Graphic*, May 7 and September 10, 1982.
32. *Daily Graphic*, October 13, 1982.
33. *Daily Graphic*, February 20 and July 22, 1982; *People's Daily Graphic*, February 2 and February 11, 1984.
34. Two letters from "All Form Four Students," Wenchi Secondary School, to the Headmaster, Staff, and School Council, with copies forwarded to the INCC, June 16 and June 18, 1982, PDC Collection.
35. *Daily Graphic*, October 26, 1982.
36. Letter from the "PDC/Students' Task Force," Adukrom, to the PNDC Secretariat, Accra, March 8, 1982, PDC Collection.
37. *Daily Graphic*, February 2 and 11, 1982.
38. *People's Daily Graphic*, August 9, 1983.
39. *Daily Graphic*, January 6, 1982.
40. "The Treasonable Acts of Yiadom Ohene Boakye and His Henchmen Liaison Officers at the Produce Buying Divisions of the G.C.M.B.," statement signed by the Interim National Defence Committee of the Produce Buying Division, [January 1982], PDC Collection.
41. *People's Daily Graphic*, August 26, 1983.
42. *Daily Graphic*, February 18 and June 10, 1982.
43. *Daily Graphic*, June 22, 1982.
44. Letter from George A. Tindaanbil, Vice-Chairman, State Insurance Corporation WDC, Sekondi-Takoradi, to the Chairman, PNDC, Accra, May 20, 1982, PDC Collection.
45. Letter from Darko Agyekum, Executive Secretary, Western Regional Council of Kwame Nkrumah Revolutionary Guards, Sekondi, to Chairman, PNDC, Accra, July 9, 1982, PDC Collection.
46. Letter to Flt. Lt. J. J. Rawlings, Chairman PNDC, from George B. Odoom, John N. Dadzie, and C. M. Ackah, State Fishing Corporation employees, Tema, February 2, 1982; letter to the Chairman, PDC, State Fishing Corporation, from S. S. Narketey, Tema, February 15, 1982; letter

to the Secretary, National Investigations Committee, State House, Accra, from George Ben. Odoom, employee of State Fishing Corporation, Tema, March 8, 1982, PDC Collection.
47. "Report on Fish Storage by Pasomahtago Ltd," to Chairman PDC, by Finance Affairs Sub-committee of SFC People's Defence Committee, February 22, 1982; "Speech by the Local Chairman of People's Defence C'ttee," transcript on SFC letterhead, February 1982, Ref # SFC/PDC/C.2, PDC Collection.
48. *Daily Graphic*, April 21, 1982.
49. "Minutes of the 3rd Management and W.D.C. Meeting Held at Head Office Board Room on Thursday 4th February, 1982," National Industrial Corporation Fabric Manufacturing Factory, Accra, PDC Collection.
50. "Report on the Investigation Carried Out on Alleged Unauthorised Collection of Textiles Materials from Store," from D. E. Ofusu, Chairman, and Joseph Charway, Secretary, WDC, NIC Fabric Manufacturing Factory, Accra, to the Secretary, PNDC, Burma Camp, February 8, 1982, PDC Collection.
51. "Resolution Adopted by Workers of SGMC Headquarters at Tarkwa on Thursday 29th July, 1982 in Connection with the Removal of Mr. R. A. S. Ofori Atta (Corporation Secretary) from Office," signed by E. J. Acquah and S. R. N. Forson, Chairman and Secretary of WDC, SGMC Hq., and F. K. Abuah and Robert K. Cole, Chairman and Secretary, Ghana Mine Workers Union; "State Gold Mining Corporation, Minutes of Meeting Held on Thursday, 22nd July, 1982 at the Office of the Managing Director," signed by P. Y. Osei, Confidential Secretary, and B. A. Barko, Chairman, Interim Management Committee, PDC Collection.
52. "State Gold Mining Corporation, Workers Defence Committees Seminar, Sat. 3rd–Sun. 4th July 1982, Report, 5th July 1982," signed by Steve Ocansey, Secretary, Organising Committee, Tarkwa Goldfields Limited, PDC Collection.
53. *Daily Graphic*, June 12 and August 6, 1982; "Address by the Ghana National Farmers Council WDC Chairman on the Official Inauguration of the WDC at the Headquarters," June 10, 1982; "Workers Defence Committee, Reminder, Six Months Leave without Allowance," from Ghana National Farmers Council WDC Secretary Faustina Nelson to GNFC Secretary-General Oheneba Osei Yaw Akoto, July 15, 1982, PDC Collection.
54. "Petition for Investigations," signed and/or thumb-printed by 31 GNFC "chief farmers" and other figures, to the Chairman, INCC, Accra, August 5, 1982, PDC Collection.
55. *Daily Graphic*, December 30, 1982.
56. Letter from the Secretary, Millet Coop Consumers Union, to the PDC, Millet Textile Corporation, Accra, March 5, 1982; letter from Mary

Tandoh, member of the Gbegbeyise-Shiabu Cooperative Society, Old Dansoman-Mpoase, to the National Investigations Committee, March 18, 1982; "Minutes of the Meeting of the Local PDC Representatives, and the Consumers Co-operative Executives with the Personnel Manager," March 31, 1982, PDC Collection.

57. Letter from F. Gidi-Kodzo Azah, Chairman, and J. I. Q. Foligar, Secretary, Kpando PDC, Kpando, to Fl. Lt. J. J. Rawlings, Chairman, PNDC, July 5, 1982; letter from Chairman F. Gidi-Kodzo Azah, PDC, Kpando, to the Acting Secretary, INCC, Accra, July 30, 1982, PDC Collection.

58. *Daily Graphic*, December 8, 1982.

59. *People's Daily Graphic*, May 18 and 31, 1983.

60. *Daily Graphic*, January 9, 1982.

61. Yao Graham, "From GTP to Assene: Aspects of Industrial Working Class Struggles in Ghana 1982–1986," in *The State, Development and Politics in Ghana*, ed. Emmanuel Hansen and Kwame A. Ninsin (London: CODESRIA, 1989), 49; Nugent, *Big Men, Small Boys*, 62–63; *Daily Graphic*, April 21, April 30, and May 15, 1982.

62. *West Africa*, May 30, 1983.

63. Kwame Ninsin, "State, Capital and Labour Relations, 1961–1987," in Hansen and Ninsin, *State, Development and Politics*, 32.

64. *Venceremos*, "official organ" of the Workers Defence Committee of the Bank of Ghana 1, no. 3 (April 26, 1982) and 1, no. 5 (June 26, 1982), PDC Collection.

65. "Resolution Passed at the End of a Two-Day Seminar for Zonal Coordinators and Workers' Defence Committees in Navrongo District Held at the Institute for Field Communication and Agricultural Training (IFCAT) on the 2nd and 3rd of July, 1982," PDC Collection.

66. Graham, "From GTP to Assene," 50–51.

67. "Report of 'MONICORD' Mission to Agri Dev't Bank," by Kojo Jamesi, to the National Coordinator, Monitoring and Coordination committee, INCC, Accra, June 10, 1982, PDC Collection.

68. *Daily Graphic*, November 27 and December 30, 1982.

69. Letter from E. K. Aboagye, Branch Secretary, Public Utility Workers Union of TUC, Electricity Corporation, to Yao Graham, INCC, Accra, May 6, 1982, PDC Collection.

70. Ronald W. Graham, "Structural Problems in the World Economy: A Case Study of the Ghana-Valco Renegotiations," in *Essays from the Ghana-Valco Renegotiations, 1982–85*, ed. Fui S. Tsikata (Accra: Ghana Publishing Corporation, 1986), 99–101.

71. "Interview Revelations & Recommendations," by E. Bukroh, INCC representative to Valco discussions, June 8, 1982, PDC Collection.

72. *Daily Graphic*, June 19, 1982.

73. *Daily Graphic*, November 4, 1982; Graham, "Structural Problems," 102.
74. Letter from John Zekpe, Ghana Textile Printing Co., Tema, to PNDC, Gondar Barracks, Accra, June 1, 1982, PDC Collection.
75. Graham, "From GTP to Assene," 52–55; *Daily Graphic*, November 15, 18, 19, and 20, 1982.
76. Nugent, *Big Men, Small Boys*, 67; *Daily Graphic*, December 15, 1982; *West Africa*, December 12, 1983.
77. *People's Daily Graphic*, April 29 and 30, 1982.
78. *West Africa*, April 1, 1985.
79. Editorial, *People's Daily Graphic*, November 30, 1983.
80. *Daily Graphic*, June 2, 1982.
81. *Daily Graphic*, February 23 and April 17, 1982; letter from the Secretary and Chairman, WDC, Rockshell International Ltd., Tema, to the National Co-ordinator, WDC, Accra, March 15, 1982; letter from Ruben Goli, Secretary, WDC, Super Paper Products Co. Ltd., Tema, to the Coordinator, INCC, Accra, March 31, 1982, PDC Collection.
82. Letter from the Chairman and Secretary, WDC, M&K Engineering (Ghana) Ltd., Accra-North, to the PNDC Press Office, Accra, undated [but with an April 19, 1982, forwarding note to the INCC], PDC Collection.
83. "Progress Report on the Activities of the Dzindziso Peoples Defence Committee," October 5, 1982, Dzindziso Buem; letter from J. O. Lewis, Dzindziso PDC Chairman, and the PDC Secretary [name illegible] to the National Coordinator, INCC, Accra, October 18, 1982, PDC Collection.
84. *Daily Graphic*, April 1, 1982.
85. Letter by the PDC Secretary and Chairman, Anlo-Afiadenyigba [addressee not indicated], May 20, 1982, PDC Collection.
86. Nugent, *Big Men, Small Boys*, 70–72.
87. Letter from Kofi Portuphy, INCC Complaints and Investigations, to Officer-in-Charge, People's Police Service, Ada Foah, May 28, 1982, PDC Collection.
88. "Urgent Report from the Ayirebi PDC" [undated and unsigned] and "Important Report from the Ayirebi PDC," by Prince Danso (secretary), Yaw Nimo (chairman), Asumadu Ampong (spokesman), and Firang Yaw David (vice-secretary), Ayirebi PDC, April 30, 1982, PDC Collection.
89. "Monthly Operational Report, Peoples' Defence Committee, Great Ningo," by Ebenezer K. Nartey, March 13, 1982, PDC Collection.
90. "Prices of Food Items," public circular signed by E. D. Nikoi, Secretary, Central Coordinating Committee of PDCs, Labadi, July 9, 1982, PDC Collection.
91. *Daily Graphic*, July 12, 1982.
92. *People's Daily Graphic*, August 4, 1983.

93. *Daily Graphic*, May 11, 1982; see also Nugent, *Big Men, Small Boys*, 80.
94. *Daily Graphic*, October 19, 1982.
95. *Daily Graphic*, November 11, 1982.
96. *People's Daily Graphic*, June 15, 1983.
97. Letter from Gab Dak SoSu, Interim Chairman, WDC of West African Examinations Council, to the Coordinator, INCC, and the Coordinator, Interim Regional Coordination Committee, Accra, June 25, 1982, PDC Collection.
98. Statement on Mamponse PDC letterhead by W. D. Hammond, Chairman, Mamponse PDC, Accra, July 23, 1982, PDC Collection.
99. In an August 16, 1982, letter, the secretary of the Oyarifa PDC offered to the general commercial manager of the UTC Department Stores in Accra a barter arrangement, proposing to exchange maize for soap, sugar, and other essential items. In the margins of the letter, an INCC leader, YAS, scribbled, "This is a serious dv/pt [development] in the consciousness of PDC executives." PDC Collection.
100. *People's Daily Graphic*, January 4, 1983.
101. *Daily Graphic*, November 1, 1982.
102. Letter from Mrs. S. B. Dickens, Secretary, Odorkor Zone 13 Medium Scale Bakers, Kaneshie-Accra, to Gyesi Ankrah, INCC, Accra, June 7, 1982, PDC Collection.
103. Letter from the Chairman and Secretary, Dawa Youth Association, to the Chairman, INCC, Accra, July 4, 1982, PDC Collection.
104. *Daily Graphic*, May 25, 1982.
105. Letter from Kwabena Otoo, Secretary, Abeka PDC, to Co-ordinator, INCC, Accra [April 15, 1982], PDC Collection.
106. *Daily Graphic*, February 22, 1982.
107. Takyiwaa Manuh, author's interview, Accra, January 20, 1999.
108. Jeffrey S. Ahlman, *Living with Nkrumahism: Nation, State, and Pan-Africanism in Ghana* (Athens: Ohio University Press, 2017), 160–74.
109. "Revolutionary Suggestion," letter from James Kow Ainooh, assistant secretary, WDC, Tema Development Corporation, Tema, to the chairman, PNDC, March 11, 1982; "Report on PDC/WDC Activities in the Brong-Ahafo Region since the Launching of the Revolution on 31st December, 1981," by Kwabena Anane-Adjei, Regional Interim Coordinator of Brong Ahafo PDCs, May 20, 1982; "Report of the B.A. IRCC—Regional Coordinators Meeting—Friday, 13th August 1982," by K. H. Akar, INCC cadres in Brong Ahafo, PDC Collection.
110. Maxwell Owusu, "Tradition and Transformation: Democracy and the Politics of Popular Power in Ghana," *Journal of Modern African Studies* 34, no. 2 (June 1996): 307.
111. Yaw Akrasi-Sarpong, author's interview, Accra, October 28, 1988.

112. *People's Daily Graphic*, July 28, 1983.
113. *West Africa*, February 14, 1983.
114. Author's field notes from visits to Mobisquad sites in the Central, Eastern, and Greater Accra regions, October–November 1988.
115. Kofi Portuphy, author's interview, Accra, October 28, 1988.
116. Owusu, "Tradition and Transformation," 335–36, 341.
117. Yao Graham, author's interview, Accra, March 14, 1999.
118. *People's Daily Graphic*, January 25, 1984.
119. Letter from Barima Ofosu Anim I, Osenasehene, on letterhead of the "Ahenfie (Osenase) Palace," Osenase, Eastern Region, to the Chairman, PNDC, Burma Camp, Accra, March 23, 1982, PDC Collection.
120. Letter from Akatsi Town Development Committee to the Regional Secretary, PNDC, Ho, July 19, 1982, signed or thumb-printed by J. M. Amekor (Chair Akatsi TDC), Torgbui Sakpaku VII (Left Wing Chief of Avenor), Torgbui Letsa Norba II, Torgbui Aho III, Torgbui Ahortor II, Torgbui Badzi III, A. K. Dogbatse (elder), Victoria Kunudzro (market women representative), PDC Collection.
121. "Report on Investigations cum Political Rally—Ekumfi Edumafa, Central Region," by Dan Gyan Ankrah, May 9, 1982, PDC Collection.
122. "Gomoa Dabenyin Peoples Defence Committee," letter by J. K. Egyakwa Amusah, of Amusah Farms Ltd., to Chairman, INCC, Accra, May 24, 1982, PDC Collection.
123. Various letters from P. K. Xenya (PDC Secretary, Battor), Togbe Torkla IV (Battor Traditional Council), and Togbe E. H. K. Hervi VI (Chairman, Battor Traditional Area), to the INCC, PNDC Chairman, and Regional Secretary, Ho, March 16–April 15, 1982, PDC Collection.
124. *Daily Graphic*, November 10, 1982.
125. Donald Ray, *Ghana: Politics, Economics and Society* (London: Francis Pinter, 1986), 80–86.
126. *Daily Graphic*, April 5, 1982.
127. Abdulai Tinorgah, author's interview, Accra, January 26, 1999.
128. *Daily Graphic*, February 26, April 1, May 1, August 31, and September 17, 1982.
129. "INCC—Invact, Full Report of the Situation in Old Ningo," report of the INCC Investigation and Action Committee, n.d. [May 1982], PDC Collection.
130. Letter by T. N. Aboegyi, Secretary, PDC, Osiabura, Volta Region, March 19, 1982 [addressee not indicated]; letter by Kokoroko Pascal, Secretary, PDC, Kodeha, to INCC Investigation Department, State House, Accra, April 6, 1982; letter by Ernest Obimpe, Acting Secretary, Vakpo Students Union, Vakpo, Volta Region, to INCC, Complaints and Investigation Department, June 30, 1982, PDC Collection.

131. "Reaction of Some Anti-revolutionists against the Tomefa Peoples Defence Committee," report by Johnson Agkeryegah, PDC, Tomefa-Tease, to INCC, Accra, July 23, 1982, PDC Collection.
132. *Daily Graphic*, April 22 and October 13, 1982; *People's Daily Graphic*, June 1, August 22, and November 2, 1983.
133. "Discipline and Productivity," August 28, 1983, in Jerry John Rawlings Jr., *Forging Ahead: Selected Speeches of Flt-Lt. Jerry John Rawlings, Chairman of the PNDC, vol. 2, January 1st 1983–December 31st 1983* (Accra: Ghana Publishing Corporation, n.d.), 32.
134. Paul Emiljanowicz and Bonny Ibhawoh, "Democracy in Postcolonial Ghana: Tropes, State Power and the Defence Committees," *Third World Quarterly* 42, no. 6 (2021): 1213–32.
135. "Press Statement: Central Workers' Defence Committee of Civil Servants Held on Tuesday, 27th April, 1982, at the Public Services Commission"; "Press Statement on Recent Pronouncements by Mr. B. B. D. Asamoah Secretary to the PNDC on the Political Direction of the 31st December, Revolution," signed by Kwasi Anhwere, Interim Publicity Secretary, Central Workers Defence Committee of the Civil Service, June 22, 1982, PDC Collection.
136. Graham, "From GTP to Assene," 62–67.
137. *People's Daily Graphic*, December 8, 1984.
138. Committee for the Defence of the Revolution, *CDR Guidelines* (Accra: Nsamankow Press, 1986).
139. *People's Daily Graphic*, January 23, 1985; *West Africa*, February 4, 1985.
140. Author's notes, CDR National Secretariat, Accra, March 8–9, 1985.
141. Kofi Marrah, author's interview, Accra, January 24, 1999.

Chapter 7: Justice Fast and Rough

Epigraph source: George Agyekum, author's interview, Accra, February 13, 1999.

1. Robert Klitgaard, *Controlling Corruption* (Berkeley: University of California Press, 1988), 187.
2. William Burnett Harvey, *Law and Social Change in Ghana* (Princeton, NJ: Princeton University Press, 1966), 237–38.
3. Ken A. Attafuah, "Public Tribunals and the Administration of Justice in Rawlings' Ghana (1982–1992)" (unpublished manuscript, 1998), 67.
4. Kwadwo Afari-Gyan, *Public Tribunals and Justice in Ghana* (Accra: Asempa Publishers, 1988), 4.
5. Harvey, *Law and Social Change*, 230–36.
6. Attafuah, "Public Tribunals," 75–79.
7. Radio and television broadcast to the nation, January 5, 1982, in Jerry John Rawlings Jr., *A Revolutionary Journey: Selected Speeches of Flt.-Lt. Jerry*

Notes to Pages 147–153

　　John Rawlings, Chairman of the PNDC, vol. 1, *Dec. 31st 1981–Dec. 31st 1982* (Accra: Information Services Department, n.d.), 12.
8. *West Africa*, August 22–28, 1988.
9. *Daily Graphic*, January 21, 1982.
10. Kwamena Ahwoi, *Working with Rawlings* (Tema: Digibooks Ghana, 2020), 22.
11. Attafuah, "Public Tribunals," 85.
12. B. F. Bankie, "The Pre and Post 31 December 1981 Legal System of Ghana: Political Change and Law Reform—Inquest for a Popular Legal Dispensation" (unpublished manuscript, 1987), 49.
13. Attafuah, "Public Tribunals," 130–31.
14. Letter from Daniel Owusu-Koranteng (coordinating secretary) and Eden Gokah (vice-coordinating secretary), Coordinating Committee of the Defence Committee, Agona Swedru, to Chairman PNDC, September 15, 1982, PDC Collection.
15. Letter from D. D. Ayeh, Secretary Amasaman PDC, Amasaman, Accra, to Chairman PNDC, July 12, 1982, PDC Collection.
16. Bankie, "Pre and Post 31 December 1981," 17; letter from Michael Nunoo, INCC, Accra, to Officer-in-Charge, Weija Police, July 6, 1982, PDC Collection; letter from Gyasi Ankrah, INCC Investigation and Complaints Department, to Commanding Officer, Military Police, Accra, June 16, 1982, PDC Collection.
17. Provisional National Defence Council, Citizens Vetting Committee Law (PNDCL 1), February 1, 1982; Provisional National Defence Council, Citizens Vetting Committee (Amendment) Law (PNDCL 18), June 30, 1982.
18. B. A. Sapati, author's interview, Accra, February 2, 1999.
19. Sapati, interview.
20. Sapati, interview.
21. *People's Daily Graphic*, February 3, 1983.
22. Data drawn from *Daily Graphic*, December 28, 1982.
23. Provisional National Defence Council, National Investigations Committee Law (PNDCL 2), February 3, 1982.
24. Emmanuel Ohene, author's interview, Accra, February 19, 1999.
25. Attafuah, "Public Tribunals," 136.
26. Baffour Agyeman-Duah, "Ghana, 1982–6: The Politics of the P.N.D.C.," *Journal of Modern African Studies* 25, no. 4 (December 1987): 627.
27. Provisional National Defence Council, Public Tribunals Law, 1982 (PNDCL 24), July 21, 1982.
28. Attafuah, "Public Tribunals," 117–18.
29. Provisional National Defence Council, Public Tribunals Law, 1982.
30. Provisional National Defence Council, Public Tribunals Law, 1984 (PNDCL 78), December 21, 1983.

31. Bankie, "Pre and Post 31 December 1981," 43–44.
32. Attafuah, "Public Tribunals," 205.
33. Agyekum, interview.
34. Kwamena Ahwoi, author's interview, Accra, March 12, 1999.
35. Agyekum, interview.
36. J. C. Amonoo-Monney, author's interview, Accra, February 3, 1999.
37. Without access to actual tribunal records, the author compiled a dataset from accounts in every available issue of the state-owned newspaper *Daily Graphic / People's Daily Graphic* from the first trials in 1982 through the end of 1987. Because the trial articles often followed a set format, it was possible to identify comparable information on the cases of 1,417 individual defendants, although not always in full detail. The sample is incomplete, however, since there were cases that were never covered in the newspaper, especially in tribunal sessions held outside Accra.
38. *People's Daily Graphic*, July 3 and October 16, 1985, and January 17, 1987.
39. *People's Daily Graphic*, August 24, August 31, and September 2, 1983.
40. *People's Daily Graphic*, November 28, 1985, and January 22, February 25, and February 27, 1987.
41. Ahwoi, interview, 1999.
42. Mike Oquaye, "Law, Justice and the Revolution," in Gyimah-Boadi, *Ghana under PNDC Rule* (Oxford: CODESRIA, 1993), 163.
43. Amonoo-Monney, interview.
44. Attafuah, "Public Tribunals," 238.
45. *Daily Graphic*, September 28, 1982.
46. *People's Daily Graphic*, June 25, 1983.
47. Agyekum, interview.
48. Ahwoi, interview, 1999.
49. *Daily Graphic*, September 16, 1982.
50. *Daily Graphic*, October 23 and December 2, 1982.
51. George Agyekum, ed., *The Judges' Murder Trial of 1983* (Accra: Justice Trust Publications, 1999), 164.
52. Oquaye, "Law, Justice and the Revolution," 162.
53. Roger Gocking, "Ghana's Public Tribunals: An Experiment in Revolutionary Justice," *African Affairs* 95, no. 379 (April 1996): 210.
54. *People's Daily Graphic*, September 19, 1984, January 5, 1985, and April 5, 1986.
55. Attafuah, "Public Tribunals," 253.
56. Attafuah, 258.
57. Ahwoi, *Working with Rawlings*, 35–36.
58. Ahwoi, interview, 1999.
59. *People's Daily Graphic*, November 1, 1985.
60. *People's Daily Graphic*, August 29, 1986.

61. Provisional National Defence Council, Revenue Commissioners Law (PNDCL 80), January 7, 1984.
62. Attafuah, "Public Tribunals," 134–35.
63. Ohene, interview.
64. "Address by Mr. Ato Dadzie, PNDC Secretary, PNDC Secretariat, on the Occasion of the Inauguration of Accra District/Community Tribunal," in Board of Public Tribunals, *Report on Operations 1988* (Accra: Board of Public Tribunals, 1989), Annex, 2.
65. Board of Public Tribunals, *Report on Operations*, 5, 14–15.
66. *People's Daily Graphic*, March 1 and November 7, 1986.
67. *People's Daily Graphic*, July 12, 1986.
68. *People's Daily Graphic*, July 11, 1987.

Chapter 8: Shifting State Agendas

1. *Daily Graphic*, July 12, 1982.
2. World Bank, *Ghana: Policies and Program for Adjustment* (Washington, DC: World Bank, 1984), xvi, 1–33; John Loxley, *Ghana: Economic Crisis and the Long Road to Recovery* (Ottawa: North-South Institute, 1988), 1–4; UNICEF, "Adjustment Policies and Programmes to Protect Children and Other Vulnerable Groups in Ghana," in *Adjustment with a Human Face*, vol. 2, *Country Case Studies*, ed. Giovanni Andrea Cornia, Richard Jolly, and Frances Stewart (Oxford, UK: Clarendon, 1988), 94–97; Tsatsu Tsikata, "Ghana," in *The Human Dimension of Africa's Persistent Economic Crisis*, ed. Adebayo Adedeji, Sadig Rasheed, and Melody Morrison (London: Hans Zell, 1990), 144–46.
3. Donald Rothchild and E. Gyimah-Boadi, "Ghana's Economic Decline and Development Strategies," in *Africa in Economic Crisis*, ed. John Ravenhill (New York: Columbia University Press, 1986), 258.
4. Provisional National Defence Council, *Preamble to Policy Guidelines of the Provisional National Defence Council* (Accra: Ghana Information Services Department, 1982), 4.
5. *Daily Graphic*, March 1, 1982.
6. *Daily Graphic*, August 21, 1982.
7. *Daily Graphic*, May 28 and 29, 1982.
8. *People's Daily Graphic*, April 28, 1983.
9. Kevin Shillington, *Ghana and the Rawlings Factor* (New York: St. Martin's, 1992), 99.
10. *Daily Graphic*, September 21, 1982.
11. *Daily Graphic*, September 7, 1982.
12. Kwesi Botchwey, *The PNDC's Programme for Reconstruction and Development* (Accra: Information Services Department, 1982), 3.
13. *People's Daily Graphic*, February 25, 1983.

14. Rothchild and Gyimah-Boadi, "Ghana's Economic Decline," 270.
15. Kojo Tsikata, author's interview, Accra, March 4, 1985.
16. Eboe Hutchful, "From 'Revolution' to Monetarism: The Economics and Politics of the Adjustment Programme in Ghana," in *Structural Adjustment in Africa*, ed. Bonnie K. Campbell and John Loxley (New York: St. Martin's, 1989), 106.
17. Ernest Harsch, "Ghana: On the Road to Recovery," *Africa Report* 34, no. 4 (July–August 1989): 24.
18. Tony Hodges, "Ghana's Strategy for Adjustment with Growth," *Africa Recovery* 2, no. 3 (August 1988): 16–21, 27.
19. World Bank, *World Development Indicators, 2000*, CD-ROM version (Washington, DC: World Bank, 2000); Ishan Kapur, Michael T. Hadjimichael, Paul Hilbers, Jerald Schiff, and Philippe Szymczak, *Ghana: Adjustment and Growth, 1983–91* (Washington, DC: International Monetary Fund, 1991); World Bank, *Ghana: Progress on Adjustment* (Washington, DC: World Bank, 1991).
20. Loxley, *Ghana*, 43–44.
21. Jon Kraus, "The Struggle over Structural Adjustment in Ghana," *Africa Today* 38, no. 4 (1991): 27–33.
22. Kweku G. Folson, "Structural Adjustment in Ghana," in *Alternative Strategies for Africa*, vol. 3, *Debt and Democracy*, ed. Ben Turok (London: Institute for African Alternatives, 1991), 102–3.
23. Yaw Asante, Frederick Nixson, and G. Kwaku Tsikata, "The Industrial Sector and Economic Development," in *Economic Reforms in Ghana: The Miracle and the Myth*, ed. Ernest Aryeetey, Jane Harrigan, and Machiko Nissanke (Trenton, NJ: Africa World Press, 2000), 246–66; Loxley, *Ghana*, 50.
24. *People's Daily Graphic*, May 5 and 13, 1983.
25. Tsikata, "Ghana," 154.
26. World Bank, *Ghana: Policies*, xvii.
27. Reginald H. Green, *Country Study 1: Ghana* (Helsinki: World Institute for Development Economics Research, 1987), 7.
28. Huudu Yahaya, author's interview, Accra, October 28, 1988.
29. Richard Jeffries, "Urban Popular Attitudes towards the Economic Recovery Programme and the PNDC Government in Ghana," *African Affairs* 91, no. 363 (April 1992): 214–15.
30. Paul Nugent, *Big Men, Small Boys and Politics in Ghana: Power, Ideology and the Burden of History, 1982–1994* (London: Pinter, 1995), 182.
31. UNICEF, "Adjustment Policies and Programmes," 100, 106, 110.
32. Loxley, *Ghana*, 26; UNICEF, "Adjustment Policies and Programmes," 98; Green, *Country Study: Ghana*, 42; Kraus, "Struggle over Structural Adjustment," 32; Hodges, "Ghana's Strategy," 27.

33. Kraus, "Struggle over Structural Adjustment," 31.
34. Mohamed Ibn Chambas, author's interview, Accra, May 4, 2000.
35. Baffour Agyeman-Duah, author's interview, Accra, May 2, 2000.
36. George Benneh, author's interview, Legon, May 8, 2000.
37. Beth Rabinowitz, *Coup, Rivals, and the Modern State: Why Rural Coalitions Matter in Sub-Saharan Africa* (New York: Cambridge University Press, 2018), 169–96.
38. *People's Daily Graphic*, April 5, 1984.
39. W. Asenso Okyere, "The Response of Farmers to Ghana's Adjustment Policies," in *The Long-Term Perspective Study of Sub-Saharan Africa: Background Papers*, vol. 2 (Washington, DC: World Bank, 1990), 79.
40. Alexander Sarris and Hadi Shams, *Ghana under Structural Adjustment: The Impact on Agriculture and the Rural Poor* (New York: New York University Press, 1991), 226.
41. Simon Commander, John Howell, and Waye Seini, "Ghana: 1983–7," in *Structural Adjustment and Agriculture: Theory and Practice in Africa and Latin America*, ed. Simon Commander (London: Overseas Development Institute, 1989), 112.
42. Ibrahim Adam, author's interview, Accra, June 15, 1993.
43. John Nabila, author's interview, Accra, May 11, 2008.
44. Commander, Howell, and Seini, "Ghana: 1983–7," 119, 123–25.
45. George J. Sefa Dei, "The Renewal of a Ghanaian Rural Economy," *Canadian Journal of African Studies* 26, no. 1 (1992): 24–53.
46. Kwame Ninsin, "Ghana beyond Crisis and Adjustment," *Africa Development* 21, nos. 2–3 (1996): 37.
47. World Bank, *Ghana: Policies*, 51.
48. Jeffrey Herbst, *The Politics of Reform in Ghana, 1982–1991* (Berkeley: University of California Press, 1993), 56.
49. *People's Daily Graphic*, May 15, 1985.
50. Tsikata, "Ghana," 147; Herbst, *Politics of Reform*, 40–41.
51. Donald Ray, *Ghana: Politics, Economics and Society* (London: Francis Pinter, 1986), 30–39; *West Africa*, September 30, 1985.
52. "Address Delivered by Mr. R. R. Beckeley, Interim Chairman of the Central Workers Defence Committee of the Civil Service, at the Inauguration of the Committee on the Restructuring of the Civil Service," June 30, 1982, attached to a July 12, 1982, letter from G. N. Baiden, Secretary Central WDC of the Civil Service, to all WDCs and heads of departments, PDC Collection.
53. Radio and television broadcast to the nation, August 28, 1983, in Jerry John Rawlings Jr., *Forging Ahead: Selected Speeches of Flt.-Lt. Jerry John Rawlings, Chairman of the PNDC*, vol. 2, *January 1st 1983–December 31st 1983* (Accra: Information Services Department, n.d.), 27–28.

54. Stephen D. Younger, "Ghana: Economic Recovery Program; A Case Study of Stabilization and Structural Adjustment in Sub-Saharan Africa," in *Successful Development in Africa: Case Studies of Projects, Programs, and Policies* (Washington, DC: World Bank, 1989), 148; Sarris and Shams, *Ghana under Structural Adjustment*, 135; *People's Daily Graphic*, July 24, 1987.
55. World Bank, *Economic Developments in 1987: A Status Report* (Accra: World Bank, 1987), 14.
56. *People's Daily Graphic*, January 19, 1987.
57. *People's Daily Graphic*, July 2, 1985.
58. *People's Daily Graphic*, April 1, 1986.
59. Nugent, *Big Men, Small Boys*, 192.
60. *People's Daily Graphic*, April 1 and April 7, 1986.
61. *People's Daily Graphic*, June 10, 1986.
62. Mamadou Dia, *Africa's Management in the 1990s and Beyond: Reconciling Indigenous and Transplanted Institutions* (Washington, DC: World Bank, 1996), 89.
63. *People's Daily Graphic*, February 21, 1986.
64. *People's Daily Graphic*, August 10, 1984.
65. *People's Daily Graphic*, September 4, 1985.
66. *People's Daily Graphic*, July 12, 1986.
67. World Bank, *World Development Indicators*.
68. Eboe Hutchful, "Military Policy and Reform in Ghana," *Journal of Modern African Studies* 35, no. 2 (June 1997): 258.
69. Kwamena Ahwoi, *Working with Rawlings* (Tema: Digibooks Ghana, 2020), 218.
70. Arnold Quainoo, author's interview, Accra, February 15, 1999.
71. Ray, *Ghana*, 148; *People's Daily Graphic*, March 13, 1985.
72. Hutchful, "Military Policy and Reform," 253.
73. Hutchful, 256.
74. Quainoo, interview.
75. Robin Luckham, "Transition to Democracy and Control over Ghana's Military and Security Establishments," in *Ghana: Transition to Democracy*, ed. Kwame A. Ninsin (Accra: Freedom Publications, 1998), 134.
76. *People's Daily Graphic*, September 24, 1985.
77. Hutchful, "Military Policy and Reform," 260, 269–70.
78. World Bank, *World Development Indicators*.
79. Major General Carl Coleman, author's interview, Accra, May 14, 2008.
80. Quainoo, interview.
81. Nugent, *Big Men, Small Boys*, 178–79, 184; Kwame Ninsin, ed., *Ghana: Transition to Democracy* (Accra: Freedom Publications, 1998), 53.
82. Ministry of Local Government, *From the Centre to the Grassroots (Excerpts from Selected Speeches on the PNDC's Decentralisation Policy)* (Accra: Venus Publications, 1991).

83. Baffour Kofi Apreko, "An Appraisal of the Implementation of the PNDC Decentralisation Policy as a Grassroots Development Strategy, with Ga District as a Case Study" (master's thesis, Institute of African Studies, University of Ghana, Legon, 1994), 82.
84. *Daily Graphic*, December 21, 22, and 23, 1982.
85. Provisional National Defence Council, *Decentralisation in Ghana* (Accra: Information Services Department, 1983), 3; emphasis in original.
86. Provisional National Defence Council, *Outlines of the Decentralisation Plan of the Provisional National Defence Council* (Accra: Information Services Department, 1984), 1.
87. *People's Daily Graphic*, November 8, 1984, and April 26, 1986.
88. *People's Daily Graphic*, October 24, 1985, October 13, October 14, and November 22, 1986, and January 27, 1987.
89. S. K. Asibuo, "Military Regime Performance in Decentralization and Local Administration for Development: A Ghanaian Case Study," *Africa Insight* 22, no. 4 (1992): 283–87.
90. Maxwell Owusu, "Tradition and Transformation: Democracy and the Politics of Popular Power in Ghana," *Journal of Modern African Studies* 34, no. 2 (June 1996): 326.
91. *Daily Graphic*, December 10, 1982.
92. Provisional National Defence Council, Chieftaincy (Restoration of Status of Chiefs) Law, 1983.
93. *People's Daily Graphic*, May 23, 1987.
94. *People's Daily Graphic*, August 19, 1986, and February 19, September 9, and December 23, 1987.
95. *People's Daily Graphic*, January 3, 1986.
96. Owusu, "Tradition and Transformation," 337, 342.
97. *People's Daily Graphic*, April 6, 1987.
98. Owusu, "Tradition and Transformation," 337.
99. Kofi Portuphy, author's interview, Accra, October 28, 1988; Huudu Yahaya, author's interview, October 28, 1988.
100. Notes from author's field trip, Mozano, Central Region, November 2, 1988; Owusu, "Tradition and Transformation," 342.
101. *People's Daily Graphic*, August 3, 1985, and April 16, 1986.
102. Edzodzinam Tsikata, "Women's Political Organisations, 1951–1987," in *The State, Development and Politics in Ghana*, ed. Emmanuel Hansen and Kwame A. Ninsin (London: CODESRIA, 1989), 85; Takyiwaa Manuh, "Women, the State and Society under the PNDC," in *Ghana under PNDC Rule*, ed. Gyimah-Boadi (Oxford: CODESRIA, 1993), 186, 189, 195.
103. Tsikata, "Women's Political Organisations," 86–87; Manuh, "Women, the State and Society," 186.

104. Tsikata, "Women's Political Organisations," 86–87.
105. Beverly J. Stoeltje, "Asante Queen Mothers: A Study of Female Authority," in *Queens, Queen Mothers, Priestesses, and Power: Case Studies in African Gender*, ed. Flora Edouwaye S. Kaplan (New York: New York Academy of Sciences, 1997), 41–71.
106. Cecelia Johnson, author's interview, Accra, November 4, 1988.
107. Tsikata, "Women's Political Organisations," 85, 89.
108. Provisional National Defence Council, (Establishment) Proclamation (Supplementary and Consequential Provisions), PNDC Law 42, Section 32, 1982.
109. *West Africa*, February 25, 1985, 347.
110. Republic of Ghana, *The Search for True Democracy in Ghana* (Accra: Public Relations Department, 1985), 10.
111. National Commission for Democracy, *Evolving a True Democracy: Summary of NCD's Work towards the Establishment of a New Democratic Order* (Accra: National Commission for Democracy, 1991), 10–11.
112. S. Y. M. Zanu, "PNDC Law 207 and the Financing of District Assemblies," in *Ghana's Local Government Law: Issues of Implementation*, ed. S. A. Nkrumah (Legon: School of Administration, University of Ghana, 1990), 33.
113. Republic of Ghana, *District Political Authority and Modalities for District Level Elections* (Accra: Ghana Publishing Corporation, 1987), 1–3.
114. Kwamena Ahwoi, author's interview, Accra, June 17, 1993.
115. *People's Daily Graphic*, December 27, 1987.
116. Herbst, *Politics of Reform*, 91–92.
117. Gwendolyn Mikell, "Peasant Politicisation and Economic Recuperation in Ghana: Local and National Dilemmas," *Journal of Modern African Studies* 27, no. 3 (September 1989): 472–73.
118. Ninsin, "Ghana beyond Crisis and Adjustment," 28; Mikell, "Peasant Politicisation," 473.
119. National Commission for Democracy, *Evolving a True Democracy*, 37, 51.

Chapter 9: Elections and Money

1. Michael Bratton and Nicolas van de Walle, *Democratic Experiments in Africa: Regime Transitions in Comparative Perspective* (Cambridge: Cambridge University Press, 1997), 7.
2. Kwame Ninsin, ed., *Ghana's Political Transition, 1990–1993: Selected Documents* (Accra: Freedom Publications, 1996), 61.
3. Ninsin, *Ghana's Political Transition*, 173.
4. Charles D. Jebuni and Abena D. Oduro, "Structural Adjustment Programme and the Transition to Democracy," in *Ghana: Transition to Democracy*, ed. Kwame Ninsin (Accra: Freedom Publications, 1998), 40.
5. *West Africa*, August 13–19, 1990.

Notes to Pages 199–206

6. Ninsin, *Ghana's Political Transition*, 12.
7. *West Africa*, August 27–September 3, 1990; Paul Nugent, *Big Men, Small Boys and Politics in Ghana: Power, Ideology and the Burden of History, 1982–1994* (London: Pinter, 1995), 201.
8. Kwame Boafo-Arthur, "The International Community and Ghana's Transition to Democracy," in Ninsin, *Ghana: Transition to Democracy*, 152.
9. Jebuni and Oduro, "Structural Adjustment Programme," 36.
10. Ninsin, *Ghana's Political Transition*, 63.
11. Paul Nugent, "Ghana: The Slow March Back towards Multipartyism," in *Africa Contemporary Record*, vol. 23, 1990–92, ed. Colin Legum (New York: Africana Publishing, 1998), B 48.
12. Ninsin, *Ghana's Political Transition*, 78.
13. *West Africa*, June 17–23, 1991.
14. Ninsin, *Ghana's Political Transition*, 141.
15. Ninsin, 134.
16. Provisional National Defence Council, Constitution of the Fourth Republic of Ghana (Promulgation) Law, 1992 (PNDCL 282).
17. *West Africa*, May 11–17, 1992.
18. Nugent, *Big Men, Small Boys*, 246.
19. Sarah Brierley, "Party Unity and Presidential Dominance: Parliamentary Development in the Fourth Republic of Ghana," *Journal of Contemporary African Studies* 30, no. 3 (July 2012): 434.
20. Joseph Ayee, "Ghana's Return to Constitutional Rule under the Provisional National Defence Council (PNDC)," *Law and Politics in Africa, Asia and Latin America* 29, no. 4 (4th Quarter 1996): 444.
21. Nugent, *Big Men, Small Boys*, 232–33; Richard Jeffries and Clare Thomas, "The Ghanaian Elections of 1992," *African Affairs* 92, no. 368 (July 1993): 356.
22. Ayee, "Ghana's Return," 449; Jeffries and Thomas, "Ghanaian Elections of 1992," 331–66.
23. Ayee, "Ghana's Return," 250–51.
24. Joseph R. A. Ayee, "The 1996 General Elections: An Overview," in *The 1996 General Elections and Democratic Consolidation in Ghana*, ed. Joseph Ayee (Accra: Department of Political Science, University of Ghana, 1998), 39.
25. Ayee, "1996 General Elections," 41–52.
26. Ayee, "1996 General Elections," 46.
27. Alexander K. D. Frempong, "Political Conflict and Elite Consensus in the Liberal State," in *Ghana: One Decade of the Liberal State*, ed. Kwame Boafo-Arthur (Dakar: CODESRIA, 2007), 147.
28. Frempong, 151–52.
29. Daniel A. Smith, "Consolidating Democracy? The Structural Underpinnings of Ghana's 2000 Elections," *Journal of Modern African Studies* 40, no. 4 (December 2002): 621–50.

30. *The Independent* (Accra), January 14, 2000.
31. *West Africa*, December 18, 2000–January 14, 2001, and January 15–21, 2001; Frempong, "Political Conflict," 153–55.
32. Daniel Treisman, "Income, Democracy, and Leader Turnover," *American Journal of Political Science* 59, no. 4 (October 2015): 927–42.
33. Emmanuel Gyimah-Boadi, "Another Step Forward for Ghana," *Journal of Democracy* 20, no. 2 (April 2009): 138–53; Lindsay Whitefield, "'Change for a Better Ghana': Party Competition, Institutionalization and Alternation in Ghana's 2008 Elections," *African Affairs* 108, no. 433 (2009): 621–41; Carter Center, "Election Observer Mission Preliminary Statement," Atlanta, GA, December 10, 2008, http://www.cartercenter.org.
34. Samuel P. Huntington, *The Third Wave: Democratization in the Late Twentieth Century* (Norman: University of Oklahoma Press, 1993), 267.
35. Kwame Ninsin, "Introduction: Understanding Ghana's Electoral Politics," in *Issues in Ghana's Electoral Politics*, ed. Kwame Ninsin (Dakar: CODESRIA, 2016), 5–6.
36. Institute of Economic Affairs, *Political Parties Code of Conduct 2012* (Accra: Institute of Economic Affairs, 2012), 4–6.
37. Mawusi Yaw Dumenu and Mildred Edinam Adzraku, *Electoral Violence and Political Vigilantism in Ghana: Evidence from Selected Hotspots* (Accra: Center for Democratic Development, 2020), vii, 1.
38. *Public Agenda*, March 7, 2001.
39. *Accra Daily Mail*, April 24, 2003.
40. Dumenu and Adzraku, *Electoral Violence*, 39.
41. *Daily Graphic*, April 3, 2013; *Ghanaian Chronicle*, September 14, 2015.
42. *Ghanaian Chronicle*, May 26, 2015; *Daily Graphic*, October 23, 2015.
43. *Daily Graphic*, April 7 and May 17, 2017.
44. *Daily Graphic*, April 7, 2017.
45. *Daily Graphic*, May 17 and October 26, 2017.
46. Dumenu and Adzraku, *Electoral Violence*, 49.
47. Emile Short, "Recommendations of the Emile Short Commission," accessed February 17, 2021, https://www.ghanaweb.com/GhanaHomePage/NewsArchive/AWW-Full-recommendations-of-the-Emile-Short-Commission-782207.
48. *Daily Graphic*, July 26, 2019.
49. Dumenu and Adzraku, *Electoral Violence*, 51.
50. *Daily Graphic*, December 11, 2020, and February 12, 2021.
51. Steve Tonah, "Theoretical and Comparative Perspectives on Ethnicity, Conflicts and Consensus in Ghana," in *Ethnicity, Conflicts and Consensus in Ghana*, ed. Steve Tonah (Accra: Woeli Publishing Services, 2007), 3.
52. *Analysis of the Pre-2020 General Elections Survey* (Legon: University of Ghana, Department of Political Science, 2020), 13.

53. George M. Bob-Milliar, "'Te nyɔgeyɛng gbengbenoe!' ('We Are Holding the Umbrella Very Tight!'): Explaining the Popularity of the NDC in the Upper West Region of Ghana," *Africa* 81, no. 3 (August 2011): 455–73.
54. Peter Arthur, "Ethnicity and Electoral Politics in Ghana's Fourth Republic," *Africa Today* 56, no. 2 (Winter 2009): 62.
55. Frempong, "Political Conflict," 155.
56. *Daily Graphic*, September 7 and 9, 2020.
57. Frempong, "Political Conflict," 157; Bob-Milliar, "Te nyɔgeyɛng gbengbenoe!," 467.
58. *Daily Graphic*, February 24, 2015.
59. UN Development Programme, *Ghana Human Development Report 2007: Towards a More Inclusive Society* (Accra: UNDP, Ghana Office, 2007).
60. Cletus Dordunoo, author's interview, Accra, May 2008.
61. Emmanuel Bombande, "Conflicts, Civil Society Organizations and Community Peacebuilding Practices in Northern Ghana," in Tonah, *Ethnicity, Conflicts and Consensus*, 205–6.
62. *Ghanaian Chronicle*, March 14 and 15, 2002.
63. Bob Kelly and R. B. Bening, "Ideology, Regionalism, Self-Interest and Tradition: An Investigation into Contemporary Politics in Northern Ghana," *Africa* 77, no. 2 (2007): 200–201.
64. Jesse Salah Ovadia, "Stepping Back from the Brink: A Review of the 2008 Ghanaian Election from the Capital of the Northern Region," *Canadian Journal of African Studies* 45, no. 2 (2011): 310–40.
65. Tonah, *Ethnicity, Conflicts and Consensus*.
66. *Daily Graphic*, March 9, 2015.
67. Joseph R. A. Ayee, "Manifestos and Agenda Setting and Elections in Ghanaian Elections," in Ninsin, *Issues in Ghana's Electoral Politics*, 83–113.
68. Eboe Hutchful, *Ghana's Adjustment Experience: The Paradox of Reform* (Geneva: UN Research Institute for Social Development, 2002), 2, 212.
69. Frempong, "Political Conflict," 145; Paul Nugent, "Living in the Past: Urban, Rural and Ethnic Themes in the 1992 and 1996 Elections in Ghana," *Journal of Modern African Studies* 37, no. 2 (June 1999): 304.
70. *Daily Graphic*, January 27, 2014.
71. *Ghanaian Chronicle*, December 2, 2005.
72. *Monitoring Abuse of Incumbency in Ghana's 2012 Elections: Final Report* (Accra: Ghana Integrity Initiative, Ghana Anti-Corruption Coalition, and Ghana Center for Democratic Development, 2013).
73. *Daily Graphic*, December 10, 2020.
74. *Monitoring Abuse of Incumbency*, 13–16.
75. *Daily Graphic*, June 24, 2020.

76. Center for Democratic Development, *Ghana's 2020 Elections: Prospects for Credibility and Peacefulness* (Accra: Center for Democratic Development, 2020), 58–59.
77. *Ghanaian Chronicle*, October 31, 2019.
78. *Ghanaian Chronicle*, April 28, 2009.
79. *Ghanaian Chronicle*, August 18, 2009.
80. Dumenu and Adzraku, *Electoral Violence*, 30.
81. Nicholas Amponsah, "Institutions and Economic Performance: Ghana's Experience under the Fourth Republic, 1992–2002," in Boafo-Arthur, *Ghana: One Decade*, 23; Ransford Edward Van Gyampo and Emmanuel Graham, "Constitutional Hybridity and Constitutionalism in Ghana," *Africa Review* 6, no. 2 (2014): 146–47.
82. *Daily Graphic*, March 16, 2017.
83. African Peer Review Mechanism, *Country Review Report of the Republic of Ghana* (Midrand, South Africa: African Peer Review Mechanism, 2005), 29, 129.
84. *Daily Graphic*, March 16, 2017; "List of Akufo-Addo Government Ministers and Political Appointees," Wikipedia, accessed December 23, 2022, https://en.wikipedia.org/.
85. *Daily Graphic*, April 13 and 25, 2017.
86. Constitution Review Commission, *Report of the Constitution Review Commission: From a Political to a Developmental Constitution* (Accra: Constitution Review Commission, 2011), 108–9, 474, 480.
87. Government of Ghana, *White Paper on the Report of the Constitution Review Commission Presented to the President* (Accra, 2012).
88. *Daily Graphic*, October 25, 2012.
89. *Daily Graphic*, August 7, 2020.
90. *Daily Graphic*, July 17, 2014.

Chapter 10: Corruption the Democratic Way

1. AllAfrica.com, January 7, 2001; emphasis in original.
2. Institute of Economic Affairs, *Presidential Debate: Strengthening the Pillars of Democracy, Tamale, November 2008* (Accra: Institute of Economic Affairs, 2010), 11.
3. *Daily Graphic*, April 22, 2016.
4. *Daily Graphic*, August 1, 2018.
5. Susan Rose-Ackerman, *Corruption and Government: Causes, Consequences, and Reform* (Cambridge: Cambridge University Press, 1999), 127–42.
6. B. A. Sapati, author's interview Accra, February 2, 1999.
7. Vitus Azeem, author's interview, Accra, May 13, 2008.
8. *Daily Graphic*, July 4, 2018.

9. *Daily Graphic*, February 2, 2022.
10. Afrobarometer, "Ghana," accessed August 22, 2021, https://afrobarometer.org/countries/ghana-1.
11. Lionel Osse and Newton Norviewu, "Ghanaians Perceive Increase in Corruption Level, Give Government Low Marks on Fighting Graft," Afrobarometer and Ghana Center for Democratic Development, news release AD333, December 4, 2019.
12. *Daily Graphic*, September 1, 2021.
13. *The Independent*, April 29, 1999; *Ghanaian Chronicle*, October 25 and November 17, 1999, January 12 and July 19, 2000.
14. *Weekly Insight*, June 19, 2000.
15. *Ghanaian Chronicle*, February 26 and November 13, 2001; *Public Agenda*, May 2, 2003.
16. *Ghanaian Chronicle*, November 7, 2001; *Accra Daily Mail*, December 11, 2001.
17. *Ghanaian Chronicle*, October 19, 2004; *Accra Daily Mail*, February 7, 2007.
18. *Accra Daily Mail*, May 1, 2001, and April 29, 2003; *The Independent*, May 3, 2001; *Ghanaian Chronicle*, May 4, 2001.
19. *Ghanaian Chronicle*, April 29, 2003
20. *Accra Daily Mail*, February 24, 2003.
21. *Daily Graphic*, June 19, 2008; *Accra Daily Mail*, June 26, 2008; *Ghanaian Chronicle*, September 18, 2008.
22. *Public Agenda*, April 10, 2006; *Ghanaian Chronicle*, May 29 and July 13, 2007.
23. *News Ghana*, July 12, 2016.
24. *Ghanaian Chronicle*, October 13, 2004.
25. *Ghanaian Chronicle*, February 13, 2006; *Public Agenda*, February 13, 2006.
26. Kwame Asamoah and Emmanuel Ababio Ofosu-Mensah, "Fruitlessness of Anti-corruption Agencies: Lessons from the Commission on Human Rights and Administrative Justice in Ghana," *Journal of Asian and African Studies* 53, no. 7 (2018): 993.
27. Commission on Human Rights and Administrative Justice, *Report of a Preliminary Investigation by the Commission for Human Rights and Administrative Justice into Allegations of Corruption and Conflict of Interest against His Excellency, J. A. Kufuor, President of the Republic of Ghana, in Respect of the Acquisition of a "Hotel" at Airport West, Accra* (Accra: CHRAJ, 2006).
28. *Palaver*, May 15, 2006.
29. "Kufuor Used Courts To Witch-Hunt His Political Opponents," *VibeGhana*, September 13, 2011.
30. Kwamena Ahwoi, *Working with Rawlings* (Tema: Digibooks Ghana, 2020), 199–200, 206.
31. *Ghanaian Chronicle*, June 26 and 29, 2009.

32. *Ghanaian Chronicle*, September 28 and October 12, 2009; *Daily Nation* (Nairobi), October 11, 2009.
33. Government of Ghana, *Ghana @50: White Paper on the Report of the Commission of Inquiry* (Accra, 2010).
34. *Ghanaian Chronicle*, April 23 and August 12, 2010.
35. Joseph Ayee, "Public Administrators under Democratic Governance in Ghana," *International Journal of Public Administration* 36, no. 6 (2013): 444; George M. Bob-Milliar and Ali Yakubu Nyaaba, "Political Transitions and Commissions of Inquiry: The Politicisation of Accountability in Ghana," *Third World Quarterly* 41, no. 10 (2020): 1758–75; *Ghanaian Chronicle*, December 8, 19, and 23, 2011, and January 26, 2012; *Public Agenda*, January 30, 2012; *Daily Graphic*, July 24, 2014, and March 12, 2015.
36. *Ghanaian Chronicle*, November 10, 2014.
37. Government of Ghana, *White Paper on the Report of the Commission of Inquiry into Payments from Public Funds Arising from Judgment Debts and Akin Matters* (Accra, 2015).
38. Government of Ghana, 37.
39. Government of Ghana, 12–16.
40. *Daily Graphic*, July 1, 2015.
41. *Daily Graphic*, July 15, 2015.
42. *Daily Graphic*, June 29, 2021.
43. *Daily Graphic*, June 29, 2018, May 12 and 13, 2020, and May 8, 2021.
44. *Daily Graphic*, August 22 and 23, 2019, and November 5, 2020.
45. Osse and Norviewu, "Ghanaians Perceive Increase in Corruption."
46. Joseph R. A. Ayee, "Ghana: Reducing Police Corruption and Promoting Police Professionalism through Reforms," in *Police Corruption and Police Reforms in Developing Societies*, ed. Kemp Ronald Hope Sr. (Boca Raton, FL: Routledge, 2015), 65–84.
47. *Daily Graphic*, May 26, 2008.
48. *Daily Graphic*, March 6, 2015; *Daily Guide Network*, January 26, 2017, https://dailyguidenetwork.com/cop-timbillah-sacked/.
49. Osse and Norviewu, "Ghanaians Perceive Increase in Corruption."
50. *Accra Daily Mail*, November 5, 2002.
51. *Daily Graphic*, October 6, December 8 and 15, 2015, and April 21 and October 28, 2016.
52. *Ghanaian Chronicle*, January 5, 2000.
53. *Daily Graphic*, February 17, 2010.
54. Republic of Ghana, *National Anti-Corruption Action Plan, (2015–2024)* (Accra, 2011), 25.
55. Georg Kell, author's interview, New York, June 2010.
56. Papa Kojo Mbir, *Premix: An Avenue for Political Corruption, Deceit, Lies and Petty Thieving* (Accra: published by author, [2005]), 7.

Notes to Pages 242–250

57. *Public Agenda*, July 2, 2004, and June 2, 2008.
58. *Daily Graphic*, March 30, 2022.
59. Sarah Kirst, "'Chiefs Do Not Talk Law, Most of Them Talk Power': Traditional Authorities in Conflicts over Land Grabbing in Ghana," *Canadian Journal of African Studies* 54, no. 3 (2020): 524.
60. *Daily Graphic*, June 4, 2014.
61. *Ghanaian Chronicle*, August 15, 2002, and May 6, 2004; *Daily Graphic*, September 23, 2013.
62. Kirst, "Chiefs Do Not Talk Law," 519–39.
63. *Ghanaian Chronicle*, September 19, 2011.
64. T. C. McCaskie, "The Life and Afterlife of Yaa Asantewaa," *Africa* 77, no. 2 (2007): 164; *The Independent*, June 1, 1999; *Daily Graphic*, January 14, 2020.
65. Edem Adotey, "Parallel or Dependent? The State, Chieftaincy and Institutions of Governance in Ghana," *African Affairs* 184, no. 473 (2019): 635.
66. Ghana Local Government Service, "Summary of 261 MMDAs," November 8, 2021, http://www.ghanadistricts.com/Home/LinkData/8370.
67. Ministry of Local Government and Rural Development, *Ghana: The New Local Government System* (Accra: Ministry of Local Government and Rural Development, 1996), 7.
68. Joseph R. A. Ayee, *Decentralization and Conflict: The Case of District Chief Executives and Members of Parliament in Ghana* (Accra: Friedrich Ebert Foundation, 1999); Kwamena Ahwoi, *Rethinking Decentralization and Local Government in Ghana: Proposals for Amendment* (Accra: Institute of Economic Affairs, 2010); Emmanuel Debrah, "The Politics of Decentralization in Ghana's Fourth Republic," *African Studies Review* 57, no. 1 (April 2014): 49–69.
69. Ayee, *Decentralization and Conflict*, 7.
70. *The Independent*, April 6, 1999.
71. *Accra Daily Mail*, October 16, 2002.
72. *Ghanaian Chronicle*, October 1, 2009, January 10, 2010, and June 16, 2011.
73. *Ghanaian Chronicle*, December 17, 2015.
74. *Daily Graphic*, November 3, 2021.

Chapter 11: Vigilance from Above and Below

Epigraph source: Daily Graphic, December 13, 2021.

1. Republic of Ghana, *National Anti-Corruption Action Plan, (2015–2024)* (Accra, 2011), 10.
2. Poku Adusei, "Towards a Transsystemic Study of the Ghana Legal System," *Global Journal of Comparative Law* 6, no. 1 (2017): 30.
3. H. Kwasi Prempeh, *The Ghanaian Judiciary and the 1992 Constitution: A Problem of Asymmetrical Jurisprudence* (Accra: Center for Democratic Development, 1999), 9.

4. Constitution of the Fourth Republic of Ghana, Article 35(8).
5. E. Kofi Abotsi, "Introspecting the Office of the Special Prosecutor's Act and Ghana's Constitutional Framework on Anti-corruption," *African Journal of International and Comparative Law* 28, no. 2 (2020): 219–43.
6. Republic of Ghana, Criminal Offences Act, 1960, Act 29, articles 239–45; Emile Short, *Empowering Ghana's Anti-corruption Institutions in the Fight Against Corruption* (Accra: Institute of Economic Affairs, 2015), 5.
7. *Daily Graphic*, October 19, 2020.
8. *Ghanaian Chronicle*, June 11, 2008.
9. Abdul Bassit Aziz Bamba, "Wilfully Causing Financial Loss to the State: A Critique of *The Republic v. Ibrahim Adam & Ors*," *University of Ghana Law Journal* 22 (2002–4): 237–49.
10. Eyram A. Adadevoh, "New Wine in New Wine Skins: The Anti-corruption Framework of Ghana," *Journal of World Energy Law and Business* 7, no. 3 (2014): 207–9.
11. *Daily Graphic*, March 29, 2022.
12. Constitution of the Fourth Republic of Ghana, Article 286.
13. *Daily Graphic*, August 16, 2017.
14. Adadevoh, "New Wine," 209.
15. *Daily Graphic*, June 11, 2013; *Ghanaian Chronicle*, June 13, 2013.
16. *Ghanaian Chronicle*, March 27, 2013.
17. Republic of Ghana, Right to Information Act, 2019 (Act 989).
18. *Daily Graphic*, September 29, 2020.
19. Republic of Ghana, *Judicial Service 2017–2018 Annual Report* (Accra, 2018), 43.
20. *Daily Graphic*, November 17, 2014.
21. Ernest Owusu-Dapaa, "An Exposition and Critique of Judicial Independence under Ghana's 1992 Constitution," *Commonwealth Law Bulletin* 37, no. 3 (2011): 532–33.
22. Open Society Initiative of West Africa, *Ghana: Justice Sector and the Rule of Law* (Dakar: Open Society Initiative of West Africa, 2007), 78, 124.
23. Prempeh, *Ghanaian Judiciary*, 14.
24. Owusu-Dapaa, "Exposition and Critique," 549–52; Open Society Initiative, *Ghana*, 55.
25. S. K. Asare, "Accounting for Judiciary Performance in an Emerging Democracy—Lessons from Ghana," *University of Botswana Law Journal* (December 2006): 101.
26. Asare, "Accounting for Judiciary Performance," 65–66, 101; Owusu-Dapaa, "Exposition and Critique," 552–53.
27. Open Society Initiative, *Ghana*, xi.
28. Lionel Osse and Newton Norviewu, "Ghanaians Perceive Increase in Corruption Level, Give Government Low Marks on Fighting Graft,"

Afrobarometer and Ghana Center for Democratic Development, news release AD333, December 4, 2019.

29. Joseph R. A. Ayee, "Notes on the Commission on Human Rights and Administrative Justice under the 1992 Ghanaian Constitution," *Verfassung und Recht in Übersee / Law and Politics in Africa, Asia and Latin America* 27, no. 2 (1994): 163–65; Kwame Asamoah and Emmanuel Ababio Ofosu-Mensah, "Fruitlessness of Anti-corruption Agencies: Lessons from the Commission on Human Rights and Administrative Justice in Ghana," *Journal of Asian and African Studies* 53, no. 7 (2018): 192, 196; Deepa Iyer, "Earning a Reputation for Independence: Ghana's Commission on Human Rights and Administrative Justice, 1993–2003" (Princeton, NJ: Innovations for Successful Societies, 2011), http://www.princeton.edu/successfulsocieties.

30. Iyer, "Earning a Reputation for Independence"; *Daily Graphic*, March 15, 2022.

31. Céline Thiriot, "Ghana: Les aléas d'un modèle," in *L'Afrique politique 1977* (Paris: Editions Karthala, 1977), 234.

32. Itumeleng Makgetla, interview with Emile Short (Princeton, NJ: Innovations for Successful Societies, 2009), http://www.princeton.edu/successfulsocieties.

33. Iyer, "Earning a Reputation for Independence," 6.

34. Iyer; Joseph A. Ayee, *The Roots of Corruption: The Ghanaian Inquiry Revisited* (Accra: Institute of Economic Affairs, 2016), 53.

35. B. A. Sapati, author's interview, Accra, February 2, 1999.

36. Emile Short, *The Anti-corruption Mandates of the Commission on Human Rights and Administrative Justice and the Serious Fraud Office: A Duplication of Functions?* (Accra: Institute of Economic Affairs, 2010).

37. *Accra Daily Mail*, January 24, 2002.

38. *Daily Graphic*, August 28, 2012.

39. *Daily Graphic*, November 23, 2013; *Ghanaian Chronicle*, November 5, 2020.

40. Kwame Ninsin, *The Corrupt Elites: Anatomy of Power and Wealth in Ghana* (Accra: Gavoss Education, 2018), 74, 77.

41. *Daily Graphic*, August 3, 2017.

42. *Daily Graphic*, November 25, 2019.

43. *Daily Graphic*, December 12, 2019, May 12 and July 3, 2020.

44. *Daily Graphic*, July 8, 2020, and March 10, 2021.

45. *Ghanaian Chronicle*, January 20, 2012; *Daily Graphic*, November 16, 2020.

46. *Daily Graphic*, November 16, 2020.

47. *Daily Graphic*, January 26, February 15, March 17, and October 10, 2022, and July 24, 2023.

48. *Ghanaian Chronicle*, December 5, 2019.

49. Republic of Ghana, National Media Commission Act, 1993 (449).
50. Ashley McCants, interview with Paul Adu-Gyamfi (Princeton, NJ: Innovations for Successful Societies, 2008), http://www.princeton.edu/successfulsocieties.
51. *Ghanaian Chronicle*, February 21, 2019.
52. National Communications Authority, "List of Authorised TV Broadcasting Stations in Ghana, as at Third Quarter 2017," accessed June 13, 2022, https://nca.org.gh/wp-content/uploads/2021/11/AUTHORISED-TV-STATIONS-Q3-2017.pdf.
53. Glenda Nevill, "Ghana: Rapidly Expanding with Changing Mindsets," The Media Online, November 4, 2016, https://themediaonline.co.za/.
54. M. F. Amadu et al., "Assessment of Newspaper Circulation and Readership in Northern Ghana," *University for Development Studies International Journal of Development* 5, no. 2 (2018): 114.
55. Jennifer Hasty, *The Press and Political Culture in Ghana* (Bloomington: Indiana University Press, 2005), 113.
56. Hasty, 139.
57. Joseph Yaw Asomah, "Democracy, the Public Sphere, and Power Elites: Examining the Ghanaian Private Media's Role in Political Corruption," *Critical Studies in Media Communication* 37, no. 3 (2020): 229.
58. Hasty, *Press and Political Culture*, 91.
59. *Ghanaian Chronicle*, April 24, 2012.
60. *Ghanaian Chronicle*, March 4 and 15, 2005.
61. Joseph Yaw Asomah, "Can Private Media Contribute to Fighting Political Corruption in Sub-Saharan Africa? Lessons from Ghana," *Third World Quarterly* 41, no. 12 (2020): 2018–23; *Ghanaian Chronicle*, May 20 and 23, 2011, October 25 and November 1, 4, and 18, 2013; *Daily Graphic*, August 28 and September 17, 2013
62. Asomah, "Can Private Media Contribute," 2020.
63. *Daily Graphic*, June 7, 2018.
64. *Daily Graphic*, November 14 and 15, 2022; *Ghanaian Chronicle*, November 17, 2022.
65. Sylvester Senyo Ofori-Parku and Kwaku Botwe, "'This Is (Not) Journalism': Corruption, Subterfuge, and Metajournalistic Discourses on Undercover Journalism in Ghana," *Journalism Studies* 21, no. 3 (2020): 398.
66. Anas Aremeyaw Anas, interview, AllAfrica.com, June 26, 2010, https://allafrica.com/stories/201006260001.html.
67. Ofori-Parku and Botwe, "This Is (Not) Journalism," 388–405.
68. *Ghanaian Chronicle*, September 13, 2018.
69. *Daily Graphic*, January 17 and 18, 2019; Joel Gunter, "Murder in Accra: The Life and Death of Ahmed Hussein-Suale," BBC Africa Eye, January 30, 2019, www.bbc.com/.

Notes to Pages 267–275

70. *Daily Graphic*, December 13, 2017.
71. *Daily Graphic*, October 26, 2017.
72. *Daily Graphic*, April 15, 2010.
73. Asomah, "Can Private Media Contribute," 2022.
74. Open Society Initiative, *Ghana*, 5, 28.
75. *West Africa*, May 29–June 4 and June 5–11, 1995; Philip D. Osei, "Political Liberalization and the Implementation of Value Added Tax in Ghana," *Journal of Modern African Studies* 38, no. 2 (July 2000): 255–78.
76. *Daily Graphic*, June 28, 29, and 30, 2022.
77. *Daily Graphic*, June 10, 2022.
78. Mostly the *Daily Graphic* and *Ghanaian Chronicle*, but also including the Ghana News Agency, *Accra Daily Mail*, *Public Agenda*, and several others.
79. Andrea Noll and Jan Budniok, "Social Protest and the Middle Class in Ghana: A Social Movement Approach of Three Cases," *Journal of Contemporary African Studies* (2021), https://doi.org/10.1080/02589001.2021.1931056; Lewis Abedi Asante and Ilse Helbrecht, "Seeing Through African Protest Logics: A Longitudinal Review of Continuity and Change in Protests in Ghana," *Canadian Journal of African Studies* 52, no. 2 (2018): 159–81.
80. *Ghanaian Chronicle*, July 2, 2014; *Daily Graphic*, July 2, 2014.
81. Panafrican News Agency, May 15, 1999.
82. Lauren Coyle Rosen, *Fires of Gold: Law, Spirit, and Sacrificial Labor in Ghana* (Oakland: University of California Press, 2020), 107.
83. *Ghanaian Chronicle*, January 17, 2003; *Public Agenda*, November 14, 2005.
84. *Daily Graphic*, June 24, 2015.
85. *Daily Graphic*, October 2 and 3, 2013; *Ghanaian Chronicle*, October 4, 2013; *Daily Graphic* and *Ghanaian Chronicle*, November 25, 2013; *Daily Graphic*, January 13, 2014.
86. *Ghana Palaver*, June 10, 2005.
87. *Daily Graphic*, February 19, 2015.
88. *Daily Graphic*, August 4 and 5 and September 22, 2021.
89. Girish Daswani, "On Cynicism: Activist and Artistic Responses to Corruption in Ghana," *Cultural Anthropology* 35, no. 1 (2020): 114, 127.
90. OccupyGhana, "Who We Are," accessed February 29, 2024, https://occupyghana.com/about/.
91. *Ghanaian Chronicle*, May 29, 2017, and August 12, 2021; *Daily Graphic*, May 27 and June 15, 2017, and January 30, April 9, and June 7, 2018.
92. Ghana Center for Democratic Development, "The CDD Story," accessed February 29, 2024, https://cddgh.org/the-cdd-story/.
93. *Daily Graphic*, August 12, 2020.
94. Ghana Integrity Initiative, *The 2010 Annual Report* (Accra: 2011), 3; Ghana Integrity Initiative, "What Is GII (TI-Ghana)," accessed February 29, 2024, https://www.tighana.org/about-gii/overview/.

95. Ghana Anti-Corruption Coalition, "Who We Are," accessed February 29, 2024, https://gaccgh.org/who-we-are/.
96. Kwame Ninsin, "Markets and Liberal Democracy," in *Ghana: One Decade of the Liberal State*, ed. Kwame Boafo-Arthur (Dakar: CODESRIA, 2007), 90.
97. South African Institute of International Affairs, "Ghana and Civil Society Clash over Allegations of Corruption," *eAfrica*, 2 (April 2004), https://saiia.org.za/research/ghana-and-civil-society-clash-over-allegations-of-corruption/.
98. *Daily Graphic*, June 14, 2013.
99. *Daily Graphic*, April 20, 2017.
100. Abeeku Essuman-Johnson, "Organized Labour and the Liberal State," in Boafo-Arthur, *Ghana: One Decade*, 214–17.
101. *Ghanaian Chronicle*, April 11, 2019.
102. *Public Agenda*, November 28, 2011; *Daily Graphic*, July 10, 2019.
103. *Public Agenda*, November 8, 2007; *Ghanaian Chronicle*, June 23, 2008; *Daily Graphic*, June 18, 2018.
104. Alhassan Atta-Quayson and Amina H. Baidoo, "Mining-Induced Violent Resistance: The Case of Salt Mining near Keta Lagoon," *Review of African Political Economy* 47, no. 166 (December 2020): 604–20.
105. *Public Agenda*, October 17, 2005.
106. *Public Agenda*, June 2, 2008.
107. Trading Economics, "Crude Oil Production: Africa," accessed August 19, 2022, https://tradingeconomics.com/country-list/crude-oil-production?continent=africa.
108. Statista, "Government Revenue from Oil in Ghana from 2019 to 2023," accessed March 6, 2023, https://www.statista.com/statistics/1295627/annual-oil-revenue-in-ghana/.
109. Efam Dovi, "Ghana's 'New Path' for Handling Oil Revenue," *Africa Renewal* 26, no. 3 (January 2013): 12–13.
110. Joe Amoako-Tuffour, *How Ghana Plans to Manage Its Petroleum Revenues: A Step towards Transparency, Accountability and Governance Standards*, Monograph 26 (Accra: Institute of Economic Affairs, 2010); Ishmael Ackah et al., "Between Altruism and Self-Aggrandisement: Transparency, Accountability and Politics in Ghana's Oil and Gas Sector," *Energy Research and Social Science* 28 (2020): 1–14; Nelson Oppong, "Ghana's Public Interest and Accountability Committee: An Elusive Quest for 'Home-Grown' Transformation in the Oil Industry," *Journal of Energy and Natural Resources Law* 34, no. 3 (2016): 313–36.
111. Ackah et al., "Between Altruism and Self-Aggrandisement," 8; *Ghanaian Chronicle*, August 4, 2014.
112. Jesse Salah Ovadia, "Ghana's Petroleum Industry: Expectations, Frustrations and Anger in Coastal Communities," *Journal of Modern African Studies* 58, no. 3 (2020): 416.

Notes to Pages 279–290

113. *Ghanaian Chronicle*, August 1, 2019.
114. Ninsin, *Corrupt Elites*, 113.
115. Ackah et al., "Between Altruism and Self-Aggrandisement," 10.
116. Reuters, September 30, 2022; *Daily Graphic*, July 20 and 27, 2023.
117. *Washington Post*, December 1, 2022.
118. Al Jazeera, December 31, 2022.

Chapter 12: For a Society Just and Fair

1. *Daily Graphic*, April 30, 2013.
2. *Ghanaian Chronicle*, October 12, 2004.
3. Michael Johnston, *Syndromes of Corruption: Wealth, Power, and Democracy* (Cambridge: Cambridge University Press, 2005), 18–19, 23.
4. Maxwell Owusu, foreword to Kwame Ninsin, *The Corrupt Elites: Anatomy of Power and Wealth in Ghana* (Accra: Gavoss Education, 2018), ix–x.
5. J. H. Mensah, chairman of Ghana's Parliamentary Accounts Committee, address to an October 13, 1999, plenary session of the Ninth International Anti-Corruption Conference, Durban, South Africa. From author's notes.
6. Michael Ofori-Mensah, "Donor Anti-corruption Reforms: Quiet Diplomacy and Its Discontents," *Governance Newsletter* (Accra: Institute of Economic Affairs) 17, no. 5 (September–October 2011); Republic of Ghana, *National Anti-Corruption Action Plan, (2015–2024)* (Accra, 2011), 6, 8, 30–31.
7. Ayodele Odusola, Giovanni Andrea Cornia, Haroon Bhorat, and Pedro Conceição, eds., *Income Inequality Trends in Sub-Saharan Africa: Divergence, Determinants and Consequences* (New York: UN Development Program, 2017), 135.
8. Odusola et al., *Income Inequality Trends*, 139, 319, 321–23.
9. Odusola et al., *Income Inequality Trends*, 335.
10. Paul Gifford, *Ghana's New Christianity: Pentecostalism in a Globalizing African Economy* (Bloomington: Indiana University Press, 2004).
11. Joseph A. Ayee, *The Roots of Corruption: The Ghanaian Inquiry Revisited* (Accra: Institute of Economic Affairs, 2016), 47–48.
12. Johnston, *Syndromes of Corruption*, 187.
13. Typed letter, March 9, 1982, from Chairman and General Secretary Senior Staff Association, Chairman and Secretary Local Union, and Chairman and Secretary PDC of the Social Security & National Insurance Trust, Accra, to the Secretary, PNDC, Burma Camp, Accra, PDC Collection.
14. Typed letter, September 14, 1982, from W. L. Lutterodt to "Mil-Co-ord., I.R.C. for P.D.C.s., Greater Accra Region," PDC Collection.

Bibliography

Archives

Balme Library, University of Ghana, Accra
Institute of African Studies, University of Ghana, Accra
Lehman and Butler libraries, Columbia University, New York
Library of Congress, Washington, DC
National Archives of Ghana, Accra
School of Oriental and African Studies, University of London

PDC Collection (Private)

A leading member of Ghana's Interim National Coordinating Committee and National Defence Committee, two national coordinating bodies of the People's Defence Committees (PDCs) during 1982–84, preserved an extensive uncatalogued collection of documents from that period. It comprises many hundreds of letters, field reports, official directives, policy statements, pamphlets, petitions, minutes, and other documents, mostly from the defense committees but also from various government institutions, farmers' organizations, trade unions, youth associations, and other groups, as well as numerous individuals. With the collector's generous permission, the documents were made available to this researcher, who read and analyzed 382 of those that seemed most pertinent. Specific documents cited in this book's reference notes include relevant identifying information; they are designated as coming from the "PDC Collection."

Author's Interviews

Adam, Ibrahim. Agriculture minister. Accra, June 15, 1993.
Agyekum, George. Public tribunal judge. Accra, February 13, 1999.
Agyeman-Duah, Baffour. Associate executive director, Center for Democratic Development. Accra, May 2, 2000.
Ahwoi, Kwamena. Tribunal coordinator, local government minister. Accra, June 17, 1993, and March 12, 1999.
Akrasi-Sarpong, Yaw. National Defence Committee member, Provisional National Defence Council liaison. Accra, March 8, 1985, and October 28, 1988.

Amonoo-Monney, J. C. Tribunal prosecutor. Accra, February 3, 1999.
Azeem, Vitus. Executive director, Ghana Integrity Initiative. Accra, May 13, 2008.
Benneh, George. Chairman, National Council for Tertiary Education. Legon, Greater Accra, May 8, 2000.
Chambas, Mohamed Ibn. Deputy minister for higher education. Accra, May 4, 2000.
Coleman, Carl. Major general. Accra, May 14, 2008.
Dordunoo, Cletus. Academic. Accra, May 2008.
Eigen, Peter. Chairman, Transparency International. Durban, South Africa, October 15, 1999.
Graham, Yao. People's Defence Committee leader. Accra, March 14, 1999.
Johnson, Cecelia. Acting general secretary, 31st December Women's Movement. Accra, November 4, 1988.
Kell, Georg. Executive director, UN Global Compact. New York, June 2010.
Manuh, Takyiwaa. Lecturer, University of Ghana, Legon. Accra, January 20, 1999.
Marrah, Kofi. Member, Committees for the Defence of the Revolution Secretariat. Accra, January 24, 1999.
Nabila, John. Northern representative on Council of State. Accra, May 11, 2008.
Ohene, Emmanuel. Staff lawyer, National Investigations Committee. Accra, February 19, 1999.
Portuphy, Kofi. Coordinator, National Mobilization Programme. Accra, October 28, 1988.
Quainoo, Arnold. Brigadier general, army commander. Accra, February 15, 1999.
Sapati, B. A. Investigator, Citizens' Vetting Committee and National Investigations Committee. Accra, February 2, 1999.
Tinorgah, Abdulai. Provisional National Defence Council secretary, Upper Region. Accra, January 26, 1999.
Tsikata, Kojo. Provisional National Defence Council special adviser. Accra, March 4, 1985.
Yahaya, Huudu. Provisional National Defence Council secretary for mobilization and social welfare. Accra, October 28, 1988.
(Positions held at time of interview or most relevant to interview topic.)

Periodicals

Accra Daily Mail
Africa Report (New York)
Catholic Standard (Accra)
Daily Graphic/People's Daily Graphic (Accra)
Ghanaian Chronicle (Accra)
Ghana Palaver (Accra)

The Independent (Accra)
News Ghana (Accra)
Panafrican News Agency (Dakar)
Public Agenda (Accra)
Weekly Insight (Accra)
West Africa (London)

Articles, Books, Reports, and Other Documents

Abotsi, E. Kofi. "Introspecting the Office of the Special Prosecutor's Act and Ghana's Constitutional Framework on Anti-corruption." *African Journal of International and Comparative Law* 28, no. 2 (2020): 219–43.

Ackah, C. A. *Akan Ethics*. Accra: Ghana Universities Press, 1988.

Ackah, Ishmael, Abraham Lartey, Theophilus Acheampong, Eric Kyem, and Gifty Ketemepi. "Between Altruism and Self-Aggrandisement: Transparency, Accountability and Politics in Ghana's Oil and Gas Sector." *Energy Research and Social Science* 28 (2020): 1–14.

Adadevoh, Eyram A. "New Wine in New Wine Skins: The Anti-corruption Framework of Ghana." *Journal of World Energy Law and Business* 7, no. 3 (2014): 202–19.

Adotey, Edem. "Parallel or Dependent? The State, Chieftaincy and Institutions of Governance in Ghana." *African Affairs* 184, no. 473 (2019): 628–45.

Adusei, Poku. "Towards a Transsystemic Study of the Ghana Legal System." *Global Journal of Comparative Law* 6, no. 1 (2017): 25–50.

Afari-Gyan, Kwadwo. *Public Tribunals and Justice in Ghana*. Accra: Asempa Publishers, 1988.

African Peer Review Mechanism. *Country Review Report of the Republic of Ghana*. Midrand, South Africa: African Peer Review Mechanism, 2005.

Afrobarometer. "Ghana," accessed August 22, 2021. https://afrobarometer.org/countries/ghana-1.

Afrobarometer / Ghana Center for Democratic Development. *Summary of Results: Afrobarometer Round 7, Survey in Ghana, 2017*. Ghana: Afrobarometer / Ghana Center for Democratic Development, n.d. https://www.afrobarometer.org/publication/ghana-summary-results-2017/.

Agbodeka, Frances. *African Politics and British Policy in the Gold Coast, 1868–1900*. London: Longman, 1971.

Agyekum, George, ed. *The Judges' Murder Trial of 1983*. Accra: Justice Trust Publications, 1999.

Agyeman-Duah, Baffour. "Ghana, 1982–6: The Politics of the P.N.D.C." *Journal of Modern African Studies* 25, no. 4 (December 1987): 613–42.

Ahlman, Jeffrey S. *Kwame Nkrumah: Visions of Liberation*. Athens: Ohio University Press, 2021.

———. *Living with Nkrumahism: Nation, State, and Pan-Africanism in Ghana.* Athens: Ohio University Press, 2017.

Ahwoi, Kwamena. *Rethinking Decentralization and Local Government in Ghana: Proposals for Amendment.* Accra: Institute of Economic Affairs, 2010.

———. *Working with Rawlings.* Tema: Digibooks Ghana, 2020.

Allman, Jean Marie. *The Quills of the Porcupine: Asante Nationalism in an Emergent Ghana.* Madison: University of Wisconsin Press, 1993.

Amadu, M. F., A. M. Mohammed, A. Alhassan, and F. Mohammed. "Assessment of Newspaper Circulation and Readership in Northern Ghana." *University for Development Studies International Journal of Development* 5, no. 2 (2018): 108–20.

Amamoo, Joseph G. *The Ghanaian Revolution.* London: Jafint Publishers, 1988.

Amoa, S. A. *University Students' Political Action in Ghana.* Accra: Ghana Publishing Corporation, 1979.

Amoako-Tuffour, Joe. *How Ghana Plans to Manage Its Petroleum Revenues: A Step towards Transparency, Accountability and Governance Standards.* Monograph 26. Accra: Institute of Economic Affairs, 2010.

Amponsah, Nicholas. "Institutions and Economic Performance: Ghana's Experience under the Fourth Republic, 1992–2002." In Boafo-Arthur, *Ghana: One Decade,* 106–27.

Analysis of the Pre-2020 General Elections Survey. Legon: University of Ghana, Department of Political Science, 2020.

Anas, Anas Aremeyaw. Interview, AllAfrica.com, June 26, 2010. https://allafrica.com/stories/201006260001.html.

Anderson, Benedict. *Imagined Communities: Reflections on the Origin and Spread of Nationalism.* London: Verso, 1991.

Andreski, Stanislav. *The African Predicament.* New York: Atherton Press, 1968.

Apreko, Baffour Kofi. "An Appraisal of the Implementation of the PNDC Decentralisation Policy as a Grassroots Development Strategy, with Ga District as a Case Study." Master's thesis, Institute of African Studies, University of Ghana, Legon, 1994.

Apter, David E. *Ghana in Transition.* Princeton, NJ: Princeton University Press, 1972.

Arhin, Kwame. "The Economic and Social Significance of Rubber Production and Exchange on the Gold and Ivory Coasts, 1880–1900." *Cahiers d'études africaines* 20, nos. 1–2 (1980): 49–62.

———. "The Search for 'Constitutional Chieftaincy.'" In *The Life and Work of Kwame Nkrumah,* edited by Kwame Arhin, 27–51. Trenton, NJ: Africa World Press, 1993.

———. "Trade, Accumulation and the State in Asante in the Nineteenth Century." *Africa* 60, no. 4 (1990): 524–37.

Arhin, Kwame, and Joseph Ki-Zerbo. "States and Peoples of the Niger Bend and the Volta." In *General History of Africa*, vol. 6, *Africa in the Nineteenth Century until the 1880s*, edited by J. F. Ade Ajayi, 662–98. Paris: UNESCO, 1989.

Armed Forces Revolutionary Council. Ghana Nationality (Amendment) Decree. AFRCD 42, September 17, 1979.

Arthur, Peter. "Ethnicity and Electoral Politics in Ghana's Fourth Republic." *Africa Today* 56, no. 2 (Winter 2009): 44–73.

Asamoah, Kwame, and Emmanuel Ababio Ofosu-Mensah. "Fruitlessness of Anti-corruption Agencies: Lessons from the Commission on Human Rights and Administrative Justice in Ghana." *Journal of Asian and African Studies* 53, no. 7 (2018): 987–1001.

Asante, Lewis Abedi, and Ilse Helbrecht. "Seeing Through African Protest Logics: A Longitudinal Review of Continuity and Change in Protests in Ghana." *Canadian Journal of African Studies* 52, no. 2 (2018): 159–81.

Asante, Yaw, Frederick Nixson, and G. Kwaku Tsikata. "The Industrial Sector and Economic Development." In *Economic Reforms in Ghana: The Miracle and the Myth*, edited by Ernest Aryeetey, Jane Harrigan, and Machiko Nissanke, 246–66. Trenton, NJ: Africa World Press, 2000.

Asare, S. K. "Accounting for Judiciary Performance in an Emerging Democracy—Lessons from Ghana." *University of Botswana Law Journal* (December 2006): 57–111.

Asibuo, S. K. "Military Regime Performance in Decentralization and Local Administration for Development: A Ghanaian Case Study." *Africa Insight* 22, no. 4 (1992): 283–87.

Asomah, Joseph Yaw. "Can Private Media Contribute to Fighting Political Corruption in Sub-Saharan Africa? Lessons from Ghana." *Third World Quarterly* 41, no. 12 (2020): 2011–29.

———. "Democracy, the Public Sphere, and Power Elites: Examining the Ghanaian Private Media's Role in Political Corruption." *Critical Studies in Media Communication* 37, no. 3 (2020): 221–37.

Attafuah, Ken A. "Public Tribunals and the Administration of Justice in Rawlings' Ghana (1982–1992)." Unpublished manuscript, 1998.

Atta-Quayson, Alhassan, and Amina H. Baidoo. "Mining-Induced Violent Resistance: The Case of Salt Mining near Keta Lagoon." *Review of African Political Economy* 47, no. 166 (December 2020): 604–20.

Austin, Dennis. *Politics in Ghana, 1946–1960*. London: Oxford University Press, 1970.

Austin, Dennis, and Robin Luckham, eds. *Politicians and Soldiers in Ghana, 1966–1972*. London: Frank Cass, 1975.

Awe, Bolanle. "Empires of the Western Sudan: Ghana, Mali, Songhai." In *A Thousand Years of West African History*, edited by J. F. Ade Ajayi and Ian Espie, 55–71. New York: Humanities Press, 1972.

Awoonor, Kofi. *The Ghana Revolution: Background Account from a Personal Perspective*. New York: Oasis Publishers, 1984.
Ayee, Joseph R. A. *Decentralization and Conflict: The Case of District Chief Executives and Members of Parliament in Ghana*. Accra: Friedrich Ebert Foundation, 1999.
———. "Ghana: Reducing Police Corruption and Promoting Police Professionalism through Reforms." In *Police Corruption and Police Reforms in Developing Societies*, edited by Kemp Ronald Hope Sr., 65–84. Boca Raton, FL: Routledge, 2015.
———. "Ghana's Return to Constitutional Rule under the Provisional National Defence Council (PNDC)." *Law and Politics in Africa, Asia and Latin America* 29, no. 4 (4th Quarter 1996): 434–52.
———. "Manifestos and Agenda Setting and Elections in Ghanaian Elections." In Ninsin, *Issues*, 83–113.
———. "The 1996 General Elections: An Overview." In *The 1996 General Elections and Democratic Consolidation in Ghana*, edited by Joseph Ayee, 35–52. Accra: Department of Political Science, University of Ghana, 1998.
———. "Notes on the Commission on Human Rights and Administrative Justice under the 1992 Ghanaian Constitution." *Verfassung und Recht in Übersee / Law and Politics in Africa, Asia and Latin America* 27, no. 2 (1994): 159–70.
———. "Public Administrators under Democratic Governance in Ghana." *International Journal of Public Administration* 36, no. 6 (2013): 440–52.
———. *The Roots of Corruption: The Ghanaian Inquiry Revisited*. Accra: Institute of Economic Affairs, 2016.
Bamba, Abdul Bassit Aziz. "Wilfully Causing Financial Loss to the State: A Critique of *The Republic v. Ibrahim Adam & Ors*." *University of Ghana Law Journal* 22 (2002–4): 237–49.
Bankie, B. F. "The Pre and Post 31 December 1981 Legal System of Ghana: Political Change and Law Reform—Inquest for a Popular Legal Dispensation." Unpublished manuscript, 1987.
Bayart, Jean-François. *The State in Africa: The Politics of the Belly*. London: Longman, 1993.
Baynham, Simon. "Divide et Impera: Civilian Control of the Military in Ghana's Second and Third Republics." *Journal of Modern African Studies* 23, no. 4 (December 1985): 623–42.
———. *The Military and Politics in Nkrumah's Ghana*. Boulder, CO: Westview, 1988.
Beckman, Björn. *Organising the Farmers: Cocoa Politics and National Development in Ghana*. Uppsala: Scandinavian Institute of African Studies, 1976.
Bennett, Valerie Plave. "Malcontents in Uniform—the 1972 Coup d'Etat." In Austin and Luckham, *Politicians and Soldiers*, 300–312. London: Frank Cass, 1975.

Bentsi-Enchill, Kwamena. *A Blueprint for the Party Game in Ghana*. Accra: Graphic Press, 1968.
Bentsi-Enchill, Nii K. "Losing Illusions at Makola Market." *West Africa*, September 3, 1979.
Betts, R. F. "Methods and Institutions of European Domination." In *General History of Africa*, vol. 7, *Africa under Colonial Domination, 1880–1935*, edited by A. Adu Boahen, 312–31. Paris: UNESCO, 1985.
Birmingham, David. *Kwame Nkrumah: The Father of African Nationalism*. Athens: Ohio University Press, 1999.
Blundo, Giorgio, and Jean-Pierre Olivier de Sardan, eds. *Etat et corruption en Afrique: Une anthropologie comparative des relations entre fonctionnaires et usagers (Bénin, Niger, Sénégal)*. Paris: Karthala, 2007.
Boafo-Arthur, Kwame, ed. *Ghana: One Decade of the Liberal State*. Dakar: CODESRIA, 2007.
———. "The International Community and Ghana's Transition to Democracy." In Ninsin, *Ghana: Transition to Democracy*, 146–63.
Board of Public Tribunals. *Report on Operations, 1988*. Accra: Board of Public Tribunals, 1989.
Bob-Milliar, George M. "'Te nyɔgeyɛng gbengbenoe!' ('We Are Holding the Umbrella Very Tight!'): Explaining the Popularity of the NDC in the Upper West Region of Ghana." *Africa* 81, no. 3 (August 2011): 455–73.
Bob-Milliar, George M., and Ali Yakubu Nyaaba. "Political Transitions and Commissions of Inquiry: The Politicisation of Accountability in Ghana." *Third World Quarterly* 41, no. 10 (2020): 1758–75.
Bombande, Emmanuel. "Conflicts, Civil Society Organizations and Community Peacebuilding Practices in Northern Ghana." In Tonah, *Ethnicity, Conflicts and Consensus*, 195–228.
Boone, Catherine. "States and Ruling Classes in Postcolonial Africa: The Enduring Contradictions of Power." In *State Power and Social Forces: Domination and Transformation in the Third World*, edited by Joel S. Migdal, Atul Kohli, and Vivienne Shue, 108–40. Cambridge: Cambridge University Press, 1994.
Botchwey, Kwesi. *The PNDC's Programme for Reconstruction and Development*. Accra: Information Services Department, 1982.
Bourret, F. M. *Ghana: The Road to Independence, 1919–1957*. Stanford: Stanford University Press, 1960.
Bratton, Michael, and Nicolas van de Walle. *Democratic Experiments in Africa: Regime Transitions in Comparative Perspective*. Cambridge: Cambridge University Press, 1997.
Brierley, Sarah. "Party Unity and Presidential Dominance: Parliamentary Development in the Fourth Republic of Ghana." *Journal of Contemporary African Studies* 30, no. 3 (July 2012): 419–39.

Buthelezi, Mbongiseni, and Peter Vale, eds. *State Capture in South Africa: How and Why It Happened*. Johannesburg: Wits University Press, 2023.

Caiden, Gerald E., O. P. Dwivedi, and Joseph Jabbra, eds. *Where Corruption Lives*. Bloomfield, CT: Kumarian Press, 2001.

Carter Center. "Election Observer Mission Preliminary Statement." Atlanta, GA: Carter Center, December 10, 2008. http://www.cartercenter.org.

Center for Democratic Development. *Ghana's 2020 Elections: Prospects for Credibility and Peacefulness*. Accra: Center for Democratic Development, 2020.

Chazan, Naomi. *An Anatomy of Ghanaian Politics: Managing Political Recession, 1969–1982*. Boulder, CO: Westview, 1983.

Clapham, Christopher. "Clientelism and the State." In *Private Patronage and Public Power: Political Clientelism in the Modern State*, edited by Christopher Clapham, 1–35. New York: St. Martin's, 1982.

Commander, Simon, John Howell, and Waye Seini. "Ghana: 1983–7." In *Structural Adjustment and Agriculture: Theory and Practice in Africa and Latin America*, edited by Simon Commander, 107–26. London: Overseas Development Institute, 1989.

Commission on Human Rights and Administrative Justice. *Report of a Preliminary Investigation by the Commission for Human Rights and Administrative Justice into Allegations of Corruption and Conflict of Interest against His Excellency, J. A. Kufuor, President of the Republic of Ghana, in Respect of the Acquisition of a "Hotel" at Airport West, Accra*. Accra: CHRAJ, April 20, 2006.

Committee for the Defence of the Revolution. *CDR Guidelines*. Accra: Nsamankow Press, 1986.

Constitution of the Fourth Republic of Ghana. Accessed March 2, 2024. https://www.judicial.gov.gh/index.php/the-constitution.

Constitution Review Commission. *Report of the Constitution Review Commission: From a Political to a Developmental Constitution*. Accra: Constitution Review Commission, 2011.

Convention People's Party. *Manifesto for the General Election, 1954*. London: National Labour Press, 1954.

Coquery-Vidrovitch, Catherine. "The Political Economy of the African Peasantry and Modes of Production." In *The Political Economy of Contemporary Africa*, edited by Peter C. W. Gutkind and Immanuel Wallerstein, 90–111. Beverly Hills, CA: Sage Publications, 1976.

Crisp, Jeff. *The Story of an African Working Class: Ghanaian Miners' Struggles, 1870–1980*. London: Zed Books, 1984.

Daswani, Girish. "On Cynicism: Activist and Artistic Responses to Corruption in Ghana." *Cultural Anthropology* 35, no. 1 (2020): 104–33.

Davidson, Basil. *Black Star: A View of the Life and Times of Kwame Nkrumah*. Boulder, CO: Westview, 1989.

Debrah, Emmanuel. "The Politics of Decentralization in Ghana's Fourth Republic." *African Studies Review* 57, no. 1 (April 2014): 49–69.
De Graft Johnson, J. C. "The Fante Asafu." *Africa* 15, no. 3 (1932): 307–22.
Dei, George J. Sefa. "The Renewal of a Ghanaian Rural Economy." *Canadian Journal of African Studies* 26, no. 1 (1992): 24–53.
Dia, Mamadou. *Africa's Management in the 1990s and Beyond: Reconciling Indigenous and Transplanted Institutions*. Washington, DC: World Bank, 1996.
Diamond, Larry. "Class Formation in the Swollen African State." *Journal of Modern African Studies* 25, no. 4 (December 1987): 567–96.
Dovi, Efam. "Ghana's 'New Path' for Handling Oil Revenue." *Africa Renewal* 26, no. 3 (January 2013): 12–13.
Dowse, Robert. "Military and Police Rule." In Austin and Luckham, *Politicians and Soldiers*, 16–36.
Dumenu, Mawusi Yaw, and Mildred Edinam Adzraku. *Electoral Violence and Political Vigilantism in Ghana: Evidence from Selected Hotspots*. Accra: Center for Democratic Development, 2020.
Ekeh, Peter P. "Colonialism and the Two Publics in Africa: A Theoretical Statement." *Comparative Studies in Society and History* 17, no. 1 (1975): 91–112.
Ekekwe, Eme. *Class and State in Nigeria*. London: Longman, 1986.
Emiljanowicz, Paul, and Bonny Ibhawoh. "Democracy in Postcolonial Ghana: Tropes, State Power and the Defence Committees." *Third World Quarterly* 42, no. 6 (2021): 1213–32.
Essuman-Johnson, Abeeku. "Organized Labour and the Liberal State." In Boafo-Arthur, *Ghana: One Decade*, 205–26.
Fitch, Bob, and Mary Oppenheimer. *Ghana: End of an Illusion*. New York: Monthly Review Press, 1966.
Folson, Kweku G. "Structural Adjustment in Ghana." In *Alternative Strategies for Africa*, vol. 3, *Debt and Democracy*, edited by Ben Turok, 96–113. London: Institute for African Alternatives, 1991.
Frempong, Alexander K. D. "Political Conflict and Elite Consensus in the Liberal State." In Boafo-Arthur, *Ghana: One Decade*, 128–64.
Frimpong-Ansah, Jonathan H. *The Vampire State in Africa: The Political Economy of Decline in Ghana*. Trenton, NJ: Africa World Press, 1992.
Ghana Integrity Initiative. *The 2010 Annual Report*. Accra: Ghana Integrity Initiative, 2011.
Ghana Local Government Service. "Ghana Districts: Summary of 261 MMDAs," accessed February 5, 2022. http://www.ghanadistricts.com/Home/LinkData/8370.
Gifford, Paul. *Ghana's New Christianity: Pentecostalism in a Globalizing African Economy*. Bloomington: Indiana University Press, 2004.
Global Integrity Report. "Global Integrity Scorecard: Ghana 2008," accessed October 16, 2011. http://report.globalintegrity.org/Ghana/2008.

Gocking, Roger. "Ghana's Public Tribunals: An Experiment in Revolutionary Justice." *African Affairs* 95, no. 379 (April 1996): 197–223.

Gold Coast. *Report of the Commission of Enquiry in Mr. Braimah's Resignation and Allegations Arising Therefrom*. Accra: Government Printing Department, 1954.

———. *Report of the Commission of Enquiry into the Affairs of the Cocoa Purchasing Company Limited*. Accra, 1956.

Goldstone, Jack A. *Revolutions: A Very Short History*. Oxford: Oxford University Press, 2014.

———. "Toward a Fourth Generation of Revolutionary Theory." *Annual Review of Political Science* 4 (2001): 139–87.

Goody, Jack. "The Over-Kingdom of Gonja." In *West African Kingdoms in the Nineteenth Century*, edited by Daryll Forde and P. M. Kaberry, 179–205. Oxford: Oxford University Press, 1967.

———. *The Social Organisation of the LoWiili*. Oxford: Oxford University Press, 1967.

Government of Ghana. *Ghana @50: White Paper on the Report of the Commission of Inquiry*. Accra: Government of Ghana, 2010.

———. *White Paper on the Report of the Commission of Inquiry into Payments from Public Funds Arising from Judgment Debts and Akin Matters*. Accra: 2015.

———. *White Paper on the Report of the Constitution Review Commission Presented to the President*. Accra: 2012.

Graham, Ronald W. "Structural Problems in the World Economy: A Case Study of the Ghana-Valco Renegotiations." In *Essays from the Ghana-Valco Renegotiations, 1982–85*, edited by Fui S. Tsikata, 87–111. Accra: Ghana Publishing Corporation, 1986.

Graham, Yao. "From GTP to Assene: Aspects of Industrial Working Class Struggles in Ghana 1982–1986." In Hansen and Ninsin, *State, Development and Politics*, 43–72.

Gray, Paul S. *Unions and Leaders in Ghana: A Model of Labor and Development*. Owerri, Nigeria: Conch Magazine, 1981.

Green, Reginald H. *Country Study 1: Ghana*. Helsinki: World Institute for Development Economics Research, 1987.

Greene, Sandra E. "Social Change in Eighteenth-Century Anlo: The Role of Technology, Markets and Military Conflict." *Africa* 58, no. 1 (1988): 70–85.

Gunter, Joel. "Murder in Accra: The Life and Death of Ahmed Hussein-Suale." BBC Africa Eye, January 30, 2019, www.bbc.com/.

Gyimah-Boadi, Emmanuel. "Another Step Forward for Ghana." *Journal of Democracy* 20, no. 2 (April 2009): 138–53.

———, ed. *Ghana under PNDC Rule*. Oxford, UK: CODESRIA, 1993.

Hagan, George P. *Destoolment: The Pattern of Tenurial Instability of Kumasi Stools*. Legon: Institute of African Studies, University of Ghana, 1972.

Hansen, Emmanuel. "The State and Popular Struggles in Ghana, 1982–86." In *Popular Struggles for Democracy in Africa*, edited by Peter Anyang' Nyong'o, 170–208. London: United Nations University, 1987.

Hansen, Emmanuel, and Kwame A. Ninsin, eds. *The State, Development and Politics in Ghana*. London: CODESRIA, 1989.

Harsch, Ernest. "Accumulators and Democrats: Challenging State Corruption in Africa." *Journal of Modern African Studies* 31, no. 1 (March 1993): 31–48.

———. "Africans Taking Action on Corruption." *Africa Recovery* 11, no. 1 (July 1997): 26–27.

———. *Burkina Faso: A History of Power, Protest and Revolution*. London: Zed Press, 2017.

———. "Corruption and State Reform in Africa: Perspectives from Above and Below." In *Good Governance and Economic Development*, edited by Karl Wohlmuth, Hans H. Bass, and Frank Messner, 65–87. Vol. 6 of *African Development Perspectives Yearbook, 1997/98*. Munich: LIT, 1999.

———. "Ghana: On the Road to Recovery." *Africa Report* 34, no. 4 (July–August 1989): 21–26.

———. *Thomas Sankara: An African Revolutionary*. Athens: Ohio University Press, 2014.

Hart, Keith. "Swindler or Public Benefactor?—The Entrepreneur in His Community." In *Changing Social Structure in Ghana: Essays in the Comparative Sociology of a New State and an Old Tradition*, edited by Jack Goody, 1–35. London: International Affairs Institute, 1975.

Harvey, William Burnett. *Law and Social Change in Ghana*. Princeton, NJ: Princeton University Press, 1966.

Hasty, Jennifer. *The Press and Political Culture in Ghana*. Bloomington: Indiana University Press, 2005.

Hayward, Fred M. "Ghana Experiments with Civic Education." *Africa Report* 16, no. 5 (May 1971): 24–27.

Herbst, Jeffrey. *The Politics of Reform in Ghana, 1982–1991*. Berkeley: University of California Press, 1993.

Hodges, Tony. "Ghana's Strategy for Adjustment with Growth." *Africa Recovery* 2, no. 3 (August 1988): 16–21, 27.

Hodgkin, Thomas. *Nationalism in Colonial Africa*. New York: New York University Press, 1957.

Howard, Rhoda. *Colonialism and Underdevelopment in Ghana*. New York: Holmes & Meier, 1978.

Huntington, Samuel P. *The Third Wave: Democratization in the Late Twentieth Century*. Norman: University of Oklahoma Press, 1993.

Huq, M. M. *The Economy of Ghana: The First 25 Years since Independence*. London: MacMillan, 1989.

Hutchful, Eboe. "From 'Revolution' to Monetarism: The Economics and Politics of the Adjustment Programme in Ghana." In *Structural Adjustment in Africa*, edited by Bonnie K. Campbell and John Loxley, 92–131. New York: St. Martin's, 1989.

———. *Ghana's Adjustment Experience: The Paradox of Reform*. Geneva: UN Research Institute for Social Development, 2002.

———, ed. *The IMF and Ghana: The Confidential Record*. London: Zed Books, 1987.

———. "Military Policy and Reform in Ghana." *Journal of Modern African Studies* 35, no. 2 (June 1997): 251–78.

———. "Reconstructing Civil-Military Relations and the Collapse of Democracy in Ghana, 1979–81." *African Affairs* 96 (1997): 535–60.

———. "A Tale of Two Regimes: Imperialism, the Military and Class in Ghana." *Review of African Political Economy* no. 14 (January–April 1979): 36–55.

Institute of Economic Affairs. *Political Parties Code of Conduct 2012*. Accra: Institute of Economic Affairs, 2012.

———. *Presidential Debate: Strengthening the Pillars of Democracy, Tamale, November 2008*. Accra: Institute of Economic Affairs, 2010.

International Monetary Fund. "Corruption Must Be Fought on Global Scale." *IMF Survey* 26, no. 18 (1997): 303–04.

Iyer, Deepa. "Earning a Reputation for Independence: Ghana's Commission on Human Rights and Administrative Justice, 1993–2003." Princeton, NJ: Innovations for Successful Societies, 2011. http://www.princeton.edu/successfulsocieties.

Jackson, Kofi Abaka. *When Gun Rules: A Soldier's Testimony*. Accra: Woeli Publishing Services, 1999.

James, C. L. R. *Nkrumah and the Ghana Revolution*. London: Allison & Busby, 1977.

Jebuni, Charles D., and Abena D. Oduro. "Structural Adjustment Programme and the Transition to Democracy." In Ninsin, *Ghana: Transition to Democracy*, 19–41.

Jeffries, Richard. "Populist Tendencies in the Ghanaian Trade Union Movement." In *The Development of an African Working Class: Studies in Class Formation and Action*, edited by Richard Sandbrook and Robin Cohen, 261–80. Toronto: University of Toronto Press, 1975.

———. "Urban Popular Attitudes towards the Economic Recovery Programme and the PNDC Government in Ghana." *African Affairs* 91, no. 363 (April 1992): 207–26.

Jeffries, Richard, and Clare Thomas. "The Ghanaian Elections of 1992." *African Affairs* 92, no. 368 (July 1993): 331–66.

Johnston, Michael. "Corruption, Inequality, and Change." In *Corruption, Development and Inequality: Soft Touch or Hard Graft?* edited by Peter M. Ward, 13–37. London: Routledge, 1989.

———. "The Political Consequences of Corruption: A Reassessment." *Comparative Politics* 18, no. 4 (July 1986): 459–77.

———. *Syndromes of Corruption: Wealth, Power, and Democracy*. Cambridge: Cambridge University Press, 2005.

Kakrabah-Quarshie, Ray. *Achievements of the Progress Party, 1969–1971*. Accra: Bekumah Agencies, 1971.

Kapur, Ishan, Michael T. Hadjimichael, Paul Hilbers, Jerald Schiff, and Philippe Szymczak. *Ghana: Adjustment and Growth, 1983–91*. Washington, DC: International Monetary Fund, 1991.

Kasfir, Nelson. "State, Magendo, and Class Formation in Uganda." *Journal of Commonwealth and Comparative Politics* 21, no. 3 (November 1983): 84–103.

Kelly, Bob, and R. B. Bening. "Ideology, Regionalism, Self-Interest and Tradition: An Investigation into Contemporary Politics in Northern Ghana." *Africa* 77, no. 2 (2007): 180–206.

Kibwana, Kivutha, Smokin Wanjala, and Okech-Owiti. *The Anatomy of Corruption in Kenya: Legal, Political and Socio-economic Perspectives*. Nairobi: Claripress, 1996.

Killingray, David. "Soldiers, Ex-servicemen and Politics in the Gold Coast, 1939–50." *Journal of Modern African Studies* 21, no. 3 (1983): 523–34.

Kimble, David. *A Political History of Ghana: The Rise of Gold Coast Nationalism, 1850–1928*. Oxford: Oxford University Press, 1963.

Kirst, Sarah. "'Chiefs Do Not Talk Law, Most of Them Talk Power': Traditional Authorities in Conflicts over Land Grabbing in Ghana." *Canadian Journal of African Studies* 54, no. 3 (2020): 519–39.

Klitgaard, Robert. *Controlling Corruption*. Berkeley: University of California Press, 1988.

Konings, Piet. "Rizculteurs capitalistes et petits paysans: La naissance d'un conflit de classe au Ghana." *Politique africaine* no. 11 (September 1983): 77–94.

———. *The State and Rural Class Formation in Ghana: A Comparative Analysis*. London: KPI, 1986.

———. "The State and the Defence Committees in the Ghanaian Revolution, 1981–1984." Unpublished manuscript, n.d.

Kpundeh, Sahr John. *Politics and Corruption in Africa: A Case Study of Sierra Leone*. Lanham, MD: University Press of America, 1995.

Kraus, Jon. "The Political Economy of Food in Ghana." In *Coping with Africa's Food Crisis*, edited by Naomi Chazan and Timothy M. Shaw, 75–118. Boulder, CO: Lynne Rienner, 1988.

———. "The Struggle over Structural Adjustment in Ghana." *Africa Today* 38, no. 4 (1991): 27–33.

Landell-Mills, Pierre, and Ismail Serageldin. "Governance and the Development Process." *Finance and Development* 28, no. 3 (1991): 14–17.

Leff, Nathaniel H. "Economic Development through Corruption." In *Bureaucratic Corruption in Sub-Saharan Africa: Toward a Search for Causes and Consequences*, edited by Monday O. Ekpo, 325–40. Washington, DC: University Press of America, 1979.

Lemarchand, René. "Political Clientelism and Ethnicity in Tropical Africa: Competing Solidarities in Nation-Building." In *Friends, Followers, and Factions: A Reader in Political Clientelism*, edited by Steffen W. Schmidt, Laura Guasti, Carl H. Landé, and James C. Scott, 149–70. Berkeley: University of California Press, 1977.

———. "The State, the Parallel Economy, and the Changing Structure of Patronage Systems." In *The Precarious Balance: State and Society in Africa*, edited by Donald Rothchild and Naomi Chazan, 149–70. Boulder, CO: Westview, 1988.

Le Vine, Victor T. *Political Corruption: The Ghana Case*. Stanford, CA: Hoover Institution Press, 1975.

Levtzion, Nehemia. "The Early States of the Western Sudan to 1500." In *History of West Africa*, vol. 1, edited by J. F. A. Ajayi and Michael Crowder, 114–51. New York: Columbia University Press, 1976.

"List of Akufo-Addo Government Ministers and Political Appointees." Wikipedia, accessed December 23, 2022. https://en.wikipedia.org/.

Loxley, John. *Ghana: Economic Crisis and the Long Road to Recovery*. Ottawa: North-South Institute, 1988.

Luckham, Robin. "Transition to Democracy and Control over Ghana's Military and Security Establishments." In Ninsin, *Ghana: Transition to Democracy*, 119–45.

Luckham, Robin, and Stephen Nkrumah. "The Constituent Assembly—A Social and Political Portrait." In Austin and Luckham, *Politicians and Soldiers*, 89–125.

Makgetla, Itumeleng. Interview with Emile Short. Princeton, NJ: Innovations for Successful Societies, 2009. http://www.princeton.edu/successfulsocieties.

Mamdani, Mahmood. *Citizen and Subject: Contemporary Africa and the Legacy of Late Colonialism*. Princeton, NJ: Princeton University Press, 1996.

Manuh, Takyiwaa. "Women, the State and Society under the PNDC." In Gyimah-Boadi, *Ghana under PNDC Rule*, 176–95.

Markovitz, Irving Leonard. *Power and Class in Africa*. Englewood Cliffs, NJ: Prentice-Hall, 1977.

Mbir, Papa Kojo. *Premix: An Avenue for Political Corruption, Deceit, Lies and Petty Thieving*. Accra: published by author, [2005].

McCants, Ashley. Interview with Paul Adu-Gyamfi. Princeton, NJ: Innovations for Successful Societies, 2008. http://www.princeton.edu/successfulsocieties.

McCaskie, T. C. "The Life and Afterlife of Yaa Asantewaa." *Africa* 77, no. 2 (2007): 151–79.
———. *State and Society in Pre-colonial Asante*. Cambridge: Cambridge University Press, 1995.
Médard, Jean-François. "L'Etat patrimonialisé." *Politique africaine*, no. 39 (1990): 25–36.
———. "Public Corruption in Africa: A Comparative Perspective." *Corruption and Reform* 1, no. 2 (1986): 115–31.
Migdal, Joel S. *Strong Societies and Weak States: State-Society Relations and State Capabilities in the Third World*. Princeton, NJ: Princeton University Press, 1988.
Mikell, Gwendolyn. *Cocoa and Chaos in Ghana*. New York: Paragon House, 1989.
———. "Peasant Politicisation and Economic Recuperation in Ghana: Local and National Dilemmas." *Journal of Modern African Studies* 27, no. 3 (September 1989): 455–78.
Ministry of Local Government. *From the Centre to the Grassroots: Excerpts from Selected Speeches on the PNDC's Decentralisation Policy*. Accra: Venus Publications, 1991.
Ministry of Local Government and Rural Development. *Ghana: The New Local Government System*. Accra: Ministry of Local Government and Rural Development, 1996.
Mkandawire, Thandika, and Adebayo Olukoshi, eds. *Between Liberalisation and Oppression: The Politics of Structural Adjustment in Africa*. Dakar: CODESRIA, 1995.
Monitoring Abuse of Incumbency in Ghana's 2012 Elections: Final Report. Accra: Ghana Integrity Initiative, Ghana Anti-Corruption Coalition, and Ghana Center for Democratic Development, 2013.
National Commission for Democracy. *Evolving a True Democracy: Summary of NCD's Work towards the Establishment of a New Democratic Order*. Accra: National Commission for Democracy, 1991.
National Communications Authority. "List of Authorised TV Broadcasting Stations in Ghana, as at Third Quarter 2017," accessed June 13, 2022. https://nca.org.gh/wp-content/uploads/2021/11/AUTHORISED-TV-STATIONS-Q3-2017.pdf.
Nevill, Glenda. "Ghana: Rapidly Expanding with Changing Mindsets." *The Media Online*, November 4, 2016. https://themediaonline.co.za/.
Ninsin, Kwame. *The Corrupt Elites: Anatomy of Power and Wealth in Ghana*. Accra: Gavoss Education, 2018.
———, ed. *Ghana: Transition to Democracy*. Accra: Freedom Publications, 1998.
———. "Ghana beyond Crisis and Adjustment." *Africa Development* 21, nos. 2–3 (1996): 25–42.

———, ed. *Ghana's Political Transition, 1990–1993: Selected Documents*. Accra: Freedom Publications, 1996.

———. "Introduction: Understanding Ghana's Electoral Politics." In Ninsin, *Issues*, 1–12.

———, ed. *Issues in Ghana's Electoral Politics*. Dakar: CODESRIA, 2016.

———. "Markets and Liberal Democracy." In Boafo-Arthur, *Ghana: One Decade*, 86–105.

———. *Political Struggles in Ghana, 1967–1981*. Accra: Tornado Publishers, 1985.

———. "State, Capital and Labour Relations, 1961–1987." In Hansen and Ninsin, *State, Development and Politics*, 15–42.

———. "Strategies of Mobilisation under the PNDC Government." In Gyimah-Boadi, *Ghana under PNDC Rule*, 100–113.

Nkrumah, Kwame. *Revolutionary Path*. New York: International Publishers, 1973.

Noll, Andrea, and Jan Budniok. "Social Protest and the Middle Class in Ghana: A Social Movement Approach of Three Cases." *Journal of Contemporary African Studies* (2021), https://doi.org/10.1080/02589001.2021.1931056.

Nugent, Paul. *Big Men, Small Boys and Politics in Ghana: Power, Ideology and the Burden of History, 1982–1994*. London: Pinter, 1995.

———. "Ghana: The Slow March Back towards Multipartyism." In *Africa Contemporary Record*, vol. 23, 1990–92, edited by Colin Legum, B 46–59. New York: Africana Publishing, 1998.

———. "Living in the Past: Urban, Rural and Ethnic Themes in the 1992 and 1996 Elections in Ghana." *Journal of Modern African Studies* 37, no. 2 (June 1999): 287–319.

Nye, J. S. "Corruption and Political Development: A Cost-Benefit Analysis." *American Political Science Review* 61, no. 2 (1967): 417–27.

Odusola, Ayodele, Giovanni Andrea Cornia, Haroon Bhorat, and Pedro Conceição, eds. *Income Inequality Trends in Sub-Saharan Africa: Divergence, Determinants and Consequences*. New York: UN Development Program, 2017.

Ofori-Mensah, Michael. "Donor Anti-corruption Reforms: Quiet Diplomacy and Its Discontents." *Governance Newsletter* 17, no. 5 (September–October 2011): 1–11. Accra: Institute of Economic Affairs.

Ofori-Parku, Sylvester Senyo, and Kwaku Botwe. "'This Is (Not) Journalism': Corruption, Subterfuge, and Metajournalistic Discourses on Undercover Journalism in Ghana." *Journalism Studies* 21, no. 3 (2020): 388–405.

Okeke, Barbara E. *4 June: A Revolution Betrayed*. Enugu, Nigeria: Ikenga Publishers, 1982.

Okyere, W. Asenso. "The Response of Farmers to Ghana's Adjustment Policies." In *The Long-Term Perspective Study of Sub-Saharan Africa: Background Papers*, 2:74–83. Washington, DC: World Bank, 1990.

Olivier de Sardan, J. P. "A Moral Economy of Corruption in Africa?" *Journal of Modern African Studies* 37, no. 1 (1999): 25–52.
Open Society Initiative of West Africa. *Ghana: Justice Sector and the Rule of Law*. Dakar: Open Society Initiative of West Africa, 2007.
Oppong, Nelson. "Ghana's Public Interest and Accountability Committee: An Elusive Quest for 'Home-Grown' Transformation in the Oil Industry." *Journal of Energy and Natural Resources Law* 34, no. 3 (2016): 313–36.
Oquaye, Mike. "Law, Justice and the Revolution," in Gyimah-Boadi, *Ghana under PNDC Rule*, 154–75.
———. *Politics in Ghana, 1972–1979*. Accra: Tornado Publications, 1980.
Osei, Philip D. "Political Liberalization and the Implementation of Value Added Tax in Ghana." *Journal of Modern African Studies* 38, no. 2 (July 2000): 255–78.
Osse, Lionel, and Newton Norviewu. "Ghanaians Perceive Increase in Corruption Level, Give Government Low Marks on Fighting Graft." Afrobarometer and Ghana Center for Democratic Development, news release AD333, December 4, 2019.
Ovadia, Jesse Salah. "Ghana's Petroleum Industry: Expectations, Frustrations and Anger in Coastal Communities." *Journal of Modern African Studies* 58, no. 3 (2020): 397–424.
———. "Stepping Back from the Brink: A Review of the 2008 Ghanaian Election from the Capital of the Northern Region." *Canadian Journal of African Studies* 45, no. 2 (2011): 310–40.
Owusu, Maxwell. "Custom and Coups: A Juridical Interpretation of Civil Order and Disorder in Ghana." *Journal of Modern African Studies* 24, no. 1 (1986): 69–99.
———. Foreword to Ninsin, *Corrupt Elites*, v–xi.
———. "Rebellion, Revolution, and Tradition: Reinterpreting Coups in Ghana." *Comparative Studies in Society and History* 31, no. 2 (1989): 372–97.
———. "Tradition and Transformation: Democracy and the Politics of Popular Power in Ghana." *Journal of Modern African Studies* 34, no. 2 (June 1996): 307–43.
———. *Uses and Abuses of Political Power: A Case Study of Continuity and Change in the Politics of Ghana*. Chicago: University of Chicago Press, 1970.
Owusu-Dapaa, Ernest. "An Exposition and Critique of Judicial Independence under Ghana's 1992 Constitution." *Commonwealth Law Bulletin* 37, no. 3 (2011): 531–60.
Pierce, Steven. *Moral Economies of Corruption: State Formation and Political Culture in Nigeria*. Durham, NC: Duke University Press, 2016.
Prempeh, H. Kwasi. *The Ghanaian Judiciary and the 1992 Constitution: A Problem of Asymmetrical Jurisprudence*. Accra: Center for Democratic Development, 1999.

Provisional National Defence Council. Chieftaincy (Restoration of Status of Chiefs) Law, 1983.

———. Citizens Vetting Committee Law (PNDCL 1), February 1, 1982.

———. Citizens Vetting Committee (Amendment) Law (PNDCL 18), June 30, 1982.

———. Constitution of the Fourth Republic of Ghana (Promulgation) Law, 1992 (PNDCL 282).

———. *Decentralisation in Ghana*. Accra: Information Services Department, 1983.

———. (Establishment) Proclamation (Supplementary and Consequential Provisions), PNDC Law 42, Section 32, 1982.

———. National Investigations Committee Law (PNDCL 2), February 3, 1982.

———. *The New Guidelines for the National Defence Committee and People's Defence Committees*. Accra: Information Services Department, 1983.

———. *Outlines of the Decentralisation Plan of the Provisional National Defence Council*. Accra: Information Services Department, 1984.

———. *Preamble to Policy Guidelines of the Provisional National Defence Council*. Accra: Ghana Information Services Department, 1982.

———. Public Tribunals Law, 1982 (PNDCL 24), July 21, 1982.

———. Public Tribunals Law, 1984 (PNDCL 78), December 21, 1983.

———. Revenue Commissioners Law (PNDCL 80), January 7, 1984.

Quantson, Kofi B. *Ghana: Peace and Stability; Chapters from the Intelligence Sector*. Accra: Napascom, 2000.

Rabinowitz, Beth. *Coup, Rivals, and the Modern State: Why Rural Coalitions Matter in Sub-Saharan Africa*. New York: Cambridge University Press, 2018.

Rathbone, Richard. *Nkrumah and the Chiefs: The Politics of Chieftaincy in Ghana, 1951–60*. Oxford, UK: James Currey, 2000.

Rawlings, Jerry John, Jr. *Forging Ahead: Selected Speeches of Flt-Lt. Jerry John Rawlings, Chairman of the PNDC*, vol. 2, *January 1st 1983–December 31st 1983*. Accra: Information Services Department, n.d.

———. *A Revolutionary Journey: Selected Speeches of Flt.-Lt. Jerry John Rawlings, Chairman of the PNDC*, vol. 1, *Dec. 31st 1981–Dec. 31st 1982*. Accra: Information Services Department, n.d.

Ray, Donald. *Ghana: Politics, Economics and Society*. London: Francis Pinter, 1986.

Republic of Ghana. Criminal Offences Act, 1960 (Act 29).

———. *District Political Authority and Modalities for District Level Elections*. Accra: Ghana Publishing Corporation, 1987.

———. *Final Report of the Commission of Enquiry on Bribery and Corruption*. Accra: Ghana Publishing Corporation, 1975.

Bibliography

———. *First [Second and Third] Interim Report of the Commission of Inquiry into Bribery and Corruption*. Accra: Ghana Publishing Corporation, 1972.

———. *Judicial Service 2017–2018 Annual Report*. Accra: Republic of Ghana, 2018.

———. *National Anti-Corruption Action Plan (2015–2024)*. Accra: Republic of Ghana, 2011.

———. National Media Commission Act, 1993 (Act 449).

———. *Report of Commission of Enquiry into Alleged Irregularities and Malpractices in Connection with the Issue of Import Licences*. Accra: Ministry of Information and Broadcasting, 1964.

———. *Report of the Ad Hoc Committee on Union Government*. Accra: State Publishing Corporation, 1977.

———. *Report of the Commission Appointed to Enquire into the Affairs of the Ghana Timber Marketing Board and the Ghana Timber Co-operative Union*. Accra: Tema State Publishing, 1968.

———. *Report of the Commission Appointed to Enquire into the Circumstances which Led to the Payment of £28,545 to James Colledge (Cocoa) Limited as Compensation for Land Acquired for the Achiasi-Kotoku Railway*. Accra: Republic of Ghana, 1962.

———. *Report of the Commission Appointed to Enquire into the Functions, Operations and Administration of the Workers Brigade*. Accra: State Publishing Corporation, 1967.

———. *Report of the Commission of Enquiry into the Affairs of the Anlo Traditional Area*. Accra: Republic of Ghana, 1969.

———. *Report of the Commission of Enquiry on the Local Purchasing of Cocoa*. Accra: State Publishing Corporation, 1966.

———. *Report of the Commission of Inquiry into Trade Malpractices in Ghana*. Accra: Republic of Ghana, 1965.

———. *Report of the Commission to Enquire into the Affairs of NADECO Limited*. Accra: State Publishing Corporation, 1966.

———. *Report of the Committee of Enquiry into Alleged Irregularities and Malpractices in the Affairs of the Tema Development Corporation*. Accra: Ghana Publishing Corporation, 1970.

———. *Report of the Committee of Enquiry into Ejura Affairs*. Accra: Ghana Publishing House, 1973.

———. *Report of the Committee of Enquiry into the Yendi Skin Affairs*. Accra: Republic of Ghana, 1969.

———. Right to Information Act, 2019 (Act 989).

———. *The Search for True Democracy in Ghana*. Accra: Public Relations Department, 1985.

———. *White Paper on the Committee Appointed to Enquire into Recent Disturbances at Prestea*. W.P. no. 8/69. Accra: Republic of Ghana, 1969.

———. *White Paper on the Interim Report of Sowah Commission of Enquiry into the Assets of Specified Persons*, W.P. no. 13/68. Accra: Republic of Ghana, 1968.

———. *White Paper on the Report of the Commission of Enquiry into Alleged Irregularities and Malpractices in Connection with the Grant of Import Licences*. W.P. no. 4/67. Accra: Republic of Ghana, 1967.

———. *White Paper on the Report of the Commission of Enquiry into Kwame Nkrumah Properties*, W.P. no. 1/67. Accra: State Publishing Corporation, 1967.

———. *White Paper on the Report of the Commission of Enquiry into the Affairs of the Anlo Traditional Area*. W.P. no. 12/69. Accra: Republic of Ghana, 1969.

———. *White Paper on the Report of the Commission of Enquiry into the Ghana Trades Union Congress Funds*, W.P. no. 7/69. Accra: Ghana Publishing Corporation, 1969.

———. *White Paper on the Report of the Committee of Enquiry into the Yendi Skin Affairs*, W.P. no. 14/69. Accra: Republic of Ghana, 1969.

———. *White Paper on the Report of the Jiagge Commission of Enquiry into the Assets of Specified Persons*, W.P. no. 3/69. Accra: Ghana Publishing Corporation, 1969.

———. *White Paper on the Report of the Manyo-Plange Commission of Enquiry into the Assets of Specified Persons*, W.P. no. 11/69. Accra: Ghana Publishing Corporation, 1969.

———. *White Paper on the Report of the Taylor Assets Committee*. W.P. no. 1/76. Accra: Ghana Publishing Corporation, 1976.

Robertson, Claire. "The Death of Makola and Other Tragedies." *Canadian Journal of African Studies* 17, no. 3 (1983): 469–95.

Rose-Ackerman, Susan. *Corruption and Government: Causes, Consequences, and Reform*. Cambridge: Cambridge University Press, 1999.

Rosen, Lauren Coyle. *Fires of Gold: Law, Spirit, and Sacrificial Labor in Ghana*. Oakland: University of California Press, 2020.

Rothchild, Donald, and E. Gyimah-Boadi. "Ghana's Economic Decline and Development Strategies." In *Africa in Economic Crisis*, edited by John Ravenhill, 254–85. New York: Columbia University Press, 1986.

Sandbrook, Richard, and Robin Cohen, eds. *The Development of an African Working Class*. Toronto: University of Toronto Press, 1975.

Sarris, Alexander, and Hadi Shams. *Ghana under Structural Adjustment: The Impact on Agriculture and the Rural Poor*. New York: New York University Press, 1991.

Savonnet, Georges. *Les Birifor de Diépla et sa region insulaires du rameau lobi (Haute-Volta)*. Paris: ORSTOM, 1976.

Scott, James C. *Comparative Political Corruption*. Englewood Cliffs, NJ: Prentice-Hall, 1972.

Shillington, Kevin. *Ghana and the Rawlings Factor*. New York: St. Martin's, 1992.
Short, Emile. *The Anti-corruption Mandates of the Commission on Human Rights and Administrative Justice and the Serious Fraud Office: A Duplication of Functions?* Accra: Institute of Economic Affairs, 2010.
———. *Empowering Ghana's Anti-corruption Institutions in the Fight against Corruption*. Accra: Institute of Economic Affairs, 2015.
———. "Recommendations of the Emile Short Commission," accessed February 17, 2021. https://www.ghanaweb.com/GhanaHomePage/NewsArchive/AWW-Full-recommendations-of-the-Emile-Short-Commission-782207.
Sindzingre, Alice Nicole. *Etat, développement et rationalité en Afrique: Contribution à une analyse de la corruption*. Travaux et documents 43. Bordeaux: Centre d'étude d'Afrique noire, 1994.
Smith, Daniel A. "Consolidating Democracy? The Structural Underpinnings of Ghana's 2000 Elections." *Journal of Modern African Studies* 40, no. 4 (December 2002): 621–50.
Smith, Daniel Jordan. *A Culture of Corruption: Everyday Deception and Popular Discontent in Nigeria*. Princeton, NJ: Princeton University Press, 2007.
South African Institute of International Affairs. "Ghana and Civil Society Clash over Allegations of Corruption." *eAfrica* 2 (April 2004). https://saiia.org.za/research/ghana-and-civil-society-clash-over-allegations-of-corruption/.
Staniland, Martin. *The Lions of Dagbon: Political Change in Northern Ghana*. Cambridge: Cambridge University Press, 1975.
Statista. "Government Revenue from Oil in Ghana from 2019 to 2023," accessed March 6, 2023. https://www.statista.com/statistics/1295627/annual-oil-revenue-in-ghana/.
Stoeltje, Beverly J. "Asante Queen Mothers: A Study of Female Authority." In *Queens, Queen Mothers, Priestesses, and Power: Case Studies in African Gender*, edited by Flora Edouwaye S. Kaplan, 41–71. New York: New York Academy of Sciences, 1997.
Tarrow, Sidney. *Power in Movement: Social Movements, Collective Action and Politics*. Cambridge: Cambridge University Press, 1994.
Theobald, Robin. *Corruption, Development and Underdevelopment*. London: MacMillan, 1990.
Thiriot, Céline. "Ghana: Les aléas d'un modèle." In *L'Afrique politique 1977*, 229–54. Paris: Editions Karthala, 1977.
Thomas, Roger G. "The 1916 Bongo 'Riots' and Their Background: Aspects of the Early Colonial Administration of Eastern Upper Ghana." *Journal of African History* 24, no. 1 (1983): 57–75.
Tilly, Charles. *Coercion, Capital, and European States, AD 990–1992*. Cambridge, MA: Blackwell, 1992.

Tonah, Steve, ed. *Ethnicity, Conflicts and Consensus in Ghana.* Accra: Woeli Publishing Services, 2007.

———. "Theoretical and Comparative Perspectives on Ethnicity, Conflicts and Consensus in Ghana." In Tonah, *Ethnicity, Conflicts and Consensus in Ghana,* 3–24.

Trading Economics. "Crude Oil Production: Africa," accessed August 19, 2022. https://tradingeconomics.com/country-list/crude-oil-production?continent=africa.

Transparency International. Corruption Perceptions Index. http://www.transparency.org/policy_research/surveys_indices/cpi.

Treisman, Daniel. "Income, Democracy, and Leader Turnover." *American Journal of Political Science* 59, no. 4 (October 2015): 927–42.

Tsikata, Edzodzinam. "Women's Political Organisations, 1951–1987." In Hansen and Ninsin, *State, Development and Politics,* 73–93.

Tsikata, Tsatsu. "Ghana." In *The Human Dimension of Africa's Persistent Economic Crisis,* edited by Adebayo Adedeji, Sadig Rasheed, and Melody Morrison, 144–61. London: Hans Zell, 1990.

Twumasi, Yaw. "The 1969 Election." In Austin and Luckham, *Politicians and Soldiers,* 140–63.

UNICEF. "Adjustment Policies and Programmes to Protect Children and Other Vulnerable Groups in Ghana." In *Adjustment with a Human Face,* vol. 2, *Country Case Studies,* edited by Giovanni Andrea Cornia, Richard Jolly, and Frances Stewart, 93–125. Oxford, UK: Clarendon Press, 1988.

United Nations Development Programme. *Ghana Human Development Report 2007: Towards a More Inclusive Society.* Accra: UNDP, Ghana Office, 2007.

Van Gyampo, Ransford Edward, and Emmanuel Graham. "Constitutional Hybridity and Constitutionalism in Ghana." *Africa Review* 6, no. 2 (2014): 138–50.

Verdon, Michel. "Political Sovereignty, Village Reproduction and Legends of Origin: A Comparative Hypothesis." *Africa* 51, no. 1 (1981): 465–75.

———. "Re-defining Pre-colonial Ewe Polities: The Case of Abutia." *Africa* 50, no. 3 (1980): 280–92.

Ward, W. E. F. *A History of the Gold Coast.* London: George Allen & Unwin, 1948.

Waterbury, John. "An Attempt to Put Patrons and Clients in Their Place." In *Patrons and Clients in Mediterranean Societies,* edited by Ernest Gellner and John Waterbury, 329–42. London: Duckworth, 1977.

Werlin, Herbert H. "The Roots of Corruption—the Ghanaian Enquiry." *Journal of Modern African Studies* 10, no. 2 (1972): 247–66.

Wesseling, H. L. *Divide and Rule: The Partition of Africa, 1880–1914.* Westport, CT: Praeger, 1996.

Whitefield, Lindsay. "'Change for a Better Ghana': Party Competition, Institutionalization and Alternation in Ghana's 2008 Elections." *African Affairs* 108, no. 433 (2009): 621–41.
Wilks, Ivor. *Asante in the Nineteenth Century: The Structure and Evolution of a Political Order*. Cambridge: Cambridge University Press, 1975.
Wilson, Louis E. "The Evolution of Paramount Chiefs among the Adangme to the End of the Nineteenth Century: The Case of the Krobo (Ghana)." *Genève-Afrique* 24, no. 2 (1986): 73–100.
World Bank. *Economic Developments in 1987: A Status Report*. Accra: World Bank, 1987.
———. *Ghana: Policies and Program for Adjustment*. Washington, DC: World Bank, 1984.
———. *Ghana: Progress on Adjustment*. Washington, DC: World Bank, 1991.
———. *Sub-Saharan Africa: From Crisis to Sustainable Growth*. Washington, DC: World Bank, 1989.
———. *World Development Indicators, 2000*. CD-ROM version. Washington, DC: World Bank, 2000.
———. *World Development Report: The State in a Changing World*. New York: Oxford University Press, 1997.
Yankah, Kojo. *The Trial of JJ Rawlings: Echoes of the 31st December Revolution*. Accra: Ghana Publishing Corporation, 1986.
Younger, Stephen D. "Ghana: Economic Recovery Program: A Case Study of Stabilization and Structural Adjustment in Sub-Saharan Africa." In *Successful Development in Africa: Case Studies of Projects, Programs, and Policies*, 128–73. Washington, DC: World Bank, 1989.
Zanu, S. Y. M. "PNDC Law 207 and the Financing of District Assemblies." In *Ghana's Local Government Law: Issues of Implementation*, edited by S. A. Nkrumah, 31–49. Legon: School of Administration, University of Ghana, 1990.

Index

Abodakpi, Dan, 231, 251
Abutia, 17
Accra, 1, 26, 46, 50, 56, 93, 97, 118, 129, 132–35, 142, 187, 244, 254, 269
Acheampong, Ignatius K., 77–86, 93, 283
Acquaye-Nortey, W. C. O., 89
Adam, Ibrahim, 175, 232
Adangme, 18
Adansi, 113, 119, 141
Addah, Mary, 227
Adjei, Agyenim Boateng, 239
Adjei, Arthur, 264
Adu-Gyamfi, Paul, 263
Adutu, Kwabena, 165
Afoko, Paul, 211
African Peer Review Mechanism, 222
Afrifa, A. A., 73, 85–86, 93
Afrobarometer, 228–29, 240–41, 257, 274
Agyapa deal, 261, 270, 276
Agyapong, Kennedy, 267
Agyebeng, Kissi, 262
Agyekum, George, 145, 148, 153, 160
Agyeman-Duah, Baffour, 174
Agyemang, Nana Akwasi, 244
Agyeman-Rawlings, Nana Konadu, 178, 190–91, 232
Ahafo Region, 214
Ahwoi, Kwamena, 153, 160, 164, 193
Aidoo, Ama Ata, 135
Aikins, G. E. K., 166
Akan, 18–27, 37, 39, 75–78, 139, 214–15
Akata-Pore, Daniel Alolga, 104, 116, 185
Akatsi, 133, 139
Akrasi-Sarpong, Yaw, 112, 115
Akuffo, Fred, 86–88, 93
Akufo-Addo, Nana, 208, 211, 222, 225–26, 229, 231–33, 238–39, 260, 286
Akwapim, 214
Akyem, 214

Alliance for Accountable Governance, 273
Alliance for Change, 268–69, 273
Amidu, Martin, 236, 261–62
Amnesty International, 152
Amonoo-Monney, J. C., 154, 159, 161
Anane, Richard, 233
Anas, Anas Aremeyaw, 1–2, 266–68, 276
Ankrah, Joseph, 72
Anlo, 17–18, 70
Annan, D. F., 192
Apaloo, F. K., 148
Appau, Yaw, 236–37
Appiah, Joe, 52
Arhin, Kwame, 163
Arise Ghana, 269–70, 276
Armah, Kwesi, 61
Armed Forces Defence Committees (AFDCs), 184–85
Armed Forces Revolutionary Council (AFRC), 90–101, 147–48
asafo, 19–20, 37–38, 136
Asante, 19–24, 26–28, 202, 214, 282
Asante, Kofi, 233
Asantehene, 20–24, 26–28, 34, 189–90, 243–44
Asanteman Council, 53
Ashanti, 28, 33–34, 37, 41–42, 176, 214
Ashanti Goldfields Corporation, 230, 271
asikafo, 20
Assamoah, B. B. D., 142
Assasie, J. Y., 143
asset declaration, 95, 251–52
Association of Local Unions (ALU), 125
Association of Recognized Professional Bodies (ARPB), 83–85
Atim, Chris Bukari, 104
Attafuah, Kenneth, 151–52, 159, 164–65, 241
auditor general, 226–27, 260–61, 275

awafia, 17
Ayariga, Mahama, 239
Ayirebi, 132, 176
Azeem, Vitus, 225

Bamba, Moctar, 233
Bawku, 36, 216
Bekoe, Nana Okutwer, III, 103, 122, 161–62
Bekoe, Samuel Ofori, 223
Benneh, George, 174
Boahen, Adu, 198, 202
Boahen, Charles Adu, 266
Boakye, Yiadom Ohene, 120
Board of Public Tribunals, 150, 153, 166
Bolgatanga, 34, 150, 211, 272
Bongo riots, 36
Boniface, Abubakar Saddique, 218
Bono East Region, 214
Bono Region, 214
Bonsu, Mensa, 22–23
Botchwey, Kwesi, 169–72
Braimah, Joseph Adam, 51
British Empire, 44–45
Brobbey, S. A., 166
Brong, 58, 75, 101, 214
Brong Ahafo Region, 58
Buadi, Joseph Adjei, 104
Bureau of African Affairs, 63–64
Burkina Faso, 106
Busia, K. A., 52, 73–77, 286

Cape Coast, 24, 26
Catholic Bishops Conference, 198
Catholic Graduates for Action, 143
cedi, 76, 101, 170, 280
Center for Democratic Development (CDD), 2–4, 174, 222, 228–29, 261, 268, 274–76
Center for Freedom and Accuracy, 276
Central Region, 139, 148, 190, 280
Central Revenue Department, 150
Centre for Civic Education, 74
chiefs, 15–26, 136–41, 189–91; colonial authorities and, 29–38, 282; corruption and, 35–36, 70–71, 98, 140–41, 158–59, 242–44; laws on, 54, 57–58, 70; popular accountability and, 19–23, 33, 37–40
Chiiri, Naa Polkuu Konkuu, 190
Christian Council of Ghana, 93, 198

Citizen Ghana Movement, 276
Citizens' Vetting Committee (CVC), 122, 148–50, 165
Coalition on the Right to Information, 253
cocoa, 51; corruption and, 64, 80, 114–15, 120, 155–56, 246–47, 280; farming and farmers, 40–41, 56, 82, 114–15, 137, 169, 175–76, 180, 214, 246; Ghana's dependence on, 56, 76; world market price of, 78, 101
Cocoa Marketing Board (CMB), 51, 155, 169, 171, 175, 180
Cocoa Purchasing Company (CPC), 51–52
Coleman, Carl, 186
colonial rule, 23–54, 282
Commission for Human Rights and Administrative Justice (CHRAJ), 201, 204, 226, 233, 241, 257–60, 262, 275
Committee for Joint Action, 273
Committees for the Defence of the Revolution (CDRs), 112, 142–44, 185
Confiscated Assets Committee, 150
Congo, 67
constitution (of 1992), 200–202, 220–22, 255, 285
Constitutional Review Commission, 222
Convention People's Party (CPP), 46–70, 99, 283
corruption: civil society groups and, 273–80; class and, 4, 11–12, 110–11, 157–59; in colonial era, 31, 35–36; definitions of, 6–8, 11, 250–51; extent of, 225–26; governance and, 2–3, 10, 14, 168, 196–97; legislation against, 250–53; military and, 80–83; political parties and, 51–53, 59–66, 74–76, 216–25, 227–29; private business and, 12, 96–97, 129–35, 155–56, 241–42; protests against, 3, 12–13, 72–73, 93–94, 98, 117–33, 269–73, 290; scandals, 229–47; surveys, 2–4, 226–29, 240–41, 257, 289
Corruption Perceptions Index (CPI), 5, 7, 226–29
Council of State, 255
courts, 145–47, 249–50, 253–57; AFRC special courts, 94–95, 100, 147, 163; court corruption, 240–41; public tribunals, 147–48, 152–66, 250

Index

Crabbe, Samuel Azu, 79
Crusading Guide, 266

Dagari, 16–17
Dagbon, 216
Dagomba, 34–36, 70
Daily Graphic, 263, 267–68
Dame, Godfred Yeboah, 251
Damuah, Kwabena, 94, 104, 115, 125
district assemblies, 187–94, 199, 244–47
Djin, A. Y. K., 52, 61
Domelevo, Daniel Yao, 252, 260–61
Dompoase Youth Association, 141
Dordunoo, Cletus, 215
Dyula, 27

Eastern Region, 141–42, 209, 214
Economic and Organized Crime Office (EOCO), 259–60, 275
Economic Community of West African States (ECOWAS), 233
economic recovery program (ERP), 170–73, 177–80
Edusei, Krobo, 51, 60–61, 63, 161–62
Eigen, Peter, 7
Ejura, 70–71
elections, 47, 53, 73, 99, 193–97, 202–8, 213–14, 217–20, 223, 225–26, 237–38, 246, 248, 275
Elmina, 26
Energy Commission, 233
Ethiopia, 90, 106
ethnicity, 11, 15, 47, 53–57, 67, 75–76, 101, 135, 139, 208–9, 212–17
Ewe, 17–18, 26, 52, 67, 75, 77, 79, 102–3, 139, 213
Ex-Servicemen's Union, 46

Fante, 19, 24–26, 29, 30–31, 33, 56, 65, 75, 213–14
Fante Confederacy, 25–26
Federation of Ghanaian Women, 135–36
fia, 17
First Republic, 55, 282–83
Fix the Country (protest movement), 273
Forest Watch Ghana, 277
Fourth Republic, 202, 204, 213
Frafra, 41

Ga, 24, 26, 56–57, 67, 75, 101

Ga Adangme Shifimo Kpee, 56–57
galamsey, 156
Gbedemah, K. A., 60, 73
Germany, 17, 23, 27–28, 34
Ghana, 15, 44, 54
"Ghana@50" scandal, 235
Ghana Anti-Corruption Coalition, 259, 268, 275–76
Ghana Bar Association (GBA), 83, 93, 150, 152, 160, 198, 200–201, 211
Ghana Broadcasting Corporation, 263, 267
Ghana Empire, 44
Ghanaian Chronicle, 253, 258, 263–65
Ghanaian Times, 263
Ghana Industrial Holding Corporation (GIHOC), 103, 124, 162
Ghana Integrity Initiative (GII), 225, 227, 259, 275–76
Ghana Investment Promotion Centre, 218, 274
Ghana Journalists Association, 267
Ghana Muslims Representative Council, 94, 124
Ghana National Farmers Council (GNFC), 3, 123
Ghana National Petroleum Corporation (GNPC), 232, 237, 278
Ghana National Trading Corporation, 120–21, 133
Ghana Ports Authority, 120, 155
Ghana Private Road Transport Union, 173
Ghana Railway Corporation, 121
Ghana Textile Printing, 128–29
Ghana Women's League for Social Advancement, 97
Ginwala, Frene, 6
gold, 2, 13, 16, 19–23, 41, 73, 112, 119, 122, 156, 240, 243, 261, 266, 271, 280
Gold Coast, 23–28, 43–44, 47
Gold Coast Independent, 36
Golden Stool, 20
Gonja, 18, 139, 272
Graham, Yao, 128
Greater Accra Region, 142, 219
Guggisberg, Gordon, 38
Guide, 264–65
Guinea, 69
Gyan-Apenteng, K., 110–11
Gyimah-Boadi, Emmanuel, 261

Index

Hailey, Lord, 36
Hamidu, Joshua, 91, 99
Hansen, Emmanuel, 114–15
Hausa, 28, 81
Ho, 131, 150, 272, 277
hozikpui, 17
Hussein-Suale, Ahmed, 1–2, 267
Hutchful, Eboe, 183, 217

India, 44
indirect rule, 29–38
Industrial and Commercial Workers Union, 125
inequality, 175, 288–89
Institute of Economic Affairs, 289
Interim National Coordinating Committee (INCC), 111–14, 116–17, 139
International Monetary Fund (IMF), 8, 71, 76, 129, 168, 199
Inter-Party Advisory Committee, 204
Iran, 88
Israel, 239
Issah, Mallam Yusif, 231–33
Issifu, Alhaji, 124–25

Jasua, 37
Jiagge, Annie, 71–72
Jiagge Commission, 63
Johnson, Cecelia, 191
journalism, 1–2
Joy FM (radio station), 265–66
Juapong Textiles Ltd., 128–29
Judicial Council, 241, 255
June Fourth Movement (JFM), 102, 104, 114

Kakari, Kofi, 22–23
kalabule, 81–83
Karikari, Kwame, 267–68
Kell, Georg, 241
Kennedy, Arthur Kobina, 238
Keta, 52, 277
Koforidua, 84, 120, 150
Konkomba, 216
konors, 18
Krobo, 18
Kufuor, John, 205–7, 214, 220, 222, 224, 230–34, 237–38, 258, 273, 286
Kumasi, 20, 23–24, 26–27, 34, 46, 53, 72, 84, 93, 150, 172, 203, 211, 214, 244, 247, 253, 269, 271–72

Kwahu, 37–38
Kwame Nkrumah Revolutionary Guards (KNRG), 104, 121
Kwei, Joachim Amartey, 104, 124, 162

labor, 41–42, 52, 65–66, 73, 76, 98, 102, 120–29, 130, 159, 172, 271, 276
Lebanese, 89, 96, 130
Lees, Captain, 29
Legon, 73, 91
Libya, 170
Limann, Hilla, 99–104, 122, 283
Lithur, Nana Oye, 262
Lobi, 16–17
LoDagaba, 40
Lugard, Lord, 32
Lumumba, Patrice, 67

Maafo, Yaw Osafo, 260
MacCarthy, Charles, 24
Mahama, John, 208, 213–14, 218, 222, 224, 237–38, 258, 260–61, 263, 265, 273
Makola market, 97
Mamprusi, 175–76, 216
Manteaw, Steve, 279
Manuh, Takyiwaa, 135–36
Manyo-Plange Commission, 63
Marfo, Isaac Adjei, 258
Marrah, Kofi, 144
Mbir, Kojo, 242
mbrantsie, 19
media, 1, 181, 197–98, 206, 233, 238–39, 242, 246–47, 262–68, 270
Media Foundation of West Africa, 263
Mensah, J. H., 287
military, 72, 77, 104, 183–87; coups, 66–68, 77, 90, 103, 184
Mills, John Atta, 206–8, 213–14, 222, 224, 234–36, 246, 261
Mobisquads, 138, 190–91
Monney, Roland Affail, 267
Mould-Iddrisu, Betty, 235, 237
Movement for Freedom and Justice (MFJ), 198–99
mpanyinfu, 20
Muntaka, Mohammed, 235
Muslim Action Party, 56

Nabila, John, 175–76
nam, 34

Index

Nanumba, 216
Nasser, Gamal Abdel, 106
National Alliance of Liberals (NAL), 73
National Anti-Corruption Action Plan, 241, 248, 288
National Canoe Fishermen's Council, 123
National Catholic Secretariat, 93
National Commission for Democracy (NCD), 192–94, 197–200
National Defence Committee, 111–16, 127–28
National Democratic Congress (NDC), 3, 195–96, 202–20, 222–25, 227–46, 251, 253, 256, 258, 260–61, 262, 264–67, 272–74, 285–86
National Development Company (Nadeco), 62–63
National House of Chiefs, 70, 189
National Industrial Corporation, 122
National Investigations Committee (NIC), 148, 151–52, 165
National Liberation Council (NLC), 69–73, 93, 189
National Liberation Movement (NLM), 53, 56–57
National Media Commission (NMC), 263, 265–68
National Mobilization Programme (NMP), 137–38, 190–91
National Muslim Task Force, 135
National Patriotic Party (NPP), 196, 202–11, 213–20, 222–25, 227–39, 242–47, 251, 253, 256, 260–69, 272–75, 285, 287
National Planning Committee, 235
National Redemption Council (NRC), 77–79
National Revenue Secretariat, 182
National Union of Ghana Students, 85, 87, 98, 201
National Youth Organizing Committee, 137
Ndoum, Kwesi, 272
New Democratic Movement, 102, 143
Ninsin, Kwame, 13, 80, 176–77, 208–9, 279
Nkrumah, Kwame, 44–70, 77–78, 282–83, 286
Nkrumahists, 202–3, 205, 272, 287
nnoboa, 78, 137
North East Region, 215
Northern Region, 80, 175–76, 178, 182, 215–16

Northern Regional Anti-Corruption Committee, 277
Northern Territories, 28, 34–38, 47, 52
Nsamankow, 24
Nunoo-Mensah, Joseph, 101, 104, 147
Nyantakyi, Kwesi, 238
Nzema, 214

Obeng, P. V., 190, 258
Obetsebi-Lamptey, Jake, 218
obirempon, 19, 21
Obuasi, 41–42, 112, 119, 271
Ocansey, Edmund, 120–21
OccupyGhana, 13, 274
Odartey-Wellington, A., 91
odomankama, 22
Office of Revenue Commissioners (ORC), 165
Ohene, Emmanuel, 151, 165
oil revenue, 277–80
Open Society Initiative of West Africa, 256–57
Opoku-Ware, Otumfuo, II, 189
Oppong, Marrieta Brew Appiah, 281
Organization of African Unity, 55, 67
Osei, Charlotte, 239
Oti Region, 213
Owusu, Maxwell, 20, 49, 136, 287
Owusu, Victor, 99
Owusum, Osei, 258

Palaver, 233–34
patronage: by colonial authorities, 30; CPP and, 47–52, 59–66, 283; in Fourth Republic, 216–23; Progress Party and, 74–76
People's Action Against Corruption, 277
People's Action Party, 73
People's Defence Committees (PDCs), 106, 109–24, 130–44, 148, 158, 160, 199
People's Movement for Freedom and Justice, 85
People's National Convention (PNC), 232
People's National Party (PNP), 99–104, 120–22, 159, 161–62
People's Progressive Party (PPP), 272
People's Revolutionary League of Ghana (PRLG), 102
People's Shops, 133–34
Peprah, Kwame, 232

Petroleum Revenue Management Act, 278–79
police, 98, 240
Popular Front Party, 99
Portuphy, Kofi, 138, 190
poverty, 173, 214, 228–29, 288
Pratt, Kwesi, Jr., 198
Prempeh, 24, 27
Prempeh, Henry Kwasi, 276
Prempeh, Osei Agyeman, II, 34
Prestea, 73
Produce Buying Division (PBD), 120, 155
Progress Party, 73–75, 99
Provisional National Defence Council (PNDC), 103–9, 112–16, 121–22, 124, 129, 133, 142–43, 162–66, 225, 283; economic policy of, 168–77, 181–83, 286; state reform, 167–68, 177–94; transition to elections, 195–202
Public Accounts Committee, 260
Public Agenda, 277
Public Interest and Accountability Committee (PIAC), 278–80
Public Procurement Authority, 239, 260
Public Utility Workers Union, 127

Quainoo, Arnold, 94, 101–4, 118, 184–87
Quality Grain Company, 231–32
Quantson, Kofi, 85
Quayson, Richard, 226

Rawlings, Jerry John, Jr., 89–90, 193; AFRC and, 90–100, 148; on corruption, 89–90, 105, 181, 223; NDC and, 202–6, 221–22, 230, 251, 258, 264–65; PNDC and, 103–9, 141–43, 147–48, 164, 169, 178–80, 197, 199–200, 283–84, 286
Revenue Watch Institute, 280
revolution, 106
Rhodesia, 67
Right to Information bill, 252–53, 276
Russia, 280

Sankara, Thomas, 106
Sapati, B. A., 149–50, 259
Sarpong, George, 265
Savannah Region, 215
Seidu, Ahmadu, 235
Sekondi-Takoradi, 65–66

Selormey, Victor, 231
Serious Fraud Office, 204, 259
Seychelles, 27–28
Short, Emile, 241, 257–58
Sierra Leone, 27
Smith, Grace, 144
South Africa, 76, 103
Soviet Union, 170, 199
Sowah Commission, 63
Special Branch, 85
special prosecutor, 261–62
State Fishing Corporation, 121–22
State Gold Mining Corporation, 122
State Insurance Corporation, 121
Statesman, 264–65
Students' Task Force, 119, 137
Subah Infosolutions, 266
Sunyani, 150, 247
Supreme Court, 250, 255–56, 268
Supreme Military Council (SMC), 79–91, 93

Takoradi, 52, 93, 130, 132
Tallensi, 34
Tamale, 119, 132, 210, 250, 277
Tarkwa, 13, 122
Techiman, 273
Teitelbaum, Donald, 234
Tema, 56, 102, 120–21, 127–28, 142, 155, 271
Tema Development Corporation, 72
Third World Network–Africa, 277
31st December Women's Movement, 191–92, 199, 203, 232
Tiger Eye, 2, 266–67, 276
Timber Cooperative Union, 61
Timber Marketing Board, 61
Tinorgah, Abdulai, 140
Togo, 17, 34, 130–31
Togoland, 28, 43, 46
Togoland Congress, 56
Touré, Samori, 27
Trades Union Congress (TUC), 46–47, 64, 76, 84, 124–29, 198, 216, 236, 276
Transparency International, 5–6, 226–28, 261, 276, 288
Trans-Volta, 46
Tsikata, Kojo, 79, 102–3, 147, 170
Tsikata, Tsatsu, 232, 256
Tuah-Yeboah, Alfred, 248

Index

Tutu, Otumfuo Osei, II, 243

Ukraine, 280
UN Global Compact, 241
Union Government (Unigov), 84–86
United Africa Company (UAC), 40, 128
United Ghana Farmers Cooperative Council (UGFCC), 64
United Ghana Farmers Council, 51
United Gold Coast Convention (UGCC), 45–47
United Nations, 289
United Nations Convention against Corruption, 11
United Party, 57
United States, 45, 67, 127, 232, 234, 274
University of Ghana, 73, 93
University of Science and Technology, 93
University Teachers Association of Ghana, 223
Upper East Region, 216
Upper Region, 126, 140
Upper West Region, 215

value added tax (VAT), 268–69

Volta Aluminum Company (Valco), 127–28
Volta Region, 141, 181, 213
Volta River, 56

Wa, 119–20, 271
West Africa, 27, 45
whistleblowers, 252
Wikileaks, 234
Winneba, 23
women, 96–97, 105, 113, 135–36, 191–92
Workers Brigade, 63
Workers Defence Committees (WDCs), 11, 13, 106, 109–13, 116, 119–33, 141–42, 160
World Bank, 7–9, 71, 76, 168, 199, 288
Woyome, Alfred, 235–37, 267

Yaa Asantewa, 28
Yahaya, Huudu, 173, 181–82
Ya Na, 34–36
Yankey, George, 232
Yankey, Sipa, 235
Yendi, 34, 70

Zuarungu, 36

Ukrainianness
Ukrainskii Kongres, 241
Union Governance (Taiger), 84–86
United Airlines Company (UAL), 49, 128
United Ibaan Farmers' Cooperative Council (UFCC), 64
United Ghana Farmers' Council
United Kodi Co-operatives Union (UKCU), 58–62
United Nations, 280
United Nations Convention against Corruption, 21
United Party, 57
United States, 40, 60, 104, 127, 244, 276
University of Ghana, 29, 59
University Teachers Association of Ghana, 224
Urbanization, 236
Uzpatevloz, 233, 240
Upper West Region, 98, 218

value added tax (VAT), 168–169

Uru, Charlotte Osei-P., 267

Volta Aluminum Company (Valco), 129–132
Volta Region, 181, 211, 217
Volta River, 56

Wa, 110–112, 217
West Africa, 272
wielkopolowcy, 232
Wieliczka, 233
Wprosta, 231
wolna gospodarka rynkowa, 265–274
Workers Brigades, 65
Workers Defence Committee (WDC), 11, 67, 109–110, 129–131, 231–235
World Bank, 3, 20–21, 70, 104, 170, 268
Wóycicka, Alicja, 235–237

Yaa Asantewa, 225
Yakubu Hamidu, 57, 91, 82
Yankey Group, 60
Yendi, 99, 215
Yendinas, 70

Zanu-Pf, 36, 39